WITTGENSTEIN'S REMARKS ON THE FOUNDATIONS OF AI

WITTGENSTEIN'S REMARKS ON THE FOUNDATIONS OF AI

Stuart Shanker

London and New York

First published 1998
by Routledge
11 New Fetter Lane, London EC4P 4EE

Simultaneously published in the USA and Canada
by Routledge
29 West 35th Street, New York, NY 10001

Typeset in Garamond by Routledge
Printed and bound in Great Britain by MPG Books Ltd, Bodmin

British Library Cataloguing in Publication Data
A catalogue record for this book is available from the British Library.

Library of Congress Cataloging-in-Publication Data
Shanker, Stuart.
Wittgenstein's remarks on the foundations of AI / Stuart Shanker.
Includes bibliographical references and index.
1. Wittgenstein, Ludwig, 1889–1951—Contributions in artificial
intelligence. 2. Artificial intelligence. I. Title.
B3376.W564S46 1998
193–dc21   97–13425

ISBN 0–415–09794–0

IN MEMORY OF E. S. REED

I think it advisable for every critic proposing to devote his life to literary scholarship to pick a major writer of literature as a kind of spiritual preceptor for himself, whatever the subject of his thesis. I am not speaking, of course, of any sort of moral model, but it seems to me that growing up inside a mind so large that one has no sense of claustrophobia within it is an irreplaceable experience in humane studies. Some kind of transmission by seed goes on here too.

(Northrop Frye, *Spiritus Mundi*)

CONTENTS

CONTENTS

PREFACE

Immersing oneself in the work of a great philosopher is very much like immersing oneself in a culture. One begins to look at philosophical problems in his or her distinctive manner: to think and speak in ways that are uniquely characteristic of that philosopher's outlook. Moreover, as one quickly discovers when visiting a foreign culture, genuine communication between rival systems involves far more than can be captured in a dictionary. How one approaches an issue, what sorts of assumptions and conventions one tacitly adopts, what sorts of arguments one finds convincing or problematic, are all subtly influenced in ways that can easily escape one's conscious awareness or control. Not surprisingly, attempts at philosophical dialogue all too often end in mutual incomprehension, if not outright hostility.

In a fundamental sense, then, examining an opposing theory from some distinctive philosophical standpoint is similar to doing anthropology. For one is not simply investigating a body of facts which are open to plain view; one is struggling to understand the language and thinking of an entirely different culture and, in the process, to better understand one's own 'languaculture' (see Agar 1994). That is, just as one is endeavouring to understand the implicit assumptions and conventions of the doctrine one is studying, so, too, one thereby hopes to expose those aspects of one's own way of thinking that are so entrenched that one does not even see them as cultural phenomena.

Thus, there were several reasons why I wanted to write this book. First and foremost was simply my desire to deepen my understanding of Wittgenstein's later writings. For I am convinced that, in order for this to occur, one constantly has to try to relate Wittgenstein's thought to relevant philosophical or scientific arguments. Moreover, the actual writing of this book mirrors the development of Wittgenstein's thought in the 1930s, as he moved from the philosophy of mathematics to the philosophy of psychology, and then sought to integrate these seemingly distant investigations. Herein lies the principal reason why I have chosen the particular topics covered in this book, and, indeed, the order in which they are presented.

My next major goal was to understand the evolution, and thence the nature, of AI; and here it is necessary to mention at the outset an important caveat. The term 'Artificial Intelligence' is applied to a great many schools of thought: everything from the early studies in information theory and logic-proving machines to the latest work in neural networks and Expert Systems. In this book, the term 'AI' has a very restricted usage: it refers to the paradigm which emerged in the late 1950s which saw in AI the glue that would bind together such diverse fields as psychology, linguistics, anthropology, neuroscience and philosophy, under the umbrella of cognitive science.

In no sense, then, is this book intended to be seen as an indictment of AI *simpliciter*; nor, for that matter, is it meant to be seen as an attack on what John Haugeland has called Good Old Fashioned AI (see Haugeland 1985). For one of the great benefits which one can derive from studying anthropology is that one learns to resist the natural tendency to view another culture's assumptions and conventions as 'wrong'. Rather, this is a book aimed at an understanding: but not just of the later Wittgenstein, or of the foundations of AI. For, above all else, this book is concerned with a particularly troubling and significant question in the philosophy of psychology.

With the benefit of hindsight it is clear that there were not one, but two, major and independently occurring revolutions in the sciences of the mind in the 1950s: the cognitive revolution, and the post-computational mechanist revolution. Each came from a strikingly different tradition. The cognitive revolution drew heavily on the work of Piaget and Vygotsky; it owed much to Gestalt psychology and the New Look in perception, and its roots can be traced back to *Denkpsychologie*. AI grew out of recursive function theory and information theory; it owed much to automata theory and cybernetics, and its roots lay in behaviourism and nineteenth-century mechanism. How could two such dissimilar, if not adverse, movements join together? And how could the concerns of the cognitive revolution have been so quickly usurped by those of AI?

To answer these questions brings me to the title of this book. Despite the obvious danger that some readers might be given the false impression that a new manuscript has been discovered in Wittgenstein's *Nachlass*, I chose this title because it seemed to me to convey two important points. The first is that the origins of AI lie in mechanist ideas that were circulating in the 1930s, some of which can be traced back to the middle of the nineteenth century. The second point is that, not only was Wittgenstein aware of them, he was indeed preoccupied with these issues. Thus, given the continuity between 'pre-' and 'post-computational' mechanist thought which I hope to demonstrate in the course of this book, it follows that Wittgenstein's remarks on mechanism have a very deep and direct relevance for the foundations of AI, and thus, for the future of cognitive science.

As I have indicated elsewhere, I see this work as a prolegomenon to

Bruner's call for a 'reorientation of the cognitive revolution' (see Shanker 1997a). Bruner has been remarkably blunt about what he sees as the threat posed by AI to the cognitive revolution. In *Acts of Meaning* he warns that AI provides a technological refuge for the spiritual behaviourist. He regards the conflict between computationalists and connectionists as little more than the latest version of the rationalist–empiricist conflict, and he concludes that only 'Time [will] tell . . . whether a sow's ear [can] be turned into a silk purse' (Bruner 1990: 8). In place of the dominant role which AI has hitherto played in cognitive science, Bruner calls for a return to what he defines as the original driving force of the cognitive revolution: a 'cultural psychology which, almost by definition, will not be preoccupied with "behavior" but with "action" . . . and more specifically, with *situated action*' (*ibid.*: 19).

In Bruner's eyes, the chief danger posed by AI is that 'To treat the world as an indifferent flow of information to be processed by individuals each on his or her own terms is to lose sight of how individuals are formed and how they function' (*ibid.*: 12). Thus, any attempt to explain a human being's development as if one were dealing with a machine that is processing information is bound to lead one down the path of reductionism. In common with Trevarthan, who has argued strongly for the interactionist view that 'the communicating interpersonal self is the very foundation for the cognitive or thinking self who will grow up to solve problems "in the head"' (Trevarthan 1993: 121), Bruner insists that 'It is man's participation *in* culture and the realization of his mental powers *through* culture that make it impossible to construct a human psychology on the basis of the individual alone' (Bruner 1990: 12).

What Bruner's recent bid to renew the cognitive revolution comes down to is the point that, if cognitive science is to succeed in explaining a human being's socioaffective, cognitive and linguistic development, it has to restore the focus onto an agent's social interactions, and away from that of a self-modifying computer program. But then, until we understand the deep conceptual reasons for why the cognitive revolution so readily succumbed to the spell cast by AI, we constantly run the risk of sliding back into computational, or some newer version of mechanist reductionism. And it is to this larger enterprise that I hope this book will in some small measure contribute.

SGS
Atkinson College, York University
June 1997

ACKNOWLEDGEMENTS

I am deeply indebted to the Canada Council, which awarded me a Standard Research Grant, and to my college, which awarded me an Atkinson College Research Fellowship and a series of research grants to pursue this work. In this respect, I must especially thank the members of my department, who graciously relieved me of my teaching duties on several different occasions.

I have benefited from the insight and advice of so many different colleagues and students in the writing of this book that I long ago gave up hope of mentioning them all by name. Moreover, one of the tacit conventions that governs our attitudes towards acknowledgements is that one should ignore all those authors to whose writings one owes an enormous debt. Thus, unmentioned here and consigned to the Bibliography are all those philosophers and AI-theorists from whom I have learnt so much.

To begin with I must thank Peter Hacker, who not only inspired and directed my great love of Wittgenstein, but who also played an instrumental role in the genesis of this book. As the Preface makes clear, I am also deeply indebted to Jerome Bruner, who has been a constant source of insight and encouragement.

Over the course of the past few years I have worked closely with Sue Savage-Rumbaugh and Talbot Taylor. Both have influenced me in ways that are difficult to fathom, let alone express. Both know how grateful I am to them for all their help.

I should also like to thank the following, all of whom have contributed to the writing of this book: Alice Ambrose, Gordon Baker, Harold Bassford, Ellen Bialystok, Rainer Born, John Canfield, Jeff Coulter, Costis Coveos, Michael Detlefsen, Laurence Goldstein, Rom Harré, John Hunter, John Shotter, Sören Stenlund, Michel Ter Hark, Stanley Tweyman, and the late Hao Wang. I must also express my gratitude to my secretaries, Lorenza Campagnolo and Elizabeth Bentham, to my unflagging research assistant, Sonia Campagnolo, and to my friend and editor, Richard Stoneman.

This book is dedicated to the memory of Edward Reed, who helped with every chapter of this book, and so much else besides.

ACKNOWLEDGEMENTS

Finally, I must thank my family: my parents, for their constant guidance and support; my sister, who has patiently (but firmly) overseen my development in psychology; and my wife, without whom none of this would be possible.

ABBREVIATIONS

Works by Wittgenstein

AWL   *Wittgenstein's Lectures: Cambridge 1932–1935*, Alice Ambrose (ed.), Oxford: Basil Blackwell, 1979.

BB   *The Blue and Brown Books*, Oxford: Basil Blackwell, 1960.

CV   *Culture and Value*, G. H. von Wright (ed.), Peter Winch (trans.), Oxford: Basil Blackwell, 1980.

GWL   *Wittgenstein's Lectures on Philosophical Psychology 1946–47*, P. T. Geach (ed.), Chicago: University of Chicago, 1989.

LA   *Lectures & Conversations on Aesthetics, Psychology and Religious Belief*, Cyril Barrett (ed.), Oxford: Basil Blackwell, 1966.

LFM   *Wittgenstein's Lectures on the Foundations of Mathematics: Cambridge 1939*, Cora Diamond (ed.), Brighton: Harvester Press, 1976.

LSD   'The Language of Sense Data and Private Experience', 1935–6, in *Philosophical Occasions 1912–1951*, James Klugge and Alfred Nordmann (eds), Indianapolis: Hackett, 1993.

LW   *Last Writings*, G. H. von Wright and Heikki Nyman (eds), C. G. Luckhardt and M. A. E. Aue (trans), Oxford: Basil Blackwell, 1982.

NB   *Notebooks 1914–16*, G. H. von Wright and G. E. M. Anscombe (eds), G. E. M. Anscombe (trans.), Oxford: Basil Blackwell, 1961.

NL   'Notes on Logic', 1913, in *Notebooks 1914–1916*, 2nd edn, G. H. von Wright and G. E. M. Anscombe (eds), G. E. M. Anscombe (trans.), Oxford: Basil Blackwell, 1979.

OC   *On Certainty*, G.E.M. Anscombe and G.H. von Wright (eds), D. Paul and G.E.M. Anscombe (trans), Oxford: Basil Blackwell, 1977.

PG   *Philosophical Grammar*, Rush Rhees (ed.), Anthony Kenny (trans.), Oxford: Basil Blackwell, 1974.

PI   *Philosophical Investigations*, G. E. M. Anscombe (trans.), Oxford: Basil Blackwell, 1958.

PR   *Philosophical Remarks*, Rush Rhees (ed.), R. Hargreaves and R. White (trans), Oxford: Basil Blackwell, 1975.

RFM   *Remarks on the Foundation of Mathematics*, G. H. von Wright, R. Rhees and G. E. M. Anscombe (eds), G. E. M. Anscombe (trans.): Oxford, Basil Blackwell, 1978.

RPP I   *Remarks on the Philosophy of Psychology*, vol. I, G. E. M. Anscombe and G. H. von Wright (eds), G. E. M. Anscombe (trans.): Oxford: Basil Blackwell, 1980.

RPP II *Remarks on the Philosophy of Psychology*, vol. II, G. H. von Wright and Heikki Nyman (eds), C. G. Luckhardt and M. A. E. Aue (trans), Oxford: Basil Blackwell, 1980.

TLP   *Tractatus Logico-Philosophicus*, D. F. Pears and B. F. McGuinness (trans), London: Routledge and Kegan Paul, 1961.

WWK   *Ludwig Wittgenstein and the Vienna Circle*, B.F. McGuinness (ed.), J. Schulte and B.F. McGuinness (trans), Oxford: Basil Blackwell, 1979.

Z   *Zettel*, G. E. M. Anscombe and G. H. von Wright (eds), G. E. M. Anscombe (trans.), Oxford: Basil Blackwell, 1967.

Other works

BL   Frege, Gottlob, *The Basic Laws of Arithmetic*, Montgomery Furth (ed. and trans.), Berkeley: University of California Press, 1964.

LI   Husserl, Edmund, *Logical Investigations*, vol. I, London: Routledge & Kegan Paul, 1970.

Logic Kant, Immanuel, *Logic*, Robert S. Hartman and W. Schwarz (trans), Indianapolis: Bobbs-Merill, 1970.

PLP   Waismann, F., *The Principles of Linguistic Philosophy*, R. Harré (ed.), London: Macmillan, 1968.

PW   Frege, Gottlob, *Posthumous Writings*, Hans Hermes, Friedrich Kambartel and Friedrich Kaulbach (eds), Peter Long and Roger White (trans), Oxford: Basil Blackwell, 1979.

1

WITTGENSTEIN'S RESPONSE TO TURING'S THESIS

The real problem is not whether machines think but whether men do.

(B. F. Skinner, *Contingencies of Reinforcement*)

§1 Turing's machines 'are humans who calculate'

The title of this chapter suggests two contentious claims: first, that Wittgenstein was aware of the developments in recursion theory which took place during the 1930s; and second, that he disputed the version of Church's Thesis (hereafter CT) that Turing presented in 'On Computable Numbers' (Turing 1936). It will be best to concede at the outset that both themes represent something of a critical liberty or, perhaps, a corollary. For the subject of this chapter is really Wittgenstein's attack on the mechanist terms in which Turing interpreted his computability results. But one of the central points that Turing made in his 1947 'Lecture to the London Mathematical Society' was that the Mechanist Thesis is not just licensed by, but is in fact *entailed* by his 1936 development of CT. Wittgenstein's argument thus demands careful scrutiny of both the relation of Turing's argument to CT, and the cognitivist implications that the founders of AI read into CT as a result of Turing's influence.

Before we consider these matters, however, we must first satisfy ourselves that Wittgenstein was, in fact, intent on repudiating Turing's mechanist interpretation of his computability thesis. It has long been a source of frustration to Wittgenstein scholars that no overt mention of this issue is to be found in *Lectures on the Foundations of Mathematics: Cambridge 1939*, despite Turing's prominent presence at these lectures. Indeed, until recently, it might have been thought that the title of this chapter makes the still further unwarranted assumption that Wittgenstein was even aware of 'On Computable Numbers'. But any such doubts were laid to rest by the discovery of an off-print of the essay in Wittgenstein's *Nachlass*, and, even more important, the following mystifying reference to Turing Machines which occurs in *Remarks on the Philosophy of Psychology*:

Turing's 'Machines'. These machines are *humans* who calculate. And one might express what he says also in the form of *games*. And the interesting games would be such as brought one *via* certain rules to nonsensical instructions. I am thinking of games like the 'racing game'. One has received the order 'Go on in the same way' when this makes no sense, say because one has got into a circle. For any order makes sense only in certain positions. (Watson)

(RPP I: §1096)

The latter half of this passage is clear enough: Wittgenstein is saying that Turing's Halting Problem is no more epistemologically significant than any other paradox in the philosophy of mathematics.[1] The confusing part is the opening sentence. On first reading, this sounds hopelessly obscure: a clear demonstration of Wittgenstein's failure to grasp the significance of Turing's Thesis *vis-à-vis* recursion theory. Yet another way of describing the goal of this opening chapter, therefore, will be to see what sense can be made of this curious remark.

To see what Wittgenstein was driving at here, we have to work our way through a prolonged discussion of the nature of calculation in *Remarks on the Foundations of Mathematics* (see §2). But before we look at this material, it will be salutary to fill in some of the background to Wittgenstein's thought. In a widely quoted passage from *The Blue Book*, Wittgenstein told his students:

> The problem here arises which could be expressed by the question: 'Is it possible for a machine to think?' (whether the action of this machine can be described and predicted by the laws of physics or, possibly, only by laws of a different kind applying to the behaviour of organisms). And the trouble which is expressed in this question is not really that we don't yet know a machine which could do the job. The question is not analogous to that which someone might have asked a hundred years ago: 'Can a machine liquefy a gas?' The trouble is rather that the sentence, 'A machine thinks (perceives, wishes)' seems somehow nonsensical. It is as though we had asked 'Has the number 3 a colour?'
>
> (BB: 47)

Whether or not Turing had read *The Blue and Brown Books*, he would almost certainly have been aware of Wittgenstein's opposition to the Mechanist Thesis. Indeed, it seems plausible to suppose that the Turing Test represents Turing's opposition to Wittgenstein's critique, using a Wittgenstein-like argument.

Wittgenstein's last point – a veiled allusion to Frege – is that, unlike the question of whether or not a gas can be mechanically liquefied, the question of whether a machine thinks is problematic in much the same way as the question of whether or not 3 is coloured; i.e. both are troubling because they transgress rules of logical grammar, and not because we do not as yet possess the means to answer them. But Turing might have regarded this argument as simply a request for the criteria whereby one would respond to each question. That is, in Turing's eyes, the proper response to make to Wittgenstein's argument might have been that, if there is — at present — no method to ascertain whether or not 3 has a colour, then the latter question might well be regarded as a category-violation. But the point of the Turing Test is to argue that there is no *a priori* reason why we should not apply the same criteria to the question of whether or not such-and-such a machine can think as to the question of whether or not such-and-such a subject can think, given that both *inferences* are based on observable behaviour. In other words, whether or not the answer is affirmative, we can at least see that the question of whether machines can (or ever will be able to) think is *empirical*.

Perhaps the most striking aspect of the above passage from *The Blue Book* is simply the date at which it was written. This was in 1933, nearly ten years before Turing began to think seriously about the Mechanist Thesis. Close to the same time, Wittgenstein wrote in *Philosophical Grammar*:

> If one thinks of thought as something specifically human and organic, one is inclined to ask 'could there be a prosthetic apparatus for thinking, an inorganic substitute for thought?' But if thinking consists only in writing or speaking, why shouldn't a machine do it? 'Yes, but the machine doesn't know anything.' Certainly it is senseless to talk of a prosthetic substitute for seeing and hearing. We do talk of artificial feet, but not of artificial pains in the foot.
>
> 'But could a machine think?' — Could it be in pain? — Here the important thing is what one means by something *being in pain* [or by *thinking*].
>
> (PG: 105)

Here is yet further evidence — already familiar from the writings of Curry and Post — that the Mechanist Thesis was in the air at least a decade before Turing began serious work on it. From Wittgenstein's point of view, 'On Computable Numbers' represents a misguided attempt to integrate independent issues in mathematical logic and the philosophy of mind. And it was precisely Turing's bridging argument which concerned Wittgenstein.[2]

Turing discusses the nature of Turing Machines ('computing machines') at two different places in 'On Computable Numbers': §§1–2 and §9. In the first instance he defines the terms of his argument, and in the second he takes up his promise to defend these definitions. Thus, in his justification, Turing naturally shifts from mathematics to epistemology, and, in so doing, he introduces a theme which constitutes the focus of Wittgenstein's remarks.

In essence, Wittgenstein objects that the mathematical and philosophical strands in 'On Computable Numbers' are not just independent of one another but, indeed, that the epistemological argument misrepresents the mathematical content. The remark that Turing's machines 'are *humans* who calculate' is only concerned with the *prose* presented at §9; but its corollary is that we must go back and look at the mathematical content of Turing's achievement in such a way as to avoid Turing's philosophical confusion.

Turing introduces Turing Machines in §§1–2 with the following argument:

> We may compare a man in the process of computing a real number to a machine which is only capable of a finite number of conditions q_1, q_2, ..., q_R which will be called 'm-configurations'. The machine is supplied with a 'tape' ... running through it, and divided into sections ... each capable of bearing a 'symbol'. At any moment there is just one square, say the r-th, bearing the symbol G(r) which is 'in the machine'. We may call this square the 'scanned symbol'. The 'scanned symbol' is the only one of which the machine is, so to speak, 'directly aware'.
>
> (Turing 1936: 117)

This reiterated warning of the anomaly – 'so to speak' and inverted commas around 'directly aware' – highlights the premise which Turing felt constrained to justify.[3] When read as a strictly mathematical affair, §§1–2 operate as an abstract outline for how to construct a machine that can be used to execute calculations, with no reason to present the argument in terms of the various cognitive terms with their attendant qualifications.

Turing's Thesis reads as follows: suppose it were possible to transform a recursive function into binary terms. It would then be possible to construct a machine that could be used to compute analogues of those functions if it used some system which could encode those '0s' and '1s'. Both the function (the table of instructions) and the argument (the tape input) must first be encoded in binary terms, and then converted into some mechanical analogue of a binary system. Turing speaks of the machine scanning a symbol, but that is entirely irrelevant to the argument; for how the binary input is actually configured and how the program/tape interact is not at issue.

Turing was not presenting here the mechanical blueprints for a primitive computer but, rather, a *computational design*, which only five years later he sought to implement using electrical signals to represent the binary code. And he did this with his version of CT, which demonstrates that:

All effective number-theoretic functions (viz. algorithms) can be encoded in binary terms, and these binary-encoded functions are Turing Machine computable.

The thesis which Turing defends at §9 is not this, however, but rather the *epistemological* premise that 'We may compare a man in the process of computing a real number to a machine which is only capable of a finite number of conditions q_1, q_2, ..., q_R which will be called "*m*-configurations".' He begins by analysing the conditions which govern human computing. The crucial part of his argument is that:

> The behaviour of the computer at any moment is determined by the symbols which he is observing, and his 'state of mind' at that moment. ... Let us imagine the operations performed by the computer to be split up into 'simple operations' which are so elementary that it is not easy to imagine them further divided. Every such operation consists of some change of the physical system consisting of the computer and his tape. We know the state of the system if we know the sequence of symbols on the tape, which of these are observed by the computer ... and the state of mind of the computer. ... The simple operations must therefore include:
>
> (a) Changes of the symbol on one of the observed squares.
> (b) Changes of one of the squares observed to another square within L squares of one of the previously observed squares. ...
>
> The operation actually performed is determined ... by the state of mind of the computer and the observed symbols. In particular, they determine the state of mind of the computer after the operation is carried out.
> We may now construct a machine to do the work of this computer. To each state of mind of the computer corresponds an 'm-configuration' of the machine ....
>
> (*Ibid.*: 136–7)

This passage raises a highly intriguing question *à propos* Wittgenstein's objection that Turing's machines 'are really *humans* who calculate'. For this looks like the exact opposite: viz. that Turing has actually defined human calculation mechanically, so as to license the application of quasi-cognitive terms to describe the operation of computing machines. So why, then, did Wittgenstein not make the converse point that 'Turing's humans are really machines that calculate'? The answer to this question, as we shall see in the following section, lies in Wittgenstein's discussion of the nature of *calculation* in Book V of *Remarks on the Foundations of Mathematics*.

5

§2 'Does a calculating machine calculate?'

In a passage that can be read as a direct response to Turing's argument at §9, Wittgenstein asks:

> Does a calculating machine *calculate*?
>
> Imagine that a calculating machine had come into existence by accident; now someone accidentally presses its knobs (or an animal walks over it) and it calculates the product 25 × 20.
>
> I want to say: it is essential to mathematics that its signs are also employed in *mufti*.
>
> It is the use outside mathematics, and so the *meaning* of the signs, that makes the sign-game into mathematics.
>
> Just as it is not logical inference either, for me to make a change from one formation to another (say from one arrangement of chairs to another) if these arrangements have not a linguistic function apart from this transformation.
>
> (RFM V: §2)

Wittgenstein's point here is that it is essential to what we call 'calculation', or 'inference',[4] that we employ a proposition like '25 × 20 = 500' in our everyday interactions, and that we don't just treat this as an interesting *pattern* (which, as Wittgenstein says elsewhere, might serve as the central motif on a piece of wallpaper). That is, we say things like 'If S owns 25 shares of XYZ which is currently trading at $20, then S must have $500 invested in XYZ'. And if asked to justify this, we do not insist on taking receipt of the certificates and counting them out; rather, we simply respond that 25 × 20 = 500.

Interestingly, Wittgenstein seems to be denying here the one part of Turing's argument that no one has ever questioned: the idea that *recursive functions are mechanically calculable*. The point that Wittgenstein is driving at is that the concept of calculation cannot be separated from its *essential normativity*. This becomes clear two passages later, when he asks us to

> Imagine that calculating machines occurred in nature, but that people could not pierce their cases. And now suppose that these people use these appliances, say as we use calculation, though of that they know nothing. Thus e.g. they make predictions with the aid of calculating machines, but for them manipulating these queer objects is experimenting.
>
> These people lack concepts which we have; but what takes their place?
>
> Think of the mechanism whose movement we saw as a geometrical (kinematic) proof: clearly it would not normally be said of

someone turning the wheel that he was proving something. Isn't it the same with someone who makes and changes arrangements of signs as [an experiment]; even when what he produces could be seen as a proof?

(RFM V: §4)

That is, we do not say that S 'calculated' or 'proved' x simply because his results may correspond with ours when we calculate or prove something. Rather, what renders an agent's action a *calculation* or a *proof*, and not just a doodle or an experiment, is his mastery of a normative practice: e.g. that he treats a proposition like '25 $\times$ 20 = 500' as a rule-governed transformation which justifies or explains his certainty that x is the case.

The 'normativity of mathematics' could justly be said to be the main subject of *Lectures on the Foundations of Mathematics* and *Remarks on the Foundations of Mathematics*. This theme is best summed up by Wittgenstein's insistence that 'A proof leads me to say: this *must* be like this' (RFM III: §30). The point of a mathematical proof is that it carves out rules of mathematical grammar: 'Let us remember that in mathematics we are convinced of *grammatical* propositions; so the expression, the result, of our being convinced is that we *accept a rule*' (*ibid.*: §27). That is, the role of a proof is to forge the internal relations which underpin our treatment of a mathematical proposition as a rule of grammar: 'For the proof is part of the grammar of the proposition!' (PG: 370). 'The proof changes the grammar of our language, changes our concepts. It makes new connexions and it creates the concept of these connexions' (RFM III: §31).

In the long discussion of calculation and rule-following in Books V and VI of RFM, Wittgenstein continually reverts to the question: Under what circumstances can I say of myself, or another individual, or a different culture, etc., that I/he/they are calculating/following a rule, as opposed to merely doodling, or conducting an experiment. He asks us to consider how

There might be a cave-man who produced *regular* sequences of marks for himself. He amused himself, e.g., by drawing on the wall of the cave:

- . — .—.—.

or

-.—..- . . . - . . . .-

But he is not following the general expression of a rule. And when we say that he acts in a regular way that is not because we can form such an expression.

(RFM VI: §41)

That is, the fact that we can map a rule onto S's behaviour does not entail that S is following that rule.

What more is needed in order for a subject to be described as 'following such-and-such a rule'?

> Let us consider very simple rules. Let the expression be a figure, say this one:
>
> |—|
>
> and one follows the rule by drawing a straight sequence of such figures (perhaps as an ornament).
>
> |—||—||—||—||—|
>
> Under what circumstances should we say: someone gives a rule by writing down such a figure? Under what circumstances: someone is following this rule when he draws that sequence? It is difficult to describe this.
>
> (*Ibid.*: §42)

The crucial point in what follows is that we do not say that S 'calculated' or 'proved' *x* because we infer that such-and-such went on in his mind; for the application of the expression 'S is following this rule' has nothing whatsoever to do with any putative 'mental events' which might accompany such regular behaviour:

> If one of a pair of chimpanzees once scratched the figure |—| in the earth and thereupon the other the series |—||—| etc., the first would not have given a rule nor would the other be following it, whatever else went on at the same time in the mind of the two of them.
>
> If however there were observed, e.g., the phenomenon of a kind of instruction, of shewing how and of imitation, of lucky and misfiring attempts, or reward and punishment and the like; if at length the one who had been so trained put figures which he had never seen before one after another in sequence as in the first example, then we should probably say that the one chimpanzee was writing rules down, and the other was following them.
>
> (*Ibid.*)

In other words, while we can only describe the chimps as following a rule if their behaviour displays more than mere regularity – i.e., while the concept of rule-following is internally related to the concept of regularity – rule-following does not reduce to mere regularity. In order to describe an agent as 'following a rule', his or her behaviour must license the application of various normative terms. For example, the agent must do such things as instruct, explain, correct, or justify his or her actions by appealing to the rule.

In Book V of RFM, Wittgenstein turns this argument directly onto the case of Turing Machines. The thrust of Wittgenstein's remarks on Turing's Thesis is that merely coming up with the 'correct results' – i.e., with the results that *we* obtain by calculation or inference – is not a sufficient condition to say of someone or something that he or she is calculating. For *calculation* is embedded in this cluster of normative concepts, none of which can be applied in the case of Turing Machines.

The common response from AI theorists to this argument is that this is precisely the point that is covered by the Turing Test. On Turing's account, all that matters is that the chimpanzees' behaviour satisfies the criteria which govern our use of the concept of calculation *vis-à-vis* human behaviour. What causes them – or for that matter, ourselves – to behave in this manner is not immediately at issue; only that the resulting behaviour satisfies the same criteria as we apply to ourselves. Hence, by parity of reasoning, if a machine can be constructed which would satisfy those same criteria, it would be no less irrelevant how it achieved this feat. We need not know whether or not it is possible to build such a machine; all that matters, in regards to the question of whether machines can think, is that there is no reason why such a contingency should be ruled impossible *a priori*.

But the crucial issue raised by Wittgenstein's attack on Turing's Thesis does not concern the Turing Test; rather, it is Turing's *analysis of calculation* which underpins the role carved out for the Turing Test. For Turing's approach to the Mechanist Thesis proceeds from a Cartesian distinction between *observed behaviour* (i.e., giving correct answers) and the *unobserved processes or states* which cause that behaviour (i.e., the 'mental states' that govern human or animal calculation, and the physical states that guide the operations of a Turing Machine). Thus, Turing assumes that the answer to the question, 'How did x arrive at the correct answer?', consists in a specification of the causal sequence of 'mental states' which can be modelled – and thence explained – on a Turing Machine.

The problem with this argument lies in the point emphasised in Book VII, §42 of RFM (quoted above), that whether or not the chimpanzees are calculating or following a rule has nothing whatsoever to do with what may have gone on in their minds (or, *a fortiori*, their brains). It is the nature of an agent's actions, or his ability to justify his action by citing the rules he is following, which govern our description of him as 'calculating' or 'following a rule'. But the answer to the question 'How did the Turing Machine arrive at x?' is indeed constituted by Turing's account of the mechanics of the system given in §1–2 (together with an account of some particular program in §§3f). Thus, Turing ignores the fact that:

the playing or calculation of a person can be justified by rules which he gives us when asked; not so the achievements of a machine, where the question 'Why do these keys spring out?' can *only* be answered by describing the mechanism, that is by describing a causal nexus. On the other hand, if we ask the calculator how he comes to his results, he will explain to us what kind of calculation he is doing and then adduce certain laws of arithmetic. He will not reply by describing the mode of action of a hidden machine, say, a machine in his brain.

(PLP: 122)

Turing's response to this last point is that how an agent may respond to the question of how he came to his results is irrelevant to the question of how he really came to his results. For the processes we are concerned with here are *pre-conscious*: i.e., not such that an agent could be aware of them. And what Turing claims to have discovered is that *calculation depends on our brains following a set of simple mechanical rules, which are such that they can also be followed by a machine*. That is, it is on the basis of the machine's ability to follow the sub-rules of the program, each of which is mechanically calculable, that he claimed to be able to build up his picture of machine intelligence.

Wittgenstein responds (in a passage which clearly harks back to Lecture XX of *Lectures on the Foundations of Mathematics*):

'This calculus is purely mechanical; a machine could carry it out.' What sort of machine? One constructed of the usual materials – or a super-machine? Are you not confusing the hardness of a rule with the hardness of a material?

(RFM III: §87)

But Turing's point was that to say 'This calculus is purely mechanical' means that the rules of calculation have been broken into a series of *meaningless* sub-rules, each of which is devoid of cognitive content, and for that reason are such that 'a machine could carry it out'.

Here, finally, is the level of the argument at which we can begin to see why Wittgenstein insisted that Turing's machines 'are really *humans* who calculate': a theme which is picked up – purged of any explicit reference to Turing – at RFM IV, §20: 'If calculating looks to us like the action of a machine, it is the *human being* doing the calculation that is the machine.' From the foregoing we know that Wittgenstein was not sanctioning here the picture of 'human calculation' Turing offered in 'On Computable Numbers'. But to see what he was after we have to consider the notion of algorithms – of effective calculation – which Turing had inherited from Hilbert, and which was indirectly responsible for the arguments contained, not just in §9, but in the post-1941 mechanist development of Turing's thought on the basis of that Thesis.

Turing felt not only that the Mechanist Thesis is entailed by his analysis of computability, but that the latter is the inexorable consequence of Hilbert's approach to the *Entscheidungsproblem*. The whole thrust of 'On Computable Numbers' derived from the fact that it was seen as the culmination of those very themes which had originally sparked off the development of recursion theory. Whether or not Turing had succeeded in clarifying the nature of effective procedures, this much at least was agreed by mathematical logicians: that Turing had succeeded in explicating the notion of computability in terms of mechanical procedures. It is to the framework of Turing's thought that we must look, therefore, if we are to grasp the import of Wittgenstein's critique.

§3 Church's Convention

I stressed in the opening section that Wittgenstein viewed the epistemological element suffusing 'On Computable Numbers' not just as independent from, but more importantly as a distortion of, its mathematical content. Indeed, it was imperative that Wittgenstein see Turing's argument in these terms; otherwise he could not – in light of his insistence that the philosopher has no business meddling in the internal affairs of the mathematician – have justified his own involvement with Turing's Thesis (see Shanker 1987a). To sustain this position demands, however, a closer look at the conceptual foundations of Turing's thought.

The key to the almost immediate success of Turing's Thesis lay in the themes which preceded it. Hilbert's original attempt to reduce transfinitary to finitary mathematical truths was a reflection of his basic epistemological premise that the human mind is bound by its 'finite limitations': an idea which naturally governed his approach to the *Entscheidungsproblem*. This is manifested in his twin demands that the processes employed in any computation must be fixed in advance, and that every computation must terminate in a finite number of steps (see Webb 1980: 75–6, 176). How, then, can one ignore the epistemological basis of subsequent efforts to provide a rigorous analysis of effective procedures?

In a sense, however, this would appear to be precisely what Church attempted. Judging from the terms in which he formally presented his thesis,[5] Church's interests were exclusively number-theoretic. We know from Kleene's and Rosser's histories of the development of Church's thought that, in his early work on the λ-calculus (around 1930), Church's goal was to construct analogues of the integers and the algorithms that can be performed on them using λ-functions (see Kleene 1981b, Rosser 1984). By 1932, Church had clarified that λ-definable functions must be effectively – i.e. algorithmically – calculable.[6] In 1933 he began to speculate that the

11

opposite might also hold: viz., that the λ-definable functions are *all* the effectively calculable functions.

In his first announcement of the thesis (in 1935), Church suggested that every effectively calculable function is λ-definable. Following Kleene's demonstration of the equivalence of λ-definability and recursiveness, Church shifted the emphasis onto the latter. Most significant of all, Church presented his 1936 version of the argument as a definition, not a conjecture:

> We now define the notion . . . of an *effectively calculable* function of positive integers by identifying it with the notion of a recursive function of positive integers (or of a λ-definable function of positive integers). This definition is thought to be justified by the considerations which follow, so far as positive justification can ever be obtained for the selection of a formal definition to correspond to an intuitive notion.
>
> (Church 1938: 100)

But what follows is somewhat confusing; for his justification is that there is no known recursive function on the positive integers for which there is not an algorithm to calculate its values; and conversely, that there is no known example of a function for which we possess an algorithm that is not recursive. Strictly speaking, these are reasons for regarding CT as a valid conjecture, rather than a useful definition. The kind of justification appropriate for the latter would be one which draws attention to the consequences of adopting such a definition, not 'evidence' for accepting its 'truth'.

When one treats CT as a definition, one has to conclude, not that it is unlikely, but rather, that it is logically impossible to discover a function on the primitive integers for which there is an algorithm which is not recursive. Any suggestion to the contrary must, on these terms, be regarded, not as (contingently) false but rather, as *meaningless*. And indeed, many have argued that Church's argument is best seen in conventionalist terms, where the inference from 'ϕ is effectively calculable' to 'ϕ is recursive' is stipulated, and Church's justification is understood as a partial attempt to defend this piece of conceptual legislation on the negative grounds that the possibility of encountering anomalies is remote.[7]

The important point to bear in mind in all this is that Church's proposed 'definition' was of 'effectively calculable function on the positive integers'. Far from representing an attempt to analyse a problematic epistemological concept, Church's intention was to delimit the range of number-theoretic functions for which there are algorithms (see Kleene 1981b: 48). That is, Church sought to employ the notion of recursiveness as the criterion for what should henceforward be deemed 'effectively calculable functions'. Should a novel method lead outside the class of general recursive functions, 'the new function obtained *cannot* be considered as effectively defined' (Kleene 1950: 320; my emphasis).

The crux of Wittgenstein's remarks on Turing's Thesis turns on a clear understanding of the logical status of this use of 'cannot'. To paraphrase what Wittgenstein says in a related context: 'Here the word "cannot" means *logical impossibility* whose expression is not a proposition but a rule of syntax. (A rule delimits the form of description.)' (WWK: 241) For:

> So much is clear: when someone says: 'If you follow the *rule*, it *must* be like this', he has not any *clear* concept of what experience would correspond to the opposite.
>
> Or again: he has not any clear concept of what it would be like for it to be otherwise. And this is very important. . . . For the word 'must' surely expresses our inability to depart from *this* concept. (Or ought I to say 'refusal'?)
>
> (RFM IV: §30)

In other words, the certainty that there could not, on Church's version of CT, be a non-recursive effectively calculable function, is grammatical, not inductive. It is its role as a rule of grammar that renders this version of CT 'unshakably certain', not 'the manner in which its truth is known'.

Even to speak of the 'truth' of CT – without drawing attention to the normative basis in which the term should here be understood – is potentially misleading, in so far as this invites the confusion that CT is a hypothesis. But whatever arguments Church might have employed to defend the adoption of his convention would have had no bearing on the logical status of CT itself. Unlike a hypothesis, it is impossible to doubt the 'truth' of Church's rule of grammar: not because it is *irrefutable*, but, rather, because the possibility of doubt has been *logically excluded*.[8] Hence Wittgenstein would have agreed with the letter if not the spirit of Kleene's claim that CT 'excludes doubt that one could describe an effective process for determining the values of a function which could not be transformed by these methods into a general recursive definition of the function' (Kleene 1950: 319).

In that case, it is misleading even to refer to CT as a *thesis*; for all this represents the fruits of grammatical clarification, not epistemological justification. When Kleene first baptised CT as such, it was on the grounds that 'such functions as have been recognized as being effectively calculable (effectively decidable), and for which the question has been investigated, have turned out always to be general recursive' (Kleene 1943: 274). But, as Kleene recognised, Church's conventionalist outlook renders such an argument strictly heuristic. Hence Kleene immediately shifted from mathematical to pragmatic considerations in his subsequent appeal that 'If we consider the thesis and its converse as definition, then the hypothesis is an hypothesis about the application of the mathematical theory developed from the definition' (*ibid.*: 274).

Kleene's overriding concern was to establish that CT 'cannot conflict with the intuitive notion which it is supposed to complete' (*ibid.*). But it is not at all clear, given the above arguments, how it could. If, *ex hypothesi*, there was no pre-existing mathematical notion of an effectively calculable function, then there was nothing with which Church's new rule – and the totality of functions thereby defined – *could* conflict. But even had this not been the case, Church's argument would simply have constituted an attempt to persuade mathematicians to *redefine* their terms. On neither account would CT assume an empirical aspect. For it was its designated role *qua* rule of grammar which determined its logical status, rather than the arguments summoned in support of that mandate. The problem with Church's approach, however, was that he offered no explanation for the fact that effectively calculable functions are *effective procedures* in the sense envisaged by Hilbert. Church had merely recapitulated Hilbert's original premise that the latter are algorithms. What was missing was some sort of elucidation of this prior assumption. And it was precisely this lacuna which Turing filled in 'On Computable Numbers'.

§4 Gödel's response to Turing's version of CT

The key to the success of Turing's version of CT was that he offered:

1 an 'analysis' of algorithmically calculable functions, which
2 emerged rather than departed from Hilbert's framework, in such a way that
3 the notion of effective procedures assumed a wider epistemological import.[9]

It was on the basis of this last point that Turing was to insist, in his 'Lecture to the London Mathematical Society', that, just as his Computability Thesis had evolved from Hilbert's formal systems, so too the Mechanist Thesis is entailed by the premise that mechanically calculable functions are Turing Machine computable.

That does not, however, mean that Turing intended his version of CT to be read in mechanist terms; only that he felt that one is forced into such a conclusion by the demonstration that algorithms are mechanically calculable. For, as has been emphasised by those who wish to treat CT as the foundation for AI, there is no suggestion in 'On Computable Numbers' that Turing Machines demonstrate or possess cognitive abilities. On the contrary, Turing was to stress that 'machine intelligence' only emerges in the shift from 'brute force' to 'learning' programs (see Chapter 2).

The crucial point here is that each of the 'instructions' of the latter demands the same – non-cognitive – execution as the former. In Dennett's words, the 'atomic tasks' of the program are putatively such that they 'presuppose *no* intelligence' (Dennett 1978: 83). It is rather the overall complexity of the program built up out of these 'mechanical sub-rules' which, as Turing saw it, forces one 'to admit that [since] the progress of the machine had not been foreseen when its original instructions were put [i]t would be like a pupil who had learnt much from his master, but had added much more by his own work. When this happens I feel that one is obliged to regard the machine as showing intelligence' (Turing 1947: 123).

The transition in Turing's thought was closely tied to the gradual shift in his interests from recursion theory to (what McCarthy was shortly to call) Artificial Intelligence. Given the guiding spirit behind the development of the former – viz., to show that all number-theoretic functions are recursively calculable – Turing felt obligated to show that all (effective) number-theoretic functions are mechanically calculable. Hence he set out to prove that his mechanical computer was every bit as powerful as a human computer. This reflects the significance of his emphasis on the term *computer*: i.e., the fact that his attention in 'On Computable Numbers' was very much confined to computation. Even in his major post-war work (the 1946 'Proposal for Development in the Mathematics Division of an Automatic Computing Engine' and the 1947 London lecture), Turing was still primarily concerned with the mechanisation of mathematical procedures: the problem of determining the 'scope of the machine', which he naturally approached within function-theoretic parameters (Turing 1946: 38f). Indeed, not just Turing's, but virtually all early interest in computers was focused on the development of machines to facilitate brute-force approaches to complex computational problems.

In 1937, Turing set out to construct a machine to help him solve Riemann's Hypothesis by calculating values of the zeta-function until an exception had been found.[10] In America, Wiener and von Neumann were similarly interested in using a machine to calculate the value of the Reynolds number. And, of course, the war accelerated interest in such machines in those areas which demanded enormous computations: not just the obvious example of cryptanalysis, but also artillery (the development of ENIAC), radar, meteorology and, towards the end of the war, the problems of implosion and the development of the hydrogen bomb.

From numerous memoirs on the origins of digital computers, we know that the general awareness that computers could be employed for more than just number-crunching – i.e., that they could be used for general symbol-manipulation – occurred some time during 1952–54.[11] But at least ten years before this, Turing had begun to speculate on a problem from which AI was rapidly to emerge. From various sources that he pieced together, Hodges demonstrated that, by 1944, Turing was primarily interested in 'the construction of a universal computer and [in] the service such a machine might render to psychology in the study of the human brain' (Turing 1959: 94). Apart from such critical factors as his meetings with Shannon, the problem which led Turing into these domains was a paradigm of formalist thought.[12]

According to Hodges, Jack Good and Turing began discussing (in 1941) the 'question of whether there was a "definite method" for playing chess – a machine method, in fact, although this would not necessarily mean the construction of a physical machine, but only a book of rules that could be followed by a mindless player – like the "instruction note" formulation of the concept of computability' (Hodges 1983: 211).[13] By 1943, Turing was seriously involved in the construction of a 'paper machine' (Turing's 'slave player'), which was unlike the earlier Turing Machines in so far as chess, according to Turing, 'requires some intelligence' to be played at all adequately (*ibid.*).

In 1936, Turing had insisted that the essence of Turing Machines is that they require no intelligence to follow their (mechanical sub-) rules. By 1946, Turing was exploring 'a very large class of non-numerical problems that can be treated by the calculator. Some of these have great military importance, and others are of immense interest to mathematicians' (Turing 1946: 41). Chief among the latter was chess:

> Given a position in chess the machine could be made to list all the 'winning combinations' to a depth of about three moves on either side. This . . . raises the question 'Can the machine play chess?' It could fairly easily be made to play a rather bad game. It would be bad because chess requires intelligence. We stated at the beginning of this section that the machine should be treated as entirely without intelligence. There are indications however that it is possible to make the machine display intelligence at the risk of its making occasional serious mistakes. By following up this aspect the machine could probably be made to play very good chess.
>
> (*Ibid.*)

Turing found in chess both the essence of the formalist epistemology under-lying his analysis of calculation in 'On Computable Numbers', and the materials for the mechanist structure which he sought to erect on this foundation. For it represented the categorial leap from brute force to self-modifying algorithms, paving the way for a shift from the crude picture presented in 'On Computable Numbers', where no intelligence was required of the Turing Machines, to one in which the machine would have to be able to 'learn' from previous positions in order to improve its quality of play. It was the latter argument which led Turing to introduce the notion of *machine intelligence* the following year in his London lecture, and then to promote a full-blown Mechanist Thesis in 1950 in 'Computing Machinery and

Intelligence'. 'On Computable Numbers' thus stands out as a turning-point, not just in Turing's thought, but, through his influence, on the mathematical transition from recursion theory into computer science, and the epistemological transition from formalism into AI.

There are numerous examples in the history of mathematics of impossibility proofs which, in the process of closing off one branch of inquiry, have served to open another. Rarely, however, has the effected transition led outside of mathematics proper into the realm of epistemology (see Shanker 1988b). But Turing could draw on no less a precedent than Gödel's second incompleteness theorem to support such a reading of his computability thesis. The fundamental problem raised by Turing's interpretation of his version of CT, therefore, is whether 'On Computable Numbers' does indeed operate as a transitional impossibility proof which, as such, provides a cognitive foundation for the Mechanist Thesis.

Nowhere could the underlying tension in Turing's extended thesis be more clear than in Gödel's response to 'On Computable Numbers'. As Davis has documented, Gödel 'insisted (as Church later reported to Kleene) that it was "thoroughly unsatisfactory" to *define* the effectively calculable functions to be some particular class without first showing that "the generally accepted properties" of the notion of effective calculability necessarily lead to this class. . . . [I]t was not until Turing's work became known that Gödel was willing to concede that this difficulty had been overcome' (Davis 1982: 12–13). But why should Gödel have resisted an argument which, as Turing himself was to remark, bore strong resemblance to Gödel's own earlier approach (see Turing 1939; cf. Gödel 1934)? Even more to the point, why should Gödel have endorsed Turing's – as opposed to Church's – version of CT in the first place, and why should he have continued to support a thesis whose consequences he so strongly disliked?[14]

Gödel's argument holds a special fascination for Wittgensteinians interested in the foundations of AI (see Neumaier 1986). This is not only for the obvious reason that his attitude towards mechanism seems to run parallel to Wittgenstein's – albeit for epistemological reasons which Wittgenstein was loath to accept – but, even more intriguingly, because these sentiments were to lead Gödel remarkably close to endorsing Hilbert's faith that 'in mathematics there is no *ignorabimus*': a theme which finds a striking echo in Wittgenstein's approach to the Decision Problem (see Shanker 1987a, 1988b). But how important is the above caveat about Wittgenstein's opposition to Gödel's epistemology?

In his 'Remarks before the Princeton bicentennial conference', Gödel credited Turing with having succeeded 'in giving an absolute definition of an interesting epistemological notion' (Gödel 1946: 84). This presents a line of thought which departs significantly from Wittgenstein's; for it shifts the focus from Church's interest in the mathematical characterisation of a class of functions, to an epistemological problem about – in Turing's terms – the mental states of the agents engaged in the calculation of those functions. The problem which this raises is: having taken this initial step, how could Gödel avoid the quandary in which he subsequently found himself *vis-à-vis* Turing's Mechanist Thesis?

Interestingly, unlike the 'Note added 28 August 1963' to 'On formally undecidable propositions' (Gödel 1934: 195), in the 1967 postscript to 'On undecidable propositions of formal mathematical systems' Gödel was careful to exclude the mechanist consequences that Turing had drawn from his version of CT. In the latter he begins by crediting Turing with having produced an illuminating account of the notion of formal system in terms of mechanical calculation:

> In consequence of later advances, in particular of . . . A. M. Turing's work, a precise and unquestionably adequate definition of the general concept of formal system can now be given. . . . Turing's work gives an analysis of the concept of 'mechanical procedure' (alias 'algorithm' or 'computation procedure' or 'finite combinatorial procedure'). This concept is shown to be equivalent with that of a 'Turing machine'. A formal system can simply be defined to be any mechanical procedure for producing formulas.
>
> (Gödel 1934: 369–70)

But he concludes with the warning: 'Note that the question whether there exist finite *non-mechanical* procedures, not equivalent with any algorithm, has nothing whatsoever to do with the adequacy of the definition of "formal system" and "mechanical procedure"' (*ibid.*: 370).

Wang's record of Gödel's *obiter dicta* has enabled us to piece together the reasoning which underlay this parenthetical remark. Wang first tells us that 'The concept of a mechanical procedure is involved in the characterization of formal systems. It seems natural to ask what mechanically solvable problems or computable functions are. This is related to the rather popular question: can machines think? can machines imitate the human mind?' (Wang 1974: 83). Overlooking the possibility that it is the assumption on which the question rests that should most concern the anti-mechanist, Wang continues: 'One often hears that in mathematical logic a sharp concept has been developed which corresponds exactly to our vague intuitive notion of computability. But how could a sharp concept correspond exactly to a vague notion? A closer look reveals that the sharp notion, often referred to as recursiveness or Turing computability, is actually not as sharp as it appears at first sight' (*ibid.*).

All this is offered by way of circumscribing the bounds of Turing's analysis of calculation in order to thwart his mechanist ambitions. And this argument, Wang explains, grew out of Gödel's reaction to Turing's post-1941 interests:

> Gödel points out that the precise notion of mechanical procedures is brought out clearly by Turing machines producing partial rather than general recursive functions. In other words, the intuitive notion does not require that a mechanical procedure should always terminate or succeed. A sometimes unsuccessful procedure, if sharply defined, still is a procedure, i.e. a well determined manner of proceeding. Hence we have an excellent example here of a concept which did not appear sharp to us but has become so as a result of a careful reflection. The resulting definition of the concept of mechanical by the sharp concept of 'performable by a Turing machine' is both correct and unique.
>
> (*Ibid.*: 84)

At this point we are clearly still operating within the parameters of recursion theory. The crux of this argument is that 'A formal system is nothing but a mechanical procedure for producing theorems. The concept of formal system requires that reasoning be completely replaced by "mechanical operations" on formulas in just the sense made clear by Turing machines' (*ibid.*). So much makes clear both why Gödel was persuaded to accept CT on the basis of Turing's Thesis, and also why he repudiated the consequences which Turing was to draw. The former question is explained by Gödel's recognition of the epistemological aetiology of Turing's argument; the latter by his objection to Turing's philosophical embellishments. But the question is: having agreed with points 1 and 2 listed at the beginning of this section, was Gödel entitled to reject Turing's reading of point 3?

As far as Gödel was concerned, Turing had only succeeded in analysing the concept of formal system (viz., as mechanical procedure). After all, in his 1947 lecture Turing vaguely claimed that he had succeeded in giving a precise definition of a 'rule of thumb' procedure in terms of 'mechanical calculability'. The issue has devolved onto the debate whether Gödel's objection that a distinction must be drawn between formal systems or algorithms and effective procedures is warranted. Thus Wang insists:

> What is adequately explicated [by Turing] is the intuitive concept of mechanical procedures or algorithms or computation procedures of finite combinatorial procedures. The related concept of effective procedures or constructive procedures, meaning procedures which can in the most general sense be carried out, suggest somewhat different elements which are related to the difference between mental and mechanical procedures.
>
> (*Ibid.*: 89)

In other words, Gödel identified mechanically with humanly effective procedures so far as finite combinatorial procedures are concerned. The former are those cases where the computation terminates (i.e. partial recursive functions). And the Halting Problem had established the existence of a class of functions where we do not know whether or not the program will terminate (Gödel's general recursive functions). But humanly effective procedures, according to Gödel, must always be capable of termination. It is not enough, however, to say that his reason for this assumption relied on the premise that humanly effective procedures must be finitely bound. Rather, Gödel seems to have shared Hilbert's belief that to grasp a problem is to know in advance that there must be an answer: something which, according to the Halting Problem, cannot be guaranteed to Turing Machines.

Wang depicts Gödel's position in terms of a *categorial* difference between mechanically and humanly effective procedures. Yet he offers no grounds for such a demarcation, other than the puzzling remark that

> The related concept of effective procedures or constructive procedures, meaning procedures which can in the most general sense be carried out, suggests somewhat different elements which are related to the difference between mental and mechanical procedures and the question as to the method by which a Turing machine or a set of equations is seen to be one which defines a Turing computable or general recursive function.
>
> (*Ibid.*)

As it stands, the argument is not convincing. For one thing, it is presented dogmatically, with no reason offered as to why effective procedures should be characterised by the criterion that we must know in advance whether or not they terminate. But in the Gibbs lecture (as quoted by Wang), Gödel appears to be interested in the slightly different objection that what is involved here is not so much a categorial as a qualitative difference: viz., mental processes *transcend* the capabilities of mechanically effective procedures. Turing's argument, according to Gödel, presents the 'following disjunction: Either the human mind surpasses all machines (to be more precise: it can decide more number theoretical questions than any machine) or else there exist number theoretical questions undecidable for the human mind.' Gödel's response was to regard 'Hilbert [as] right in rejecting the second alternative. If it were true it would mean that human reason is utterly irrational by asking questions it cannot answer, while asserting emphatically that only reason can answer them' (*ibid.*: 324–5).

Webb shows that it is simply irrelevant, as far as the parallels between effective and mechanical procedures are concerned, whether or not we know in advance that they will terminate. For

> whether a procedure literally 'can in the most general sense be carried out' does not depend on whether or not its termination can

be constructively guaranteed in advance, *but only on the execution of its atomic tasks*. If I can actually follow some procedure, however general, step by step, this would surely not be changed by forgetting that termination had been constructively proved. . . . Why should mental procedures require any more assurance of their termination than mechanical ones?

(Webb 1980: 224–5)

Indeed, Webb argues that, far from being a liability, the Halting Problem is the saving feature of the Mechanist Thesis, and that Turing's undecidable sentences should be seen as the 'guardian angels of computability theory' (*ibid.*: 202, 208). For without them the mechanist would be confronted with a strongly determinist account of thought. But the upshot of the Halting Problem is that to describe a Turing Machine as rule-governed is not at all to say that we can predict for all Turing Machines how they will terminate. In fact, as Turing was to emphasise in his account of mechanical chess, the whole point of learning programs is that it is often impossible to foresee how they will evolve (see Turing 1947: 122ff). One may thus sympathise with Gödel's stand, which harks back to the inspiring theme of Hilbert's Paris lecture that there is no problem in mathematics, however intractable it might at first appear, which cannot be resolved if only the right point of view from which to attack it is discovered. But the question Webb raises is whether Gödel provided any reason to deny the possibility of cultivating a similar ability in a self-modifying system.

Whatever one might feel about the mechanist conclusions which Webb draws from this objection, it must be conceded that he has successfully clarified a crucial aspect of Gödel's argument. According to Gödel, *thought* and *mechanical calculation* are partially co-extensive processes (viz., for the case of partial recursive functions). They diverge because of the epistemological constraints that exist for the latter (i.e. the premise that algorithmic calculability must be finitely bound), and the unbounded possibilities open to the former. But what about Gödel's initial premise? What does it mean to say that thought and mechanical calculation are *partially co-extensive processes*? In conceding this, has Gödel already admitted the very premise which lands him in the dilemma from which he could find no other escape than platonism?

This is very much the question that formed the starting-point for Wittgenstein's approach to Turing's Thesis. As Wittgenstein saw it, the real problem posed by Turing's version of the Mechanist Thesis lies in the epistemological framework that Turing inherited and augmented in his work on the *Entscheidungsproblem*. And it is precisely this element which, unlike Gödel, Wittgenstein tackled head-on. Wittgenstein's primary objectives were thus to clarify whether:

21

1   calculation can be analysed as consisting in a set of mental processes which may (or may not) be partially co-extensive with mechanical procedures; and
2   whether Turing's post-1941 development of the Mechanist Thesis rests on a misinterpretation of his computability results, the seeds of which were sown in Turing's 1936 presentation of his mechanical version of CT.

§5 The emergence of 'machine intelligence'

In the cosmology of AI, the higher cognitive forms only appeared when heuristic systems emerged from their primitive algorithmic origins. In the eyes of the founders of AI, 'Heuristic problem-solving, when successful, must, obviously, be rated as a higher mental activity than the solving of problems by some more or less automatic procedure. We are, therefore, probably justified in attaching the label of artificial intelligence to machine methods and machine programs that make use of heuristic procedures' (Samuel 1962: 14).

To do full justice to this argument, we shall have to look more closely, in Chapter 2, at the basic AI premise that 'Learning is any change in a system that produces a more or less permanent change in its capacity for adapting to its environment' (Simon 1984: 118). Given such a starting-point, it follows that there is no categorial difference between 'biological learning systems' – i.e. human beings – and 'ideal learning systems' – i.e. computer programs (*ibid.*). But in so far as the mastery of a rule must constitute the foundation for any theory of learning, our concern in the remainder of this chapter will be Turing's introduction of the notion of *mechanical rule-following*.

It is important to distinguish from the start between the AI view of rule-following and what one finds in computer science. Knuth describes how his

> favorite way to describe computer science is to say that it is the study of *algorithms*. An algorithm is a precisely defined sequence of rules telling how to produce specified output information from given input information in a finite number of steps. A particular representation of an algorithm is called a *program* . . . . Perhaps the most significant discovery generated by the advent of computers will turn out to be that algorithms, as objects of study, are extraordinarily rich in interesting properties and, furthermore, that an algorithmic point of view is a useful way to organize knowledge in general.
>
> (Knuth 1976: 38)

Elsewhere Knuth explains that 'an algorithm is a set of rules or directions for getting a specific output from a specific input. The distinguishing feature of an algorithm is that all vagueness must be eliminated; the rules must describe operations that are so simple and well defined they can be executed by a machine' (Knuth 1977: 63).

So far there is nothing here with which the Wittgensteinian philosopher need take strong exception. For all that Knuth is saying is that:

1   an algorithm consists of a set of rules, which
2   are all of roughly the same – i.e. trivial – complexity, and
3   together yield a specific output from a specific input.

On this reading, algorithms constitute a special sub-set of the class of functions (where functions are seen as rules for mapping arguments onto values). What distinguishes them in function-theoretic terms are 1 and 2 above.

Note that no mention is made here of the idea that a machine follows these 'simple' rules. But, as far as the founders of AI were concerned, the whole point of reducing rules to a series of utterly simple sub-rules was that the latter are such as can be followed by a machine. Thus, when the AI theorist discusses algorithms, the emphasis is on the idea that the 'Instructions given the computer must be complete and explicit, and they must enable it to proceed step by step without requiring that it comprehend the result of any part of the operations it performs. Such a program of instructions is an algorithm. It can demand any finite number of mechanical manipulations of numbers, but it cannot ask for judgments about their meaning' (Chaitin 1975: 47).

To appreciate the full implications of this interpretation of algorithms, we need to return to the assumption which lies at the heart of the 'justification' presented at §9 of 'On Computable Numbers'. The difference between Turing's 'slave' and 'learning' programs lies in the shift from fixed to self-modifying algorithms. In the case of the former, the Turing Machine repeatedly performs the same elementary steps *ad infinitum* (or *finitum* as the case may be). In the latter case, the Turing Machine alters its program by employing heuristics which enable it to augment its knowledge-base and/or store of rules, and thence the range and sophistication of the tasks it can execute. Thus, the crux of Turing's post-computational version of the Mechanist Thesis is that 'machine intelligence' is strictly a function of – emerges from – the complexity of a self-modifying heuristic program.

According to this doctrine, AI had 'to face the fact that a "human computer" does need intelligence – to follow rules formulated in a language he must *understand*' (Webb 1980: 220). So, in order to provide a 'non-question begging' analysis of calculation, 'the smallest, or most fundamental, or least sophisticated parts must not be supposed to perform tasks or follow procedures requiring intelligence' (Dennett 1978: 83). Thus,

Turing's analysis of calculation is said to have 'succeeded just because it *circumvented* the problem of how a computer can understand ordinary language' (Webb 1980: 225). For without 'meanings' to deal with, 'these atomic tasks presuppose no intelligence [and] it follows that a non-circular psychology of computation is possible' (*ibid.*: 220). Hence the epistemological significance of Turing's version of CT is said to lie in his having demonstrated that algorithms can be described as:

> complex systems of meaningless sub-rules, each of which can as such be applied purely mechanically.

One of the issues arising from this 'analysis' of calculation which has most captivated contemporary philosophers of mind is whether *understanding* can be built up out of the 'syntactical instructions' that man and machine are both said to follow (see Searle 1980). But the problem which concerned Wittgenstein lay in the prior assumption that, by scanning, printing, and erasing symbols on its tape, a Turing Machine can be said to be *following* 'meaningless sub-rules'. There are two interlocking assumptions operating in this conception of algorithms which Wittgenstein scrutinised:

1   that it is intelligible to speak of a species of *meaningless rule*;
2   that the concept of *mechanically following a rule* is equivalent to the concept of *following a mechanical rule*.

We shall look at item 1 in the remainder of this section, and item 2 in the final section of this chapter.

In order to come to grips with the notion of a 'meaningless rule', we first need to recognise that there is an important distinction between describing a subject as following the sub-rules of an algorithm, and describing a subject as grasping the algorithm itself. Wang cites the example of how a pupil can learn how to apply a Euclidean algorithm correctly without comprehending how it works: 'Giving an algorithm for solving a class K of problems and a problem belonging to K, anybody can solve the problem provided he is able to perform the operations required by the algorithm and to follow exactly the rules as given. For example a schoolboy can learn the Euclidean algorithm correctly without knowing why it gives the desired answers' (Wang 1974: 90). The problem that concerns us here is the supposition that 'a schoolboy can learn the Euclidean algorithm correctly without knowing why it gives the desired answers'. For it would seem that this credits the child with an ability which he is then immediately said not to possess.

In general, we describe a subject as having mastered a rule if the subject is able to explain, justify, correct, etc., his actions *by reference to that rule*. The case of algorithms is no different. To master an algorithm involves more than just executing each of its sub-steps without grasping the overall pattern or function of these 'atomic tasks'. Someone who learned all the individual rules for the chess-pieces without ever grasping that the point of the game is to mate their opponent's king would not yet have learnt how to play chess. Likewise we would not say that a pupil had mastered the rules of long division if he were to tell us that he didn't know how to proceed when no remainder was left. So, too, all one can say in Wang's example is that the schoolboy has learned how to apply what, for him, is a set of independent rules; but to learn how to apply each of these 'atomic rules' does not in itself amount to *learning the algorithm*.[15]

This still leaves us, however, with the problem of what is involved in speaking of the schoolboy as 'learning how to apply each of the sub-rules of the algorithm'. The crucial point here is that exactly the same sort of criteria apply to the pupil's mastery of each of the sub-rules, *qua* rules, as apply to the algorithm itself. That is, to describe S as having mastered a sub-rule entails that he possesses the same sort of abilities as outlined above. The *simplicity* versus *complexity* of a rule has no bearing on the normativity of rule-following. Clearly, therefore, Turing's argument must somehow be seen to overcome this obstacle, and this brings us up against one of the major premises in his Thesis: the idea that there is such a thing as a 'meaningless sub-rule'. The obvious question one wants to ask here is, what sort of rule would a *meaningless rule* be: a rule which, by definition, has no meaning: which stipulates nothing? This certainly looks like a contradiction in terms; in which case, one wants to know how such a radical thesis could have been so readily and uncritically accepted.

Of the many factors involved in the reception of Turing's Thesis, the one that particularly stands out is the importance of Hilbert's epistemological framework. Gödel maintained that

> The concept of formal system requires that reasoning be completely replaced by 'mechanical operations' on formulas in just the sense made clear by Turing machines. More exactly, a formal system is nothing but a many valued Turing machine which permits a predetermined range of choices at certain steps. The one who works the Turing machine can, by his choice, set a lever at certain stages. This is precisely what one does in proving theorems within a formal system.
>
> (Wang 1974: 84)

Ironically, Wittgenstein would have agreed with the opening premise of this argument, but significantly, not at all in the manner intended.

As we saw in the preceding section, Gödel felt that Turing had successfully analysed the concept of *formal system*: i.e. that Turing Machines manifest the mechanical essence of the symbolic transformations which characterise a formal system. Wittgenstein's response to this point was that, if anything, Turing Machines manifest the *non-mathematical* character of 'formal systems', in so far as 'it is essential to mathematics that its signs are also employed in *mufti*' (RFM V: §2). This is quite a large (and important) issue. Among other things, it demands careful consideration of the relationship between mathematical propositions, the well-formed formulae of a formal system, and the manner in which Hilbert tried to bridge the gap between syntax and semantics with 'interpretations' (see Shanker 1988b). For our purposes, it suffices to note that the reason why Wittgenstein would agree that 'The concept of formal system requires that reasoning be completely replaced by "mechanical operations" on formulas in just the sense made clear by Turing machines' is that the concept of *reasoning* is fundamentally incompatible with that of *formal system*.[16]

That is, it is misleading to speak of a 'mechanical *deduction*'; for the two concepts involved here – *inference* and *sign manipulation* – cannot be fused together. One can speak of correctly *transforming* signs (according to the rules of the system), but not of *deducing* one string of meaningless marks from another. We say that S has grasped that q follows from p if S is able to explain the nature of the conceptual relationship between the meaning of q and p: i.e. that p *entails* q.

Thus, to return to the passage on calculation examined in the first section, if someone were accidentally to press the knobs '25', '×', and '20' of a calculating machine and obtain the result 500, they would not thereby have *calculated* the product of 25 × 20. For

> You aren't calculating if, when you get now this, now that result, and cannot find a mistake, you accept this and say: this simply shews that certain circumstances which are still unknown have an influence on the result.
>
> This might be expressed: if calculation reveals a causal connexion to you, then you are not calculating. . . . What I am saying comes to this, that mathematics is *normative*.
>
> (RFM VII: §61)

Similarly, if by a series of carefully scripted stimuli we were able to cause a subject to turn a switch off and on in such a way that the subject's actions could be used to produce results that we obtain by applying an algorithm, that would not mean that the subject was 'tacitly' applying that algorithm. For being caused to turn a switch off and on is not the same thing as following the simple instruction 'Turn the switch on whenever you see *x*'.

The standard AI response to this argument is that Wittgenstein has ignored the most critical aspect of Turing's Thesis: viz., the distinction between describing what the agent is aware of doing – e.g. the sorts of things which the agent might say if asked 'Why did you φ?' – and what is going on in the agent's mind/brain when he was φing. That is, at the level of *human action* it might be illicit to speak of a 'meaningless sub-rule', but at the *pre-conscious* level of information-processing, this is the only kind of rule which a brain could follow. Thus, the ultimate issue that concerns us here is whether Turing succeeded in analysing – i.e. in reducing – the concept of *calculation* to a level where Wittgenstein's objections simply do not apply.

§6 'Mechanical rule-following' versus 'Following a "mechanical rule"'

At the heart of AI is the belief that 'What Turing did around 1936 was to give a cogent and complete logical analysis of the notion of "computation".' Thus it was that, although people have been computing for centuries, it has only been since 1936 that we have possessed a satisfactory answer to the question: 'What is a computation?' (Davis 1978: 241). According to this view,

> Turing based his precise definition of computation on an analysis of what a human being *actually* does when he computes. Such a person is following a set of rules which must be carried out in a *completely mechanical manner*. Ingenuity may well be involved in setting up these rules so that a computation may be carried out efficiently, but once the rules are laid down, they must be carried out in a mercilessly exact way.
>
> (*Ibid.*: 243; emphasis added)

In other words, an agent's ability to calculate reduces to the mechanical application of sub-rules at the cerebral level. It has also been suggested that the sub-rules of an algorithm must be treated as meaningful in some unique sense, which would allow one to speak of symbolic systems as possessing their own intrinsic 'meanings', and thus, of 'brain symbols as having original meaning' (Haugeland 1985: 119).

Even Wang, who was so opposed to the Mechanist Thesis, conceded that:

> The intuitive notion of an algorithm is rather vague. For example, what is a rule? We would like the rules to be mechanically interpretable, i.e. such that a machine can understand the rule (instruction) and carry it out. In other words, we need to specify a language for describing algorithms which is general enough to describe all mechanical procedures and yet simple enough to be interpreted by a machine. . . . What Turing did was to analyze the human calculating act and arrive at a number of simple operations which are obviously mechanical in nature and yet can be shown to

27

be capable of being combined to perform arbitrarily complex mechanical operations.

(Wang 1974: 91)

But this argument assumes the very point which it sets out to establish: viz., that an algorithm breaks down the act of following a rule (e.g. calculating) into a set of *non-cognitive instructions*, such as can be 'followed' by a machine. That is, Turing's analysis reduces *calculation* to a level where there is no difference between *following a rule mechanically* and *following a 'mechanical rule'*: i.e., where the 'utterly simple rules' of algorithms are collapsed into 'simple mechanical rules'.

The first thing to note here is that an algorithm is not a *precise formulation* of the rules of calculation; rather, it is a *different* set of rules from the original which it is intended to supplant. Davis's Doubling Program,[17] for example, is completely different from *squaring*, inasmuch as it employs addition and subtraction instead of multiplication. To be sure, the outcome of the program corresponds to the results yielded by the rules for squaring. But what matters here is how we learn and apply the two systems of rules.

The fact that we can use the rules of addition and subtraction rather than multiplication for the purposes of doubling – as opposed to squaring – does not entail that, when squaring, what we *actually* – i.e. 'tacitly', or 'preconsciously' – do is add. If, in answer to the question 'How did you calculate that the square of 125 is 15,625?', a subject responds: 'I multiplied 125 × 125 in my head', he tells us which rules he was mentally following. The fact that the same answer can be obtained by a doubling program does not license the AI claim that, in fact, the subject's answer is wrong, or only partially correct, in so far as Turing showed us that the proper answer is that his brain must have added 125 to itself one hundred and twenty-five times. All that is involved here is the fact that one set of rules may prove to be more efficient than another in a different context or for different purposes.

Indeed, why does Turing speak of 'sub-rules' at all here? The answer is that, in order to make his reductionist analysis of calculation at all convincing, Turing had to make it type-homologous. That is, he had to maintain that algorithms decompose rules into their 'normative components'. But the reduction of calculation to a species of 'non-cognitive atomic tasks' cannot, *ex hypothesi*, be entirely homologous; for the whole point of reducing rules to sub-rules is to remove the 'normative element' which characterises the rule proper.

The argument runs into two different obstacles here. First of all, as we saw in the preceding section, no matter how simple a rule might be, this does not serve to remove its 'semantic content'. A typical rule in Davis's Doubling Program is:

> Go to step i if 0 is scanned.

But this rule is anything but *meaningless*. Granted, it is so simple that one can envisage an agent doing it mechanically after a short while (*infra*). But, however simple this rule might be, it does indeed tell one what to do.

The only way one can remove this statement's 'normative content' is by treating it as a description of the events that occur at such-and-such a point in the program, rather than as a rule. And then one can argue that, just as scanning a '0' causes the program to go to step i, so too such-and-such a neural stimulus causes such-and-such a neural response. Thus, Turing suggests that the (human) computer's 'state of mind' is the causal intermediary between observed symbols and subsequent action.

Certainly, the above statement looks like a rule – i.e. like an *instruction* – but what it actually describes on this causal picture is how:

A '0' activates the transit mechanism.

But then, this has nothing whatsoever to do with *rule-following*; it simply shows one how to break down a complex mechanical action – e.g. registering twice as many '1s' as were originally configured on a tape – into its sub-components. Moreover, the term chosen here is entirely apposite; for these mechanical operations are indeed subject to 'breakdown', but not to negligence, mental lapses, or plain misunderstanding. Hence they are *immune from error*: not because they are infallible, but, rather, because it makes no sense to speak of *error* here. For to be *capable of making a mistake* presupposes the ability to follow a rule. But Turing simply glosses over this fundamental conceptual demarcation when he argues that:

> the machine has certain advantages over the mathematician. Whatever it does can be relied upon, assuming no mechanical 'breakdown', whereas the mathematician makes a certain proportion of mistakes. . . . My contention is that machines can be constructed which will simulate the behaviour of the human mind very closely. They will make mistakes at times . . .
>
> (Turing 1959: 129)

The basic problem with Turing's 'analysis' is that the normativity of calculation disappears altogether. For he wants to postulate an entirely new species of 'rule': one that is *embodied in the brain*, and thus acts as a causal mechanism. Turing can then argue that normative behaviour can be reduced to a sequence of causal processes which, because they are cerebral, lie beyond a subject's awareness. Hence, one can use a Turing Machine as a *model* of these 'pre-conscious' causal processes.

As we shall see in Chapter 3, this argument ushered in a new version of psychologism, which served as one of the central reasons why the founders of the cognitive revolution were so drawn to AI. For the moment, however, our concern is with the manner in which Turing obscures the difference between using a mechanical process as a substitute for a normative practice, and seeing that mechanical process as a model of that normative practice. That is, our concern is with Wittgenstein's argument that *'There are no* causal connexions in a calculation, only the connexions of the pattern. And it makes no difference to this that we work over the proof in order to accept it. That we are therefore tempted to say that it arose as the result of a psychological experiment. For the psychical course of events is not psychologically investigated when we calculate' (RFM VII: §18).

One cannot emphasise enough the importance of Turing's demonstration that, given their (binary) encodability, recursive functions are ideally suited to mechanical implementation. But to mechanise rule-governed behaviour is to *substitute* a mechanical process for a normative practice. Even to speak of the machine's operations as *calculations* only serves to distort the categorial shift which occurs when mechanical devices displace normative activities.[18]

The danger here is that of supposing that, because, for example, a sorting machine can be built to do the same thing as an agent following an utterly simple rule (e.g. 'Discard all the apples without a stem'), the steps in the machine provide a model of the 'mechanics' of the agent's normative behaviour. But an account of the machine's operations can only explicate why the machine produced its results: not whether or not these were correct. For only the rules of sorting can establish this, and it is for that reason that they are said to be *antecedent* to the machine's operations. Likewise, the rules of calculation establish the criteria which determine when we shall say that the result arrived at by a Turing Machine is correct or incorrect.

The ultimate question which this raises, therefore, is: What is the difference between *mechanically following a rule*, and *following a 'mechanical rule'*? According to AI, the answer is: none. For example, after introducing the reader to Turing's computability thesis at the beginning of *Gödel, Escher, Bach*, Hofstadter remarks:

> Here one runs up against a seeming paradox. Computers by their very nature are the most inflexible, desireless, rule-following beasts. Fast though they may be, they are nonetheless the epitome of unconsciousness. How, then, can intelligent behaviour be programmed? Isn't this the most blatant of contradictions in terms? One of the major theses of this book is that it is not a contradiction at all.
>
> (Hofstadter 1980: 26)

The terms of this passage should be scrutinised long before one considers Hofstadter's efforts to surmount the paradox.

The first thing to notice is that it is not at all clear what the opening part states. What does it mean to describe a computer as 'desireless': something which, as it happens, has no desires, or rather, something of which it is absurd to speak of desires? Second, Hofstadter assumes the very point which, according to Wittgenstein, is the crux of the issue: that computers are 'rule-following beasts'. We shall only look now, however, at the third of the assumptions that Hofstadter makes here: that the issue somehow hinges on a computer's lack of 'consciousness'. It is the same point that Davis is making in the passage quoted at the beginning of this section, and almost certainly what Turing had in mind at §9 of 'On Computable Numbers', which is that there can be mechanical analogues of the 'preconscious' processes that govern a subject's behaviour when calculating mechanically.

Wittgenstein did not deny the possibility of an agent's performing certain calculations mechanically; but he is careful to clarify what this actually means. Thus he remarks: 'One follows the rule *mechanically*. Hence one compares it with a mechanism. "Mechanical" – that means: without thinking. But *entirely* without thinking? Without *reflecting*' (RFM VII: §60). This is a theme which recurs throughout Wittgenstein's remarks on rule-following. We speak of following a rule mechanically all the time: e.g. when driving a car. The question is, why describe this behaviour in normative terms: i.e., what distinguishes this behaviour from genuine automatic (e.g. autonomic) behaviour?

Suppose we are dealing with reflexes. If an agent is asked, for example, why he blinked, his answer – should he be capable of giving one – will be in strictly causal terms, and, as such, subject to confirmation or falsification. But suppose that the agent responds: 'I didn't blink, I winked, and I did so because I was taught to wink whenever x occurs.' In this latter case we shall describe the agent as following a rule, not because we are framing some hypothesis about what may have gone on in his brain, but rather, because he offers a rule as the *grounds* for his action.

Certainly, when we calculate, many of the familiar rules are performed unreflectingly. But the point that Wittgenstein is making at RFM VIII, §60, is that it is the agent's ability to cite the rules of calculation if called upon to explain or justify his results, which warrants our describing him as *calculating*. The point here is not that to follow a rule demands that one be conscious of the fact that one is following that rule; rather, it is that we describe an agent's behaviour in normative terms if the agent is capable of justifying (correcting, explaining, etc.) his actions *by reference to the rule*. Ultimately, therefore, the fallacy committed by Turing in his epistemological interpretation of his version of CT was to move from the indisputable simplicity of the sub-rules of an algorithm to the conclusion that such procedures are such that they can be *followed by a machine*. For the fact that we might follow such rules unreflectingly in no way licenses the conclusion that they are 'non-cognitive', and *a fortiori*, such that a machine could 'follow' them.

To be sure, Turing presented a picture of algorithms in which 'Ingenuity may well be involved in setting up these rules so that a computation may be carried out efficiently, but once the rules are laid down, they must be carried out in a mercilessly exact way' (Davis, 1965). But then, exactly the same thing may be said of the traffic code. What matters here is the fact that a mechanical device for sign-manipulation is no more a 'rule-following beast' than an abacus.

This last point brings us full circle to Wittgenstein's insistence that Turing's machines 'are really *humans* who calculate'. As if to corroborate Wittgenstein's insight, Turing was later to write:

> It is possible to produce the effect of a computing machine by writing down a set of rules of procedure and asking a man to carry them out. Such a combination of a man with written instructions will be called a 'Paper Machine'. A man provided with paper, pencil, and rubber, and subject to strict discipline, is in effect a universal machine.
>
> (Turing 1948: 9)

If this later argument seems to suffer from circularity, it is entirely because of the pressures built into 'On Computable Numbers'.

It was noted at the outset that, from Wittgenstein's point of view, 'On Computable Numbers' must be seen as a hybrid paper: it begins with a mathematical analysis of functions, but then strays into an inquiry into the cognitive processes of those who use them to calculate. In the first part of 'On Computable Numbers', Turing provides a unique insight into the criterion implicit in earlier attempts to delimit the range of number-theoretic functions for which there are algorithms. In the second part of the paper, he shifts to a conceptual analysis of calculation. The crux of Wittgenstein's response to Turing's interpretation of the epistemological significance of his mechanical version of CT is that the only way Turing could synthesise these disparate elements was by investing his machines with cognitive abilities *ab initio*: that is, by assuming the very premise which he subsequently undertook to defend.

The next step in our investigation of Turing's influence on the origins of AI will be to consider the manner in which Turing sought to reconcile his theory of machine intelligence with contemporary theories of learning. To conclude this prolegomenon, however, we have still to resolve why Turing should have presented these mechanical operations in quasi-cognitive terms in the first place. That is, why did Turing preface his mathematico-logical achievement with the analogy that 'we may compare a Turing Machine to a man in the process of computing'?

To dismiss the 'justification' presented in §9 of 'On Computable Numbers' as nothing more than an example of the philosophical confusions that can arise when mathematicians venture into prose in order to interpret the significance of their results would be to abandon what is perhaps the most important feature of this entire issue: viz., the manner in which the inner dynamics of the exercise upon which Turing had embarked were responsible for his subsequent involvement in the Mechanist Thesis. For Turing did not approach CT in order to promote the Mechanist Thesis; on the contrary, the latter interest evolved from his version of CT, and it is for that reason that the foundations underlying Turing's thought are as significant as the content of his computability results.

Indeed, the very controversy which continues to surround AI is proof of the enduring strength of that epistemological framework – and the problems obdurately tied to it. It was ultimately because formal systems were seen to demand an epistemological counterpart to the role which understanding plays *vis-à-vis* mathematical propositions that Church's convention was found wanting. And so it was that, because of the framework he inherited, Turing was led into the justification presented at §9, and his 'analysis' hailed as 'an absolute definition of an interesting epistemological notion' (Gödel 1946). Those who still wish to build a computational empire on the basis of such troubling precedents would do well to pause first on the significance of Wittgenstein's ever-timely warning that 'One keeps forgetting to go right down to the foundations. One doesn't put the question marks *deep* enough down' (CV: 62).

2

THE BEHAVIOURIST ORIGINS
OF AI

[The psychologists who] considered themselves to be mechanists tended to be something else. I don't know if there's a
word for them. There should be – let's say simplists. Striking
examples are people like Pavlov and Watson and the whole
family of people who believed in conditioning as a basis for
learning, the mechanical associationists. Although on the
surface they could be considered mechanists because they seem
to talk more openly about the mind being a machine, their
real trouble is that their image of the machine is precomputa-
tional.

(Marvin Minsky, quoted in Pamela McCorduck's
Machines Who Think)

§1 Turing's two questions

Turing's celebrated 1950 paper, 'Computing Machinery and Intelligence', is
dominated by the *philosophical* question that Turing asks at the outset: *'Can
machines think?'* It is a question whose import cannot be divorced from the
resounding success of Turing's version of Church's Thesis (see Chapter 1).
Moreover, if judged by the amount of interest which it has aroused, this
question surely stands unrivalled in post-war analytic philosophy. And yet,
as far as the foundations of AI are concerned, there is a definite sense in
which this question places the emphasis on the wrong issue. Indeed, there is
even a sense in which it places the emphasis on the wrong issue as far as
Turing's own interests are concerned. For over and over again we find him
returning to the *psychological* question: *Can thought be mechanically explained?*
This is a very different and, in many ways, a much more significant matter.

These two questions belong to very different traditions. The former was a
central concern of English mathematicians in the nineteenth century (e.g.
Babbage, Jevons and Marquand); the latter a mainstay of empiricist
psychology in Germany, England and America. But Turing regarded these
two questions as intimately connected: in fact, he thought that in answering

the one you would, *ipso facto*, be answering the other. The result was a remarkable synthesis: not only did Turing succeed in merging recursive function theory and psychology, but, within psychology itself, he brought together two distinct – and even hostile – schools of thought under the banner of *post-computational mechanism*. But while Turing's conception of automata may have been strikingly original, his approach to the analysis of thought pursues themes that can be traced back to the Greeks.

Admittedly, it is difficult to view the question 'Can machines think?' as anything other than a modern phenomenon (which, in philosophical terms, means Cartesian). But the question 'Can thought be mechanically explained?' is another matter. The succession of mechanical metaphors of mind – *qua* hydraulic pipes, clock, telegraph system, telephone exchange, feedback circuit, serial and parallel computer – are part of a tradition that stems from a persisting picture of a *mechanist continuum* (see §2). Locke's argument that 'In all the visible corporeal world we see no chasms or gaps. All quite down from us the descent is by easy steps, and a continued series that in each remove differ very little one from the other' (Locke 1690: III vi §12); Whytt's claim that 'in all the works of nature, there is a beautiful gradation, and a kind of link, as it were, betwixt each species of animals, the lowest of the immediately superior class, different little from the highest in the next succeeding order' (Fearing 1930: 75); Herrick's premise that there is 'an unbroken graded series from the lowest to the highest animal species' (*ibid.*: 179); and George's insistence that there is a cognitive continuum, 'with simple negative adaptation (habituation, or accommodation, and tropisms, which are orientating responses and are known to be mediated by fairly simple physico-chemical means) at one end, and maze-learning, puzzle-box learning . . . and ape-learning . . . in stages of increasing complexity, leading to human learning at the other end' (George 1962: 180), all spring from the same source as that which led to Aristotle's maxim in *De Generatione Animalium* that 'Nature orders generation in regular gradation' (Aristotle 1938: 186).

It is precisely this psychological issue, however, from which the question of whether machines can think inadvertently serves to deflect attention. Turing repeatedly insists that his sole concern is with 'the meaning of the words "machine" and "think",' and that it is his faith in 'semantic progress' which leads him to express his belief 'that at the end of the century the use of words and general educated opinion will have altered so much that one will be able to speak of machines thinking without expecting to be contradicted' (Turing 1950: 133, 142). Most of the papers he wrote towards the end of his life begin with a defence of 'machine intelligence'. His 1947 'Lecture to the London Mathematical Society', 'Intelligent Machinery' (1948), 'Computing Machinery and Intelligence' (1950), and his 1951 BBC lecture 'Can Digital Computers Think?' all begin by making the same point: Turing's repeated claim that he was 'not interested in developing a *powerful* brain . . . just a *mediocre* brain' (Hodges 1983: 251), and that 'if a machine is expected to be infallible, it cannot also be intelligent' (Turing 1947: 105).

The concept of *machine* had already undergone radical changes. At the beginning of the nineteenth century it had been confined to the static motions dictated by Newtonian mechanics, but by the 1870s the concept had so evolved as to encompass the homeostatic systems conceived by Claude Bernard. These developments were essential to the transition in the mechanist/vitalist debate from the Life Sciences to the Human Sciences that took place in the nineteenth century: i.e. the transition from the question whether the body can be explained in mechanical terms to the question whether the mind can be so explained.

The problem faced by both physiological and psychological mechanists at the turn of the century was the same: it stemmed from the widespread doubt that machines would ever approximate the creative aspect of mental phenomena. The key word here is 'ever', which signifies that the issue was regarded as empirical. The obvious solution would, in G. H. Lewes's words, be to 'think through the essentials of such a mechanism'. But 'An automaton that will learn by experience, and adapt itself to conditions not calculated for in its construction, has yet to be made; till it is made, we must deny that organisms are machines' (Lewes 1877: 436).

This is precisely the problem which was continuing to preoccupy and frustrate mechanists fifty years on; and, indeed, might have remained beyond the reach of their ambitions had Turing not completed the mathematical transformation of the concept of machine. As we saw in the opening chapter, what Turing proved in 'On Computable Numbers' is that an 'effective function' is an algorithm that can be so encoded (e.g. in binary terms) as to be machine-executable. But for the advocates of strong AI, Turing had proved far more than this: what he had really accomplished was to transform machines into a species of 'rule-following beasts' (Hofstadter 1980). And the manner in which he was said to have achieved this feat was by postulating a category of 'meaningless (sub-) rules' which could guide the operations of a machine (and/or the brain), thereby providing the rudiments for a new understanding of 'machine', and thence, the creation of artificial intelligence.

For almost three decades, philosophical discussions of Turing's contributions to the origins of AI centred on his preoccupation with strong AI, the nature of consciousness, and the significance of the Turing Test. It is not difficult to account for the overwhelming response which these issues elicited. Turing's argument spoke directly to the anxieties of a society that had just lived through a terrifying war, only to find itself in a world that had not just been transformed, but was continuing to change at a rate never before experienced in ways that few had envisaged. Turing's was the bold and, to many, the reassuring voice of the new vanguard; but the message was as old as the Renaissance: technological advances cannot be halted, man must adapt to the inexorable march of progress. And so there followed a flurry of articles and books in which AI-theorists rhapsodised and humanists anguished, all of them mesmerised by the debate over man's position on the Scala Naturae. Archetypal issues clearly die hard.

With all of the rhetoric about the computational possibilities being opened up, or the singular phenomenological characteristics of human experience, it was easy to overlook the fact that, in order to defend his philosophical thesis – viz., his proof that, if not quite yet, at some point in the future, machines will indeed be capable of thought – Turing was led deeper and deeper into the development of an appropriate psychological theory: viz., that *thinkers compute*. By the time he came to write 'Computing Machinery and Intelligence' he was explaining how his real goal was that of 'trying to imitate an adult human mind' (Turing 1950: 155). The result was a sublimely simple mechanist theory whose appeal lay in its claimed ability 'to resolve complex psychical phenomena into more elementary processes' – a sentiment which, significantly, was expressed fourteen years before the publication of 'On Computable Numbers' (Rignano 1923).

Turing's psychological theory represents a marriage of *Denkpsychologie* and behaviourism. His basic idea is that thinking is an effective procedure (because the brain is a digital computer): i.e., the mind proceeds, via an unbroken chain of mechanical steps, from a to ω, even though the subject himself may only be aware of a, δ, ξ, and ω. By mapping the subject's thought-processes onto a program designed to solve the same problem, we can thus fill in the intervening – *subconscious* – steps. This is the thesis underlying Turing's observation in 'Can Digital Computers Think?' that 'The whole thinking process is still rather mysterious to us, but I believe that the attempt to make a thinking machine will help us greatly in finding out how we think ourselves' (Hodges 1983: 442).

To be sure, there is nothing particularly novel about this picture of the unconscious mind. As a matter of fact, Hadamard's *The Psychology of Mathematical Invention* is about little else. Hadamard cites story after story to establish how all the important creative work in mathematical discovery is unconscious (see Hadamard 1945). But Hadamard's book also vividly illustrates why Turing's psychological thesis was to have such a profound and widespread impact. For, on traditional theories of the *cognitive unconscious*, the problem of 'insight' was simply shifted down a level, where any amount of extraordinary cognitive abilities that escaped the conscious mind could be attributed to the unconscious. But Turing's argument claims to take no such metaphysical step; for the processes occurring 'beneath the threshold of consciousness' are all said to be Turing-Machine computable. But then, by placing the emphasis on the question of whether machines can think, Turing only manages to blur the crucial demarcation-lines between materialism and mechanism: between breaking the machine down into its component parts, and using the machine as a psychological paradigm for understanding how the mind works.

Newell and Simon were perhaps the first to realise the significance of this point. Indeed, it was partly for that reason that they were initially opposed to the name 'artificial intelligence'.[1] For they were not interested in the philosophical question of whether or not machines can be said to think; rather, they wanted to place the emphasis firmly on psychological explanation. As they explained in 'GPS: A Program which Simulates Human Thought':

> We may then conceive of an intelligent program that manipulates symbols in the same way that our subject does – by taking as inputs the symbolic logic expressions, and producing as outputs a sequence of rule applications that coincides with the subject's. If we observed this program in operation, it would be considering various rules and evaluating various expressions, the same sorts of things we see expressed in the protocol of the subject. If the fit of such a program were close enough to the overt behaviour of our human subject – i.e. to the protocol – then it would constitute a good theory of the subject's problem-solving.
>
> (Newell and Simon 1963: 283)

It is easy to see how this argument could have been read as an expression of strong AI: if the computer can solve the same problems as man – and what's more, do so in exactly the same steps – then it would have satisfied the demands for the attribution of 'intelligence'. But the psychological significance of the argument is contained in the last line: in the claim that such a program would constitute a *theory* of problem-solving. The reasoning here is straightforward: given that thinking is an effective procedure, then, if a program simulates a subject's 'overt behaviour' and the 'fragments' of his thinking-process which he observed and reported, that program will have explained the 'hidden processes' that brought about the subject's behaviour.

The essential details of Newell and Simon's argument had already been sketched by Turing. This is the reason why we find Turing spending so much time during this period on the development of chess programs. Chess served as the ideal medium for the computational simulation/explanation of those processes which a subject (or rather, a subject's mind) employs when solving problems, where this was seen as a matter of grasping a problem, tentatively experimenting with various methods of solution, selecting a favoured route, and then verifying the success of the chosen means. What made chess so suitable for this purpose was the fact that the decision-making procedures leading up to a move are highly amenable to hierarchical recursive analysis: a player thinks through a problem by shuttling back and forth between sub- and primary-goals as he first formulates a plan, calculates the permutations, deduces whether any of these will implement the strategy he has in mind, and if none of these succeeds in realising the overall goal, formulates a new plan and repeats the process.[2] Most important of all is the fact that chess afforded the perfect environment in which to map out the goal-directed pattern of the mechanical procedures that constitute problem-solving in a fixed domain: given the prior assumption that these are moves within a calculus. The resulting models may of course be far removed from anything one might encounter in ordinary chess play; but the fact that we may not be aware of such processes was thought to be merely a confirmation of the limits of introspection (see Chapter 4).

If Turing's major accomplishment in 'On Computable Numbers' was to expose the epistemological premises built into formalism, his main achievement in the 1940s was to recognise the extent to which this outlook both harmonised with and extended contemporary behaviourist thought. Turing sought to synthesise these diverse mathematical and psychological elements so as to forge a union between 'embodied rules' and 'learning programs'. Through their joint service in the Mechanist Thesis each would validate the other, and the frameworks from whence each derived. What is all too often overlooked by cognitivists, however, is the fact that, by providing the computational means for overcoming the impasse in which mechanism found itself before the war, Turing was committed to the very framework – as defined by its set of assumptions – which had created it. As important as Turing's version of Church's Thesis was for the foundations of AI, no less significant was the behaviourist thesis which provided the means for the transformation of Turing's 'slave machines' into 'intelligent automatons'. It is to the latter thesis that we must look, therefore, in order to understand, not simply the genesis, but more importantly the presuppositions of AI. For it suggests that the gulf between pre- and post-computational mechanism may not be nearly so great as has commonly been assumed.

§2 Turing's behaviourist ambitions

The main reason why it is so tempting to speak of a 'post-computational mechanist revolution' is because of the contrast between behaviourist and AI attitudes towards the role of 'mental states' in the explanation of actions. But before we accept the radical divergence commonly postulated between 'pre-' and 'post-computational' mechanism, we should consider the extent to which Turing saw himself as working within the framework of behaviourism: as taking the behaviourist account of problem-solving a step further by treating 'mental states' as 'machine-state configurations', thereby allowing for a reductionist explanation of such higher-level activities as chess-playing and theorem-proving. This enables one to see that the route leading from Huxley's 'sentient automatons', through Jevons and

Marquand's 'reasoning machines', to Hull and Turing's 'learning systems', displays far more continuity than is commonly recognised.

In order to understand the significance of Turing's contribution to the evolution of behaviourism, we need to return to the theme that the thought-experiment machines portrayed in 'On Computable Numbers' are not credited with cognitive abilities as such; on the contrary, they are explicitly referred to as 'devoid of intelligence'. The routines that they execute are described as 'brute force': a reminder, not just of the repetitive strategy they use to solve computational problems, but also that they belong to the intellectual level of the brutes – with all the Cartesian overtones which this carries. In Turing's words, these machines 'should be treated as entirely without intelligence'. But, he continues, 'There are indications . . . that it is possible to make the machine display intelligence at the risk of its making occasional serious mistakes' (Turing 1946: 41). Just as we can say of a student exposed to 'teachers [who] have been intentionally trying to modify' his behaviour that 'at the end of the period a large number of standard routines will have been superimposed on the original pattern of his brain', so too, 'by applying appropriate interference, mimicking education, we should hope to modify the machine until it could be relied on to produce definite reactions to certain commands' (Turing 1959: 14).

The key to accomplishing this feat lies in the introduction of 'learning programs': self-modifying algorithms that revise their rules in order to improve the range and sophistication of the tasks they can execute, thereby satisfying Lewes's demand for an automaton capable of adapting to conditions not calculated for in its construction. The obvious problem which this argument raises, however, is whether, or in what sense, such programs can be described as 'learning' and, should this be deemed inappropriate, how Turing could have assumed that 'self-modifying' means the same thing as 'learning'. But before this issue can be explored, there lies the prior question of why Turing should have seized on this particular notion in order to implement his mechanist ideas.

There are several reasons why *learning* assumed such importance in mechanist thought *vis-à-vis* both of the 'traditions' outlined in §1. In mythopoeic terms, the automaton only springs to life once it displays the ability to recognise and master its environment (at which point humanist anxieties invariably surface in the form of the creator's loss of control over this now autonomous being). In both physiological and psychological terms, questions about the nature of learning dominated the mechanist/vitalist debates during the nineteenth century. And in terms of the history of AI, the first, and in some ways most potent objection raised against the Mechanist Thesis was voiced nearly a century before the invention of computers.

In her Notes on Menabrea's 'Sketch', Ada Lovelace cautioned that Babbage's 'Analytical Engine has no pretensions whatever to *originate* anything. It can do whatever we *know how to order it* to perform. It can *follow* analysis; but it has no power of *anticipating* any analytical relations or truths. Its province is to assist us in making *available* what we are already acquainted with'[3] (Lovelace 1842: 284). As he makes clear in 'Computing Machinery and Intelligence', the crux of Turing's version of the Mechanist Thesis turns on the very premise which Lovelace denies in this passage. 'Who can be certain', Turing asks, 'that "original work" that he has done was not simply the growth of the seed planted in him by teaching, or the effect of following well-known general principles' (Turing 1950: 150). The important point is that, granted that the operations of a machine can be guided by rules (however simple these might be), it should be possible to develop programs of sufficient complexity to warrant the attribution of intelligence. It was this argument which was to have so dramatic an effect on mechanist thought. For Turing was to insist that the essence of a 'learning program' is its ability to simulate the creative aspect of human problem-solving (see Turing 1947: 103–4).

To serve as a defence of machine intelligence, this argument must assume that 'learning' 'denotes changes in the system that are adaptive in the sense that they enable the system to do the same task or tasks drawn from the same population more efficiently and more effectively the next time' (Simon 1983: 28). On first reading, this statement looks like little more than a strained attempt to tailor the concept of *learning* so as to mesh with that of *mechanical rules*. For, if all that learning amounted to were the adaptation of something to its environment, we should then be forced to conclude that not just machines, but, indeed, the simplest of organisms are capable of some primitive form of learning. But far from seeing this as an *objection*, the mechanist will respond: Exactly, that is the whole point of the theory!

One cannot simply assume, therefore, that Turing only succeeded in subverting the concept of learning in his zeal to reduce it to a level commensurate with the minimal 'cognitive abilities' possessed by his machines. For such a charge would fail to do justice to the manner in which AI evolved from the union of mathematical and mechanist thought, and the extent to which the latter had come to dominate learning theory. Moreover, it would ignore the conceptual evolution of *machine* which underpins this outcome, and the bearing which this had, not just on Turing's psychological program, but as a result of his influence, on automata theory and thence AI. But most serious of all, it would obscure the extent to which behaviourist presuppositions were absorbed into the fabric of AI.

This behaviourist orientation is particularly evident in 'Intelligent Machinery', the report which Turing completed for the National Physical Laboratory in the summer of 1948. The purpose of this paper was to defend the claim that self-modifying algorithms can legitimately be described as 'learning programs'. The opening premise recalls Pavlov and Lashley's theory that what we call 'learning' is the result of new neural pathways brought about by conditioning (see Pavlov 1927: 4ff). According to Turing, 'the cortex of the infant is an unorganized machine, which can be organized by suitable interfering training' (Turing 1948: 120). By enabling the system to modify its own rules, Turing thought he had demonstrated how Turing Machines could in principle simulate the formation of neural reflex arcs that takes place during conditioning. The ensuing argument then expands on this notion of conditioning in terms of the 'Spread of Effect' experiments inspired by Thorndike.

In Turing's eyes, the most important element in this behaviourist theory is the idea that learning consists in neural stimulus–response connections. He takes it as a given that 'The training of the human child depends largely on a system of rewards and punishments. . . . Pleasure interference has a tendency to fix the character, i.e., towards preventing it changing, whereas pain stimuli tend to disrupt the character, causing features which had become fixed to change, or to become again subject to random variation.' Accordingly, 'It is intended that pain stimuli occur when the machine's behaviour is wrong, pleasure stimuli when it is particularly right. With appropriate stimuli on these lines, judiciously operated by the "teacher", one may hope that the "character" will converge towards the one desired, i.e., that wrong behaviour will tend to become rare' (*ibid.*: 121).

The concepts of extinction and positive reinforcement on which Turing placed so much emphasis in his 'learning'-based version of the Mechanist Thesis were thus directly culled from behaviourist writings: it was by employing 'analogues' of pleasure and pain stimuli that he hoped 'to give the desired modification' to a machine's 'character' (*ibid.*: 124). As he put it in 'Intelligent Machinery, A Heretical Theory':

> Without some . . . idea, corresponding to the 'pleasure principle' of the psychologists, it is very difficult to see how to proceed. Certainly it would be most natural to introduce some such thing into the machine. I suggest that there should be two keys which can be manipulated by the schoolmaster, and which can represent the ideas of pleasure and pain. At later stages in education the machine would recognize certain other conditions as desirable owing to their having been constantly associated in the past with pleasure, and likewise certain others as undesirable.
>
> (Turing 1959: 132)

The mechanist metaphor would now appear to be twice removed from the established meaning of 'learning'. Where behaviourists had taken the liberty of depicting *habituation* as a lower form of *learning*, Turing went a step further and added the premise that machines display 'behaviour', which as such can be 'conditioned' by 'analogues' of 'pleasure and pain stimuli', in what can reasonably be described as 'training'. Yet Turing was not alone in this move; at much the same time Hull was arguing that 'an automaton might be constructed on the analogy of the nervous system which could learn and through experience acquire a considerable degree of intelligence by just coming in contact with an environment' (Hull 1962: 820).

Far from being a coincidence, the affinity between Turing's and Hull's thinking is a consequence of their shared outlook towards the nature of problem-solving. This thinking is exemplified – and was to some extent inspired – by Thorndike's experiments on the 'learning curve'. Thorndike designed a puzzle box to measure the number of times a cat placed inside it would randomly pull on chains and levers to escape. He found that when practice days were plotted against the amount of time required to free itself, a 'learning curve' emerged which fell rapidly at first and then gradually until it approached a horizontal line which signified the point at which the cat had 'mastered the task'. According to Thorndike, his results showed how animal learning at its most basic level breaks down into a series of brute repetitions which gradually 'stamp' the correct response into the animal's behaviour by creating 'neuro-causal connections'. But repetition alone does not suffice for the reinforcement of these connections; without the concomitant effects produced by punishment and reward, new connections would not be stamped in.

One's immediate reaction to Thorndike's experiment might be that this manifestly constitutes an example of anything but *learning*. But to appreciate the full force of Thorndike's argument, you have to imagine that you were shown a cat that had already been conditioned quickly freeing itself from a puzzle box. Let us suppose that one's natural inclination here would be to say that the cat had clearly learnt how to free itself. The whole point of the experiment is to show us, in an artificial condition, exactly what processes had led up to this outcome. To speak of 'insight' here is completely vacuous; and so too, Thorndike wants us to conclude, must it be in all other cases of animal behaviour.

The radical behaviourists then extended this argument to apply to man as well. That is, we only speak of 'insight' when we are unfamiliar with the processes that have led up to the results we have witnessed. Thus, the familiar mentalist concepts whereby we describe human behaviour are no less illicit in our context than in an animal context. Whatever their poetic or heuristic value, they should be thoroughly eliminated from a rigorous science of behaviour.

Herein lies the thrust of the behaviourist version of the *continuum picture* outlined in §1. The crucial point is the idea that *learning* consists in the formation of stimulus–response connections which require no intelligence. A plant that turns its leaves towards the sun can be said to have 'learned' how to maximise its photosynthesis; a dog that is conditioned to salivate at the sound of a bell can be said to have 'learned' that it is about to be fed. The 'higher' forms of learning – e.g., learning how to speak, how to count, how to solve logical problems – are distinguished from these lower forms by the complexity of the stimulus–response connections forged in the organism's brain. But the mechanical nature of the atomic associations which form the basis for all levels of 'learning' remain identical. This provides the rationale for describing what had hitherto been regarded as disparate phenomena – as *reflexes* as opposed to *reflexive* phenomena – as constituting a *learning continuum* ranging from simple negative adaptation, habituation, accommodation and tropisms, through animal and infant learning, to the highest reaches of education and scholarship.

Turing's Thesis was thus tailor-made for behaviourism. For, as we saw in §1, the epistemological significance of his computational version of Church's Thesis was said to consist in the demonstration that algorithms are complex systems of 'meaningless sub-rules', each of which can as such be applied purely mechanically. The essence of Turing's version of strong AI is that *machine intelligence* is a function of the complexity of the program which the computer follows, rather than the individual steps of the algorithm. The difference between 'slave' and 'learning' programs lies in the shift from fixed to self-modifying algorithms. In the former, the Turing Machine repeatedly performs the same elementary steps; in the latter it alters its program, using heuristics which enable it to augment its knowledge-base and/or store of rules, and thence the range and sophistication of the tasks it can execute.

As we saw in Chapter 1, it was this argument which, according to the established AI interpretation of Turing's Thesis, enables us 'to face the fact that a "human computer" does need intelligence – to follow rules formulated in a language he must *understand*' (Webb 1980: 220). In order to provide a 'non-question begging' analysis of computation, 'the smallest, or most fundamental, or least sophisticated parts must not be supposed to perform tasks or follow procedures requiring intelligence' (Dennett 1978: 83). Thus, 'Turing's analysis [of computation] succeeded just because it *circumvented* the problem of how a computer can understand ordinary language' (Webb 1980: 225). Without 'meanings' to deal with, 'these atomic tasks presuppose no intelligence', from which 'it follows that a non-circular psychology of computation is possible' (*ibid.*: 220). But not just a psychology of computation; rather, a psychology of thinking *simpliciter*. For, provided the lowest level of the 'learning continuum' can be simulated, there is no *a priori* reason why machines should not be capable of ascending this cognitive hierarchy. And this was exactly the theme which Turing exploited in the 1940s in his defence of the Mechanist Thesis. In so doing he saw himself as providing the crucial definition of 'mechanical' on which the behaviourist theory of learning rests, and as a result, opening the door to a future populated with thinking machines.

§3 The continuum picture

One of the major philosophical questions that emerges as one reads through later writings on the Mechanist Thesis is whether, by forging a union between recursive function theory and psychology, and within psychology, between *Denkpsychologie* and behaviourism, Turing was surmounting or subsuming the conceptual problems that afflicted the latter, and to what extent this can be said to have impinged on AI. The *continuum picture* which Turing embraces is putatively one in which the 'higher forms' of learning are built up out of simpler components. But in actual fact, the theory proceeds in the opposite direction: i.e., it is only by presupposing that the concept of learning can be divorced from the concept of normativity that the application of 'learning' to mechanical processes can then proceed.

The key to this move lies in treating the criteria — what an agent says or does — that govern the application of *learning* as evidence of some hidden event in an organism's central nervous system. For example, being able to do sums correctly, to cite the rules of multiplication to explain or justify one's results, to correct an error by appealing to the appropriate rule, etc., are all criteria for describing S as 'having mastered the rules of multiplication'. But the continuum picture treats such behaviour as evidence of the formation of synaptic connections that constitute what, in 'folk psychological' discourse, is called *knowing how to multiply*. Hence, an organism undergoing cellular division also provides us with evidence that it has learnt how to multiply, albeit at a much lower stage on the continuum. But, far from seeing this consequence as a drawback of the theory, the mechanist greets this as a validation of the continuum picture.

According to the continuum picture, therefore, the criteria governing 'higher' applications of *learning* can be hived off from declining stages until one reaches an 'atomic level' where 'learning' is said to be purely a function of the assimilation and accommodation of stimuli. In other words, the theory postulates that it makes sense to speak of 'learning' in the absence of any normative behaviour: i.e., in the absence of the very possibility of explaining, teaching, correcting or justifying one's actions. Given that a plant, or a dog, no less than a child, can respond to discriminably different stimuli, a child's ability to learn how to speak, to count, to apply colour or shape or psychological concepts, etc., is said to be simply the end-result of a more complicated causal nexus of exactly the same sort as guides the plant's or the dog's behaviour. (And note that it does indeed make sense on this picture to speak of the plant's 'behaviour'.) The prior question of whether, or in what sense, we can speak of a plant or a dog as *learning how to distinguish* between discriminably different stimuli — as opposed to *reacting* to these stimuli — is an issue which the continuum picture dismisses with the simple expedient of placing problematic uses of the concept in question in inverted commas.

'On Computable Numbers' is filled with such inverted commas. Turing tells us that a Turing Machine is 'so to speak, "directly aware"' of the scanned symbol. 'By altering its m-configuration the machine can effectively remember' [the inverted commas are missing here] 'some of the symbols which it has "seen" (scanned) previously' (Turing 1936: 117). Here Turing conforms to the precedent established by Jacques Loeb, who demonstrated that when *Porthesia chrysorrhoea* are exposed to a source of light coming from the opposite direction to a supply of food, they invariably move towards the former (and perish as a result). In Loeb's words, 'Heliotropic animals are . . . in reality photometric machines': not that far removed, as it happens, from Turing Machines (Loeb 1912: 41). For Loeb designed his experiments to undermine the vitalist thesis that all creatures are governed by an unanalysable instinct for self-preservation. His conclusion was that 'In this instance the light is the "will" of the animal which determines the direction of its movement, just as it is gravity in the case of a falling stone or the movement of a planet' (*ibid.*: 40–1). Since it is possible to explain, 'on a purely physico-chemical basis', a group of 'animal reactions . . . which the metaphysician would classify under the term of animal "will",' the answer to no less than the 'riddle of life' – viz., the nature of free will – must lie in the fact that 'We eat, drink, and reproduce not because mankind has reached an agreement that this is desirable, but because, machine-like, we are compelled to do so' (*ibid.*: 35, 33).

Loeb treats tropisms as quantitatively, not qualitatively different from the mastery of a concept: they are simply a more primitive form of 'equivalence response'. For, on the continuum picture, concepts are 'the mediating linkage between the input side (stimuli) and the output side (response). In operating as a system of ordering, a concept may be viewed as a categorical schema, an intervening medium, or program through which impinging stimuli are coded, passed, or evaluated on their way to response evocation' (Harvey *et al.* 1961: 1). To be sure, on the folk-theoretical level of psychological discourse, to say that 'S possesses the concept ϕ' may be to say that S is able to do such-and-such; but this remark is seen as nothing more than the name of a problem, and the task of cognitive science is to explain in causal terms what this 'ability' consists in.

The reason why the mechanist has no qualms about, for example, describing caterpillars as 'learning' where the light was coming from is because of his fundamental assumption that, when we describe an organism as 'acquiring knowledge', 'we suppose that the organism had some specific experience which caused or was in some way related to the change in its knowledge state' (Bower and Hilgard 1981: 13). And this is where Turing's claim that 'To each state of mind of the [human] computer corresponds an "m-configuration" of the machine' (Turing 1936: 137) stepped in. With the benefit of this reduction of *mental states* to *machine states*, and the step-by-step interaction of these 'internal configurations' with external input, AI was in a position to reintroduce the various cognitive concepts, hierarchically arranged, at each successive stage on the phylogenetic continuum.

Turing could thus defend his speaking of a chess program as 'learning' from its past 'mistakes' on the grounds that this use of 'learning' is no different from the sense in which Loeb, Thorndike and Pavlov had employed the term. What we have to remember here is the reductionist animus of these early behaviourists. Thorndike and Pavlov were not guilty of unwittingly failing to distinguish between *learning* and *conditioning*. The whole point of their theories is that what we refer to in ordinary language as 'animal learning' is in fact merely a species of mechanical behaviour, which can thus be explained without appealing to any 'mentalist' concepts. Turing simply concluded that whatever is true of animal 'learning' applies, in virtue of the continuum picture, to human learning.

It is precisely this reductionism – as it applies to the explanation of human behaviour – which Bruner is reacting to in his recent repudiation of AI (see Bruner 1990: 4ff). But if one is to challenge the eliminative results of the continuum picture, then it is the picture itself that must be scrutinised (see Shanker 1992, 1993a). For it is not AI *per se* that is the problem here: it is the mechanist framework which underpins the succession of mechanical models described in §1 – a framework which sees adaptation and accommodation as simpler versions of human learning. Moreover, there is no *a priori* reason why the AI-theorist should be barred from referring to the continuum of S-R connections (assuming there is such a continuum) as a 'learning' continuum. The problem lies, rather, in the failure to distinguish between this technical use of 'learning' – what we might call 'learning$_{s-r}$' – and what is normally meant by 'learning'. For this in turn leads to the incoherent assumption that the continuum picture explains *what one really means* when one talks about learning in paradigmatic contexts. But the concept of learning cannot be divorced from its essential normativity, where this use of 'cannot' is the logical.

So the question of whether the behaviour of any particular organism can be described as a primitive form of learning depends on whether or not the organism can be described as benefiting from training or experience, as responding to correction and instruction, as acquiring simple and complex skills, etc. To be sure, there are myriad situations where it is difficult to decide whether one should speak of *learning* or of *conditioning*. But it is not the case that the further one moves from paradigmatic contexts, the more difficult it becomes to make such a decision; rather, it is only the so-called 'borderline' cases that are problematic. Thus, we might distinguish between the questions:

1 Has Kanzi *learned* the meaning of 'bubbles': can he use and respond to the use of words to initiate or participate in the appropriate routines? (See Savage-Rumbaugh *et al.*, 1993)

2   Did Pavlov's dogs *learn* that food was imminent when a bell sounded?
3   Is the ability of lichen to survive in the most inhospitable of environments a *skill*?
4   By correcting a program, have we *trained* it to φ? Is this really comparable, as Turing so readily assumes, to the use of punishment and rewards in the training of a human child?

In the first case, and possibly the second, the issue is decided by further testing; but in 3 and 4 the issue will only be resolved by clarifying the logical grammar of *learning*.

What makes 1 and possibly 2 so difficult is the fact that, typically, it is a subject's ability to respond appropriately to the use of 'φ', to master the rules for the use of 'φ', and to explain the correct use of 'φ', that licenses our describing S as having 'learned x'. The fact that we speak of 'primitive' instances where a subject's ability, for example, to explain the correct use of 'φ', may be severely limited, does not entail that any form of causal regularity (e.g., a tropism, or a thermostat) can be described as displaying evidence of having 'learned x'. It is precisely because it makes no sense to speak of a dog that salivates involuntarily at the sound of a bell as responding 'correctly' or 'incorrectly' to the signal that it makes no sense to try to reduce *learning* to the same terms. A dog which salivates at the sound of a doorbell has no more made a *mistake* than has an electric door that fails to open when its photo-electric beam is crossed.

The central issue underlying all these questions is whether the behaviourists established what learning consists in at the 'primitive' level, or rather demonstrated that the primitive behavioural responses that they studied should be explained in mechanical, as opposed to normative terms. Indeed, were they really seeking to explain the concept of *learning*, or were they simply attacking its indiscriminate use by comparative psychologists at the turn of the century? By conditioning an animal to do such-and-such and then extinguishing that conditioned response, they showed how inappropriate it would be to describe such behaviour in normative terms. But that hardly entails that there are *no* circumstances in which it makes sense to describe an animal as having learned something: that the concept of animal learning – indeed, *learning simpliciter* – reduces to the concept of conditioning. If anything, the upshot of their experiments is that they sharpened the criteria for speaking of 'conditioning'. But that only serves to reinforce the categorial distinction between *learning* and *responding to a stimulus* by reminding us that the difference between a tropism and, for example, learning how to count, is one of kind, not degree, in so far as it only makes sense to speak of explaining the latter in normative terms, whereas a tropism can only be explained in causal terms.

As remarked above, that is not to deny that in certain circumstances it may be difficult to distinguish between a conditioned response and a normative action. But this argument does not amount to the thesis that there are *degrees of normativity* – a continuum of ever more 'normative behaviours'. Instead, the argument draws attention to the simple fact that there are countless cases – with human infants as much as non-human primates – where we might be unable to agree on the proper description of the behaviour in question. But this sort of impasse does not signify that we lack sufficient evidence to categorise the behaviour in question; rather, it provides us with a profound insight into the nature of the meta-discursive discussions about language which themselves constitute an essential part of language. For the distinction between 'learning x' and 'being conditioned to do x' is variably realised, explained, justified and enforced. But the (variable) fact of this distinction gives us no justification for assuming that there *must* be a corresponding distinction in the phenomena we are studying. Or that, because the linguistic distinction is variable and indeterminate, therefore the phenomenal distinction *must* also be so, with gradient differences between *being conditioned to do x* and *learning x*. Nor are we justified in assuming that, if the phenomenal distinction can't be found in the mind, it must therefore be in the behaviour, so that there are gradient variable differences between *behaviour that amounts to being conditioned to do x* and *behaviour that amounts to learning x*.

It is in on the basis of the grammatical proposition that *The concept of learning is internally related to the concept of normativity*, therefore, that we clarify how it makes no sense to describe Turing's machines as 'learning' – as opposed to 'learning$_{s-r}$' – how to play chess: i.e. how there are no justificational criteria for the attribution of 'learning' to get a foothold here. That does not mean that we should expect there to be a hard and fast line between the use of causal and the use of normative terms in all behavioural contexts. When studying a child's – or for that matter, an ape's – linguistic development, for example, it is often difficult to judge where exactly reacting ends and learning begins. But to speak of 'language learning' none the less presupposes that it makes sense to describe the child or ape as mastering the rules for the use of 'p', as opposed to responding in a consistent manner to the sound of 'p'. That is, if we are to make the transition from describing a child's (or an ape's) behaviour in causal terms to describing it in normative terms, his (or its) actions and reactions must warrant our speaking of him (or it) as, for example, 'beginning to use or to respond to the use of "p" *correctly*' (see Savage-Rumbaugh *et al.* in press).

This argument illustrates the full gravity of the charge being levelled here, that the continuum picture does not genuinely attempt to 'build up' from bottom to top, but rather, proceeds in the opposite direction. By *presupposing* that learning can be treated as the same sort of process as assimilation or accommodation – that habituation constitutes a species of cognition – the mechanist has already assumed that, for example, when caterpillars are attracted to a light, this signifies a change in their 'knowledge state'. But knowledge is not a state, much less one that is caused by external stimuli and whose inception and duration can be measured, or that can be equated with a change in behaviour. After all, one can behave in a certain way without knowing what one is doing, or, conversely, one can conceal what one knows. Nor is it the case that 'we infer someone's knowledge from inputs to him and outputs from him, and we *infer* learning caused by an experience because of before-to-after changes in his inferred knowledge' (Bower and Hilgard 1981: 14). For we do not *infer* that a child who is able to answer all the addition and subtraction questions put to him knows how to count. Rather, such behaviour is a criterion for what is called 'knowing how to count'; and when a child can perform these sums we *see*, rather than *infer*, that he has learnt how to count.

Like *understanding*, to which it is so intimately connected, the concept of *learning* embraces a wide spectrum of abilities that are loosely based on the development of different kinds of skills, and not 'cortical connections' (assuming that there even is such a thing). To learn how to speak is different from learning a second language; to learn how to tie one's shoelaces is different from learning how to play a Bach fugue. But these different uses of 'learning', which progress from simple to compound skills, from practice and drill to experience and understanding, do not license one to 'descend' still further, to the point where we can treat the following statements

- 'The thermostat clicked on'
- 'The leaves of the plant turned towards the sun'
- 'The pigeon pecked the yellow key in order to get a food pellet'
- 'Kanzi pressed the "drink" lexigram in order to get a drink'
- 'S has learned how to play the Toccata and Fugue in D-minor'

as all similar in kind, and only distinguished only by their ascending mechanical complexity.

In so far as descriptions of reflex actions (e.g., responding involuntarily to the sound of the word 'red') shade into descriptions of reflexive actions (e.g., explaining what 'red' means), in the same sort of way, say, that red shades into purple, it makes sense to say that causal descriptions of behaviour – in terms of training, reacting, associating, echoing or imitating words – shade into normative descriptions of behaviour – in terms of learning, understanding, following, appealing to, explaining or teaching the rules for the use of words. Different kinds of training lead into different kinds of normative practice (e.g., how we are taught to count, to describe colours, or objects, or pains, or actions). The different kinds of practice result in different kinds of concepts, and to seek to reduce this heterogeneity to a common paradigm – e.g. the so-called 'functional' definition of concepts (see Chapter 5) – is to embrace the mechanist framework which ultimately results in eliminative materialism or reductionism.

Behaviourism and AI are converse expressions of this point. Both proceed from the assumption that there is a continuum leading from reflexes to reactions to concept-acquisition, and that the only way for psychology to explain the mechanics of learning is by having a uniform grammar of description: in the case of behaviourism, by reducing all explanations of behaviour to the terms that apply to reflexes, and in the case of AI, by reading the attributes which apply to higher-level cognitive abilities and skills into the lowest levels of reflex actions (e.g., the brain is said to make hypotheses, the nervous system to make inferences, the thermostat to possess knowledge and beliefs). This is why it is so often argued these days that AI is just a form of neo-behaviourism; for the fact is that, although the AI-scientist may approach 'learning theory' from the opposite point of view from the behaviourist, he does so because he shares the same framework as the behaviourist. Thus, on both approaches, we end up with caterpillars – and even thermostats – that 'think'.

This brings us back to the different problems involved in the philosophical question 'Can machines think?' and the psychological question 'Can thought be mechanically explained?' To talk about the 'mechanics of learning' is to refer to the importance of drill, repetition and systematic training, while still allowing scope for creativity and inculcating intrinsic motivation. We are no more interested in neurophysiology when concerned with the mechanics of learning arithmetic than we are interested in kinaestheiology when we speak of mastering the mechanics of tennis. Merely designing a program that matches and even predicts the mistakes a child will make hardly satisfies the criteria for describing that program as having learnt how to count. And it in no way *entails* that the operations of that program must shed light on what must be going on in the child's mind when he learns how to count.

The problem here has nothing to do with semantic conservatism. It lies rather in the fact that, far from *explaining* it, the continuum picture only serves to *undermine* the normative foundation on which the concept of learning rests: the criteria which govern descriptions of a child as an *agent*, whose actions are intentional, purposive, conscious and voluntary. This is what Turing's version of the Mechanist Thesis is all about. Turing's Thesis only works as a psychological programme – a 'model of how the mind works' – on the basis of the reductionism inherent in the continuum picture. The problems that arise here have nothing to do with any shortcomings of computationalism. They are concerned, rather, with the question of whether, because of its grounding in the continuum picture, AI distorts the nature of the normative practices which it seeks to explain. There is no need to delve into social or cultural psychology to see the force of this point (but see Shanker and Taylor forthcoming): the core of Turing's argument – his 'analysis' of computation – amply demonstrates the manner in which the framework drives the theory, rather than the other way round.

§4 Wittgenstein's discussion of 'reading' *vis-à-vis* Turing's analysis of 'calculation'

On the argument being sketched here, which will be developed further in the following chapters, the union which Turing forged between recursive function theory and behaviourism was grounded in an archetypal epistemological picture. Furthermore, it was this epistemological picture which served to establish AI as the paradigm for the burgeoning field of Cognitive Science. For the cognitive revolution was driven by the premise that 'Good correspondence between a formal model and a process – between theory and observables, for that matter – presupposes that the model will, by appropriate manipulation, yield descriptions (or predictions) of how behaviour will occur and will even suggest forms of behaviour to look for that have not yet been observed – that are merely possible' (Bruner 1959: 368). The big appeal of AI lay in the hope that 'perhaps the new science of programming will help free us from our tendency to force nature to imitate the models we have constructed for her' (Bruner 1960: 23).

Turing was responding, in effect, to a challenge that had been laid down by Kant, and which had preoccupied psychologists throughout the latter half of the nineteenth century. Kant had insisted that psychology could 'become nothing more than a systematic art'. It could 'never [be] a science proper', since it is 'merely empirical' (Kant 1970: 7). What he meant by this last remark is that, because psychology is based on evidence yielded by the 'inner sense', it could not (*pace* taxonomic botany) become a true science – i.e. a science on the paradigm of mechanics – since the latter requires the mathematisation of its subject matter.

What Turing was doing in 'On Computable Numbers' – even if he did not become fully aware of the fact until about five years later – was attempting to lay the foundation for just such a *science* by showing how, through the use of recursive functions, mental processes could indeed be mathematised. More is involved here, however, than simply establishing the *bona fides* of computational psychology. More to the point, Turing was responding – using the tools which Hilbert had developed – to the epistemological problems that result from Kant's picture of the mind confronted with, and forced to make sense of, reality.

Kant saw his basic task as that of explaining the rule-governed manner in which the mind imposes order on the flux of sensations that it receives (see the opening pages of the *Logic*). The power of Turing's Thesis lay in the idea that he was able to analyse these rules in such a way as to dispel the air of metaphysical speculation surrounding Kant's argument. For Turing's 'embodied rules' seemed to open up the prospect of a mechanist explanation of the *connections* between:

- perception (input) and behaviour (output)

- forming and applying a concept
- mastering and being guided by a rule
- acquiring and exercising an ability
- hearing a sound or seeing a mark and grasping its meaning
- forming an intention to φ and φing.

But the question of how to close the so-called 'gaps' presented in this list are classic epistemological problems; and the thought-experiment whereby Turing sought their solution was no more a piece of psychology than the Transcendental Aesthetic.

We saw in the preceding chapter how, according to Davis, 'What Turing did around 1936 was to give a cogent and complete logical analysis of the notion of "computation". . . . Thus it was that although people have been computing for centuries, it has only been since 1936 that we have possessed a satisfactory answer to the question: "What is a computation?"' (Davis 1978: 241). It is important to see how accurately Davis has represented the tenor of Turing's argument. It was intended to be read as a *reductive conceptual analysis*, whose epistemological significance is said to lie in the demonstration that algorithms can be defined as complex systems of 'meaningless sub-rules', each of which can as such be applied purely mechanically, and from which Turing's psychological thesis is said to follow.

Far from basing his 'precise definition of computation on an analysis of what a human being actually does when he computes' (*ibid.*), Turing based his 'analysis' on a Kantian epistemological picture of what the human being's *mind* must be doing when he computes. Calculation, according to Turing, is a cognitive process, large parts of which are hidden from introspection. We can only infer the nature of these pre-conscious operations from an agent's observed behaviour and self-observations. (Kant presents a similar conception of *inference* in the *Logic*.) Given that the phenomena to be explained in psychology are so strongly analogous to those with which physics deals, is it any wonder that both disciplines should be seeking good correspondence between a formal model and a process – between theory and observables?

It is precisely because his thought-experiment represents an attempt at conceptual analysis that Turing's Thesis has been the source of so much philosophical discussion. And perhaps the most pertinent such investigation is that conducted by Wittgenstein. Interestingly, Turing's thought-experiment shares some affinities with Wittgenstein's use of artificial language-games to clarify a concept – particularly Wittgenstein's discussion of 'reading machines' at §§156ff in *Philosophical Investigations*, which bears an uncanny resemblance to Turing's argument.[4] Moreover, Turing's reductionist thesis exemplifies not just the target which Wittgenstein is attacking, but the larger point that he is making at §§122–33 of the *Investigations*, about the dangers of philosophical theorising.

The hardest thing to get clear about in Wittgenstein's discussion of *reading* is its purpose. Wittgenstein introduces this theme in the midst of his investigation into the nature of understanding. If the discussion of *reading* is to help clarify the nature of *understanding* it obviously cannot presuppose understanding. Thus Wittgenstein dwells on reading at its most mechanical: viz., 'reading out loud what is written or printed'. But this is not an early version of the call for a 'presuppositionless psychology' (see Dennett 1978). Wittgenstein was not looking for the 'atomic units' out of which understanding is 'composed'. Rather, he uses a form of primitive language-game in order to clarify some of the problems involved in reductionist analyses of psychological concepts.

The parallel between Wittgenstein's 'reading-machines' and Turing's computing machines is striking. *Reading* (*counting* at PI §§143ff) can serve as an example of a rule-governed procedure at its most mechanical. The case Wittgenstein wants to consider is where the agent 'function[s] as a mere reading-machine: I mean, read[s] aloud and correctly without attending to what he is reading.' Here is a possible key to Wittgenstein's remark at §1096 of *Remarks on the Philosophy of Psychology* (Volume I): 'Turing's "Machines". These machines are *humans* who calculate.' That is, what Turing is doing in his thought-experiment is imagining people performing the most routine of calculating tasks in order to analyse the concept of calculation. But, whereas Turing's goal was indeed 'to break calculation down into its elementary psychic units', Wittgenstein was looking to clarify the criteria which license us in speaking of possessing a cognitive ability at its most primitive level, and the bearing which this has on reductionism.

The target in Wittgenstein's discussion is the continuum picture. Wittgenstein distinguishes between three broad uses of the term 'read':

1 Causal, as this applies to a machine reading signs
2 Primitive, as this applies to someone who does not understand a word of what he is reading
3 Paradigmatic uses of 'read' (i.e. understanding what one is reading).

Wittgenstein argues that there are many situations in which it is difficult to distinguish between items 2 and 3 (e.g., a child learning how to read, a politician reading from a cue card). And now the interesting question is: does (or could) a similar ambiguity exist between items 1 and 3? Is the machine-use just a further extension of the primitive use – as the continuum picture stipulates – and, if so, is this because the internal mechanisms guiding the machine's operations are a simpler version of the internal mechanisms guiding the organism? Could we therefore learn about the 'processes of reading' involved in items 2 and 3 by studying the machine's processes?

Wittgenstein's response to this problem is to clarify the criteria which govern the application of 'reading' in primitive contexts. He looks at the case in which we would say that 'S read p' even though he had no idea as to the meaning of p. Even in a limiting case like this, we still demand some criterion to distinguish between 'S read p' and 'It only seemed as if S read p' (e.g., 'The parrot read the sign' and 'It only seemed as if the parrot read the sign'). That is, no matter how primitive the context, we insist on being able to distinguish between ϕ*ing* and *seeming to* ϕ. The question, then, is: On what basis do we draw this distinction? Do (or could) neural considerations play any role here? Could our judgement that someone is reading be overturned by neurological evidence? And could the neurophysiologist tell us what is going on in the subject's mind when he is reading?

Wittgenstein makes the distinction between *reading* and *seeming to read* (pretending to read, memorising the words, repeating sounds) as hazy as possible. We are at that indeterminate point in a pupil's training where no one – not the pupil, nor his teacher – can say exactly when he started to read. The argument is intended to take up the point made in §149. The question Wittgenstein posed there is: What is the relation between what we call 'the possession of an ability' (or 'the acquisition of a concept') and what we call 'the exercise of that ability' (the 'application of that concept'). If we treat this relation as causal – i.e. possession causes exercise – then we shall be drawn into treating *understanding* (*reading, calculating*) as a mental state or process, and thence, into the construction of 'hypothetical mind-models' to explain how that hidden state or process causes the agent's observed behaviour:

> [A] state of the mind in this sense is the state of a hypothetical mechanism, a mind model meant to explain the conscious mental phenomena. (Such things as unconscious or subconscious mental states are features of the mind *model*.) In this way also we can hardly help conceiving of memory as of a kind of storehouse. Note also how sure people are that to the ability to add or to multiply . . . there *must* correspond a peculiar state of the person's brain, although on the other hand they know next to nothing about such psycho-physiological correspondences. We regard these phenomena as manifestations of this mechanism, and their possibility is the partic-ular construction of the mechanism itself.
>
> (BB: 117–18)

The conclusion which Wittgenstein draws in §149 of *Philosophical Investigations* is that the pair of concepts, conscious/unconscious, has no bearing on the relation between possession/exercise of an ability (acquisi-tion/application of a concept). Wittgenstein returns to this theme in §156. We look for the difference between possessing and not possessing the ability to read in 'a special conscious mental activity', and, because we cannot find any unique phenomenon to distinguish between *reading* and *seeming to read*, we conclude that the difference must be unconscious, where this is construed as either a mental or a cerebral activity. ('If there is no difference in what they happen to be conscious of there must be one in the unconscious work-ings of their minds, or, again, in the brain' (PI: §156).) This, according to Wittgenstein, is a paradigmatic example of the 'metaphysical "must"'. For, if we construe the relation between 'knowing how to read' and 'reading' as *causal* – i.e. if we construe the *grammatical relation* between 'possessing the ability to φ' and 'φing' (viz., that doing x,y,z constitute the criteria for what we call 'φing') as causal (viz., the 'ability to φ' consists in a state-configuration which causes a system to x,y,z) – then we shall be compelled to identify the 'two different mechanisms' which *must* distinguish reading from seeming to read.

In the *Brown Book*, Wittgenstein remarks how the failure to observe this logical distinction proceeds from a picture of the agent as being 'guided by the signs'. From this it seems to follow that we can only understand the nature of the 'mental activity' in which reading consists 'if we could look into the actual mechanism connecting seeing the signs with acting according to them. For we have a definite picture of what in a mechanism we should call certain parts being guided by others. In fact, the mechanism which immediately suggests itself . . . is a mechanism of the type of a pianola' (BB: 118). The problem with this picture has nothing to do with machines lacking consciousness, or with an illicit use of 'reads'. For, regard-less of whether or not it makes any sense to speak of machines as being conscious, there is indeed a sense in which we can say that, for example, a pianola is 'guided by' the notes that it 'reads'. But then, is the pianola 'guided by' the notes that it 'reads' in the same way that a child is guided by the rules he has been taught (i.e., the way the child goes through these rules in his mind, checks to see if this instance applies, automatically repeats certain mnemonics, etc.)?[5]

The continuum picture presupposes that these two uses of 'being guided' are indeed the same; but only because it presupposes that the sense in which it applies to the child can be *reduced* to the sense in which it applies to the machine. On the mechanist argument which Turing embraces, to say that the child learning how to read is guided by the rules he has been taught is to say that these rules have been 'embodied' in his brain. That is, the child is guided *in exactly the same way* as the machine is guided by its program. Only the differing complexity of their internal state-configurations accounts for their divergent 'reading abilities'.

Nowhere does Wittgenstein suggest that the kind of use which Turing makes of inverted commas should be deemed illicit. For who has made the philosopher the custodian of good grammar? Can we not understand what Turing is saying? The point is not that it makes no sense to speak of a Turing Machine as 'reading' or 'calculating'. It is that this machine-use of 'reading' or 'calculating' is categorially different from the normative sense in which we use it for children and adults – even in its most primitive applications. *Reading* is indeed a family-resemblance concept: a family which ranges from the infant responding to flash cards to a philosophy class reading the *Investigations* or a navigator reading the stars. But when we speak, for example, of a scanner 'reading' a bar code, this is not a *still more primitive extension* of an infant reacting to signs.

The mechanist insists that the only difference between the scanner 'reading' a bar code and someone reading something mechanically lies in the operations of the internal mechanisms guiding their respective actions. Accordingly, it should be possible to design a system that would perfectly simulate – and thus explain – the operations of the mechanism guiding the human reading-machine. Wittgenstein responds: 'By calling certain creatures "reading machines" we meant only that they react in a particular way to seeing printed signs. No connection between seeing and reacting, no internal mechanism enters here' (BB: 121). Neurophysiological evidence has no bearing on the application of 'reading mechanically'; it can neither corroborate nor undermine its use. What misleads us into thinking otherwise is 'the idea of a mechanism that works in a special media and so can explain special movements. . . . But what is of interest to us in reading can't be essentially something *internal*' (PG: 99). That is, 'The distinction between "inner" and "outer" does not interest us' when clarifying the concept of *reading* in paradigmatic or in primitive contexts. The criteria for describing an agent as 'reading' or as 'reading mechanically' lie in his behaviour and the situation in which this occurs: i.e. we call acting thus-and-so in such-and-such circumstances 'reading' or 'reading mechanically'.

In PI §157, Wittgenstein returns to the theme that, in certain contexts, the description of behaviour in causal terms shades into the description of behaviour in normative terms.[6] Causal descriptions of behaviour – of conditioned responses, associations, repeating sounds – merge into normative descriptions of behaviour; of reading or calculating (of being able to cite the rules one has followed in reading or calculating). But, despite the subjective nature of applying psychological concepts in primitive contexts, the terms that apply to conditioned responses do not carry over into the description of rule-following behaviour, even though it may at times be difficult to identify where 'reacting' ends and 'reading' begins. The crucial point here is that this indeterminacy in the use of psychological concepts does not license the shift to speaking of a mechanist continuum, such that the sole difference between machine-uses, primitive uses and paradigmatic uses, is one of degree and not of kind. We do indeed speak of an agent 'reading like a machine', but only when we want to signal his failure to attend to what he was reading, or to describe the manner in which he was reading (in a monotone, without pauses or inflections, etc.).

To illustrate the significance of this point, Wittgenstein presents us with the grammatical observation that 'it makes no sense' to ask a question like

'What was the first word S read?'. This distinguishes the two 'mechanical' uses of 'reading' described above: the primitive (2) and the machine-use (1). For the question 'What was the first symbol the scanner read?' is the easiest thing in the world to answer. Here we have another reminder of the different uses of 'reading', and more importantly, of the fact that the relation between possession and exercise is not causal. If it were, then the question would make perfectly good sense in both normative and causal contexts.[7]

§158 of PI ties this argument in to the attack on causal theories of meaning and understanding initiated at §6 (cf. PG: 117–18, 190). The mechanist misconstrues the grammatical proposition that we cannot speak of 'a first word in S's new state' as an empirical claim; maybe, he suggests, this is only a temporary difficulty. But the mechanist is only drawn into this position because he is already captivated by the idea that the connection forged in training (between S's possessing the ability to φ and his φing) is causal rather than grammatical. And if the changes in S's behaviour are brought about by changes in his internal mechanism, then it must be possible to say or predict what he has read/learnt if only we could read the brain's secrets: i.e. the changes occurring in 'learning'.[8]

Wittgenstein's response to this argument is grounded in his remarks on psychophysical parallelism (see Shanker, 1993b). His concern here is with the source of the 'must' underpinning the mechanist argument: viz., the misconception of the relation between possession and exercise of an ability (concept). Neurophysiological knowledge would not explain but rather presupposes independent criteria for using 'reading' ('calculating'). That is, we could only look for the neural events that take place during the exercise of an ability – i.e. we can only speak of mapping neural events onto behavioural acts – if we have independent criteria for saying 'Now he is φing'. The mistake here is that of supposing that neurophysiological models of 'internal mechanisms' (based on whatever paradigm, be it that of dynamics, physiological, computational, connectionist) are essential to the 'analysis' of a psychological concept.

The standard mechanist response to this argument is to ask: Can we not at least assume that it is possible to map what is going on when an agent is reading onto his neural processes? So much is involved in this seemingly innocent question. Every time I read the *Investigations* I understand something different: is the same thing happening in my brain every time I read the book, or something different? And what about everyone else's brain? Is it conceivable that different agents might experience different neural processes while reading the *Investigations*? If you answer 'yes', then does that mean that a concept must be defined according to the brain that is using it? And if you say 'no' – as Turing does – then what is the source of the 'must' driving your conceptual analysis? But most important of all, even if everyone did experience the same neural processes when reading, say, §571 of the *Investigations*, would this constitute an *analysis* of what reading that passage consists in, or just a *correlation*?

Suppose a Turing Machine (or an 'android') were indeed able to 'pass' the Turing Test: this would only be the case on the basis of its satisfying the criteria that govern the application of 'reading' or 'calculating' – as Turing himself, and countless mechanists following in his footsteps, have endlessly insisted. The machine's internal operations would be completely irrelevant to this issue; they could neither undermine nor corroborate such a judgement. But in that case, why should we suppose that these same operations could serve as a paradigm of what *reading* or *calculating* consist in? That is, how does Turing pass from his mechanist to his psychological thesis?

The answer lies in the use which he makes of the continuum picture: i.e. in the presupposition that *learning* consists in the formation of synaptic connections. For Turing could then assume that the machine's 'behaviour' only satisfies our criteria for saying that it is 'calculating' because its internal operations are isomorphic with those guiding the human computer when he passes the Turing Test. Thus, given that the human computer's behaviour is the end-result of mechanical processes, and that any machine can be simulated by a Turing Machine, it follows that the Mechanist Thesis and Turing's psychological thesis are internally related: *that machines can be said to think precisely because thinkers compute.* But then, these very 'processes' said to be guiding the human subject are themselves the product of the assumption driving this argument: viz., that the criteria governing the use of 'read' and 'calculate' can be transformed into evidence of (embodied) effective procedures, which as such must be isomorphic with those guiding the machine.

The picture operating here is that of reading or calculating as consisting in the mental rule-governed transformation of input data. The connections forged in teaching are these 'embodied' rules. In PI §163, Wittgenstein argues that this notion of 'rule-governed' is empty. These are 'hidden' rules, rules that are inaccessible to both observer and agent. Wittgenstein's point is not simply that any number of possible rules could be formulated to satisfy the required transformation; more importantly, it is that this indeterminacy can be stretched to a point where it is impossible to distinguish between rule-governed and non-normative behaviour. His intention is not to force us into the sceptical conclusion that 'reading' or 'calculating' are not rule-governed procedures; rather, it is to emphasise that these rules, *qua* rules, must be public. Hence the question raised by the passage is: what misleads us into postulating these 'hidden rules'? And the answer is: the epistemological framework underpinning the Mechanist Thesis – the premise that *there is a gap between input and action in the exercise of an ability which must be bridged by a series of internal operations.*

PI §164 brings us to the heart of this issue. The passage ties in to the family-resemblance argument at §§65ff. Here the mechanist is accused of looking for the 'hidden essence' of 'deriving' or 'reading'. But the 'essence' of these concepts is that there is no 'hidden essence'. Hence the mechanist is guilty of trying to define what can only be explained. (Bear in mind that the point of these discussions is to clarify the concept of understanding.) Here is the source of Davis's claim that Turing succeeded in presenting 'a cogent and complete logical analysis of the notion of "computation"': i.e. the idea that Turing succeeded in defining the essence of computation.

Instead of asking 'What does computation consist in?', we might begin our investigation of the nature of computation by considering 'What justifies our use of "calculating" in such-and-such a context?'. Waismann has the latter question in mind when he asks in *Principles of Linguistic Philosophy*: 'What, then, is the difference between a causal connection and a transition in a calculus? What is the difference between a calculation formed by a machine, and that made by a person? Or else between a musical box playing a tune and a person playing it?' The answer lies in a statement of the categorial distinction between reasons and causes *vis-à-vis* the use of 'calculation' or 'reading':

> the playing or calculation of a person can be justified by rules which he gives us when asked; not so the achievements of a machine, where the question 'Why do these keys spring out?' can *only* be answered by describing the mechanism, that is by describing a causal nexus. On the other hand, if we ask the calculator how he comes to his results, he will explain to us what kind of calculation he is doing and then adduce certain laws of arithmetic. He will not reply by describing the mode of action of a hidden machine, say, a machine in his brain.
>
> (PLP: 122)

The way that Waismann has phrased this argument invites the mechanist response that a machine could be programmed to perform exactly the same linguistic acts; but, as we have just seen, such an objection is beside the point. For what matters here are the criteria for distinguishing between justification and causal explanation. That is, the important distinction here is between applying the rules which logically determine whether we can describe a subject as having *read* or *calculated* x, and explaining the causes (if there are any) of a subject or a machine saying or writing 'x'.

The idea that Turing succeeded in giving the first cogent and complete logical analysis of calculation turns not just on his success in resolving Church's Thesis, but, on an even more fundamental level, on the persisting strength of Kant's epistemological picture of the hidden rule-governed processes whereby the mind makes sense of reality. It is precisely this epistemological picture which Wittgenstein's argument is designed to subvert. This is why he insists that it is 'necessary to look and see how we carry out [calculations] in the practice of language; what kind of procedure in the language-game [calculating] is' (RFM I: §17). That is, to paraphrase what Waismann says about concepts at pp. 227–8 of *Principles of Linguistic Philosophy*, we need to recognise that 'what we call "calculating" comes into existence only by its incorporation in language; that it is recognizable not by one feature but by a number, which, as it were, constitute its facets'. Hence, to get clear about what calculating 'consists in' we need to clarify the rules governing the use of 'calculate'. This is the reason why Wittgenstein remarks, *vis-à-vis* the clarification of psychological concepts, that 'It is very noteworthy that *what goes on* in thinking practically never interests us' (Z: §88). And that is exactly the area where Turing's 'analysis' has had its greatest influence.

Not only does Wittgenstein's argument lead us to query from yet another angle the manner in which Turing sought to analyse the concept of calculation (viz., as recursive 'mental process'), but it also brings into question the whole basis of Turing's interpretation of the logical relation in which algorithms stand to inferring, reasoning, calculating and thinking. To be sure, this barely touches the surface of the issues inspiring the information-processing approach to thinking: in particular, the basic epistemological picture of the mind sundered from and forced to make sense of reality. But it does reflect some of the philosophical problems involved in interpreting the relation in which programs stand to speaking aloud protocols (see Chapter 4).

It also sheds light on the import and relevance of the puzzling argument in *Philosophical Grammar* that begins with the question: 'if thinking consists only in writing or speaking, why shouldn't a machine do it?' and concludes with the warning that 'It is a travesty of the truth to say "Thinking is an activity of our mind, as writing is an activity of the hand"' (PG: 105–6). As the foregoing discussion makes clear, this passage bears directly on Turing's initial 'analysis' of calculation and his subsequent attempt to base an 'analysis' of *thinking* on this flawed foundation. Moreover, the very fact that Wittgenstein broached this topic five or six years before the publication of 'On Computable Numbers' provides an important insight into the conceptual environment which shaped Turing's attitude towards the Mechanist Thesis; for the themes which most concerned Wittgenstein in the early 1930s also served as the springboard for Turing's 'post-computational' entry into the philosophy of psychology.

Here is the reason why Turing's writings continue to attract such deep philosophical interest. Turing brought to the fore the consequences of the epistemological framework that has virtually governed psychology from its inception. But that framework is itself the product of an archetypal picture – to which Kant, no less than Descartes, was responding – of the relation between thought and reality. Turing's version of the Mechanist Thesis can either be seen as the crowning achievement of that framework, or as a *reductio* that forces us to reassess these epistemological premises. Similarly,

Turing's psychological thesis can either be seen as one more step in mechanism's technological advance (one that has already been displaced), or as forcing us to reassess the consequences of seeking to establish psychology on this epistemological foundation: i.e. *of trying to resolve epistemological problems psychologically*. Thus, our task in the following chapters will be to look more closely at the reasons why Turing's neo-behaviourist version of the Mechanist Thesis could have had the appeal that it did for the founders of the Cognitive Revolution.

3

THE RESURGENCE OF
PSYCHOLOGISM

'There's no use trying,' said Alice: 'one *can't* believe impossible
things.' 'I daresay you haven't had much practice,' said the
Queen. 'When I was your age, I always did it for half an hour
a day. Why, sometimes I've believed as many as six impossible
things before breakfast.'

(Lewis Carroll, *Alice in Wonderland*)

§1 AI and the rise of cognitive psychologism

The 'linguistic turn' is well and truly over in philosophy; we have now
entered the phase of the 'cognitive turn'. This is evidenced not just by the
fact that the philosophy of language is viewed as part of the latter, larger
enterprise; still more important is the decline in fortunes that logic has
suffered in the process. It used at one time to be thought that the task of
philosophical logic was to describe how the mind works; then, following
Frege's 'devastating critique' of psychologism, it became that of describing
how language works. Now it is neither, and even the prescriptivist conception of logic is under threat. For what good are 'rules of right reasoning'
when Nature is so strong and 'rules of thumb' so much more effective?

The terms in which the founders of analytic philosophy are said to have
repudiated psychologism have also been dismissed: not so much because of
any qualms over Frege's Platonism or Husserl's '*Evidenz*', as because the
problem with classical psychologism is said to be empirical, not conceptual.
If anything, given the lack of experimental work in the psychology of
reasoning, and the distinguished reputation which logic enjoyed at the time,
classical psychologism is seen as an entirely reasonable first attempt at a
'cognitive science'. And yet, for all the significance which cognitivists attach
to deposing anti-psychologism, no one actually feels obligated to examine
any of the arguments in question. At most, one is presented with a few
quotations from Boole and a brief mention of Frege and Husserl's criticisms.
Meanwhile, the one figure who many analytic philosophers feel has
contributed most to our understanding of the issues involved has gone

missing from this discussion. In the present chapter I shall undertake to remedy this omission and consider the significance of Wittgenstein's later thoughts on the philosophy of logic for psychologism, both classical and cognitive.

If ever there was a testing-ground for AI's vaunting ambition to resolve philosophical problems empirically, it is here. The debate over psychologism has long been regarded – by analytic philosophers at any rate – as the quintessential philosophical affair. But today we find it high on the agenda of cognitive scientists, anthropologists, linguists and social scientists. Only belatedly has analytic philosophy become aware of the existence, much less the importance, of these interests.

In Oxford in the late 1970s there was a feeling that we need not concern ourselves with these 'external' matters. Ours was a time of parochial self-confidence. If there was one thing of which we were certain it was that empirical studies could have no bearing on so central an issue in the philosophy of logic. Indeed, we were raised on the dogma that 'in order to arrive at the conception of a systematic theory of meaning, it was necessary first [for Frege] to defeat psychologism, to expel psychology from logic' (Dummett 1973: 684). But the truth is that psychologism had never been 'decisively overthrown'; it had merely shifted to other arenas: to social anthropology (which was perhaps its natural abode), to the psychology of reasoning, and to genetic epistemology.

Most important of all, for the purposes of this book, is the fact that psychologism has been revived by AI, albeit in a significantly altered form. In his entry on 'The Laws of Thought' in the *Oxford Companion to the Mind*,[1] Gregory explains that

> A deep question is how far laws of thought are innate . . . and how far they are learned, and are products of particular cultures, societies, and technologies. . . . If laws of thought are innate – inherited – it now appears that they can be modified: there are few, if any, limits to how or what we may think. At present, it seems that we shall not be able to specify effective laws of thought in detail before there are adequate computer programs for solving problems – including problem-solving that is not strictly and explicitly logical.
>
> (Gregory 1987: 430)

If not for the quotation from Boole with which he begins this entry, one might assume that Gregory has merely seized on an unfortunate way of talking about problem-solving strategies and reasoning biases. The quotation makes it clear, however, that it is indeed the *laws of thought* with which we are meant to be dealing.

Traditionally, what philosophers have understood by the 'laws of thought' are the three Aristotelian laws of logic: viz., the laws of identity, noncontradiction, and excluded middle. Gregory would appear to be saying that these laws of thought are only *contingently* true: i.e. he is suggesting that it may be the case that, because of the way that our brains are presently configured to process information, we all believe that 'not both p and not-p', but it is conceivable that future generations may begin to reason differently, should the information-processing structure of the human brain continue to evolve. Indeed, a cognitivist might ask whether this isn't precisely the lesson that we've learnt from Darwin: viz., that no one can predict the course of evolution. Doesn't the argument that the laws of thought must be Aristotelian presuppose a 'just-so' conception of evolution which sees the thought-processes of *Homo sapiens* as the culmination of primate development?

Lest there be any question as to whether this return to psychologism represents something of an oversight on the part of AI scientists, one need only encounter Boden's disdain for the idea that 'the logician who falls prey to psychologism has been seduced by a temptress of disreputably easy virtue' (Boden 1981), to realise that AI-theorists are quite intentionally challenging the very foundation of analytic philosophy: the principle that logic and psychology are *categorially* divorced from one another. Here, according to the canons of AI, is a clear and vital instance where the full weight of empirical evidence has overthrown a cherished principle of *a priori* reasoning.

This argument raises all sorts of philosophical problems: problems about the nature and interpretation of this 'empirical evidence'; about the proper understanding of this '*a priori* principle'; about its 'justification'; and about the 'mechanics' of reasoning. But above all else, we need to clarify in what sense AI is committed to psychologism, and why this should be the case. For if we can establish why AI-theorists are so drawn to psychologism, this will shed considerable light on the nature of AI as a psychological theory.

§2 Classical and cognitive psychologism

Whatever the problems involved in AI's reading of psychologism (*infra*), it does serve to bring out one very important point: as pivotal as the debate over psychologism was for the philosophy of logic, it is of just as much significance for the philosophy of psychology. For, if the failure to distinguish between logic and psychology induces one to misconstrue the nature of logical truths, so, too, *pari passu* does it undermine one's understanding of psychological explanation. Analytic philosophy's repudiation of psychologism would thus, if vindicated, be doubly important.

Humphrey went so far as to claim that 'Husserl's main endeavour was to free logic from the shackles of psychology. Equally he has succeeded in freeing psychology from the shackles of logic' (Humphrey 1951: 78). It is useful to be reminded that there are two sides to psychologism, and that these are far more intimately connected than the 'act/object of thinking' distinction, made famous by Frege, would lead one to believe. But, from

AI's point of view, Humphrey was wrong on both scores – at least, as far as concerns Frege and Husserl's argument. Thus, the basic question which AI raises is: If there are compelling reasons to question the assumption that Frege and Husserl succeeded in 'refuting' psychologism, are we not thereby compelled to reconsider our attitudes towards the formal separation between psychology and logic?

Such an argument adds an important factor to our understanding of psychologism. There is a tendency for analytic philosophers to focus exclusively on the consequence of treating the laws of logic as psychological generalisations for our understanding of the nature of logical propositions and rules of inference. If logicians have ignored the converse psychological dimensions of the argument, they have done no less than the majority of classical psychologicians themselves (with Wundt being the most notable exception). Indeed, as we saw in Chapter 2, the whole history of AI is one in which only subsequently did the founders of AI, whose initial interest was in the development of mechanical procedures for proving theorems and playing chess, become interested in the psychological implications of their work. And, as we shall see in this chapter, the very nature of the formalist framework in which these pioneers were operating encouraged them to approach this issue psychologistically.

Our understanding of this issue is hampered, however, by the fact that, for all the work that has been done on the rise of scientific materialism in nineteenth-century German philosophy, relatively little has been written on the interrelated growth of psychologism, even though its role in the evolution of post-computational mechanism has proven to be equally, if not more significant. Fortunately, an invaluable history of psychologism has recently been published (see Kusch 1995). One of the more important lessons to be learnt from Kusch's work is how careful we must be when interpreting and assigning the term 'psychologism'. Nowhere could the significance of this point be more clear than in the case of AI.

Johann Erdmann coined the neologism 'psychologism' to describe Eduard Beneke's transcendental conception of logic. In England, this Kantian theory was adopted by Sir William Hamilton, whose *Lectures on Metaphysics and Logic* provoked a strong attack from John Stuart Mill in *A System of Logic* and *An Examination of Sir William Hamilton's Philosophy*. Mill's argument had a profound influence on contemporary German philosophers and psychologists, largely because it provided the scientific materialists and mechanist reductionists with the means to fight off what they saw as the surge of 'mystery-mongering' being promulgated by the 'Back to Kant' movement. The resulting *naturalist* conception of philosophy then sparked off what Wundt castigated in 'Psychologismus und Logizismus' as a 'logicist' reaction in the last decades of the century – by which he was referring to the growing 'mathematical imperialism' which sought to subjugate both logic and psychology under its sway.

We shall look in greater detail in the following sections at the background, nature and limitations of Frege and Husserl's anti-psychologism, and at Hilbert's formalist precursor of cognitive psychologism. For the moment we need to see how the basic problem with AI's renunciation of anti-psychologism is that it focuses exclusively on Frege and Husserl; and, indeed, how the AI reading of psychologism proceeds through Frege and Husserl's eyes. The problem here is that several of the key figures singled out by Frege and Husserl as psychologicians not only rejected the allegation, but actually insisted that it was Frege and Husserl who were guilty of the charge. In fact, 'naturalism', or the 'psychological conception of logic' (as Frege scrupulously referred to it), was actually conceived as an antidote to Kantian 'transcendental' psychologism (a term coined by Husserl). Describing the naturalists as psychologicians is thus rather like accusing the logical positivist of metaphysics.

Husserl argued that there are two species of psychologism, *transcendental* (or Kantian) and *naturalist*, which both proceed from a misconception of the nature of logical truths. To this distinction must now be added a third species of psychologism. For, although there are few today (but there are some!) who would subscribe to the transcendental psychologistic thesis that the laws of logic describe the operations of the mind, there are a large number who support the *cognitive* version of psychologism, which maintains that we can learn how the mind works by mapping verbal protocols – transcripts of everything a subject says while solving some problem – onto a very different kind of formal model: viz., a computer program.

To appreciate the significance of this shift from classical to cognitive psychologism, we might compare Gregory's *Companion* article on the 'Laws of Thought' to what he first said about the same passage from Boole's *The Mathematical Analysis of Logic* when he originally quoted it in *Mind in Science*:

> For Boole, appropriate laws of logic are rules by which the Mind works. It is thus possible to discover how the Mind works by looking at the most effective rules of logic.
>
> I am inclined to believe that such arguments must be treated cautiously, for it might be that explicitly formulated rules of logic are powerful just because the Mind does not normally work in this way – so it gets a special boost.
>
> (Gregory 1981: 229)

The irony in this passage is that Gregory is quite right to seize on Boole as an exemplar of the psychologism that AI is seeking to revive. But then, Boole was not a naturalist, and clearly not the focus of Frege and Husserl's critique (see §§4, 5). What this quotation really demonstrates is the Kantian underpinnings of AI (see §3).

The schema (Figure 3.1) of the history of psychologism illustrates this point: Should this schema be presented as a circle, rather than in linear terms, with AI marking a return to the beginning? The fact that Gregory refers in the quoted passage from *Mind in Science* to the 'laws of logic', and not, as he does in the *Companion* entry, to the 'laws of thought', certainly confirms the importance of the link between transcendental psychologism and AI. Strictly speaking, this shift from speaking of the 'laws of thought' to the 'laws of logic' was the target of Mill's attack on Hamilton. According to Mill, the problem with Hamilton's argument was that it confused the laws of thought, which are psychological generalisations, with the laws of logic, which are precepts (see §4). But AI doesn't so much represent a return to transcendental psychologism as a synthesis of transcendental and formalist psychologism.

Like the transcendental psychologicians, the founders of AI were arguing that you can use a formal model to discover how the mind works. And, like the naturalist psychologicians, they were arguing that the classical laws of logic are precepts rather than psychological generalisations (whose utility as such is due to the fact that the human mind is not a classical logical machine). But, whereas the naturalist psychologicians based their argument on an analysis of the nature of logic (*qua* 'art'), the founders of AI were suggesting that the problem with transcendental psychologism is simply that it had inadequate formal tools with which to work. In other words, they were saying that the problem with both naturalist psychologism and with Frege and Husserl's attack on naturalist psychologism is the same: both mistook an empirical shortcoming for a conceptual mistake.

Thus AI seeks to incorporate elements from both transcendental and naturalist psychologism. From transcendental psychologism it takes the idea that the task of cognitive science is to discover 'a correspondence between a mental operation and some formal model of that operation – be it a model stated in terms of a logical calculus as in [Inhelder and Piaget's *The Growth of Logical Thinking*] or in terms of idealized strategies as in . . . *A Study of Thinking*' (Bruner 1959: 368). The reason why transcendental psychologism failed, according to AI, was simply because its models were too impractical, given the constraints of 'cognitive economy' on the human information-processing system.

From naturalist psychologism AI takes the idea that cognitive science must discover laws of thought that conform to the reality of human thinking (e.g., the type of problems we can solve, the time it takes us to do so, etc.). And like the naturalist psychologician, the AI-theorist is fully prepared to question whether these 'laws of thought' are innate or acquired, and to envisage the possibility of their changing over time, or for species. All that is putatively at stake is whether computational models provide the most suitable vehicle for understanding how our minds work *at the present time*.

AI was not the first to treat the debate over transcendental psychologism

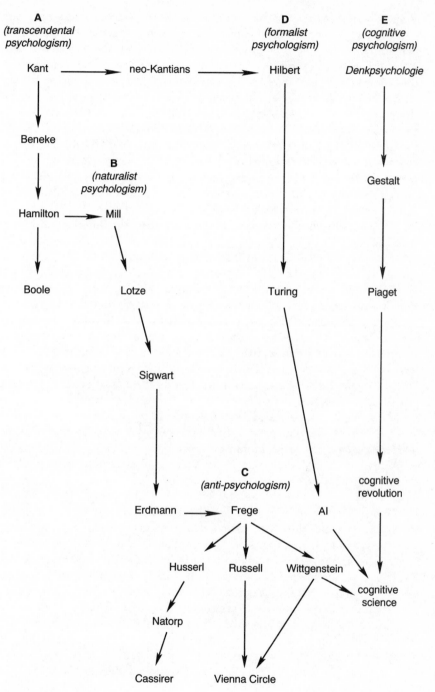

Figure 3.1

as an empirical matter. At the turn of this century, Störring was attempting to prove that human beings do not reason syllogistically in order to establish that thinking is not a 'logical process'. Transcendental psychologicians responded that all examples of thinking which appear to contain 'gaps' in their deductive chain of reasoning can be explained as harbouring unconscious enthymemes. The chief reason why German psychologists of thinking, from the Würzburg School to Gestalt, paid so much attention to the conflict between 'syllogistic' and 'actual' thinking was in order to settle the question of whether or not *inference* could be treated as a logical mental process. It was widely assumed that, if it could be shown that thinking is at least in part non-deductive – i.e. that human reasoning is governed by a different set of rules which are efficient in some contexts but break down in others – then this would suffice to refute the mechanist theory (dating back to Boole, Babbage, Jevons and Marquand) that the mind is a logical machine.

This was the tradition which to a large extent inspired the 'cognitive revolution' (see Shanker 1996). Thus the reason why AI had such an immediate impact on psychologists of thinking was because it seemed to demonstrate that, even though inference consists primarily of 'rules of thumb' rather than deductive procedures, this is no obstacle to treating reasoning as a mechanical procedure. For the computationalist is only committed to the premise that mental processes cannot be mapped onto logical procedures, not that they cannot be mapped onto effective procedures as defined by Turing (i.e. algorithms). Hence Turing's version of Church's Thesis seemed to offer cognitive psychologicians a much more powerful type of formal model – one which, *as it happens*, can be run on a computer – to discover the 'hidden' or 'unconscious' processes that occur during what, on the surface, look like 'gaps' in human reasoning.

As Newell and Simon put it in 'GPS: A Program which Simulates Human Thought':

> We may then conceive of an intelligent program that manipulates symbols in the same way that our subject does – by taking as inputs the symbolic logic expressions, and producing as outputs a sequence of rule applications that coincides with the subject's. If we observed this program in operation, it would be considering various rules and evaluating various expressions, the same sorts of things we see expressed in the protocol of the subject. If the fit of such a program were close enough to the overt behaviour of our human subject – i.e. to the protocol – then it would constitute a good theory of the subject's problem-solving.
>
> (Newell and Simon 1963: 283)

Far from being a drawback, it turns out to be blessing for cognitive psychologism that verbal protocols are invariably full of pauses, false steps, fresh starts, flashes of insight, and sudden solutions of a problem (see Chapter 4). Any attempt to run a computer program along similar lines would quickly grind to a halt. But if an agent's brain is seen as some sort of computational information-processing device, then the fragmentary evidence presented in the subject's verbal protocol must be treated as the *conscious elements* of a mental program whose *underlying operations* are *pre-conscious*: i.e. 'inaccessible to introspection', but inferrable from the corresponding steps in a computer program that is mapped onto the protocol. And this premise – the correspondence between mechanical procedures and 'pre-conscious mental processes' – is precisely what AI took over from transcendental psychologism.

AI thus offered to the vanguard of cognitive scientists, who, while they may not have been terribly interested in strong AI, were none the less predisposed to embrace psychologism, the possibility of advancing beyond what was seen at the time as Piaget's 'relatively static, unnecessarily static' group-theoretic model (Bruner 1960: 23). This new school was drawn to AI by the hope that 'perhaps the new science of programming will help free us from our tendency to force nature to imitate the models we have constructed for her' (*ibid.*). The key to the union that was so quickly forged between AI and cognitive psychology, therefore, lies in the premise that 'human reasoning is supported by a kind of thematic process rather than by an abstract logic. The principal feature of this thematic process is its pragmatic rather than its logical structure. It consists of a tendency to work with and to prefer empirically reasonable propositions, whether as hypotheses or as conclusions' (Bruner *et al.* 1967: 104).

It may seem, however, that cognitive science was confronted with an insuperable obstacle here; for, as Gardner notes:

> Cognitive science was conceived in the shadow of contemporary logic. . . . [B]oth early work on computers and the model of the neuron as a logical circuit encouraged a view of thought as logical. Furthermore, the first generation of cognitive scientists embraced a model of human beings that was decidedly rationalistic. Jerome Bruner, Herbert Simon, Allen Newell, and Jean Piaget all elected to investigate issues involving the abilities of human beings to reason validly.
>
> (Gardner 1985: 361)

In other words, the problem was to show how one can use 'the most logical of tools' to model problem-solving when there is so much evidence to suggest that 'we do not normally rely on logical deduction – not even when we are solving problems of apparently logical types. People (including logicians) not only make mistakes in probabilistic and everyday thinking . . . but often do not use logic where one might expect them to do so' (Boden 1988: 175–6).

AI's answer was that the logical calculus (= high-level language) sets out the construction and transformation rules according to which a program must be written, and establishes the 'problem-space' within which the gulf between starting point and goal must be bridged. This 'problem-space' is said to be isomorphic with 'a sort of maze of mental activity through which we [i.e. our minds] must wander, searching for a solution' (Lesgold 1988: 190). The program, like the brain of a human problem-solver, then has to select, from a wide range of possible choices, a route that seems likely to lead to the goal (according to pre-determined but self-modifying heuristics).

A program need not, however, choose the best possible route in order to simulate human reasoning (i.e. a chess program need not compete at the grandmaster level in order to qualify as a model of ordinary chess-thinking). This point was clearly spelled out by Turing in 'Computing Machinery and Intelligence':

> The processes of inference used by the machine need not be such as would satisfy the most exacting logicians. . . . For at each stage when one is using a logical system, there is a very large number of alternative steps, any of which one is permitted to apply, so far as obedience to the rules of a logical system is concerned. These choices make the difference between a brilliant and a footling reasoner, not the difference between a sound and a fallacious one.
>
> (Turing 1950: 29)

That is, we can use a computer to simulate the rules that the human mind follows, bearing in mind that the choices made by either system need not be optimal in order for the decision to be deemed intelligent.

In short, the AI response to Frege and Husserl's anti-psychologism is that, far from being *incoherent*, the classical psychologicians had entirely the right idea about inferring the hidden 'processes of inference' from formal models, but were frustrated in their endeavours by the limitations of their model, which assumed a deductive rigour that oversimplifies and might even be foreign to mental processes. But that does not preclude the possibility of using more sophisticated mathematical tools to model 'actual thinking' (cf. Bruner 1983: 112). Viewed as a psychological programme, therefore, AI embraces the fundamental premise that 'Good correspondence between a formal model and a process – between theory and observables, for that matter – presupposes that the model will, by appropriate manipulation, yield descriptions (or predictions) of how behaviour will occur and will even suggest forms of behaviour to look for that have not yet been observed – that are merely possible' (Bruner 1959: 368). What cognitive psychologism really presupposes, however, is that there are *pre-conscious mental processes* with which mechanical procedures can be correlated.

The challenge from AI to analytic philosophy's embargo on classical psychologism begins to take on an extremely interesting dimension. AI theorists have trumpeted the fact that they are questioning not just analytic philosophy's conception of psychology, or even of logic, but indeed, of itself: of the role of philosophy *vis-à-vis* cognitive science. Philosophical arguments are seen as *a priori theories* which may or not be fruitful, depending on the turns that psychological paradigms and technologies may take. But there is another way to read all this. One could argue that its attitude towards psychologism establishes a continuity between AI and classical *epistemological* theories which calls into question AI's very claim to constitute a *bona fide* science. No matter which side one might wish to take on this issue, it illustrates just how vital is a grounding in the debate over psychologism for an understanding of the foundations of AI.

§3 Psychologism as conceived by Kant

In this section we shall investigate the Kantian foundations of cognitive psychologism. The matter is of considerable historical interest: it enables us to see, first, what Mill – and in his footsteps, the naturalist psychologicians – were objecting to; and thence, the crux of Frege and Husserl's anti-psychologism. It allows us to appreciate why Hilbert was to claim that 'The formula game that Brouwer so deprecates has, besides its mathematical value, an important general philosophical significance' (Hilbert 1927: 475). It sheds important light on what mechanists regard as the cognitive implications of Turing's Thesis, and the behaviourist slant which Turing imposed on Hilbert's Kantian intentions. And it shows us how familiar Wittgenstein was with this epistemological tradition, and the bearing that this has on some of the more opaque remarks in his writings on logic and inference.

Historical rewards thus abound, but still more is involved. For the overriding issue here is the persistence of a Kantian picture which has been amplified by AI, even elaborated in ways that *prima facie* run contrary to some of Kant's most famous precepts, but remains Kantian none the less. We must not suppose, however, that the mere charge of 'Kantian metaphysics' serves as some sort of indictment of AI. There may still be some institutions around where positivist attitudes remain so entrenched that such is the case. But one of the more salutary effects of the cognitive revolution has been the extent to which it has tempered philosophers' polemical zeal. We are also reminded that, to a Kantian, to have one's argument labelled metaphysical is steep praise indeed. And, as we have already seen, to have one's theory labelled psychologistic is something of a badge of honour in contemporary AI circles.

In order to satisfy the complex demands being imposed on this analysis of cognitive psychologism, it is clearly not enough to approach this as a straightforward descriptive or hermeneutic exercise along the lines that, for example, when Hilbert speaks of using proof theory to describe 'the activity of our understanding, to make a protocol of the rules according to which our thinking actually proceeds' (Hilbert 1927), what he has in mind is the fulfilment of Kant's vision of a pure general logic that will provide a 'canon of understanding' – although this is indeed an essential aspect of Hilbert's argument (see §7). Nor are we interested in simply noting important parallels between the psychology of reasoning and Kant's applied general logic. What we are really interested in here is the part that goes missing in the *First Critique*: the key presuppositions which underpin the 'givens' that Kant outlines in the very first paragraph of the book.

In other words, we are looking for the epistemological framework governing Kant's conception of the faculty of understanding – and thence, of logic – and the abiding role which this has played in the evolution of cognitive psychologism. Here especially our interest is critical, not descriptive. In general, we are after the fundamental problems involved in this epistemological framework, and for the purposes of this chapter, its particular significance for assessing psychologism – be it classical or cognitive. To see the force of this point, one need only start with the Introduction to the chapter on Transcendental Logic in the *First Critique*.

Kant spells out here the epistemological picture which those following in his footsteps take for granted. He first reiterates his basic claim that knowledge originates through the interaction of sensibility and understanding. ('The understanding can intuit nothing, the senses can think nothing. Only through their union can knowledge arise' (Kant 1933: B76).) One can only apprehend an object via concepts, and it is only via apprehension that concepts are called into operation. 'Commonly, one also calls sensibility the *lower*, the understanding, however, the *higher* faculty; on the ground that sensibility gives the mere material to thinking, the understanding, on the other hand, disposes of this material and brings it under rules and concepts' (*Logic*: 40).

Numerous writers have commented on the psychological overtones – and limitations – of this argument (see, e.g., Kitcher 1990). Kant infers from the possibility of experience the categories which we must possess and the cognitive processes we must apply to generate knowledge from sensations. Thus he presents us, in the Objective and Subjective Deductions, with a body of synthetic *a priori* propositions about how the mind works: where the 'mind' under discussion is that of the 'transcendental subject'.

This approach is similar – but certainly not identical – to Piaget's 'epistemic subject' – similar in the sense that neither Kant nor Piaget wants to be seen as engaged in psychology. The categories and generative mechanisms which Kant attributes to the mind are said to be shared by all agents, regardless of sex, age, culture or environment. To appreciate the difference between their two views, however, one need only recall Piaget's criticisms of Kant's transcendental epistemology. Piaget complained that concepts, on Kant's theory, are fixed and invariant. There is no consideration given to development: to the dynamics of 'epistemological change'. Moreover, the categories which govern judgement are not discovered inductively on Kant's theory but, rather, are established by *a priori* proofs (see Piaget 1965).

The perception and evaluation of Kant's theory as quasi-psychological – as constituting a 'transcendental psychology' – are based on the epistemological framework which governs his argument. Kant assumes *ab initio* (read B1 of the *First Critique*) that the mind is bombarded by a flux of sensations which must be synthesised and organised: in contemporary terms, a mass of information that must be 'transformed, reduced, elaborated, recovered, and used' (Neisser 1967: 4). To do this, the mind – the faculty of understanding – must be governed in its operations by the fundamental laws of logic.

Kant's 'absolutely necessary rules of thought without which there can be no employment whatsoever of the understanding' is the logical structure through which all information must be processed. Pure general logic can only disclose these 'necessary rules' if it

> abstracts from all content of the knowledge of understanding and from all differences in its objects, and deals with nothing but the mere form of thought.
>
> As pure logic, it has nothing to do with empirical principles, and does not, as has sometimes been supposed, borrow anything from psychology, which therefore has no influence whatever on the canon of the understanding.
>
> (Kant 1933: A54)

If we are to see Kant as espousing a form of psychologism, therefore, we must be careful not to confuse his argument with the type of naturalist psychologism that Kant goes to such pains to refute in the *Logic*.

The *Logic* opens up with a theme which is as familiar to modern readers as it was to Kant's peers. All of nature, he argues, is rule-governed, and nowhere could this be more true than in regards to the operations of the human mind. But we are 'not conscious of' the rules that we follow in thinking or in speaking a language (*Logic*: 13). We can only 'gradually come to cognize them through experiments and long use of our powers' (*ibid.*).

Next, we get the quintessential Kantian argument that the *understanding* is the faculty of thinking: it is 'bound in its acts to rules we can investigate' (*ibid.*). It is the source of the contingent 'thinking rules' which we use to solve problems in various disciplines (*ibid.*). Our interest, *qua* philosophers, is not in these 'applied thinking rules', but in the general, necessary rules whereby the understanding constructs the latter. These necessary rules are 'those without which no use of the understanding would be possible at all': those which make thinking possible (*ibid.*: 14).

In order to discover these necessary rules, we must abstract from the contingent rules that we follow in a particular discipline. For the 'objects' of a domain affect the manner in which we think about them. But the necessary rules are those that apply to any and every domain. These 'necessary rules of thought in general' concern solely the *form*, not the substance of thinking (*ibid.*: 14–15). And the 'science of the necessary laws of the understanding and reason in general . . . we call logic' (*ibid.*: 15). Pure general logic provides us, therefore, with a 'canon of the understanding and of reason' (*ibid.*: 16). What Kant means by this is that pure general logical propositions are prescriptive: they are not empirical generalisations about how we think, but, rather, they serve as norms for how one should think if one is to arrive at the truth.

This distinction is crucial to Kant's attack on the type of naturalist psychologism – itself a reaction to Kantian transcendental psychologism – that was to flourish in the latter part of the nineteenth century. The problem with naturalist psychologism, according to Kant, is that it fails to distinguish between the contingent rules of thinking that are *described* in applied logic, and the necessary rules *prescribed* by pure logic. The rules of thinking that obtain in specific sciences are a product of the interaction between the necessary rules of thinking and the objects of a specific domain. Naturalism, according to Kant, misconstrues the empirical generalisations yielded by the psychology of reasoning (as Kant himself comes very close to calling it (see *ibid.*: 21)) as necessary and universal (synthetic *a priori*) truths. 'In logic we do not want to know how the understanding is and thinks, and how it hitherto has proceeded in thinking, but how it ought to proceed in thinking' (*ibid.*: 16).

What is, perhaps, most important about this argument is how Kant undertakes to ground the normativity of pure general logical propositions. Obviously it cannot be by introspection. Apart from Kant's (distinctively modern-sounding) complaints about the unreliability of 'inner perception', this would simply return him to naturalism. But Kant does not deny that pure general logical propositions are descriptive; what he argues is that they describe, not the rules of actual thinking or reasoning, but, rather, the necessary rules which the faculty of understanding follows.

This amounts to an entirely different species of psychologism: what (following Husserl) we might call *transcendental psychologism*, provided we do not confuse this with *transcendental psychological generalisations*. For Kant would have dismissed the latter notion as a contradiction in terms. Psychological generalisations, for Kant, are by definition contentual: they are based on the interaction of sensibility and understanding and are known by introspection. A proposition like 'One cannot believe both p and not-p' can in no sense be seen as a psychological generalisation. Pure logical propositions about the necessary rules of the understanding are rather *abstract generalisations* that are discovered *a priori*.

There is an interesting remark in the *Logic* in which Kant explains how 'The rules of logic . . . must be taken not from the *contingent* but from the *necessary* use of the understanding, which one finds, without any psychology, in oneself' (*ibid.*). In fact, what he means is: which one *cannot* find with psychology (cf. Kant 1933: A52ff). But it is his emphasis here on the mind's internal workings which is most arresting. 'One cannot believe both p and not-p' is said to be a generalisation about 'the rules that bind the understanding' (*ibid.*: A152). It is universal and necessary precisely because it is not psychological.

What Kant means by this is that a generalisation like 'One cannot believe both p and not-p' is prior to a proposition like 'One cannot believe that the earth is flat and that it is a sphere': where 'prior' is to be construed literally – viz., the former proposition describes a rule that is *experientially antecedent* to trying and being unable to believe that the earth is both flat and spherical. These rules are mental mechanisms. The latter is grounded in the former because this is how the faculty of understanding operates (as can only be revealed by philosophy).

Applied general logic (the psychology of reasoning) is thus parasitic on pure general logic. It 'is a representation of the understanding and of the rules of its necessary employment *in concreto*, i.e., under the accidental subjective conditions which may hinder or help its application, and which are all given only empirically' (*ibid.*: A54; cf. *Logic*: 21). Hence psychological generalisations presuppose the synthetic *a priori* truths yielded by pure general logic about the laws of thought (viz., the fundamental laws of logic), the generative mechanisms of thought (viz., apprehension, reproduction and recognition), and the categories whereby the mind synthesises and constructs knowledge from sensations.

This creates the obvious problem for Kant of reconciling his transcendental psychologism with the phenomenon of applied thinking errors (*Irrtum*). Kant's examples of 'judgement errors' in the *First Critique* are largely concerned with the phenomenon of visual illusions, but we could just as easily cite an example like the 'reasoning bias' recorded by Peter Wason in his 'selection task' experiment (see Wason 1980). Indeed, Cohen describes the performance errors documented by bias-theorists as 'cognitive illusions' which a subject is, in principle, capable of detecting and correcting, which are due, perhaps, to a lack of intelligence, education, attention, etc. (see Cohen 1981).

It might seem to the cognitivist that Kant's most obvious solution would have been to exploit the distinction between the necessary and the contingent rules of the understanding – the rules which the understanding follows *in abstracto* and *in concreto* – in order to combine a transcendental psychologism with a contentual psychology of reasoning. That is, to argue that the *understanding*, governed by the Laws of Logic, constructs domain-specific rules which may not themselves obey the Laws of Logic: perhaps to compensate for the limitations of sensibility (imagination) *vis-à-vis* the peculiar demands of reality. 'Errors' would then be nothing more than the result of a clash between divergent processing rules. But Kant tells us that one of the most basic synthetic *a priori* propositions discovered by transcendental logic is that the mind *cannot* follow contra-logical rules. Hence the source of reasoning errors must lie in some other mental activity. And as we have already seen, applied thinking is defined as the product of sensibility interacting with the understanding.

Kant's own solution to the problem of reasoning errors anticipates Cohen's. He locates the source of these errors in the faculty of sensibility: not, that is, that they can be attributed to sensibility alone ('Because the senses do not judge at all') but rather, 'in the unnoticed influence of sensibility upon the understanding, or, more exactly, upon judgment' (Kant 1933: A294). He tells us that what this amounts to is our propensity to mistake merely subjective grounds for objective grounds.[2]

It might be tempting to conclude that Kant's transcendental psychologism is an idly turning wheel *vis-à-vis* his applied logic, but in fact it plays a crucial role. The mind as studied by the philosopher is like a thought-experiment machine designed to run in a frictionless state. Operating it in the real world means that all sorts of things are going to go wrong. But we will never be able to diagnose the cause of these *malfunctions* by simply opening up the casing and peering inside. We can only understand how it ought to run by considering what it would be like to use it in this ideal state: in modern terminology, by formalising the rules followed by the ideal thinker/cogniser – the rules of competence as opposed to performance.

In some ways, though, talk of an 'ideal thinker/cogniser' is inappropriate. To many it suggests a picture of an unrealisable goal for which all of us are unconsciously striving (because of biological programming) but fall short of achieving, due to various inherited or acquired cognitive biases. To some it suggests a model of how the mind works in 'ideal circumstances'. But what Kant was searching for are the necessary rules which must govern the faculty of understanding, even when the distortions induced by actual reasoning conceal the fact. Kant was not postulating the existence of 'pure abstract objects' – a domain of Platonic entities such that reasoning about them is distortion-free, thereby enabling us to see how the mind works.[3] Kant's position was rather that the only way to uncover the necessary rules governing the understanding is by abstracting from ordinary reasoning via transcendental deduction.

This argument suggests an interesting way of reading the debate between Cohen and cognitive scientists that erupted in the early 1980s. Many of the commentators on Cohen's 1981 paper in *Behavioral and Brain Sciences* were openly mystified about Cohen's intentions. What, they wondered, is to be gained by arguing that cognitive biases disguise an underlying rationality? This, they felt, is surely a manifestation of philosophy's innate conservatism. The hard-nosed AI scientist has no such qualms about accepting the apparent irrationality of the human subject, as revealed by reasoning experiments and corroborated by successful programs; certainly no desire to engage in what he sees as a strictly semantic debate over the concept of rationality.

From a Kantian perspective, however, the thrust of Cohen's argument is not to minimise the importance of Wason's or Tversky and Kahnemann's results: it is to reorient our attitude towards their psychological significance. Cohen's point is that, by abandoning a logical framework, you misconstrue the source of reasoning errors. The mind is much more complicated than the picture suggested by cognitive heuristics. Reasoning is a product of interacting mental components. The bias-theorist thus oversimplifies the psychological complexity involved in judgement and reasoning.

To the AI-theorist this is complexity without a purpose. Its sole rationale is a 'given' which there is no reason to adopt. Nature loves simplicity. Indeed, the guiding principle underlying AI is to 'define thinking or problem solving in such a way as to relate them to, not separate them from, simpler processes' (Duncan 1959: 397).[4] Remove the assumption that the mind is a logical machine and there is no need to complicate our explanation of the mechanics of judgement and reasoning with problems about representation.

The reaction to Cohen's argument forewarns us that few AI scientists are going to regard the study of Kant's transcendental psychologism as anything other than a purely historical matter. But what concerns us here is not the rival claims of transcendental versus naturalist, static versus developmental, or logical versus computational models: it is the presupposition that a formal model can be used to reveal the mind's hidden processes. The source of this premise is *epistemological*, not psychological. Indeed, this epistemological source determines how the cognitivist defines 'psychology', regardless of whether this be from a Kantian, a naturalist, a Piagetian, or a computational point of view.

It is precisely here where the issue of psychologism enters. Kant introduces four fundamental premises which, in turn, raise the two basic problems that define psychologism:

1   given that the mind is divorced from reality, and
2   that the mind's information about reality must be organised,
3   it follows that thinking and reasoning, like all natural phenomena, are (partially hidden) rule-governed (psychic) processes, and
4   that the task of logic is to explain both how we do think (applied general logic) and how we ought to think (pure general logic).

The metaphysical problems which this raises are:

1« what is the nature and source of the necessity that governs our thinking-processes? And:
2« how can we model the rules which, unconsciously, we must follow in thinking (and in speaking a language), or which prevent us from thinking in certain ways, try as we might?

For Kant, it is the constitution of the faculty of understanding which accounts for 1«. Given, according to Kant, that the operations of the faculty of understanding conform to Aristotle's fundamental laws of thought, it follows that classical logic provides the missing steps in our reasoning: the rules the mind must follow in reasoning of which we are not aware. It is precisely this 'given' which AI insists has been overturned by empirical findings. The only certain thing we can say about thinking, according to AI, is that it must proceed by mechanically simple steps – steps which themselves demand no intelligence. But the logic of the configuration of these steps is heuristic.

As significant as this shift may be from Kant's Aristotelian model to a computational model of the laws of thought, the latter approach remains resoundingly metaphysical, with the *brain* taking the place of the *epistemic subject*. Before AI theorists recoil at this suggestion, they should consider whether they have in fact abandoned the Kantian reliance on necessary laws, or are simply less forthright about this feature of their argument. To be sure, no AI scientist is about to argue that the brain must be a serial or parallel computer; the premise is rather that, most likely for reasons of efficiency, it was natural for the brain – given its propensity to binary encodability – to evolve in some such manner. But this is a 'top-down', not a 'bottom-up' approach; or, to put this in more familiar philosophical terms, the reasoning here is *a priori*, not *a posteriori*.

The AI theorist insists that, given, thanks to Turing, that we can simulate all 'processes of inference' computationally, we can infer from such models the steps which the mind/brain *must* have gone through at those pre-processing and/or processing stages which are 'inaccessible' to self-observation. How different is this from Kant's attempt to reason back from the nature of a cognitive task to the operations that must have been performed by the understanding? Kant's conception of applied general logic as describing how we think in some particular domain (e.g. how we solve chess problems) *as informed by* the necessary rules postulated by transcendental logic is very much the picture that we will find in Selz and de Groot and in Newell and Simon (see Chapter 4). If computationalists are guilty of a philosophical sin, therefore, it is that of assuming that what they are doing is purely inductive – that protocols validate their models – while remaining oblivious to the crucial role which they assign, via 'pre-conscious processes', to the *computational "must"*'.

The AI theorist may think he is abandoning Kant's attitude towards pure logic, or, at the very least, reversing the subsidiary relation between applied and pure logic (between psychology and logic), but neither is the case. Indeed, it is striking to see just how Kantian the theory remains. AI substitutes 'computational psychology' for 'applied general logic' in (4) above (while retaining the 'normativity' conception of pure logic), and 'programs' for Kant's logical model in (2«). But in many other respects the argument remains Kantian. Indeed, even the shift from Kant's Aristotelian model of the laws of thought to computational models of cognitive heuristics can be accommodated within Kant's conception of logic. For one of the things to bear in mind here is Kant's claim in the Preface to the second edition of the *First Critique* that his transcendental arguments are subject to 'confirmation or refutation by experiment' (Kant 1933: Bxixff). In light of this oft-repeated claim, perhaps Kant's appeal to the classical laws of logic should not be seen as dogmatic; if the 'science of metaphysics' (philosophy) advances another logic, so be it.

To grasp the continuity in psychologistic thinking, we need to place Kant's theory within the larger context of his influence on the evolution of psychology in the nineteenth century. This was really twofold. To begin with, there is the familiar point that Kant's attack on the possibility of a true – i.e. a Newtonian – science of psychology stimulated attempts to systematise (mathematise) the subject. But this must be seen in conjunction with Kant's transcendental psychologism. For the latter played no less crucial a role in establishing the framework from which AI evolved. What Kant was saying is that you cannot hope to understand the inner workings of the mind using self-observation. But that does not entail that we are barred from understanding the mind's inner workings. Nor does it entail that psychology is irrelevant to this enterprise. It is from self-observations that we must 'abstract' in order to discover the mind's hidden workings.

The subordinate relationship posited by Kant between applied and pure general logic thus provides an essential complement to Harré's claim that cognitivism presupposes a 'Hertzian' model of psychological explanation (see Harré 1990). In essence, a Hertzian conception of psychology is one which claims that a psychology confined to introspection and behavioural reports is condemned to remain purely descriptive. In order to constitute a genuinely *explanatory* science, it must infer from these observable phenomena the generative mechanisms which brought them about. It is in this sense that we speak of basing the concept of psychological explanation on the paradigm of physics.

Not only is this theme already present in Kant's writings (in fact, this is exactly what he says in the *Anthropology*), but, even more importantly, we can see how Kant's transcendental psychologism *demanded* a Hertzian conception of psychology. For the very notion of 'pre-conscious cognitive processes' presupposes that the problem facing psychology is that the generative processes underlying cognition occur 'beneath the threshold of introspection': *must*, according to the Objective and Subjective Deductions, occur beneath the threshold of introspection, since they supply the conditions that make introspection possible. (In other words, it makes no sense to suppose that we could so train our powers of introspection as to be able to attend to these hidden processes.)

The argument rests, therefore, on a Cartesian picture of introspection as a form of perception, but further assumes that a subject only has privileged access to fragments of her thought or reasoning-processes. The task of psychology thus becomes that of constructing formal models which will fill in the 'gaps' in the subject's self-awareness of her reasoning processes. And this is precisely the theme which the naturalists were to reject: not because of any qualms over the downgrading of introspection; not even because of doubts about the notion of 'unconscious inferences' (which is integral to Mill's theory of perception, and which in turn may have been a key source for Helmholtz's *unbewusster Schluss*); but because the role here assigned to the laws of logic struck naturalists as the consequence of removing the laws of thought from the realm of experience.

§4 'Logic is a part, a branch, of psychology'

As was remarked in the opening section, it is highly significant that, when AI-theorists talk about psychologism, they invariably cite Boole's *Laws of Thought* as their paradigm. But when Frege and Husserl attacked psychologism their attention clearly lay elsewhere. Frege is the more reticent of the two when it comes to providing names. It is Husserl's list in *Logical Investigations* that provides us with an indication of the philosophers that he and Frege wanted to attack: viz., 'Mill, Bain, Wundt, Sigwart, Erdmann and Lipps' (LI: 146). In other words, the 'naturalists'.

It is a school of thought in which Boole was seldom (if ever) included. Frege saw Boole as a member of the English school that was primarily interested in the construction of reasoning machines. Hence in his long article on 'Boole's Logical Calculus and the Concept-script' he associates Boole with Jevons, not with the naturalists, and chastises Boole for supposing that our 'thinking as a whole [could be] coped with by a machine or replaced by purely mental activity' (Frege 1979: 35). This was the central theme in the debate over mechanist theories of reasoning at the turn of the century; but it played at best a minor role in the concurrent debate in the philosophy of logic over psychologism. Moreover, whereas Boole's argument remained Kantian, that of the naturalist psychologicians was largely inspired – as Husserl stresses – by Mill.[5]

Boole begins *The Laws of Thought* with the psychologistic claim that the

'science of Logic' should be founded on 'the fundamental laws of those operations of the mind by which reasoning is performed' (Boole 1947: 1).
Gregory draws from this passage the conclusion that 'For Boole, appropriate
laws of logic are rules by which the Mind works. It is thus possible to
discover how the Mind works by looking at the most effective rules of logic'
(Gregory 1981: 229). In fact, what Boole argued is that 'The laws of
thought, in all its processes of conception and of reasoning, in all those operations of which language is the expression or instrument, are of the same
kind as are the laws of the acknowledged process of Mathematics' (Boole
1947: XXII §11). The key themes here are the Kantian ideas that:

1   logic is the science of conception (categorisation and judgement) and
     reasoning; and
2   the hidden rules of the mind's operations can be inferred from a formal
     calculus.

Much as he may have sympathised with the former thesis, the latter was
to be one of Mill's primary targets in his rejection of the Kantian tradition
in the philosophy of logic. This argument had an enormous influence on
nineteenth-century German philosophy and psychology. Both the *System of
Logic* and *An Examination of Sir William Hamilton's Philosophy* went through
several printings in Germany. For the purposes of this chapter, it is the
Examination which is the more important of the two texts, primarily because
it supplied the framework for the naturalists' response to the 'Back to Kant'
movement.

As Mill repeatedly emphasises, Hamilton developed Kant's conception of
the distinction between pure and applied logic (which Hamilton calls 'logic'
and 'psychology' respectively). This is manifest in the following quotation
from Hamilton's *Lectures on Metaphysics and Logic*, which Mill quotes in the
Examination:

> When philosophy, by a reflective abstraction, analyses the necessary
> from the contingent forms of thought, there results a science, which
> is distinguished from all others by taking for its object-matter the
> former of these classes; and this science is Logic. Logic, therefore, is
> at last fully and finally defined as the science of the necessary forms
> of thought.
>
> (Mill 1873: 357)

Psychology, according to Hamilton, is the science of the contingent forms of
thought.

Mill first tries to show that this argument is self-contradictory. Given
that psychology is 'the science of all mental phænomena' (which 'includes
thinking'), how can one argue that there is another, distinct science which

treats of a domain of thought excluded from psychology (*ibid.*: 357)? On Hamilton's own definition, logic must rather be a subset of psychology. This leads to Mill's well-known remark (quoted by Husserl) that 'so far as it is a science at all, [Logic] is a part, a branch, of Psychology' (*ibid.*: 359). That is, logical laws, according to Mill, are about psychological processes (such as judgement, reasoning and inference). Psychology thus provides the theoretical foundations of logic.

The next step in Mill's argument is to invert Hamilton's Kantian conception of the logic/psychology distinction. Given that psychology analyses those 'modes in which, and the conditions subject to which, by the constitution of our nature, we cannot but think' (*ibid.*: 358), it follows that it is psychology that treats of the 'necessary properties of thought' – 'the properties which all thoughts possess, which thought must possess, without the possession of which it would not be thought' (*ibid.*: 357). According to Mill, therefore, the exact opposite from what Kant concluded is the case: viz., 'The necessary Laws of Thought . . . are precisely those with which Logic has least to do, and which belong the most exclusively to Psychology' (*ibid.*: 359).

Mill's argument turns on what he regards as a fatal ambiguity in Hamilton's theory. Hamilton treats the 'laws of thought' as referring both to 'necessities of nature' and to 'precepts' (*ibid.*: 358). But missing from Hamilton's argument is Kant's thesis that the laws of logic are prescriptive because they describe the operations of the faculty of understanding *in abstracto*. Take away this foundation and all one is left with is the argument which we find today amongst cognitive psychologicians that 'one learns how to *use* formal logic as a prosthetic device with which to check one's reasoning' (Bruner 1983: 112).

Mill concludes that, freed from this 'metaphysical prejudice', we can see how 'There is nothing to prevent us from thinking contrary to the laws of Logic: only, if we do, we shall not think rightly, or well, or conformably to the ends of thinking, but falsely, or inconsistently, or confusedly' (Mill 1863: 359). Thus we get Mill's conclusion that *psychology describes the necessary forms of thought* – how we must think given the nature of our mental constitution – whereas *logic is an art* – 'a collection of precepts or rules for thinking' – designed to counter the mind's often wayward results (*ibid.*). But to say that the laws of logic are prescriptive does not rule out that they form a subset of psychology's descriptive laws of thinking. The laws of correct thinking, according to Mill, are those which are in accord with the constitution of our minds (the necessary properties of thought).

Mill repeatedly makes it clear that he accepts the Kantian form/content distinction (sensations are given which the mind must organise). 'What the mind adds to these, or puts into them, is Forms of Thought' (*ibid.*: 360). What the mind 'puts in' is structure. 'The Forms of Thought are Conception, Judgment, and Reasoning: Logic is the Science of the Laws

84

(meaning the rules) of these three operations' (*ibid.*). This last point may seem somewhat confusing, given the above logic/psychology distinction; but Mill goes on to explain that 'Logic becomes the science of the precepts for the formation of concepts, judgments, and reasonings' (*ibid.*: 361). In other words, psychology describes how we *do* categorise, judge, reason and infer; logic prescribes how we *should*.

Mill refuses, however, to speak of the laws of identity, contradiction, and excluded middle as 'laws of logic'; rather, he refers to them as 'The Fundamental Laws of Thought'. For these laws, he insists, express 'actual necessities of thought' (*ibid.*: 372). It is impossible to believe both p and not-p. But this is because belief is a conscious mental state. Hence the nature of this necessity – *qua* necessity – must be psychological. 'The Law of Contradiction is a principle of reasoning in the same sense, and in the same sense only, as the Law of Identity is. It is the generalization of a mental act which is of continual occurrence, and which cannot be dispensed with in reasoning' (*ibid.*: 378).

Thus Mill concludes that it is indeed possible for a subject to think both p and not-p if he does so 'unconsciously': i.e., if he is not aware that his mental states *p* and *not-p* are contradictories. The task of logic is then simply to establish that this is the case; the constitution of the human mind will then take care of the rest. For, 'when once he is made to see that there is a contradiction, it is totally impossible for him to believe it' (*ibid.*: 373). That is, only 'acts of belief' can be true or false, and accordingly, can contradict one another. Hence the law of contradiction refers to the psychological generalisation that it is impossible to sustain contradictory mental states: impossible to experience the mental state of believing p and disbelieving p. And we discover this 'law' by introspection: i.e. it is impossible to observe these contradictory mental states in the same consciousness.[6]

It is easy to see how this theory tied in with scientific materialism. Mill presupposes that logic, like ethics, can be reduced to physics: i.e. that 'every "ought" rests on an "is".' The law of contradiction is not prescriptive *as opposed to* causal: it is prescriptive precisely *because* it is causal. Thinking according to the laws of logic will cause you – will cause your mind – to arrive at the truth. But then, how does Mill explain the phenomenon of 'thinking falsely, or inconsistently, or confusedly' (*ibid.*: 359)? The answer is straightforward: other psychological factors must have overridden the operations of the fundamental laws of thought, causing the thinking-process to arrive at erroneous beliefs. These other factors cause us to think irrationally. For, given that it is a necessary property of thought to observe the law of contradiction, someone who fails to recognise p and not-p as contradictories is prevented from thinking rationally by some intervening psychological cause (e.g. powerful emotion).

Take away 'the groundwork, and justifying authority' of the fundamental laws in the operations of the mind of the transcendental subject, and you take away their absolute (universal and sempiternal) necessity. This sets the stage for Mill's enunciation of the basic principle of naturalist psychologism:

> Whether the three so-called Fundamental Laws are laws of our thoughts by the native structure of the mind, or merely because we perceive them to be universally true of observed phænomena, I will not positively decide: but they are laws of our thoughts now, and invincibly so. They may or may not be capable of alteration by experience, but the conditions of our existence deny to us the experience which would be required to alter them. Any assertion, therefore, which conflicts with one of these laws – any proposition, for instance, which asserts a contradiction, though it were on a subject wholly removed from the sphere of our experience, is to us unbelievable. The belief in such a proposition is, in the present constitution of nature, impossible as a mental fact.
>
> (*Ibid.*: 381)

The most we can say is that the 'fundamental laws of thought' are necessary for us, here and now; these are, after all, psychological generalisations. Perhaps other creatures might be so mentally constituted that contradictory mental states can co-exist in a single consciousness.

The major consequence of this argument is that a sharp distinction is introduced between Mill's naturalist and Boole's transcendental psychologism. For Mill is removing logic's role as the model of how the mind works: of the unconscious rules which the mind must follow in categorising, judging, and reasoning. The only way to discover the rules one is following is by attending to them. Mill does not deny the phenomenon of unconscious rule-following, but he construes the concept of the *unconscious* on the model of Hartley's *secondarily automatic motions* ('the effort of attention, after becoming less and less, is finally null, and the operation, originally voluntary, becomes, in Hartley's language, secondarily automatic' (*ibid.*: 363)). He thus introduces a crucial shift, from Kant's 'pre-conscious' (logical) rules which the mind must follow, to associationism's unconscious rules that we acquire in the course of learning how to think and speak: rules which, through habit, we become unaware of following.

Mill's problem, however – as is evidenced by his tendency to slip back into describing logical propositions in the very terms he has proscribed – is that he has no basis for universalising his normative conception of logic. When Gregory confronts this problem he argues:

> it might be that explicitly formulated rules of logic are powerful just because the Mind does not normally work in this way – so it gets a special boost. Just this is so for hand tools: they are so effective because the hands are not like them. If our hands had

screwdriver-like fingers, we would not need screwdrivers. So possibly Boole's and later logics are useful just because the Mind does not normally work this way.

(Gregory 1981: 229)

But whereas Gregory speaks only of the 'efficacy' of formal logic, Mill dwells on the theme that the rules of logic are precepts for arriving at the *truth*. It is not that logic supplies a *useful* problem-solving tool; logic is rather the art 'of correct thinking, and the Science of the Conditions of correct thinking' (Mill 1873: 361). But truth has been tied to the 'acts of belief' of the thinking subject; hence what are precepts for one culture might not be for another (since it would not lead to what count as truths for them). The naturalist psychologicians simply ignored the sceptical and relativist implications of this argument for the philosophy of logic. Frege and Husserl did not.

§5 The laws of truth are 'boundary stones set in an eternal foundation'

Analytic philosophers have tended to dwell on Frege's responsibility for the 'demise' (substitute 'remission') of psychologism, but apart from a few scattered remarks in the review of Husserl's *Philosophie der Arithmetik*, the opening sections of *Foundations of Arithmetic*, the preface to *Basic Laws*, and 'Thoughts', Frege's most important reflections on psychologism – in his various attempts at a textbook on logic – went unpublished (see PW: *passim*). It was Husserl who had by far the greater impact on contemporary philosophers and psychologists (see Kusch 1995).

Husserl devoted almost the whole of the first volume of *Logical Investigations* to his attack on psychologism. Still, many analytic philosophers will argue that Frege should be given the lion's share of the credit for the 'refutation' of psychologism, in so far as Husserl's conversion to anti-psychologism came about as a result of Frege's critical review of *Philosophie der Arithmetik*. Whether or not this was actually the case (see Føllesdal 1958, Mohanty 1982, Bell 1990, Dummett 1991), what is clear is that Frege and Husserl must be read together in order to appreciate fully the analytic attack on psychologism.[7]

Perhaps the best known of Frege's writings on psychologism is his preface to *Basic Laws*, which contains the attack on Benno Erdmann's 'psychological conception of logic'. Even before one considers the nature of Frege's critique of psychologism, one should be asking why it is that he begins his most important work in this fashion. Was this solely a case of getting clear on what he regarded as the correct way to view the nature of logic, or did Frege have some larger purpose in mind?

The answer to this question can be found in the 1897 version of 'Logik'.

Frege explicitly argues there that 'Psychological treatments of logic arise from the mistaken belief that a thought (a judgement as it is usually called) is something psychological like an idea. This view leads necessarily to an idealist theory of knowledge' (PW: 143). Thus, in Frege's eyes, the debate over psychologism not only raises fundamental questions about the nature of logical truth, but further, about the nature of thought and its relation to language.

To understand Frege's critique of psychologism we need to go back to Mill's response to the question: Why is it impossible to believe both p and not-p? As we saw in §4, Mill's answer was: Given that thinking is a mental process, and that psychology studies the operations of the mind, it follows that the explanation of this *mental phenomenon* must be psychological. Hence the law of thought 'No one can think both p and not-p' must be a psychological law. But when Mill says that 'Logic is a part, a branch, of psychology', he is not suggesting that the laws of logic are psychological generalisations. For recall that the 'necessary Laws of Thought' are said by Mill to be psychological generalisations. The laws of logic, Mill argues, are rather precepts of correct reasoning. Thus, Mill draws a fundamental distinction between the *psychological generalisation* 'No one can believe both p and not-p' (because of the way our minds are constituted) and the *logical precept* 'No one should try to believe both p and not-p' (if one wants to think in accord with the rest of humanity).

Frege responds that logic is a science, not an art; the task of logic is 'to discern the laws of truth' (Frege 1918: 1). From these 'laws of truth there follow prescriptions about asserting, thinking, judging, inferring' (*ibid.*). That is, we can think of the laws of truth as 'prescriptions for making judgments; we must comply with them in our judgments if we are not to fail of the truth' (PW: 143). Mill, according to Frege, recognised that it is only in this 'prescriptive' sense that one can refer to the laws of logic as 'laws'. But Mill then sought to ground this fact in our mental constitution. Thus, Mill argued that the laws of logic prescribe how we ought to think because he thought that, like laws of nature, they 'define the actual course of events' (*ibid.*: 145).

It is because he is so wary about confusing these prescriptive and descriptive senses of the term 'law' that Frege is reluctant to sanction the expression 'Fundamental Laws of Thought', as opposed to what he regards as the perfectly legitimate 'Fundamental Laws of Thinking'.[8] Frege spells this point out in his attack on Achelis: there are *laws of thinking* – which means, contrary to Kant's famous objection, that you can have a science of psychology in the natural scientific sense – and there are *precepts of thought* (which follow from the science of logic). But what you cannot have are 'norms of thinking': viz., logical rules that describe how the mind works.

This, according to Frege, is the fallacy committed by the psychological logicians (*ibid.*: 146): viz., the failure to observe the categorial distinction between two such statements as:

1 Whenever human beings believe that p is the case, and they believe that the conditional 'If p then q' obtains, they invariably conclude q; and
2 p. & p —>q. —> q.

Item 1 is a psychological generalisation which may or may not be true, or whose truth-value may change over time, or for subjects.[9] But item 2 describes a logical truth that must always be the case, regardless of where or when or by whom it is grasped.

Husserl picks up on this argument in his endorsement of the prescriptivist conception of logic. He distinguishes between *using the laws of logic as norms* and *describing them as norms*. He rejects the latter thesis – which he sees as intrinsically psychologistic – on the grounds that this distorts the 'thought-content' of the laws of logic. The laws of logic should not be seen as rules that tell us how we should think; for this would render their content 'real' as opposed to 'ideal'. The distinction here, he explains in his reply to Palágyi, is between 'pure and empirical generality' (Husserl 1903: 39). What he means is that the laws of logic do not assert anything about the world; they are rather abstract 'theoretical truths' whose *absolute generality* serves to ground the various rules of inference (LI: 170).

The argument is intended to apply both to transcendental and to naturalist psychologism, which Husserl sees as obverse sides of the same coin. The former speaks of 'generic human nature' (the faculty of understanding) while the latter focuses on actual human nature. But both sides are equally guilty of trying to deduce 'the ideal from the real, or, more precisely, the necessity of laws from the contingency of facts' (*ibid.*: 146). Both sides (and perhaps Frege as well?) misconstrue the relation between logic and psychology ('pure' and 'applied' logic) because both presuppose that the contrast that concerns us in the philosophy of logic is between *laws of nature* and *prescriptive laws*. In fact, the opposite to a law of nature is an *ideal law* (*ibid.*: 175). An 'ideal law' is not a norm which *tells you* to do such-and-such; it is rather a generalisation about the concept of truth. Thus, the laws of logic are ideal laws which we treat as precepts.

The crucial question which both Frege and Husserl felt needed to be cleared up is: Why were naturalist philosophers led to confuse the laws of logic with laws of thinking? Frege's answer was that, although thinking is a mental process, that does not mean that what you think *about* are mental entities: i.e. that words are names of ideas or mental representations. If that were the case, then the relations between signs would be psychological and the laws governing those relations would be psychological: i.e. the laws of logic would amount to psychological generalisations rather than precepts. But the laws of logic are true timelessly, invariantly, and independently of anyone's actually thinking them. Indeed, it is precisely because of the cate-gorial distinction between logical truths and the laws of thinking that we use logical truths as laws (i.e. as precepts).

What Frege is saying, therefore, is that the mentalism underpinning naturalist psychologism undermines the prescriptivist conception of logic that Mill wanted to establish.[10] As Frege sees it, the real lesson to be learnt from psychologism is that words and sentences must stand for something objective rather than subjective: i.e. words do not stand for ideas, and sentences do not stand for combinations of ideas. Moreover, the reason why naturalist philosophers were drawn into a psychological conception of logic was because they had relied on a faulty tool: on ordinary language, which is deeply imbued with psychological overtones.

In what is an obvious allusion to Mill, Frege remarks: 'if we see the task of logic to be that of describing how men actually think, then we shall natu-rally have to accord great importance to language. But then the name logic is being used for what is really only a branch of psychology' (PW: 143).[11] The only way that logic will be able to attain Kant's goal of 'saying what holds with the utmost generality for all thinking, whatever its subject-matter' (*ibid.*: 128) is if it adopts a *concept-script*. For the primary task of logic is to 'free us from the fetters of language' (*ibid.*: 143), and, *a fortiori*, psychology. Only thus can one preserve the objectivity of truth.

Frege adopts a sceptical strategy in his attack on psychologism. He endeavours to convince us that psychologism would render communication impossible and the concept of truth nonsensical. He starts out by complaining that philosophers have inconsistently and indiscriminately used the word 'idea' to refer to both a subjective and an objective entity (Frege 1959: 37). He insists that, for the sake of clarity, the term 'idea' should be restricted to its subjective use: viz., as referring to mind-dependent images or sensations that are privately owned and unshareable. On this (standard) view, no two people can have the same idea when they hear a word; for 'It is so much of the essence of any one of my ideas to be a content of my consciousness, that any idea someone else has is, just as such, different from mine' (Frege 1923: 361). But then, how can this epistemological common-place be reconciled with one's ability to communicate one's thoughts, or with the fact that a thought is true independently of anyone's believing it to be so? How could something so ephemeral as an idea account for the time-lessness of true thoughts (see PW: 133)?

Frege is hereby challenging the fundamental premise of the telementa-tional view of language: the idea that language is a structured system of arbitrary vocal sounds whereby thoughts are transferred from one person's mind to another. He is not, however, challenging the basic view that language serves as a medium for the communication of thoughts; nor is he challenging the Cartesian view of the epistemic privacy of mental states. What he is arguing is that, if words were the names of ideas (as subjectively understood), and sentences stood for combinations of such ideas, then genuine communication could never take place (see *ibid.*: 134). The fact is, however, that genuine communication between speakers is a common occurrence. Hence the only conclusion one can draw is that words do not stand for ideas and sentences do not stand for combinations of ideas. And the only other option available to us, according to Frege, is Platonism: i.e. the thoughts expressed by sentences 'are neither things in the external world nor ideas. A third realm must be recognized.'

Thus we get Frege's famous argument that signs have both a *sense* and a *reference*: a 'mode of presenting' a referent – i.e. the thought expressed by a sentence – and a truth-value. The thoughts that are communicated by sentences must be something objective; for 'The being of a thought [lies] in the possibility of different thinkers' grasping the thought as one and the same thought' (Frege 1923: 376). How else, Frege asks, could we account for the phenomenon of contradiction? That is, if the thought expressed by a sentence were a subjective entity, then no two people could have the same thought, in which case they could never contradict one another. Contradiction can only occur when 'it is the very same thought that one person is asserting to be true and another to be false' (PW: 133). Frege concludes that the only way the possibility of contradiction can be explained is if we see thoughts as objective, mind-independent entities that we grasp when we think (see *ibid.*: 145). And 'This view,' Frege tells us,

> is in harmony with many of our ways of talking. For do we not say that the same thought is grasped by this person and by that person? And that each person has the same thought over and over again? Now if thoughts only came into existence as a result of thinking or if they were constituted by thinking, then the same thought could come into existence, cease to exist, and then come into existence again, which is absurd.
>
> (*Ibid.*: 137)

Frege's critique of psychologism thus turns on the distinction – which Mill himself had emphasised – between the *act of thinking* and the *object of thinking* – and thence, between psychology and logic. The *object of thinking* is said to be whatever is thought or believed – what is true or false, where truth is conceived of as being wholly independent of what is believed to be true. Frege insists that, given the *objectivity* and *sempiternality* of truth, the 'objects of thinking' could not possibly be ideas. It was by treating the objects of thinking as ideas that psychologism had confused the *descriptive laws of human thinking* with the *prescriptive laws of logic*.

Frege and Husserl both accept that the laws of thinking can fluctuate wildly from species to species, but that the laws of truth must – logically must – remain invariant. This is the point that lies behind Husserl's remark that: 'No one *can* believe in a contradiction, no one *can* take something both to be and not to be – no one, that is, who is rational, to add an obvious qualification. The impossibility concerns anyone who wishes to judge rightly and no one else. It does not therefore express a psychological compulsion' (LI: 119). Why the 'obvious qualification'? The answer is because someone who believed the contradiction would, *contra* psychologism, still be thinking: would still be grasping and combining thoughts. He would just not be thinking rationally. The mistake the psychologicians made was to equate a psychological process – thinking, judging, reasoning, inferring, asserting, etc. – with a logical process (proof).

Frege and Husserl are both more than willing to accept that there might be beings who think in radically different ways than we do, and thus whose fundamental laws of thinking would be markedly different from our own.[12] Indeed, they both accept that there might be beings – in Frege's words 'madmen' and in Husserl's words 'angels' – who violate the laws of logic, although *we* cannot conceive what this 'hitherto unknown kind of madness' would be like (BL: xvi; see LI: 161). The mistake which the naturalist psychologicians made was to conclude from this possibility [*sic*] that such beings would therefore have different but equally valid laws of thought.

To understand the motivation for this argument, we have to go back to Book II vii §5 of Mill's *System of Logic*. Mill starts out by stating his accord with Hamilton that 'inconceivability is no criterion of impossibility'. But Hamilton cites this maxim to establish the *a priori* character of the laws of contradiction and excluded middle. While accepting the principle that 'There is no ground for inferring a certain fact to be impossible, merely from our inability to conceive its possibility', Mill felt that he must establish the *a posteriori* character of these 'fundamental Laws of Thought'. His solution, as we saw in the preceding section, was that the law of contradiction should be seen as 'one of our first and most familiar generalizations from experience. The original foundation of it I take to be, that Belief and Disbelief are two different mental states, excluding one another. This we know by the simplest observation of our own minds' (Mill 1963: 277).[13]

Frege and Husserl's attention was fixed on this argument. If the laws of logic were a necessary property of our thinking, then we couldn't make sense of the suggestion that there might be beings who could think otherwise. To be sure, our minds may be so constituted that we cannot imagine what it would be like to violate the laws of logic, but that, they felt, is a very different matter from supposing that it would be impossible to violate the laws of logic. An apposite comparison here, Husserl tells us, is to the fact that, even though it is impossible for *us* to see infra-red colours, it is possible that other beings might see those colours (LI: 161). But, for psychologism, the failure to observe the logical/psychological distinction ('ideal' versus 'real' laws) means that inconceivability *is* a criterion of impossibility.

As Husserl sees it, the very fact that we can understand the passage from

Erdmann's *Logik* which he quotes in *Logical Investigations* clearly demonstrates that psychological possibility is categorially distinct from logical possibility. By confusing them, psychologism is forced into the position that such beings would have different logical laws: i.e. that the laws of logic are psychological generalisations. But the impossibility of imagining different 'logical principles' – as opposed to the impossibility of imagining different thought-processes – is logical: i.e. it violates the very essence of *truth* to suppose that beings who think differently from us would be thinking according to different laws of truth. So what Frege and Husserl are saying is: we can conceive of a well-regulated society (the heavenly choir) or an anarchic state (bedlam) where it is common to think both p and not-p; but such thoughts must – logical 'must' – be 'wrong'. For 'Whoever judges differently, judges quite wrongly, no matter what species of mental creatures he may belong to' (*ibid.*: 159).

It is because of the picture that they inherit from Kant of thinking as a *hidden mental process* that Frege and Husserl uncritically accept that it is just as conceivable that some creature might have a different *cognitive system* from us as a different digestive system. They regard this as merely a psychological hypothesis. But how we must describe the results of such thought-processes are fixed by the laws of logic. That is, it is not a *fact*, it is a *logical truth*, that we could not accept what they were thinking as rational. So, on this argument we can understand the supposition that madmen or angels might think both p and not-p, but it makes no sense to suppose that the conclusions of such acts of thinking could be *correct*. (Husserl vacillates between calling such 'acts of judgment' 'wrong' and 'irrational'.) A 'judged content' is said to be 'true eternally', which means: the 'fundamental logical principles [are true] without regard to time and circumstances, or to individuals and species' (*ibid.*).

As we shall see in the following section, Wittgenstein was to devote a great deal of thought to this argument, not so much in order to expose its weaknesses as to bring out what he saw as the important insight that Frege was struggling to articulate. According to Wittgenstein, what Frege had recognised is the connection between the fact that we treat the laws of logic as 'boundary stones set in an eternal foundation' and the categorial distinction between citing a logical truth to justify one's judgement and treating a logical truth as the cause of one's making that judgement.[14] But the problem with Frege's argument, as Wittgenstein shows us, is that his thinking (and Husserl's) still remained clouded by psychologistic presuppositions. This comes out most clearly in Frege and Husserl's discussion of the source of our knowledge that logical truths are indeed logical truths.

Frege and Husserl both respond that we know this fact by 'inner evidence'. But doesn't this mean that the argument simply collapses back into psychologism? To forestall this objection, they argue that the use of this perceptual metaphor should not mislead one into supposing that 'inner evidence' is the name of a subjective experience. And it seemed that the only way to establish this conclusion was to embrace realism (via the now familiar argument that the answer to certain mathematical conjectures – e.g. Goldbach's Conjecture – 'may transcend all human cognitive capacity' but it is logically possible that 'the problem *has* a solution' (*ibid.*: 191)). The '*ideal* relations [between concepts] and laws [which obtain in logic and mathematics] make up an independent realm' (*ibid.*: 192). The 'inner evidence' involved in grasping a logical truth – grasping that it is a *logical truth* – is both that of seeing these relations and seeing that these relations hold independently of our seeing them.

Frege is content to dismiss the question of how we achieve this feat as a psychological issue: 'It is enough for us that we can grasp thoughts and recognize them to be true; how this takes place is a question in its own right' (PW: 145). But then, what is to stop Frege's 'madman' from claiming that he, too, grasps the 'thought' 'p & not-p' and recognises that it is true? Husserl's attempts to resolve this issue are no more helpful (see LI: 51). The problem he is grappling with is how to use experiential terms to describe something that he does not want to reduce to an experience: viz., the grasping of a logical truth. The act/object distinction means that our 'grasping' can in no way impinge on the status of a logical truth *qua* logical truth. But this is the result of the appeal to 'inner evidence', for the argument comes down to a phenomenological distinction between two kinds of 'inner experience': that of the 'mediately' and the 'immediately self-evident'. Thus, the argument ends up on a strikingly psychologistic note: logic is the science of 'ideal laws' and 'theoretical truths' whose status as such is grounded in the 'clarity and distinctness' of a thought.

Wittgenstein was to remark in the *Tractatus* that 'it is remarkable that a thinker as rigorous as Frege appealed to the degree of self-evidence as the criterion of a logical proposition' (TLP: 6.1271). It might be tempting to respond that Frege's appeal to 'intuition' should only be seen as a negative thesis: solely the consequence of recognising the confusions inherent in psychologism. For is Frege not constantly warning us not to take his Platonism too literally (see PW: 137, 148)? But what is most important here is the fact that Frege and Husserl saw realism as the only viable alternative to psychologism. The flight to realism and the appeal to 'inner evidence' are really symptomatic of a deeper problem in the Cartesian framework in which both the psychologicians and Frege and Husserl approached the foundations of logic.

Frege and Husserl defend their recourse to realism as the sole alternative to psychologism, but in fact their attack on psychologism turns on their realism: on a series of fairly standard criticisms of idealism. Moreover, the Platonism creates a host of problems in its own right: e.g. how 'thoughts', which are objective but not spatio-temporal or perceptible, are apprehended and communicated – that is, what it is to grasp a thought, and how a community of speakers establishes that it has grasped one and the same thought. Thus, in seeking to overcome the scepticism and relativism which the psychologistic view of logic entails, Frege and Husserl land us with a metaphysical problem about the nature of thoughts and classical sceptical problems about other minds.

It is hardly any wonder, then, that AI-theorists should be so dismissive of the so-called 'Fregean refutation of psychologism' which analytic philosophy has embraced. After all, not only does Frege and Husserl's anti-psychologism leave us with problems that are every bit as puzzling as those raised by psychologism, but, even worse, they land us in a dilemma which, from the AI point of view, is intolerable. For the upshot of Frege and Husserl's argument is that logic studies the relations between thoughts, but can shed no light on the workings of the mind; while psychology studies the workings of the mind, but can shed no light on the relation between thoughts. But before we can consider the cognitivist alternative to this anti-psychologistic paradox, we must first address what, for the philosophy of logic, is perhaps the most important question raised by Frege and Husserl's attack on psychologism: viz., the question whether their argument really serves to clarify the nature of the laws of logic and the relation in which they stand to rules of inference.

§6 Logic constitutes what we understand by 'thought'

The focus in this section is on Wittgenstein's later remarks on the foundations of logic. This means, unfortunately, that the *Tractatus* must get short shrift. The problem is not that the *Tractatus* has too little to offer on the score of anti-psychologism; quite the contrary, it is that it has too much. The *Tractatus* represents a comprehensive attempt to work out an anti-psychologistic philosophy of logic (see TLP: 4.1121) whose relevance to Wittgenstein's later approach to logic is profound (see Baker 1988). But it would take us too far outside the scope of the present work to detail the differences between Wittgenstein's *Tractatus* response to psychologism and the position he subsequently worked out. For our main concern in this chapter is with cognitive psychologism. Thus we must bypass Wittgenstein's early writings on the nature of logic – from which anything psychological is banished – and concentrate instead on the later works.

In particular, our major concern in this section is with Wittgenstein's argument that, because he remained committed to the premise that the laws of logic are *externally* related to thinking, Frege developed a conception of logic that has more in common with psychologism than he realised. We saw in §3 how Mill had accepted Hamilton's claim that the fundamental laws of thought are *abstract generalisations* but concluded from this that they are *ipso facto* empirical. Frege (and Husserl) agreed that the laws of thought are significant generalisations, but insisted that they are not 'real': not about how the mind of the actual or the epistemic subject works. On Wittgenstein's reading, Frege's attempt to provide a realist alternative to naturalist psychologism was the result of his accepting the basic epistemological premise that logical truths are *substantial*.

In his discussion of this problem, Wittgenstein focuses on the framework which seems to force us into one of the positions canvassed by the main schools in the nineteenth-century debates in the philosophy of logic (viz., Kantianism, nominalism, naturalism, realism and formalism). Wittgenstein's strategy in this issue is similar to that which he adopts in his remarks on the foundations of mathematics. Indeed, this is the reason why the two themes are intermingled in the first book of *Remarks on the Foundations of Mathematics*. He does not question the merits of any of the particular alternatives but, rather, he scrutinises the nature of the problem which each theory was designed to resolve. We should, therefore, approach Wittgenstein's writings on the foundations of logic on the same footing that we approach his writings on the foundations of mathematics: viz., with the awareness that, as Max Black put it, 'a critic of the game is not another player' (Black 1965).

The obvious starting-point is Wittgenstein's well-known remark: 'Frege says in the preface to *Grundgesetze der Arithmetik*: " . . . here we have a hitherto unknown kind of insanity" – but he never said what this "insanity" would really be like' (RFM I: §152). In typical fashion, Wittgenstein's intentions here are anything but obvious. Does he mean to accept that the issue is, at least in part, empirical? If so, what does it matter if Frege was unfamiliar with the work of social anthropologists? At least Wittgenstein should have known from his reading of Frazer's *Golden Bough* what kind of 'alternative logics' are possible in primitive cultures. Indeed, doesn't Wittgenstein himself suggest that 'We can imagine human beings with a "more primitive" logic, in which only for certain sentences [e.g. indicative] is there anything corresponding to our negation', and the doubling of the operator is seen 'as mere repetition, never as cancelling the negation' (RFM: App. I, §8)?

To understand the point Wittgenstein is making about Frege's antipsychologism at RFM I §152, we have to go back to what he says at RFM I §132: 'Frege calls it "a law about what men take for true" that "It is impossible for human beings . . . to recognize an object as different from itself". – When I think of this as impossible for me, then I think of *trying* to do it.' The first part of this passage may seem somewhat troubling, since Frege regards the law of identity as a 'law of valid inference', or, later, a 'precept of correct thinking'. But Wittgenstein is making a more subtle and a more significant point. According to Frege, the psychological counterpart of the law of identity *may* constitute a 'fundamental law of our thinking'. Wittgenstein's concern here is with the psychologistic assumption underpinning this thesis, which manifests itself in the 'inconceivability' argument (see §5) – hence the importance of the latter sentence in this quotation.

The argument to which Wittgenstein is alluding occurs in the Introduction to *Basic Laws* (BL: xivff). This begins with Frege's emphasising the distinction between 'being true' and 'being taken to be true' (the categorial difference between the laws of logic and the laws of thinking). Frege's so-called *Grundgedanke* is: 'I understand by "Laws of Logic" not psychological laws of takings-to-be-true, but laws of truth' (*ibid.*: 13). It is clear that, in the passage which Wittgenstein cites, Frege is talking about psychological laws of thinking. Frege's point is that, *qua* fundamental law of thinking, the law of identity is something that he, as a philosopher, need 'neither support nor dispute'; for 'what we have here is not a logical consequence' (*ibid.*: 15). That is, it may be the case that all human beings believe that p = p, but philosophers need not concern themselves with the question of whether or not this empirical generalisation is true. All that concerns the philosopher is the *law of truth* that p = p.

It is significant that Wittgenstein should have picked up on this theme and not the more obvious Platonism. In part, this was because to have challenged the latter might have created the impression that Wittgenstein was merely opting for an anti-realist position in the foundations of logic debate, and thus, trying to inculcate scepticism, when his real purpose was to scrutinise the framework underlying psychologism. Implicit in his criticism is the point that the psychologicians were right to try to relate the laws of logic to *thinking*, and that the problem with Frege's (and Husserl's) argument is that it only purchases logical purity at the price of completely severing this relationship; and, in the process, retains a psychologistic conception of mental processes.

Wittgenstein felt that, as important as Frege's writings may be for advancing our understanding of the nature of logic, his thought remained tethered to the psychologistic assumption that the impossibility preventing us from imagining what contra-logical thought would be like is psychological: e.g. the same as that which prevents us from seeing (as opposed to counting) that:

|||||||||||||||||

has fifteen strokes.[15] Were the impossibility of imagining 'p ≠ p' psychological, then one could indeed 'think of *trying* to do it'. But it is impossible to attempt such a feat: not because of our 'cognitive constitution', but because we *logically exclude* the possibility of 'trying to do so'. 'Here "I can't imagine the opposite" doesn't mean: my powers of imagination are unequal to the task. These words are a defence against something whose form makes it look like an empirical proposition, but which is really a grammatical one' (PI: §251).

In other words, the statement 'One can't imagine p ≠ p' is like the statement 'One can't imagine moving the castle diagonally in chess', rather than the statement 'One can't imagine what it would be like to live in a monochromatic world'.[16] For a statement like 'The castle is moved horizontally and vertically' does not describe how the castle is moved but, rather, stipulates how it should be moved. Thus, to speak of *trying to imagine* the castle moving diagonally would be the result of misconstruing this normative utterance as an empirical proposition.[17] To be sure, one can imagine someone wrongly believing that the castle moves diagonally (i.e. one can imagine someone misunderstanding the rules of chess). And one can imagine a game quite similar to chess in which the castle does move diagonally; but then, this would be to imagine a different game from chess.

What Wittgenstein is saying here is that the premise Frege shared with the psychologicians is that the statement 'We could not understand other cultures who think according to different laws of logic' is empirical: i.e. it is a result of our 'mental constitution'. And it is precisely because of this common ground that the cognitivist is mystified by the status which Frege and Husserl's anti-psychologism enjoys among analytic philosophers. For the cognitivist feels that we can learn something important about how our mind works from the fact that we can't imagine what such a culture's 'thought-processes' would be like. Rips, for example, begins a recent paper on 'Deduction' by asking us to imagine a culture that embraced the rule 'modus shmolens': viz., from p. & p →q they infer ¬q. He suggests that 'people who violate principles like modus ponens would be unfathomable. How could we convince them or teach them? How could we understand what they believe?' (Rips 1988: 146). In true psychologistic fashion, he concludes that the reason why one can't imagine what this would be like is because 'Modus ponens and other inference principles like it are so well integrated with the rest of our thinking – so central to our notion of intelligence and rationality – that contrary principles seem out of the question' (*ibid.*: 117). Thus the fact that *we* can't imagine what it would be like to infer ¬q from p. & p →q, even though this is *conceivable* [*sic*], is said to reveal an important fact about the structure of our information-processing system.

If, contrary to this cognitive psychologistic argument, *modus ponens* doesn't represent a generalisation about the way that members of our society learn or are conditioned to reason, or the way that the human 'information-processing system' has evolved, in what relation do the rules of inference stand to thinking? Wittgenstein explains:

> The laws of inference do not compel [someone] to say or to write such and such like rails compelling a locomotive. And if you say that, while he may indeed *say* it, still he can't *think* it, then I am only saying that that means, not: try as he may he can't think it,

but: it is for us an essential part of 'thinking' that – in talking, writing, etc. – he makes *this sort* of transition.

(RFM I: §116)

That is, we can say (construct a fairy tale in which) 'There might be a culture that followed the rule "modus shmolens"', just as we can imagine a teapot that speaks; but in neither case can we really understand what this would mean. But what is the nature of this use of 'cannot'? The crux of Wittgenstein's argument is that, in Frege's eyes, it is empirical; for Frege treated understanding as a mental phenomenon (a mental process or state). Hence, the explanation of our inability to imagine what such 'thought-processes' would be like must, according to Frege, be psychological. But if we encountered a culture that 'spoke' in a way which seemed to violate the laws of logic, we would neither say that they 'think differently from us' nor that they 'think wrongly'; rather: 'In that case we shan't call it [thinking]' (*ibid.*). That is, whatever function a statement like 'The castle moves diagonally' might play, it can't be that of determining what counts as playing chess[18]; and so too, whatever an agent is doing when uttering 'p. & p →q. → ¬ q', it can't be described as 'thinking'.

There are, of course, countless examples of speakers saying contradictory things in everyday life. The deliberate use of such constructions may direct us, depending on the circumstances, to look for some hidden irony or ambiguity in a speaker's utterances, or to question whether the speaker is deliberately obfuscating, or is merely confused or being silly. A neurologist might treat such utterances as manifestations of some localised cerebral damage. A developmental psychologist might treat such word-games as an important stage in an infant's acquisition of language. But the one thing we cannot make sense of, given the *internal relation* between the *laws of logic* and *thinking*, is the suggestion that a society might 'follow the rule' p. & p →q → ¬ q. This last statement is not an empirical generalisation, based on our 'mental constitution'. It is a grammatical observation about the connection between the *laws of logic* and the concept of *thought*.

This picture of logic as that which constitutes 'what we understand by "proposition" and by "language"' (RFM I: §134) was intended to overthrow four basic themes comprising Frege and Husserl's conception of logic:

1 First and foremost is that Frege and Husserl did not repudiate the premise that logical propositions are significant generalisations. What they did reject was the psychologistic assumption that logical propositions describe the workings of the mind. Rather, what logical propositions describe, according to Frege and Husserl, are the logical relations that hold between independently existing logical objects.
2 On Frege and Husserl's conception of logic, the role of logical proofs is to derive one substantial proposition from another.

3   Frege and Husserl see logical propositions as abstractions whose *absolute generality* serves to ground all the various rules of inference.
4   Frege and Husserl regard rules of inference as standing in an external relation to independently existing truths: i.e. they are treated as 'technical norms' for attaining truth. Hence remove the Platonist conception of truth from their argument and one is left with instrumentalism and possibly relativism.

The heart of Wittgenstein's response to these four themes can be found in lectures XXIX–XXX in *Lectures on the Foundations of Mathematics*. Wittgenstein begins by telling his students that he 'wants to say something about logical propositions – considered as laws of thought' (LFM: 275). He makes the point that, on the psychologistic conception of logic, the *generality* connoted by the term 'law' is empirical, whereas for Frege and Husserl it was supposed to be 'abstract' (or 'ideal'). But, if we remove the presupposition that logical propositions are *expressions of thoughts*,[19] it is clear that the terms 'law of logic' and 'law of thought' must be understood in some other sense. For, as he had shown in the *Tractatus*, logical propositions are tautologies: they are devoid of content. '– and we call this a *law of thought*. But isn't this queer?' After all, a tautology 'doesn't seem to say anything about *thinking*. So why should we call it a law of thought?' (*ibid.*: 277).

In the *Tractatus*, Wittgenstein had leaned towards the view that the very notion of a 'law of logic' or a 'law of thought' is the illicit result of treating logical propositions as some form of significant generalisation. By 1939 he was more interested in clarifying what earlier philosophers might have meant by these terms. The reason why this is such a difficult issue is because, on the psychologistic conception of logic, rules of inference are collapsed into logical propositions. Rule of inference are treated as describing either:

•   the rules which govern the faculty of understanding;
•   the rules whereby human beings *do* reason; or
•   the rules whereby humans *ought* to reason.

We saw in §5 how Husserl sought to fight his way clear on this issue; on Wittgenstein's argument, one could say that the reason why he ultimately failed is because of his preconception of logical propositions as significant 'theoretical truths'.

Wittgenstein's objection to psychologism thus has nothing to do with any so-called instance of the 'Naturalist Fallacy', for Frege is just as much at fault as Erdmann in the failure to distinguish between logical propositions and rules of inference. How could a construction which conveys no information be treated as a rule: especially, a rule about '&' or '→' when it uses these operators? A tautology such as 'p. & p →q. →q' does not *tell* us how to use

'&' and '→', nor does it *say* that *q* can be *inferred* from *p. & p →q*' (*ibid.*). In this respect, 'We can say then that "p. & p → q. → q" is not a law of thought. But if you say that this *is a tautology* – then you could call that a law of thought. The law of thought is the statement that that expression *says nothing, all the information is cancelled out,* etc. And we get the *"follows"* from saying that this is a tautology' (*ibid.*).

In other words, it is the fact *that* 'p. & p →q. →.q' is a tautology which signifies that q follows from 'p. & p →q'. To grasp the rule of inference *that* 'p. & p →q. →.q' *is a tautology* just is to grasp that q follows from 'p. & p → q'. To understand the rules governing '&' and '→' is to understand that the truth of 'p' and 'p →q' is grounds for asserting 'q'. To understand a logical operator is to understand the rules of inference which it licenses. And, most important of all, to understand these formulations is to understand that they are *grammatical propositions*, not psychological or metaphysical generalisations. According to Wittgenstein, this is the point that Frege and Husserl were striving for, but were prevented from realising because of the experiential gloss which, like their psychologistic predecessors, they imposed on the use of 'understand', 'think', 'infer', etc., in these grammatical articulations.

Wittgenstein concludes that, in general, we might say that any expression 'if p then q' is a rule of inference if and only if the corresponding expression 'p →q' is a tautology: it is by determining which propositions are tautologies that what is called 'thinking' ('inferring', 'reasoning') is formulated. Thus Wittgenstein explains how 'We can conceive the rules of inference . . . as giving the signs their meaning, because they are rules for the use of these signs. So that the rules of inference are involved in the determination of the meaning of the signs. In this sense rules of inference cannot be right or wrong' (RFM VIII: §30). For rules of inference are rules of grammar which, as such, are antecedent to truth. They no more describe how the mind works than do logical propositions; rather, they stipulate how certain expressions are to be used.

This argument marks just as significant a reorientation in our understanding of the expression 'rule of inference' as it does of 'logical proposition'. Gone is the restriction of the term to formal rules such as *modus ponens* and *modus tollens*. On this approach, the inference 'if x is red than x is not green (blue, . . .)' is a paradigm rule of inference. Wittgenstein was well aware of the argument that such inferences are really enthymemes (with a suppressed premise based on the colour-exclusion statement). One of his main concerns was to remove any need for appealing to this (or any other) form of depth analysis. For this, he felt, distorts the logical nature of rules of inference *qua* rules of grammar: the rules whereby we explain, teach, correct, justify the use of concept-words.

Another of Wittgenstein's concerns was to overthrow the traditional conception of rules of inference as technical norms. For the relation between rules of inference and truth is internal, not external: rules of inference do not *enable* us to arrive at the truth, they *determine* what we call deriving one truth from another (AWL: 138–9). Moreover, this argument overturns the fundamental assumption – shared by all parties to the foundations of logic dispute – that rules of inference must somehow be grounded in logical propositions. It was this premise that encouraged the psychologistic conception of logic as a 'normative science': i.e., logical propositions must be such that their absolute generality or abstractness, or their status as transcendental or psychological generalisations, serves to justify all the various rules of inference: i.e. to prescribe how we ought to reason if we are to arrive at the truth. But the upshot of Wittgenstein's account of logical propositions is that rules of inference cannot be grounded in 'pseudo-propositions' devoid of content.

In the *Tractatus* there was no problem about justifying rules of inference, since these had already been abolished as a result of the conception of entailment as an internal relation between propositions. In his later work, Wittgenstein shifts to the view that we cite a rule of inference to justify a deduction because entailments are reflections of rules of grammar. Internal relations are reflections of explanations of the rules of grammar which formulate how expressions are to be used, and what we call 'recognising an entailment' is equivalent to ('runs along the same tracks as') what we call 'acknowledging a rule of inference'. These, it must be stressed, are grammatical propositions, not psychological generalisations (see Baker 1988: 130ff).

Psychologism is the consequence of construing such grammatical propositions experientially,[20] thereby treating logic as 'a kind of ultra-physics, the description of the "logical structure" of the world, which we perceive through a kind of ultra-experience (with the understanding e.g.)' (RFM I: §8). This last parenthetical remark makes it clear that Wittgenstein intended his investigations into the nature of logic to be seen as applying to the epistemological tradition extending from Kant all the way up to Russell (whose ill-fated theory of 'logical experience' in *Theory of Knowledge* was one of Wittgenstein's primary targets in the *Tractatus*): an epistemological tradition which applies as much to the cognitive significance attributed to formal models by AI as it does to the nineteenth-century debate over the foundations of logic. And, as we shall see in the next section, the link between these two concerns – between mathematics and psychology, and between classical and cognitive psychologism – was forged by a formalist whose claim to be seen as one of the founders of AI has yet to be fully appreciated.

§7 Hilbert's protocol

One of the more interesting contributions to the foundations of AI has never actually been recognised as such, and was certainly not so intended. But Hilbert's defence of proof theory, prompted by Brouwer's attack on what the latter saw as the trivialising effect of reducing mathematics to 'a game played with symbols', is grounded in a psychologistic conception of

reasoning. Hilbert's resulting statement on 'the general philosophical significance' of proof theory marks the formalist advent of cognitive psychologism
(Hilbert 1927).

For all the work that has been done on the Frege–Hilbert controversy
over the nature of axiomatic systems, relatively little has been said about the
similarities in their attitudes towards language and thought. The origins for
this common ground lie in the late nineteenth-century mathematical
mistrust, created by the foundations crisis, of both reasoning and the
linguistic instruments used to capture and convey the mind's activities. In
the simplest terms, we are presented with three separate realms – those of
thought, language, and reality – each of which was thought to be externally
related to, but isomorphic with, the others. It is only because they conceived
of language and thought as externally related to one another that Frege and
Hilbert could treat language as a *vehicle* for the communication of thoughts,
and, *a fortiori*, worry about the 'defects' of ordinary language for scientific or
mathematical purposes.

To be sure, Hilbert insisted that we can discover truths about reality
which can in principle be rigorously organised (e.g. axiomatised).[21] Whether
this applies to all the truths discernible by the mind is, as Gödel was to
argue (see Wang 1974), another matter. But both Frege and Hilbert felt that
reasoning and ordinary language are unreliable: the former because we
frequently misuse the laws of logic, and 'no one, though he speak with the
tongue of angels, will keep people from negating arbitrary assertions,
forming partial judgments, or using the principle of excluded middle'
(Hilbert 1967c: 379); and the latter because, in Lotze's words, 'Speech may
pass over much that thought, in order to be complete, must include' (Lotze
1887: V, iii, §4). Moreover, given the fact that 'we think in sentences'
(Hilbert 1927),[22] the limitations of ordinary language may actually exacer-
bate the mind's natural imperfections.

It was because of this growing loss of faith in the reliability of reasoning
and the language in which this is conducted that Frege saw his concept-
script as the ideal instrument to compensate for the saltations of intuition.
But Hilbert was not interested in merely developing a reasoning tool whose
power would reside in its ability to counteract the mind's natural tendencies.
Rather, Hilbert's rationale for 'the axiomatic method' was the psychologistic
claim that 'Forging ahead towards the ever deeper layer of axioms [in the
formation of a theory] we attain ever deepening insights into the essence of
scientific thinking itself' (Hilbert 1917: 12).

Hilbert first broached this theme in his celebrated 'Paris Lecture', deliv-
ered at the second International Congress of Mathematicians in 1900.
Hilbert chose to use the occasion to respond to Emil Du Bois-Reymond's
stunning 'act of apostasy' of 1872 (see Shanker 1992). Hilbert was a student
at the University of Berlin at a time when all of Germany was preoccupied
with Emil Du Bois-Reymond's declaration that 'as regards the enigma[s]

what matter and force are, and how they are to be conceived [and how "the brain gives rise to thought", the scientist] must resign himself once for all to the far more difficult confession – "IGNORABIMUS!"' (Du Bois-Reymond 1874: 32). Hilbert was presenting in his Paris lecture, not just the mathematicians', but in a more profound sense, his generation's response to Du Bois-Reymond.

Hilbert begins by attacking Paul Du Bois-Reymond's attempt to extend his brother's remarks on the limits of our knowledge of nature to questions concerning the continuum (see Du Bois-Reymond 1882). But Hilbert uses his conviction in the solvability of the Continuum Hypothesis to attack Emil's larger thesis. He makes this clear at the end of his prefatory remarks, where he extends the problem from one appertaining solely to mathematics to science in general. He then seeks to show how his faith in the solvability of all problems which we are capable of framing is vindicated by the mathematical use of impossibility proofs.[23] It is an argument which formally dismisses Du Bois-Reymond's scepticism (without, it must be stressed, challenging Du Bois-Reymond's attack on scientific materialism).

Given the tone of Hilbert's opening remarks, it would be tempting to see the Paris Lecture as nothing more than an expression of the scientific exuberance infusing science at the dawn of the new century. But far more is involved here. Throughout Hilbert's later writings we encounter the same themes: 'There is,' he argues in 'Naturerkennen und Logik', 'no *Ignorabimus* for the mathematician, and, in my opinion, none too for natural science in general' (Hilbert 1930: 15). On a still stronger note, 'Knowledge of Nature and Logic' – a title which was no doubt intended to recall Du Bois-Reymond's lecture – ends with the remark which Hilbert was to recommend for his epitaph: 'Instead of the foolish *Ignorabimus*, our slogan is, on the contrary: We must know. We will know' (*ibid.*: 15–16).

This is not so much a paean to the inexorable march of science, or the boundless power of thought, as a comment on the mind's cognitive structure. For Hilbert felt that the epistemic subject is so constituted that the mind cannot rest content with an unanswered question. There is a 'strong need' – a 'fundamental urge' – to find the answer to unsolved problems, and to discover the ultimate axioms on which all scientific thinking is based (see Hilbert 1917). Different methods for answering unsolved questions, or different ways of formulating such questions, must be endlessly pursued until a solution is discovered and the problem can be laid to rest.

The obvious question which this counter-affirmation raises is: What is the nature of this 'must'? The answer, as Detlefsen has shown, can be found in Kant's discussion of reason in the Transcendental Dialectic (see Detlefsen 1992). Kant speaks of how the role of reason is 'to prescribe to the understanding its direction towards a certain unity of which it has itself no concept, and in such manner as to unite all the acts of the understanding, in respect of every object, into an *absolute* whole' (Kant 1933: A326–7).

Similarly, Hilbert describes how 'our thought proceeds from unity and seeks to produce unity' (Hilbert 1930). The axiomatic method thus responds to Kant's claim 'that in inference reason endeavours to reduce the varied and manifold knowledge obtained through the understanding to the smallest number of principles and thereby to achieve in it the highest possible unity' (Kant 1933: B361).

'There is a strong need,' Hilbert explains in 'Axiomatic Thinking', 'which makes itself felt in the individual branches of knowledge, for the basic propositions that are regarded as axioms to be grounded themselves.' 'Through progressing to ever deeper layers of axioms we obtain ever deeper insight into the essence of scientific thought, and this will make us ever more conscious of the unity of our knowledge' (Hilbert 1917). But when Hilbert talks of axioms as expressing a 'form of thinking', he does not mean that they are confined to providing a representation of mathematical thought. Rather, the axiomatic method 'treats of the form of thought in general' (Kant 1933: A55). The 'unity' from whence and towards which thinking proceeds – as revealed by proof theory – is the ultimate set of 'laws which the understanding employs when, in thinking, it relates [representations] to one another' (*ibid.*: A56).

Hilbert's Kantian intentions go still further: not just the goal, but the actual vehicle for its attainment, conforms to Kant's dictates. For the axiomatic method represents an attempt to realise Kant's vision of a pure general logic that would provide a 'canon of the understanding'. We saw in §3 how Kant's 'absolutely necessary rules of thought without which there can be no employment whatsoever of the understanding' can be seen as the logical structure through which all information must be processed. But 'pure general logic' can only disclose these 'necessary rules' if it 'abstracts from all content of the knowledge of understanding and from all differences in its objects, and deals with nothing but the mere form of thought' (*ibid.*: A 54).

Hilbert's formalism is precisely this: an attempt to represent the *form of thought* by abstracting all content from mathematical propositions. The correspondence involved in proof theory is not just between the formulas of an object system and mathematical propositions. Hilbert was arguing for the much stronger thesis that the rules of the formal system are isomorphic with those underlying mathematical thought. The correlation involved here, therefore, is said to be between *formal procedures* and *mental processes*.

This argument raises the standard problem with which all psychologistic theories must deal. Given that these 'necessary rules' are isomorphic with those of a logical system (whose axioms are consistent), this confronts Hilbert with the same problem as Kant: viz., How does one account for the phenomenon of reasoning errors if the mind is governed by the laws of logic? Once again, Hilbert's solution follows Kant's lead. As we saw in §3, Kant located the source of reasoning errors in the faculty of sensibility (in our propensity to mistake merely subjective for objective grounds). Similarly, Hilbert asks:

> has the contentual logical inference ever deceived and abandoned us anywhere when we applied it to real objects or events? Contentual logical inference is indispensable. It has deceived us only when we accepted arbitrary abstract notions, in particular those under which infinitely many objects are subsumed. What we did, then, was merely to use contentual inference in an illegitimate way; that is, we obviously did not respect necessary conditions for the use of contentual logical inference.
>
> (Hilbert 1967c: 376)

Hence by introducing *ideal propositions* (e.g. deploying the logical choice function in order to reduce the role of the quantifiers in a formalised proof to applications of the transfinite axiom) we counteract 'the unnoticed influence of sensibility upon the understanding, or, more exactly, upon judgment' (*ibid.*).

We can now begin to appreciate the 'general philosophical significance' which Hilbert was to claim for proof theory. Given that the rules of contentual inference are indeed – as Kant taught – Aristotelian, but that this fact is concealed by the use of imperspicuous concepts, we can use proof theory to discover the 'forms of thought'. In 'On the Infinite', Hilbert describes how, 'In the logical calculus we possess a sign language that is capable of representing mathematical propositions in formulas and of expressing logical inference through formal processes' (*ibid.*: 381). And in 'The Foundations of Mathematics' he insists that 'The formula game that Brouwer so deprecates has, besides its mathematical value, an important general philosophical significance. For this formula game is carried out according to certain definite rules, in which the *technique of our thinking* is expressed' (Hilbert 1967c: 475).

In a passage that could have been written by any contemporary AI-scientist, Hilbert explains how 'These rules form a closed system that can be discovered and definitively stated. The fundamental idea of my proof theory is none other than to describe the activity of our understanding, to make a protocol of the rules according to which our thinking actually proceeds' (*ibid.*). Here is as clear a statement as one could wish of Hilbert's Kantian intentions. But it is not just the role assigned to the axiomatic method (pure general logic) that he shared with Kant; this shared approach is grounded in Kant's basic epistemological picture of the mind confronted by and forced to make sense of reality (cf. Hilbert 1967c: 367; and 1927: 464).

This shared epistemological outlook is particularly evident in Hilbert's attack on logicism, in which he emphasises that

Kant already taught – and indeed it is part and parcel of his doctrine – that mathematics has at its disposal a content secured independently of all logic and hence can never be provided with a foundation by means of logic alone; that is why the efforts of Frege and Dedekind were bound to fail. Rather, as a condition for the use of logical inferences and the performance of logical operations, something must already be given to our faculty of representation, certain extralogical concrete objects that are intuitively present as immediate experience prior to all thought.

(Hilbert 1967c: 376)

As a criticism of logicism this argument presupposes the psychologistic principle that the laws of logic are those rules which the mind uses to frame judgements about these extralogical concrete objects. But they are only called into operation by the presence of sensory information (representations) needing to be processed ('concepts without intuition are blind').

What, then, is the status of logical truths? For Kant, logical propositions are prescriptive because they describe the necessary rules which the faculty of understanding follows. But for Hilbert, the distinction between synthetic *a priori* and *a posteriori* propositions disappears, and in its place we have the distinction between *contentual* (real) and *ideal* propositions. 'p v ¬p' is not a synthetic *a priori* proposition but, rather, an *ideal proposition* which is used to transform real propositions. Ideal propositions are contentless: they are simply part of an effective method for computing which real propositions are true. That is, they are regulative devices whose epistemic utility consists in the efficiency that they bring to contentual reasoning: to establishing the class of true real propositions. Thus we simply bypass the debate over the foundations of logic, since no problem of justification *vis-à-vis* logical truths arises: there are no 'logical generalisations' to ground.

The question which remains, however, is 'Why should ideal propositions have this epistemic utility?' At times Hilbert sounds like he is supporting a Kantian position (i.e. subscribing to transcendental psychologism). But, overall, the tone is more sympathetic to naturalist psychologism. For example, when he is explaining the problems that arise 'In the domain of finitary propositions, in which we should, after all, remain' (where 'the logical relations that prevail are very imperspicuous, and this lack of perspicuity mounts unbearably if "all" and "there exists" occur combined or appear in nested propositions'), he concludes that 'one could attempt to determine the logical laws that are valid for the domain of finitary propositions; but this would not help us, since we just do not want to renounce the use of the simple laws of Aristotelian logic' (Hilbert 1967c: 379).

There are two things to notice here. First, Hilbert says 'Do not': not *cannot*. And second, he continues to speak of the 'laws' of Aristotelian logic, which forces us to ask in what sense he thought that these laws are 'laws'.

The answer must be in line with the distinction Hilbert draws between contentual and ideal propositions. That is, we must distinguish between two different senses of the term 'laws'. When the laws of logic are instantiated in ideal propositions they are 'laws of truth': rules for transferring truth from one real proposition to another. But when they are instantiated in real propositions they are 'laws of thought': rules governing the epistemically efficient operation of our minds.

This argument stands in an interesting relation to Wittgenstein's treatment of logic in the *Tractatus*. According to the picture theory, the fundamental logico-syntactical demarcation is between bi-polar empirical propositions and mono-polar tautologies and contradictions. Unlike Hilbert's Kantian picture of 'abstracting' content, the whole force of Wittgenstein's conception of tautologies and contradictions as 'pseudo-propositions' in which all information cancels out lies in his truth-conditional theory of molecular propositions. But what is most interesting, *vis-à-vis* Hilbert's argument, is how Wittgenstein conceives of the role of proof in logic as strictly that of transforming and generating tautologies: i.e., they are proofs *that* an expression is a logical truth, not proofs *of* the truth of a logical proposition.

As was noted in the preceding section, Wittgenstein leans in the *Tractatus* towards the position that the very notions of a 'law of logic' or a 'law of thought' are the confused result of treating logical propositions as some sort of significant generalisation. But, for Hilbert, the laws of logic, when instantiated in real propositions, are indeed laws of thought. Whether this is to be construed in Kantian terms, or as natural laws of what Lipps had referred to as 'the physics of thought', remains unclear. But it is no doubt significant that there is insufficient evidence to determine whether Hilbert's endorsement of the argument at A 54 of the *First Critique* extended to the second paragraph (viz., Kant's further claim that, 'As pure logic, it has nothing to do with empirical principles, and does not, as has sometimes been supposed, borrow anything from psychology, which therefore has no influence whatever on the canon of the understanding').

Hilbert's apparent agnosticism on this issue reminds one of the early Wittgenstein when he argues that what interests logic is only the unasserted proposition (i.e. that 'Assertion is merely psychological' (NB: 95–6)). Hilbert seems to be saying that the status of the (contentual) laws of logic is not something to be settled *a priori* (certainly there can be no doubt about Hilbert's desire to avoid what he called Kant's 'anthropomorphic garbage'), and there is no need for the logician to get bogged down in such psychological matters. Whether or not we can imagine cultures who would think according to different laws of logic, all that matters is that, since their inception, Aristotle's laws have been found to be such effective reasoning tools, and that by introducing regulative devices to ensure their efficient operation, we maximise *our* potential to discover truths: an argument which clearly anticipates the passage from Gregory's *Mind in Science* quoted in §2.

How ambitious were Hilbert's intentions? His claim that 'the fundamental idea of my proof theory is none other than to describe the activity of our understanding, to make a protocol of the rules according to which our thinking actually proceeds' makes it sound like he was proposing to reverse Mill's dictum: i.e. seeking to demonstrate that 'Psychology is a part, a branch, of (mathematical) Logic' (and in the process, refute Kant's exclusion of psychology from the ranks of natural science on the grounds that it cannot be mathematised). In 'Naturerkennen und Logik', Hilbert insists that 'even in everyday life we employ methods and concepts that require a high degree of abstraction and are comprehensible only because of the unconscious application of the axiomatic method' (1930: 4). This sounds as if Hilbert is saying that proof theory can be used to make a protocol of the rules that we use for theoretic purposes. But on the basic Kantian epistemological picture which Hilbert adopts, virtually all judgement involves theory-construction. Hence, proof theory can be used to make a protocol, if not of thinking *simpliciter*, at least of its core problem-solving and categorisation processes.

As far as the foundations of AI are concerned, we can detect the outlines here of Turing's thesis that reasoning (problem-solving) can be reduced to computation. And by leaving open the issue of transcendental versus naturalist psychologism, Hilbert paved the way for the shift from using algorithms instead of the logical calculus to 'model' this reduction (where, significantly, the latter tool was very much the product of Hilbert's *Entscheidungsproblem*). We can thus see how, working within an essentially Hilbertian framework, Turing could have provided the bridge, not just from pre- to post-computational mechanism, but, in a fundamental sense, from classical to cognitive psychologism as well.

This is a consequence of the fact that what begins as a method for mapping logical procedures onto mental processes soon turns into the reverse; for, given the isomorphism postulated by Hilbert between the mind of the epistemic subject and the logical calculus, we can employ the latter to fill in the 'gaps' in our self-observations of the former, where these 'gaps' are a result of the fact that we tend to 'apply, especially in first attacking a problem, a rapid, unconscious, not absolutely sure combination, trusting to a certain arithmetical feeling for the behavior of the arithmetical symbols, which we could dispense with as little in arithmetic as with the geometrical imagination in geometry' (Hilbert 1984b: 277). Thus the logical calculus can be used as a model for disclosing the hidden mechanics of the mind: the computational steps which occur in the logical calculus become the paradigm for the steps that must occur in finitary reasoning, regardless of a subject's ability to perceive such mental operations. If Wittgenstein's discussion of classical psychologism is to have any bearing on cognitive psychologism, therefore, it is precisely this argument which it must address.

§8 What is inferring?

> The propositions of logic are 'laws of thought', 'because they bring out the essence of human thinking' – to put it more correctly: because they bring out, or show, the essence, the technique, of thinking. They show what thinking is and also show kinds of thinking.
>
> (RFM I: §133)

If quoted in isolation, the above passage could almost serve to establish Wittgenstein as a *bona fide* member of the family of psychologicians (no doubt from the transcendental side). In one of the more problematic passages in his writings on logic, Wittgenstein even goes so far as to suggest that 'The laws of logic are indeed the expression of "thinking habits" but also of the habit of *thinking*. That is to say they can be said to show: how human beings think, and also *what* human beings call "thinking"' (*ibid.*: §131). The latter observation about the constitutive nature of the laws of logic *vis-à-vis* 'thinking' seems clear enough (see §5); it is the prior remark which is troubling.

It is difficult to say who Wittgenstein might have had in mind when he refers to 'thinking habits'. Husserl uses the expression 'thought-habits' to mean something like what we would now call 'reasoning biases' (see LI: 130; cf. Evans 1989). Another possible source can be found in James's *Principles of Psychology*. 'Habits of thinking' occurs in a quotation from Locke (James 1890: I 563). What James understood by this is the manner in which the thought of A is followed in the next moment by the thought of B (*ibid.*: I 553f). But then, according to James, such localised associations are to be explained in terms of the experiences of the individual (*ibid.*: 565), whereas Wittgenstein seems to be referring to the sort of cultural 'thinking-habits' postulated by the psychologicians.

Perhaps the most likely source for Wittgenstein's allusion to 'thinking-habits' is Hilbert; for these are exactly the terms that Hilbert employed in 'The Logical Foundations of Mathematics', and the drift of this passage appears to be to respond to Hilbert's conception of the relation between a formal system and thinking. Moreover, an annotated copy of 'The Logical Foundations of Mathematics' was found in Wittgenstein's *Nachlass*, which suggests that the overlap between Wittgenstein's discussion of the relation between the propositions of logic and inferring, and Hilbert's conception of the protocol provided by the logical calculus, may be more than coincidental. But if Hilbert was indeed Wittgenstein's target here, it is not so much because of any impact he might have had on the philosophy of logic, but because of the slide into cognitive psychologism which his argument entails.

We can begin to see what Wittgenstein has in mind at RFM I §131 from the argument at RFM I §8, where he identifies as one origin of the picture of logic as 'a kind of ultra-physics' an ordinary inference like 'The stove is smoking, so the chimney is out of order again.' This is an example of the sort of 'thinking-habit' to which Wittgenstein is alluding. In other words, the laws of logic bring out that we tend to think elliptically. But then, what exactly does 'elliptical' mean?

The answer to this question lies in the parenthetical remark: 'And *that* is how this conclusion is drawn! Not like this: "The stove is smoking, and whenever the stove smokes the chimney is out of order; and so . . . ".' The latter is the type of argument which a subject might produce if asked to justify the prior inference; and it is in light of this that we call the prior reasoning 'elliptical'. But if the subject's reasoning is construed as a mental process, then the way is open to arguing that the latter argument must be what went on *in the subject's mind*. That is, *modus ponens* becomes a paradigm for the 'preconscious inferential steps' through which the subject's mind *must* have progressed.

The larger point that Wittgenstein is making here is that psychologism is not just the result of misconstruing the grammatical propositions whereby we formulate or explain the rules governing the use of meta-linguistic terms as empirical propositions; this tendency is itself the result of treating meta-linguistic terms like 'understanding' or 'inferring' as the names of mental processes. In what is perhaps an admonition directed at himself, Wittgenstein asks: 'What is the difference between inferring wrong and not inferring? between adding wrong and not adding? Consider this' (RFM VI: §48). Frege, Russell and the early Wittgenstein would have all responded that whether a subject had *wrongly inferred* '¬q' from 'p. & p →q', or had *not inferred* '¬q' from 'p. & p →q' but had performed some other mental act,[24] is a psychological and not a logical issue. For they all regarded *inferring*, *reasoning* and *judging* as mental processes, and hence, the concern of psychology and not of logic.

This is precisely the starting-point for the AI defence of cognitive psychologism. For the early AI-theorists saw themselves as merely responding to the challenge laid down by the founders of analytic philosophy. On this reading, Frege never *refuted* psychologism but, rather, simply threw the ball into psychology's court. Indeed, we might say that psychologism is defined by the premise that the answer to the question 'What is inferring?' will consist in the description of a mental process.[25] What kind of mental process the psychologician takes *inferring* to be will depend on her epistemological orientation. That is, the method whereby a psychologician seeks to discover the 'hidden processes of inference' – e.g., by transcendental deduction, by introspection, by a formal model that supplies the 'missing steps' in one's stream of conscious experiences – establishes where she is situated on the psychologistic spectrum.

The root of the problem here, Wittgenstein states in a related discussion in *Philosophical Grammar*, is that 'We say that understanding is a "psychological process", and this label is misleading, in this as in countless other cases. It compares understanding to a particular *process*. . . . And our next step is to conclude that the essence of the process is something difficult to grasp that still awaits discovery' (PG: 74–5). That is, the seemingly innocuous premise that understanding or inferring are psychological processes prompts us to analyse them as we would any physical process. Only 'now the analogy which was to make us understand our thoughts falls to pieces. So we have to deny the yet uncomprehended process in the yet unexplored medium' (PI: §308; cf. Z: §446).

'The grammar of a mental state or process,' Wittgenstein explains in *Philosophical Grammar*, 'is in many respects similar to that of e.g. a brain-process. The principal difference is perhaps that in the case of a brain-process a direct check is admitted to be possible; the process in question may perhaps be seen by opening the skull. But there is no room for a similar "immediate perception" in the grammar of mental process. (There is no such move in this game.)' (PG: 82) The AI-theorist might be tempted to respond that AI does not merely observe brain-processes, but a system of neural impulses whose *logical structure* constitutes what we are searching for when seeking to analyse a mental process like inference [*sic*]. But Wittgenstein's argument goes deeper than this 'ordinary language philosophy' reading suggests; for he points out that what we need to get clear about here is:

> what inferring really consists in: We shall perhaps say it consists in the transition from one assertion to another. But does this mean that inferring is something that takes place when we are making a transition from one assertion to another, and so *before* the second one is uttered – or that inferring consists in making the one assertion follow upon the other, that is, e.g., in uttering it after the other? Misled by the special use of the verb 'infer' we readily imagine that inferring is a peculiar activity, a process in the medium of the understanding, as it were a brewing of the vapour out of which the deduction arises.
>
> (RFM I: §6)

The 'special use of the verb "infer"' to which Wittgenstein is alluding is that of a dynamic process-verb. That is, inferring is something that one can do well or poorly, slowly or quickly, successfully or unsuccessfully, etc. And it is just such uses of the term which encourage the psychologistic view of inference as a mental process.

Wittgenstein responds to this view of inference in a particularly dense argument presented at RFM I §17. He first outlines the epistemological consequences of this conception:

> When we ask what inferring consists in, we hear it said e.g.: 'If I have recognized the truth of the propositions . . . , then I am justified in further writing down . . . '. – In what sense justified? Had I no right to write that down before? – 'Those propositions convince me of the truth of this proposition.' But of course that is not what is in question either.

If inferring 'q' from 'p. & p →q' were a mental process, then its justification could only be grounded in some (putatively 'basic') experience that will counter the claims of philosophical scepticism: e.g. the 'experience' of recognising or grasping a true thought. But, as Frege and Husserl both emphasised, the truth of an inferred thought cannot depend on the 'epistemic stance' which one takes towards it, for that would render truth both relative and subjective.

Wittgenstein next broaches the theme which he is to spell out at RFM I §§131 and 133: ' "The mind carries out the special activity of logical inference according to these laws".' To this Wittgenstein responds: 'That is certainly interesting and important; but then, is it true? Does the mind always infer according to *these* laws?' The purpose of this rhetorical question is not to reinforce some ulterior sceptical motive, or to defend a psychologistic belief in 'other modes of reasoning'. Rather, the point is that on a psychologistic conception of inference it is perfectly legitimate to ask such a question. This opens up the prospect of a mind subject to 'logical malfunction' in much the same way that an engine may suddenly begin to misfire (or a signal detection system begin to manifest *biases*). And it encourages us to speculate about the 'conceivability' of a different kind of mind which follows a different set of laws.

On the classical psychologistic view of inference, the laws of logic are somehow hard-wired into the human brain, and it is this which causes the human mind to reason in a logical manner. Herein lies the answer to Hilbert's question of how the logical calculus can provide a protocol for the 'activity of thinking': viz., the laws of logic *represent* the manner in which human beings think because their neurological embodiment literally *causes* human beings to think in that manner. (Why the brain should have evolved in this manner is an empirical matter.) But, as we saw in §5, Frege objected to this argument that if the *grounds* of an act of reasoning are reduced to its *causes*, then 'justification in the proper sense is not possible; what we have in its place is an account of how the conviction was arrived at' (PW: 147), and something like general consensus among a community of language-speakers will be said to establish whether or not that conclusion is 'correct' (cf. LI: 103f).

Waismann expands on this argument in *Principles of Linguistic Philosophy*. 'What,' he asks, 'is the difference between a causal connection and a transition in a calculus? What is the difference between a calculation formed by a machine, and that made by a person? Or else between a musical box playing a tune and a person playing it?' The answer lies in the fact that:

> the playing or calculation of a person can be justified by rules which he gives us when asked; not so the achievements of a machine, where the question 'Why do these keys spring out?' can *only* be answered by describing the mechanism, that is by describing a causal nexus. On the other hand, if we ask the calculator how he comes to his results, he will explain to us what kind of calculation he is doing and then adduce certain laws of arithmetic. He will not reply by describing the mode of action of a hidden machine, say, a machine in his brain.
>
> (PLP: 122; cf. RFM I: §119)

In other words, the rules of inference, or calculation, are *antecedent* to the machine's operations: they establish the criteria which determine when the machine is performing properly or malfunctioning (see Chapter 1).

The way that Waismann has phrased this argument might invite the AI response that a machine could be programmed to perform exactly the same linguistic acts as ourselves, and conversely, that we can easily manipulate and predict how a calculator will 'explain' his results (see Nisbett and Wilson 1977). But such an objection would miss Waismann's point. For, whether we would say of such a system that it had 'justified its result' or that it had 'produced a justification for its result' – a distinction, incidentally, which involves far greater complexity than the narrow limits that a simple language-game such as blind interaction permits – what matters here is the fact that we make such a categorial distinction.

That is, we distinguish between describing a subject as having 'inferred' or 'calculated' x, and describing the causes (if there are any) of a subject's uttering the sound (or writing the mark) 'x' (say, as the result of an automatic response to a stimulus). These two levels of discourse – the normative and the causal – are not only independent of one another, but, indeed, they are mutually exclusive. Thus, assuming that it were possible to identify a neural sequence in a subject's brain that preceded the uttering of 'x'[26] – say, a causes b and b causes c – and further, suppose that the neural sequence $a \rightarrow b \rightarrow c$ could be mapped onto the steps in some program, this would in no way entail that S had *inferred* x, or that a computer operating that program had 'inferred' x. For what establishes whether or not S had inferred x are the sorts of things that S says to justify or explain his result. A neuroscientist who observed $a \rightarrow b \rightarrow c$ would have absolutely no grounds for distinguishing between saying that S had *inferred* x, or that such-and-such had *caused* S to utter 'x'.

But could one not argue that the putative 'neural sequence' – and, *a fortiori*, the program onto which it is mapped – *explains* in what inferring consists? In which case, it is tempting to conclude that the concept of inference should – at least in scientific contexts – be abandoned altogether, on the ground that an appropriate neuropsychological account will exhaust everything that can or need be said about an agent's behaviour. But then, this eliminativist conclusion rests on the psychologistic premise that we are analysing the 'mental process' of inferring. Thus Wittgenstein insists that what we really need to do here is 'look and see how we carry out inferences in the practice of language; what kind of procedure in the language-game inferring is.' For our basic problem is that we are 'in the dark about what following and inferring really consists in; what kind of fact, and what kind of procedure, it is. The peculiar use of these verbs suggest to us that following is the existence of a connexion between propositions, which connexion we follow up when we infer' (RFM I: §19).

This picture of a series of mental acts, each of them systematically related to the preceding step, constitutes the essence of the psychologistic conception of inference (see PG: 100). Unlike the case of physical processes and activities, however, 'When we say: "This proposition follows from that one" . . . "to follow" is being used *non-temporally* (and this shows that the proposition does not express the result of an experiment)' (RFM I: §103). This objection represents the heart of Frege and Husserl's attack on psychologism: viz., when we say that 'q' follows from 'p. & p. $\rightarrow$ q', we do not mean that p occurred at t_1 and q at t_2, or that if we think p, and then think p $\rightarrow$ q, we will find ourselves thinking q.

Psychologism cannot accept this point. For, given the assumptions that inferring consists in the mental process of grasping the relations between thoughts, and being guided in this process by neurally embodied rules of inference, then the mental process of inferring can be no less a temporal operation than the mechanical process of working with a logical calculus: or the 'm-configuration alterations' of a Turing machine.[27] That means that to say that S inferred 'q' from 'p. & p. $\rightarrow$ q' is indeed to say that *first* S processed 'p', *then* 'p $\rightarrow$ q', and *then* 'q'.

Wittgenstein draws our attention to the fact that this argument capitalises on a critical aspect of the overlap between 'infer' and physical process-verbs: viz., that inferring can be extended over time; have a beginning, middle and end; be interrupted and resumed; or broken down into stages that occur one after another. Given the formal manner in which one presents or justifies one's inferences, it is tempting to assume that the 'process of inferring' consists in the transformation of these propositions in 'the medium of the mind'. It then seems natural to conclude that this 'exper-

115

ience' must be such that it can guarantee the reliability of its results. And this could only be the case if inferring consisted in an unbroken chain of transformations, each of which is self-evidently or directly true (in the same way as is supposed to apply to the 'gapless' proofs of an axiomatic theory).

In addition to being a process-verb, 'infer' is also a success-verb. This feature of its use prompts the objection: 'But we surely infer this proposition from that because it actually follows! We ascertain that it follows.' To this, Wittgenstein responds: 'We ascertain that what is written here follows from what is written there. And this proposition is being used *temporally*' (*ibid.*: §23). That is, we can say when, or where, S realised that q follows from p. & p →q. The point of this cryptic remark is not to resurrect the 'act/object' distinction; it is to draw attention to the importance of distinguishing between rules of inference and their application: i.e. to the fact that the logical connections laid down in grammar constitute the grounds for their temporal uses. But 'ascertain' is no more being used to describe an experience than 'infer' or 'grasp'. Rather, it is used to signify that S can transform an expression according to a rule of grammar (*ibid.*: §9).

For example, we ask a pupil what is entailed by 'p. & p →q', and after some delay he answers 'q'. When we say that he *ascertained* that the latter follows from the former, or that it took him five minutes to *see* the answer, we are not alluding to some psychological process that occurred in his mind which took five minutes (a mental process which presumably becomes faster with experience). In this normative practice, we cite the rule of inference as the criterion for describing his action as that of having *ascertained* that 'q' follows from 'p. & p →q'. And should his subsequent behaviour reveal that he had only guessed the correct answer, this does not corroborate the psychologistic premise that inferring is after all a mental process, but, rather, demonstrates that the criteria governing the use of 'ascertain' ('grasp', 'recognise', 'see', etc.) are defeasible.

This brings us to the point where we can appreciate the obscure argument that Wittgenstein presents at the outset of his discussion of inference in *Remarks on the Foundations of Mathematics*. He beckons us to

> look at what happens here. – There is a transition from one proposi-
> tion to another *via* other propositions, that is, a chain of inferences;
> but we don't need to talk about this; for it presupposes another kind
> of transition, namely that from one link of the chain to the next.
> Now a process of forming the transition may occur between the
> links. There is nothing occult about this process; it is a derivation of
> one sentence from another according to a rule; a comparison of both
> with some paradigm or other, which represents the schema of the
> transition; or something of the kind. This may go on on paper,
> orally, or 'in the head'. – The conclusion may however also be drawn
> in such a way that the one proposition is uttered after the other,

without any such process; or the process may consist merely in our saying 'Therefore' or 'It follows from this,' or something of the kind. We call it a 'conclusion' when the inferred proposition *can* in fact be derived from the premise.

(*Ibid.*: §6)

What Wittgenstein is saying here is that, e.g., someone who is working through a proof by writing down (saying out loud or to himself) 'By hypothesis it is the case that a. By axiom 1 it follows that b. By *modus ponens* it follows that c . . . ' is going through the process of applying the axioms and rules of inference of a system to a given problem. But the process involved here is logical, not psychological: it is the process of *deriving* one proposition from another according to a paradigm. What the agent is doing here is justifying (explaining, or articulating) the steps he is taking by appealing to the axioms and rules of inference; and it is only if these steps do conform to these axioms and rules of inference that we say 'In the second step he inferred from the first axiom that b, in the third step he inferred by *modus ponens* that c . . . '. That is, it is only if the subject's behaviour satisfies the criteria governing the use of the meta-linguistic expression in question that we describe him as having *inferred* (ascertained, etc.) that p entails q.

But these utterances are not a sufficient condition for describing a subject as having inferred that p entails q; for someone might repeat the various steps mechanically without grasping what they were saying, or we might simulate them in a program. Nor are they a necessary condition; for one need not go through this laborious process. A prodigy might immediately (and consistently) supply an answer, and, provided this was correct, we will describe him as having inferred q. But that does not mean that his *brain* (quickly) went through the same logical process as that which the more ponderous thinker employs; for what one says or writes in arriving at some conclusion are *criteria* for the application of 'infer', not *manifestations* of a hidden process.

These criteria make no allowance for what – if anything – may have been going on in one's mind while working on a problem. For example, Einstein reported that he often visualised the solution to a problem. But that does not mean that *inference in Einstein's case* consisted in the transformation of mental images. Herein lies one root of the persisting psychologistic theme that inference consists in the construction and manipulation of mental models. The criteria governing the use of 'infer' are solely concerned with whether one proposition follows from another: in the logical sense that 'it *can* be derived' by a series of transformations according to paradigms. This is the reason why 'It is very noteworthy that *what goes on* in thinking practically never interests us' (Z: §88), and why Wittgenstein goes on to ask: 'Isn't it the same here as with a calculating prodigy? – He has calculated right if he has got the right answer. Perhaps he himself cannot say what went on in

117

him. And if we were to hear it, it would perhaps seem like a queer caricature of calculation' (*ibid.*: §89).

Wittgenstein constantly returns in his later writings on the philosophy of logic and psychology to the question: 'What do the calculating boys do? Yet we say they calculate' (GWL: 150). For the phenomenon of the autistic savant might be seen as an extreme version of the problem that seems to confront us when trying to explain what inferring consists in. Our picture of *calculating in the head*, Wittgenstein remarks, is one in which calculation is 'as it were submerged, and goes on *under* the mirror surface of the water. (Think of the sense in which water '*consists*' of H and O.)' (RPP I: §97). The statement 'S multiplied 16 × 17 in his head' seems to function as the description of an activity, and what else could this activity be if not a psychological process? But 'This is the point at which I go wrong. For I now want to say: "*This* process in the mind corresponds to *this* process on paper. And it would then make sense to talk of a method of projection according to which the image of the sign was a representation of the sign itself"' (PI: §366). That is, given the psychologistic premise that *calculating in the head* is a mental process, it is compelling to see the formal calculation as a model for the pre-conscious cognitive processes that *must* have gone in the subject's mind (see PG: 99). Just as it is compelling for AI, *qua* psychologistic theory, to see a computer program as a model for the pre-conscious processes that go on in a subject's mind.

The key to resolving this issue, Wittgenstein explains, is to see that *calculating in the head* (inferring) is no more a psychological process than is *calculation* (inference). To be sure, there are many things that *may* go on in one's mind when calculating in the head; e.g. one might visualise writing the figures down, or one might say the various steps to oneself. But nothing at all might have gone on in one's mind without undermining the use of this expression. For the possibility of such 'mental accompaniments' has no bearing on the use of 'calculating in the head'. Hence 'The thing is: we have got to get down to "What is reporting? What is describing?" because you report to me the above sort of things' (GWL: 251).

The crucial thing we have to recognise is that an expression like 'I multiplied 16 × 17 in my head' is not based on any criteria. One of the distinguishing features of 'calculating in the head' is that, like 'infer', it is primarily used in the case of a correct result; a wrong result has the same effect on 'I calculated x in my head' as 'You dreamt it' has on 'I have been to grandma' (*ibid.*: 150). But, significantly, the use of 'calculate in the head' is also tied to context: to a speaker's mathematical abilities, and the problem at hand. We would be puzzled, for example, if Erdos had ever reported that he had calculated the sum of 4 × 3 in his head; but puzzled in a different way if a two-year-old was to make the same claim. For 'Only if you have learnt to calculate – on paper or out loud – can you be made to grasp, by means of this concept, what calculating in the head is' (PI: 216).

The same point applies to inference. That is, it only makes sense to say that an agent *inferred* 'q' from 'p' if p entails q and if the agent is capable of explaining or justifying his result. Thus, we might draw from this grammatical observation the corollary that there is not a *continuum of inference*, ranging from the lowest life forms up to man. For the paradigm uses of 'infer' severely limit the use of the term in primitive contexts: a point which has profound implications for AI's attempt to postulate an 'atomic level' of information-processing, not simply because it exposes the illegitimacy of describing causal sequences in normative terms, but, more importantly, because it challenges the reductionist premise on which this argument is built.

Wittgenstein is not, however, suggesting that the answer to his frequently posed question 'And what does inferring consist in?' is: 'In the transformation of a proposition according to paradigm.' Rather, he intends for us to see how the question itself is misleading: the consequence – or perhaps origin – of the misguided psychologistic search for the mental processes underlying the activity of inferring. Instead of asking what inferring *consists in*, one might ask: 'What are the criteria governing the use of "infer"?' 'What are the consequences of using the term "infer"?'

Given Wittgenstein's immediate purpose in this argument, which is to clarify the dangers of treating the grammatical propositions whereby we explain the use of meta-linguistic expressions as empirical propositions, and, *a fortiori*, the confusions that result if these meta-linguistic terms are construed as the names of psychological processes, it is clear why this issue should have played such a crucial role in the normative conception of mathematical propositions and proofs which Wittgenstein developed in *Remarks on the Foundations of Mathematics* (see Shanker 1987a). It is not at all surprising, therefore, to encounter virtually the same arguments in the discussion of *calculation* in the midst of the inquiry into the nature of *thinking* in *Philosophical Investigations*, *Remarks on the Philosophy of Psychology*, and *Lectures on the Philosophy of Psychology*. Indeed, one of the reasons why *calculation* was to dominate Turing's approach to the Mechanist Thesis was precisely because the *progressive* overtones are so pronounced in the 'special use of the verb "calculate"': if anything, even more so than is the case with 'infer'.

Not only does Wittgenstein's argument lead us to query from yet another angle the manner in which Turing sought to analyse the concept of calculation as a recursive 'mental process', but it also brings into question the whole basis of AI's interpretation of the relation in which programs stand to problem-solving (*inferring*, *reasoning*, and *thinking*). To be sure, this barely touches the surface of the issues inspiring the AI approach to the psychology of thinking. But it does reflect some of the philosophical problems involved in interpreting the relation in which programs stand to speaking aloud protocols. It enables us to appreciate just how deep a question it is why AI was led to ponder the question of 'how far laws of thought are innate and how far they are learned' (Gregory 1987: 430). And, finally, it sheds some light on the puzzling argument in *Philosophical Grammar* that begins with the question 'if thinking consists only in writing or speaking, why shouldn't a machine do it?' and concludes with the warning that 'It is a travesty of the truth to say "Thinking is an activity of our mind, as writing is an activity of the hand"' (PG: 105–6). As we shall see in the next chapter, this passage bears directly on AI's early concern with the nature of *creativity*. Moreover, the very fact that Wittgenstein broached this topic five or six years before the publication of 'On Computable Numbers' provides an important insight into the conceptual environment which shaped AI. For, as will become increasingly evident in the sequel, the themes which most concerned Wittgenstein in the early 1930s also served as the springboard for the 'post-computational' entry into the psychology of thinking.

4

MODELS OF DISCOVERY

People say again and again that philosophy doesn't really progress, that we are still occupied with the same philosophical problems as were the Greeks. But the people who say this don't understand why it has to be so. It is because our language has remained the same and keeps seducing us into asking the same questions.

(Wittgenstein, *Culture and Value*)

§1 Eureka!

Explaining the nature of insight has served more than perhaps any other single issue to define the reductionist character of AI as a psychological programme. This is true historically as much as it is conceptually. For one of the first 'mysteries' that the founders of AI addressed was the so-called 'aha experience'. In part this was simply because the nature of creativity had dominated the psychology of thinking for much of the twentieth century (*infra*). But perhaps even more to the point, it was the kind of problem which the debate over creativity presented that made it so appealing to the founders of AI.

Contemporary attitudes towards creativity have been largely shaped by the nineteenth-century Romantic picture of genius, which in turn was grounded in classical Greek myths about inspiration (see Abrams 1953). This is precisely why the founders of AI found the nature of insight to be such an enticing issue. For it seemed to them to present a direct confrontation between *myth* and *science*. That is, AI would succeed in explaining that which 'folk theory' deemed to be inexplicable. If one were to reject the very possibility of a mechanist explanation of creativity – on purely *a priori* grounds – this could only be because one was in the grip of some sort of 'ordinary language inertia'.

On this reading, the various myths which constitute our picture of creativity – e.g., the myths of genius, or inspiration, or the moment of insight – are construed as a form of *pre-scientific*, and thus primitivist, way of

121

thinking about thinking (see Weisberg 1986). This is the reason why there is a distinctly pejorative undertone to the AI use of the word 'myth', rendering it closer to an antonym for 'truth' rather than a synonym for 'fable'. But what if the conflict between myth and science is categorially different from the conflict between a *bona fide* 'naive theory' like phrenology and science? That is, what if the Romantic explanation of creativity belongs to a completely different genre than Gall's explanation of Gluck's creativity (viz., as the result of an enlarged 'artistic structure' in his brain)? What implications, if any, would this have for the attempt by the founders of AI to explain the nature of creativity in mechanist terms?

To answer this question, we must first consider how Romanticism perceives creativity. The paradigm account of sudden inspiration has long been the following tale:

> While Archimedes was considering the matter [of how to ascertain the amount of gold in Hiero's crown] he happened to go to the baths. When he went down into the bathing pool he observed that the amount of water which flowed outside the pool was equal to the amount of his body that was immersed. Since this fact indicated the method of explaining the case, he did not linger, but moved with delight he leapt out of the pool, and going home naked, cried aloud that he had found exactly what he was seeking. For as he ran he shouted in Greek: heure'ka heure'ka.
>
> (Vitruvius 1934)

This story has epitomised Western attitudes towards inspiration for nearly two millennia: the fortuitous occurrence of events, the sudden moment of insight, the exhilaration and distraction that comes with an unexpected discovery, and, above all, the utter mystery of the unconscious processes involved. How did Archimedes make the connection between the over-flowing water when he stepped into the bath and the problem which Hiero II had set him? How is it that no one else had ever seen that the volume of an irregular solid could be measured by the displacement of water? And then there is 'Eureka': more than just an avowal, it has become the emblem for one of the mind's most closely guarded secrets.

The Greeks did, however, have an explanation for what happens when the mind suddenly finds the answer to a question for which it had been searching: insight was regarded as a gift of the Muses, its origins were 'divine'. Of course, in empirical terms, this explains nothing. But then, this was certainly not intended as a *scientific theory*. If anything, it served to highlight the Greeks' belief that there are some things which cannot be scientifically explained. The problem this outlook leaves us with, however, might be said to be that of explaining the nature of this 'cannot'.

According to the Greeks, the essence of insight is that it comes from some supernatural source, unpredicted and unfettered. Socrates tells Ion:

> The poet is a light and winged and holy thing, and there is no invention in him until he has been inspired and is out of his senses, and the mind is no longer in him. The gift which you possess of speaking excellently about Homer is not an art, but . . . an inspiration; there is a divinity moving you, like that contained in the stone which Euripides calls a magnet, but which is commonly known as the stone of Heraclea. . . . In like manner the Muse first of all inspires men herself; and from these inspired persons a chain of other persons is suspended, who take the inspiration. For all good poets, epic as well as lyric, compose their beautiful poems not by art, but because they are inspired and possessed.

In other words, the origins of insight are *unconscious* and, hence, unexplainable.

To the founders of AI, such an argument reeks of obscurantism. They agreed that the secret of creativity was locked in the unconscious, but, like all other secrets of nature, they saw this as a mystery which begs to be explained in mechanist terms. The Greek–Romantic picture of the unconscious as something other-worldly, or transcendental, is precisely the sort of thinking that underlies AI's scientistic reading of 'the myth of creativity'. Indeed, Plato's own analogy in the above passage seems to reinforce the AI point that we are dealing here with a *folk theory*.

Thus, the founders of AI would have regarded what Socrates says to Ion about the poet as being no different in kind from what Gall had to say about cerebral protrusions. For that very reason, the founders of AI were confident that, should AI be able to give a fully scientific explanation of the unconscious processes that bring about a 'moment of insight', it would thereby have established a precedent for the psychology of thinking *tout court*, on the ground that the processes underlying problem-solving – whether 'creative' or otherwise – are largely unconscious. And in so arguing, AI could claim to be following in, rather than trampling over, the footsteps of the Romantic poets.

The idea that there is a parallel between the unconscious processes underlying poetic creation – where poetry was seen, in Romantic terms, as the perception and representation of the hidden truths of Nature – and those involved in problem-solving, began to emerge around the middle of the nineteenth century. It was thought that, in both cases, 'inspiration could be explained as a more or less intermittent outburst into the conscious mind of psychic material, which had been stored in the subconscious mind' (Ellenberger 1970: 168). But interest at the turn of the twentieth century was beginning to swing from the poetic to the scientific end of the creativity spectrum. Thus, where Mill had written in the 1830s on Wordsworth and Coleridge, in the 1930s it was Helmholtz and Poincaré who were receiving all the attention. This was largely due to the fact that research on scientific and mathematical discovery fits in naturally with the emphasis on problem-solving in the psychology of thinking. But it also reflects the growing dominance of technology in the twentieth century, with its attendant pre-occupation with the pedagogic problem of how best to cultivate a scientific mind.

This shift from poetic to scientific creativity involved a dramatic reorientation in the manner in which the phenomenon of inspiration was approached. In Mill and Carlyle's writings on creativity, the emphasis is on the 'poet-philosopher' or the 'poet as hero'. The great figures, such as Wordsworth and Coleridge, were seen, not just as exceptional, but even as abnormal beings. As far as Mill and Carlyle were concerned, it may in principle be possible to understand how their minds work, but there could be no question of trying to implement such discoveries in one's own mental life. At best one can merely strive to understand what it is that the 'poet-philosopher' is able to perceive.

This attitude carried over to some extent into the twentieth century: most noticeably in theories of mathematical platonism (see Hardy 1967). But there was a noticeable change in the psychology of thinking in regard to the nature of creativity and problem-solving. Helmholtz's and Poincaré's memoirs were valued, not so much for what they revealed about these two extraordinary individuals, but, rather, for what they can tell us about how the mind solves problems: namely, that the great discoveries 'cannot be produced by chance alone . . . [T]here can be no doubt of the necessary intervention of some mental process unknown to the inventor, in other terms, of an unconscious one' (Hadamard 1945: 20). That is, 'to the unconscious belongs not only the complicated task of constructing the bulk of various combinations of ideas, but also the most delicate and essential one of selecting those which satisfy our sense of beauty and, consequently, are likely to be useful' (*ibid.*: 32).

Hadamard's argument was meant to be read as a challenge to that venerable tradition in the nineteenth century which saw consciousness as a supernumerary faculty which 'picks out' from the multitude of ideas presented to the mind 'certain ones as worthy of its notice and suppresses all the rest' (James 1879: 9). On this picture, reasoning was regarded as 'but another form of that selective activity which appears to be the true sphere of mental spontaneity' (*ibid.*: 12). The very term 'selective activity' was thought to presuppose the adjective 'conscious'.

Thus, the fundamental objection commonly voiced to Jevons and Marquand's 'reasoning machines' was that, while such devices might be capable of simulating 'mechanical reasoning' (e.g. computing the multiplication tables), they could never reach the levels of 'creative reasoning'. For the latter mental process is characterised by the mind's ability to choose between different ideas; and this ability was regarded as the quintessential *conscious act*.[1] To be sure, how the actual process of selection takes place, and how the conscious mind *knows* when the unconscious mind has hit upon a fruitful combination, still remained profound mysteries. But at least it seemed clear that the key to discovering the nature of creativity lay in unlocking the secrets of the unconscious mind.

As can be clearly seen in 'The Processes of Creative Thinking', this approach to creativity constituted the starting-point for Newell and Simon's theory of General Problem Solving (GPS). Newell and Simon tell us that GPS was designed to explain 'the unconscious processes that are supposed to occur during "incubation", the imagery employed in creative thinking and its significance for the effectiveness of the thinking, and above all, the phenomenon of "illumination", the sudden flash of insight that reveals the solution of a problem long pursued' (Newell *et al.* 1959: 1). The crux of Newell and Simon's argument was that introspectionist theories of creativity had failed because they overlooked the crucial problem-solving processes which lie *beneath the threshold of consciousness*.

These processes are said by AI to provide 'the machinery that makes consciousness possible' (Johnson-Laird 1988: 15). The 'machinery' intended here is not, however, simply neural: it is 'that class of psychological events that are at the time unknown to the [subject] but that actively affect [his] behavior' (Shevrin and Dickman 1980: 422). The key word here is 'psychological'. The point is that 'all categories of descriptive terminology applicable to conscious experience can also be applied to unconscious processes: perception, judgment, thought, affect, motivation, and so forth' (*ibid.*). Thus, the patron saints of AI were Mill and Helmholtz, not James and Titchener; for it was to those who saw consciousness as somehow derivative from the unconscious, rather than the reverse, that the founders of AI looked for inspiration.

§2 The 'cognitive unconscious'

At the end of the nineteenth century, one of the leading problems in the psychology of thinking was to explain 'moments of insight': i.e., cases where one suddenly finds the answer to a problem, or the name, face, word, etc., for which one was searching. In the so-called 'cult of the unconscious' sweeping Europe at the time (see Ellenberger 1970), it became increasingly common to assign the mechanics of this phenomenon to the unconscious, with consciousness enjoying the fruits of this subliminal process. Transcendental arguments were paramount here; but amid the various Romantic views competing for attention – which, like Plato's account in the *Ion*, treated insight and creativity as ineffable – there emerged a radical new use of the term 'unconscious' to designate *inferential processes that take place in the brain*: what Carpenter referred to as *unconscious cerebration* (see Carpenter 1891).

This notion of 'unconscious inferences' owed much to Helmholtz's inferential theory of perception. According to the standard empiricist theory of perception which shaped Helmholtz's thinking, there is a 'gap' between the retinal patterns of stimulation that we experience and the objects that we see. This 'gap', Helmholtz argued, must be filled by 'cerebral inferences': i.e. the brain must frame *hypotheses* on the basis of the data it has stored from past experiences and the information it is currently processing (see Helmholtz 1971b). But then, why not extend this argument to the problem of creativity? Insight, no less than perception, could be treated as the end-result of 'unconscious inferences'. One could thus explain the 'Aha phenomenon' as the result of the fact that, although one is not consciously thinking about a problem, the brain continues to work away on it. Should it hit upon a solution, this will be instantly recognised by the faculty of consciousness.

Thus was born the theory of the 'cognitive unconscious'. There was nothing particularly radical about describing cerebral processes as 'unconscious'; for the cerebral processes that were assumed to be parallel with (and to underlie) the association of ideas – the so-called 'habits of the brain' – had long been described as 'unconscious'. What was so striking about this new theory was the suggestion that cerebral processes could also be described in cognitive terms: i.e. that one could talk about the *unconscious inferences* that take place in the brain during perception or problem-solving.

This theory was immediately challenged by Cartesians, who argued that it confused two distinct levels of psychological activity: the *neural* and the *mental*. James, for example, insisted that

> So far, then, from perception being a species of reasoning properly so called, both it and reasoning are co-ordinate varieties of that deeper sort of process known psychologically as the association of ideas, and physiologically as the law of habit in the brain. *To call perception unconscious reasoning is thus either a useless metaphor, or a positively misleading confusion between two different things.*
>
> (James 1890: II, 113)

As far as AI is concerned, this merely amounts to the standard 'ordinary language' objection. Indeed, from Turing on, AI-theorists have dismissed objections to the 'cognitive unconscious' as the result of 'semantic conservatism'. Thus Gregory insists that

> Until recently the notion of unconscious inference seemed to many psychologists to be self-contradictory – as if it used to be assumed that consciousness is necessary for inference to be possible. Perhaps

126

again through the influence of computers . . . this objection no
longer has force. To hold that 'unconscious inference' is a self-
contradictory notion now appears as mere semantic inertia.

(Gregory 1973: 51)

But it was not the notion of *unconscious inference* which late nineteenth- and
early twentieth-century psychologists found disturbing; it was the notion of
unconscious reasoning. As we shall see, herein lies an important distinction
between 'pre-' and 'post-computational mechanism'.

Mill's argument that 'what we are conscious of is constructed out of what
we are not conscious of' (Mill 1873: 275) had a profound influence on
Helmholtz's thesis that perception is the end-result of an *unbewusster Schluss*.
Thus, we must be wary of Gregory's suggestion that Helmholtz had antici-
pated the idea that these unconscious processes are computational (Gregory
1986: 54). For there can be no denying the fact that Helmholtz's conception
of 'unconscious inference' was firmly rooted in nineteenth-century empiricism.[2]

This is most clearly borne out by the fact that Helmholtz was forced to
renounce the terms of his original argument by the idealist response to the
first edition of *Physiological Optics*.[3] While the argument which Helmholtz
presented in 'The Facts of Perception' (1878) is not quite the 'recantation'
which James suggested (see James 1890: II 111n), it was certainly the 'qualification' which Schlick and Klein described (see: Helmholtz 1977: 175f;
Klein 1977: chapter 3). In 'The Recent Progress of the Theory of Vision'
(1868), Helmholtz had explained how the term 'unconscious judgments',

> though accepted by other supporters of the Empirical Theory, has
> excited much opposition, because, according to generally-accepted
> psychological doctrines, a *judgment*, or *logical conclusion*, is the culmi-
> nating point of the conscious operations of the mind. But the
> judgments which play so great a part in the perceptions we derive
> from our senses cannot be expressed in the ordinary form of logi-
> cally analyzed conclusions, and it is necessary to deviate somewhat
> from the beaten paths of psychological analysis in order to convince
> ourselves that we really have here the same kind of mental operation
> as that involved in conclusions usually recognised as such.
>
> (Warren and Warren 1968: 130)

Disturbed by the manner in which this idea was being exploited by the
proponents of a *noumenal unconscious*,[4] Helmholtz carefully avoided the terms
of his earlier argument. The problem that remained, however, was: How
does one account for the apparent independence of the brain – for that fact
that, as Cobbe put it, 'the brain can sometimes think without us' (Cobbe
1883: 353) – without opening the door to the transcendental ego?

127

It is not entirely clear how Helmholtz wished to respond to this dilemma. At times he seems to incline towards a Romantic view of the unconscious.[5] Yet he was not about to assign those powers to the 'automatic unconscious' – so called because of the Cartesian overtones – which were deemed to lie irrevocably beyond the capacities of reasoning machines: viz., creativity and adaptativeness. After all, Helmholtz's unconscious was so stupid that, even when experience had demonstrated that something was a visual illusion, it persisted in its 'fallacious reasoning'.

In any event, it is clear that he was only abandoning the phrase *unbewusster Schluss*: not the underlying thesis that it is legitimate to speak of cerebral processes in cognitive terms. Thus, in the second edition of *Physiological Optics* (1894) he insisted that he 'even now finds the name up to a certain limit, to be still admissible and significant' (Helmholtz 1977: 176). The reason for this, as he explained in 'The Origin of the Correct Interpretation of our Sensory Impressions' (also 1894), was that

> these associations of perceptions in the memory actually take place in such a manner, that at the time of their origin one is not aware of it, or is aware only in such a manner that one remembers to have observed the same process frequently before. . . . The memory of earlier cases with the accompanying circumstances can emerge more distinctly during the first repetitions of rarer observations of this kind, so that the mental process here acquires a greater analogy to conscious thought.
>
> (Klein 1977: 55–6)

This passage indicates that Helmholtz had backed off from his initial strong position of treating the cerebral processes underlying 'perceptual judgment' as literally a species of inferring, and was now only prepared to describe them as *analogous* to the steps which occur in conscious inference.

Both the differences and the similarities between Helmholtz's and contemporary versions of the 'cognitive unconscious' come out most clearly here. Helmholtz's intention was to synthesise the nineteenth-century mechanist conception of the unconscious *qua* reflex movement with the nineteenth-century conception of inference as a 'psychic activity' (in which we see in our mind's eye how ideas are logically related). His argument proceeds from the Hartleian theme that, through habituation, processes which were initially conscious can become secondarily automatic.[6] This applies to *all* conscious experiences: i.e. to reasoning as much as to perception. Hence the argument supplies an answer to the question of what happens in the mind when one is suddenly aware of the solution to a problem. Strictly speaking, the answer is: solely that. But since a 'moment of insight' must always be the conclusion of an inference, it must be the culminating point of unconscious – i.e. cerebral – processes which are isomorphic with, *and can thus be inferred from*, the corresponding steps which would have occurred had the inference been conscious.

The fact that these cerebral processes can be described in cognitive terms was not thought to entail, however, that they are autonomous. On the contrary, the whole thrust of the empiricist framework was to exclude such a premise (which was seen as bolstering metaphysics). Helmholtz's argument was thus no more intended to make the pre-Freudian suggestion that there are two separate and independent cognitive realms than that the same range of activities can be attributed to the brain as apply to the mind. Rather, his point was that the 'basic process which underlies all that can truly be called thinking' occurs both with and without awareness (Warren and Warren 1968: 220). That is, the chain of inferences leading up to the solution of a problem can be either conscious or unconscious. In the latter case, only the last link in this chain is present to consciousness. But the fact that the brain can execute 'unconscious inferences' does not mean that the brain can engage in *unconscious reasoning*: a suggestion which even the proponents of the 'cognitive unconscious' regarded as 'self-contradictory'.

To understand this last point, we need to move deeper into the murky waters of the empiricist conception of consciousness. The basic themes in the empiricist picture of the mind were:

- to be mental is not necessarily to be volitional but it is *ipso facto* to be conscious (i.e. transmitted to the Sensorium);
- unconscious processes are those which occur in the nervous system that are not transmitted to the Sensorium; hence to be unconscious is to be neither volitional nor mental;
- reflex actions must be involuntary, but they need not be unconscious;
- hence there can be automatic mental changes: reflex actions that are not initiated by the Will but are transmitted to the Sensorium;
- to be volitional is necessarily to be mental (conscious); hence there can be no 'unconscious Will' (such as Schopenhauer and Hartmann had championed).

On this picture of consciousness, reasoning was seen as a *volitional* and thus a conscious mental activity. Or rather, reasoning was seen as consisting of two elements: rigidly following syllogistic rules, and choosing premises or hypotheses. The latter type of activity was seen as the hallmark of the Will. But we are still left with the mystery of what the Will is and how it sets the cerebrum into motion (see James 1890). Thus, in so far as the Will plays a crucial role in reasoning (and not just the Will, although it was seen as paramount, but also such arcane phenomena as imagination and intuition), the operations of the cerebrum 'can scarcely be designated as Reasoning processes, since "unconscious reasoning" seems a contradiction in terms' (Carpenter 1891: 517).

The proponents of the 'cognitive unconscious' were only prepared to argue that the syllogistic component of reasoning can be 'mechanised'. That is, just as one is conscious of what one is doing when learning a skill like playing the piano, but with practice attention can be focused elsewhere while the motor cortex continues on with the activity, so, too, in reasoning the brain can follow rules that were consciously acquired but have since become automatic. But nineteenth-century mechanists agreed with Cartesians that 'The intervention of unconscious processes in the creative act is a phenomenon quite different from the automatization of skills; and our unawareness of the sources of inspiration is of a quite different order from the unawareness of what we are doing while we tie our shoestrings or copy a letter on the typewriter' (Koestler 1975: 156).

The constant theme in turn-of-the-century writings in the psychology of thinking was that the essence of reasoning lay in the selection of premises, and that this is a capacity that can no more be assigned to the brain than to 'reasoning machines'. Indeed, the very fact that Jevons and Marquand's 'logical machines' were seen as simulating the mechanical actions of the 'automatic unconscious' was cited as both justifying and at the same time as limiting the claim that they could be described as 'reasoning machines'. As Peirce put it: 'the value of logical machines seems to lie in their showing how far reasoning is a mechanical process': that is, the extent to which rule-following becomes automatic. But one must not exaggerate the significance of this achievement, for 'Even syllogistic reasoning in its higher varieties . . . requires a living act of choice based on discernment, beyond the powers of any conceivable machine; and this sufficiently refutes the idea that man is a mere mechanical automaton endowed with an idle consciousness.'[7]

Helmholtz's argument thus conformed with – and contributed to – the nineteenth-century mechanist thesis that we can infer the nature of the unconscious inferences underlying certain cognitive acts from what would have to have occurred in consciousness for the same results to have obtained. Far from being – in AI terms – the 'machinery that makes consciousness possible', the 'cognitive unconscious' as originally conceived was constrained by the conscious. Indeed, as far as psychology proper was concerned, intro-spection was still thought to remain supreme in the study of problem-solving.

To be sure, the 'pre-computational' mechanists felt that it is difficult to separate the effects of 'self-observation' from those of 'inner perception' (hence the need espoused by Wundt for trained subjects). And they insisted that introspective reports are every bit as fallible as ordinary perceptions (hence Wundt's demand for stringent experimental checks). But they were not hostile to the basic Wundtian conception of psychology as an introspec-tionist science (bearing in mind that Wundt himself had subscribed to the theory of unconscious inference and had come to share Helmholtz's qualms; see Klein 1977: 57f).

There are clearly substantial differences, therefore, between 'pre-' and 'post-computational' conceptions of the 'cognitive unconscious', particularly in regard to the central AI claim that we *cannot* be aware of the preconscious processes – including *selective* processes, such as the serial or multi-channel filtering of information – that make conscious experience possible.[8] In this respect, Helmholtz should be seen as a precursor rather than a progenitor of AI. Furthermore, 'unconscious inferences' are no longer regarded as secondarily automatic. And, of course, AI is not tethered to the halter of introspection. But the fact that Helmholtz did not foresee the rise of information theory (which, interestingly, can be traced back to his discovery of the principle of the conservation of energy) does not mitigate where his greater significance for this issue lies. For, in a fundamental sense, what matters here is not so much whether Helmholtz fits comfortably into the modern mechanist fold as the reasons why computationalists have been drawn to treat him in this fashion.

Both the psychologistic conception of reasoning which guided Helmholtz, and his argument that we can infer the nature of unconscious cerebral processes that take place in perception or reasoning from an external paradigm, are central to the AI enterprise. In early mechanist writings on the 'cognitive unconscious', it is syllogisms and calculations which were called into service as the paradigms for the 'hidden processes' that were said to lead up to the sudden solution of a problem (cf. Montmasson 1931: 48f, 78f). As we shall see in §4, the AI models are rather more sophisticated. But as striking as the swing from tachistoscopes to computers may be, what has remained constant are the fundamental assumptions that inferring is a mental process, and that 'moments of insight' are caused by antecedent (unbroken) chains of unconscious processes, the nature of which can be discovered from some formal model.

§3 The role of chess in the evolution of AI

The obvious problem with the theory of the 'cognitive unconscious' was that it raised far more questions than it (putatively) answered. To begin with, there was the puzzling question of how conscious inferences become 'secondarily automatic' (whatever that actually means) and, further, how these two systems – the brain and the conscious mind – are able to communicate with one another. That in turn raised a troubling question about what exactly consciousness is, and how it is able to exert control over the brain, or to separate the wheat from the chaff of neural processes. But the issue that most concerned psychologists of thinking at the time was that the theory of the 'cognitive unconscious' could only be used for problems which the subject already knew how to solve: i.e. it could not account for the phenomenon of creativity. It was one thing to insist that, in cases of the 'Aha phenomenon', the brain must have solved the problem, and that since x (such-and-such a calculation, proof, etc.) constitutes a solution of the problem, this *must* have been what the brain inferred; but quite another to explain *how* the brain knew that x constituted a solution to the problem when this was something which had entirely eluded the conscious mind.

Poincaré seized on this point in 'Mathematical Discovery'. In both his review of Hilbert's *Grundlagen* and his attacks on logicism, Poincaré had made clear where his anti-mechanist sympathies lay as far as the foundations of mathematics were concerned. The purpose of his memoir was to take this crusade a step further by entering the debate in the psychology of thinking over the nature of creativity.

Poincaré begins his argument with the familiar nineteenth-century theme that 'Discovery is discernment, selection' (Poincaré 1913: 58). But his point was not that such a process must *ipso facto* be conscious; rather, he insists that the real problem posed by the 'moment of insight' is how the 'subliminal ego' should have chosen, from the myriad possibilities available, just that combination of ideas which is 'most interesting or useful' (*ibid.*). It is this which 'is most mysterious. How can we explain the fact that, of the thousand products of our unconscious activity, some are invited to cross the threshold, while others remain outside?' (*ibid.*).

Clearly, Poincaré argues, this phenomenon cannot be explained in terms of what mathematicians refer to as 'brute force' techniques. (Poincaré cites the example of Eratosthenes' sieve.) For 'The combinations so obtained would be extremely numerous, useless, and encumbering' (*ibid.*: 57). The only thing one can say with any certainty is that 'The real work of the discoverer consists in choosing between those combinations with a view to eliminating those that are useless, or rather not giving himself the trouble of making them at all' (*ibid.*). Poincaré maintains that this point applies just as forcefully – if not more so – to the unconscious as to the conscious mind. And even if one argues that the 'conscious Ego' delimits the number of permutations which the 'subliminal Ego' examines, one is still left with the mystery of the 'aesthetic sensibility' displayed by the processes of 'unconscious selection' (*ibid.*). But then, this takes us right back to where we started in §1, with Socrates' speech to Ion, only, with the brain taking the place of the Muses.

At the beginning of the twentieth century the debate over creativity had reached a stalemate. Psychiatrists were divided over the merits of 'cerebral' versus 'dynamic' models of the unconscious (see Münsterberg 1910). Psychologists of thinking were united in their opposition to 'trial-and-error' explanations of creativity, but completely uncertain about how else to proceed.[9] Philosophers were insisting that only they were qualified to explain the transcendental character of the unconscious. And 'hard-nosed behaviourists' were insisting that such issues were at best irrelevant, and at worst unanswerable.[10]

AI stepped into this impasse with a computational method of reconciling trial-and-error reasoning with a mechanist account of the 'preconscious processes' that bring about a 'moment of insight' (*infra*). But the seeds for this resolution of the debate over the nature of creativity had already been laid half a century before: by Poincaré himself. Poincaré had argued that:

> The rules which must guide this [unconscious] choice are extremely subtle and delicate, and it is practically impossible to state them in precise language; they must be felt rather than formulated. Under these conditions, how can we imagine a sieve capable of applying them mechanically?
>
> (Poincaré 1913: 57)

Note that Poincaré is not denying the possibility of discovering such 'unconscious rules'; he is merely pointing to what he saw as the enormous difficulty of such a task. But then, AI theorists could respond that Poincaré was thinking of his own experiences in the recherché realms of higher mathematics.[11] What if the great 'subtlety and delicacy' of his thinking was actually a consequence of the complexity of these mathematical domains? Perhaps if one were to begin by looking at simpler contexts, it would be possible to lay the groundwork for studying the 'unconscious rules' that govern our thinking in all domains?

This was the thinking behind Turing's argument that 'at each stage when one is using a logical system, there is a very large number of alternative steps, any of which one is permitted to apply, so far as obedience to the rules of a logical system is concerned. These choices make the difference between a brilliant and a footling reasoner, not the difference between a sound and a fallacious one' (Turing 1950: 29). Thus we arrive at the fundamental argument that, if AI begins with the simplest of cases, it can show how the 'processes that occur in human problem solving can be compounded out of elementary information processes, and hence . . . can be carried out by mechanisms' (Newell *et al.* 1958: 152). With all the attention which the strong mechanist thesis attracted during the 1960s, it was natural to overlook the fact that the rider at the end of this quotation was not only meant to defend the thesis of 'artificial intelligence', but, even more important, was meant to elucidate the mechanics of the 'cognitive unconscious'. For what the founders of AI were saying was that, even in the case of 'toy domains', the brain cannot be confined to trial-and-error methods – as could easily be demonstrated with a brute-force approach to playing chess.[12]

This brings us back to the theme, touched on in the opening chapter, that chess programming was to play an instrumental role in the evolution of AI. As we saw in Chapter 1, Turing was originally interested in the 'question of whether there was a "definite method" for playing chess – a machine method, in fact, although this would not necessarily mean the construction of a physical machine, but only a book of rules that could be followed by a mindless player – like the "instruction note" formulation of the concept of computability' (Hodges 1983: 211). There is nothing to suggest that Turing had read widely in the psychology of chess, or that (in the beginning) he saw in chess anything other than a suitable laboratory system for the study of 'definite methods'. But it is clear that he had read widely in chess theory, a field which early on had adopted the convention of presenting game strategies in the form of rules.

Bearing in mind the fact that reasoning was universally seen as a rule-governed 'mental activity', it was natural for Turing to assume that these rules represent the manner in which advanced chess players mentally solve chess problems. But, rather than attempting to reformulate and encode these rules in binary terms, Turing set about coming up with a 'definite method' for playing chess at the most rudimentary level. Once he had accomplished this goal, he could then try to show how this method would 'learn' from playing chess, and gradually improve in much the same way that a human chess player – that is, that the brain of a human chess player – improves.

Thus, the crux of the post-computational mechanist response to Poincaré's insistence that 'discovery is discernment, selection' was that:

1   the rules which guide the brain's choice at each stage of operating with a logical system can be stated in a precise language: viz., the language of recursion theory;
2   the 'subtlety and delicacy' of the 'cognitive heuristics' governing reasoning (see Evans 1989) is due to the fact that these rules are self-modifying and highly 'plastic'.

In other words, the complexity of human reasoning is partly a function of the heuristics governing problem-solving, and partly a function of the complexity of the domains in which these heuristics are applied (see Simon 1969b).

It is highly significant that chess served as the vehicle to work out this rapprochement between mechanism and the psychology of thinking. Interest in the psychology of chess at the turn of the century had been largely confined to the study of prodigies; hence the subjects were primarily chess masters, and the methodology strictly introspectionist (see Binet 1894, Cleveland 1907). The shift in attitudes towards the psychology of chess – from a science based on self-observation to one based on experimental paradigms – had begun prior to and entirely independent of Turing, and largely as a result of Otto Selz's work on the 'laws of cognitive activity'.

Proceeding on the basis of the Würzburg School's approach to the psychology of thinking, Selz undertook to confirm the existence of directed associations (i.e. the manner in which an *Aufgabe* influences a subject's response to a stimulus). Where Selz's particular importance for the foundations of AI lies is in his insistence that

The individual analysis of task-conditioned thought processes always shows an uninterrupted chain of both general and specific partial operations which at times cumulatively (A + B + C) and at times in a stepwise fashion (B after failure of A) impel the solution of the task. These operations are continued until a solution is found or up to a momentary or lasting renunciation of the solution.

(Simon 1982: 153)

Although Selz's writings were relatively unknown among English-speaking psychologists, the work of one of his followers, Adriaan De Groot, had an immediate and profound impact on the evolution of GPS.[13]

De Groot sought to implement Selz's ideas in an exhaustive investigation into how a broad spectrum of chess-players set about solving board problems. His primary finding was that, as Selz had outlined, such problem-solving processes are based on a linear chain of operations: a point which, as De Groot noted in the Epilogue to the English translation of *Thought and Choice in Chess* (which was published thirty years after the original Dutch publication), rendered his research highly compatible with the requirements of chess programming. As far as the foundations of AI are concerned, it is perhaps even more significant that Newell and Simon were to arrive at similar results from the complete opposite direction (i.e. from their work on the Logic Theorist), with no prior awareness of De Groot's work: a point to which they gave due prominence at the end of the 1950s.

At the outset of *Thought and Choice in Chess*, De Groot cites Selz's dictum that the psychologist's goal must be to deliver 'a complete (literally: "gapless") description of the causal connections that govern the total course of intellectual and/or motor processes' in problem solving (De Groot 1965: 13). Thus, De Groot saw his major problem as that of explaining the phenomenon of pauses in a player's reports followed by a new approach. For 'It is often during these very pauses that the most important problem transformations appear: the subject takes a "fresh look" at the entire problem' (*ibid.*: 184).

De Groot approaches this task on the basis of the fundamental assumption that thinking is an 'internal process or activity': that the 'external form' of the protocols 'provides important cues for hypothesizing on the inner, operational structure of the process, i.e., on the dynamics of the development of problem and solution, of rational choice and decision' (*ibid.*: 100). The key word here is 'cues'; according to De Groot, 'the most salient deficiency of the protocol is its *incompleteness*.' This is said to be a result of the fact that:

(i) 'Phases and/or steps in the course of the thought process remain *under the threshold* of the subject's awareness and are therefore not found in the protocol'

(ii) 'Quite often *thoughts move so quickly* that the spoken word cannot keep up with them. The subject is then either forced to skip steps or to deliberately slow down his thinking (if possible) which thereby disturbs the thought process'

(iii) '*Not all thought is immediately verbalizable* thought'.

(De Groot 1965: 81–2)

He also mentions the standard concerns that:

(iv) speaking aloud distracts from or distorts the thinking process;
(v) verbal reports are merely epiphenomena (controlled by a separate centre from that which governs problem-solving);
(vi) several external factors can influence verbal reports (ranging from *Aufgabe* and motivation, to training, distraction, fatigue and cultural background).

The picture of the mind which guides De Groot is thus one in which we *cannot* – where this use of 'cannot' is meant to be psychological – hope to capture the full range of our thoughts in the net of language: either because so much of the thinking-process is subliminal, or is too rapid or too intricate for our powers of introspection, or is simply of a nature that outstrips the present possibilities of linguistic expression. De Groot concedes to the Wundtians that, with training, it might be possible to ameliorate some of these deficiencies; but he insists that no amount of laboratory experience can enable a subject to discern all of the steps involved in problem-solving, especially those leading up to the sudden solution of a problem.

It is no surprise, then, that De Groot should have been so drawn to AI: and vice versa. For long before he had heard of algorithms, De Groot was arguing that a 'subject's thinking is considered one continuous activity that can be described as a *linear chain of operations*' (*ibid.*: 54), and that 'transitional phases have to be assumed in order to understand the progress of the thought process even though the written protocol gives no indication at all' (*ibid.*: 113). Hence he seized on the computational definition of thinking as an *effective procedure*,[14] with its corollary that programs can serve as the paradigm for what *must* occur in thinking, regardless of the subject's ability to articulate – or even be aware of – such processes.

On this modified Selzian conception of Protocol Analysis, computer models provide not just an invaluable but, in fact, a *necessary* adjunct to thinking-aloud experiments. Without them, De Groot insists, psychology could never hope to overcome the inherent limitations of introspection, and thus could never hope to explain 'moments of illumination', or to account for the mind's ability to solve problems of enormous computational complexity in a small amount of time. Given that thinking and algorithms are both 'linear chains', it follows, according to De Groot, that we can hypothesise from a program what must have been going on during the pauses in the player's mind. For there can be no such lacunae in the computer model: a program with such 'gaps' would literally grind to a halt, and the same must hold true for thinking, *given that it, too, is an effective procedure.*

This harmony between De Groot's and Newell and Simon's approach to Protocol Analysis sheds further light on the fact that AI stands in the psychologistic tradition of Mill and Helmholtz, not the introspectionist tradition of Binet and Cleveland (see Chapter 3). According to AI, a subject's verbal reports provide a fragmentary glimpse into the operations of his mind: and an essential key to the sequence of steps that must intervene between problem-orientation and solution.[15] Hence the AI-scientist's task becomes one of mapping a program onto a subject's verbal protocol in order to infer from the former 'the rules according to which his thinking actually proceeds' (see Chapter 2). For the key steps in the program – the end-results of nested sub-routines – were thought to be isomorphic with the end-results of a subject's 'unconscious cerebrations', as manifested in the subject's moves or reports. That is, given the premise that mechanical and mental procedures are both effective, it seemed straightforward to the founders of AI to argue that programs could supply the 'missing steps' in reasoning: i.e., that they could provide a model of the mind's 'inner' workings in problem-solving, and thus could explain how the 'process of incubation' leads up to a 'moment of illumination'.

It is easy to see why the role played by Protocol Analysis in early AI must have seemed such a positive development to those early cognitive scientists whose roots lay in the cognitive revolution. On the face of it, a *mechanist explanation of creativity* seems to be a contradiction in terms. This is not simply because of the way we ordinarily speak about creativity; the deeper problem is that, by its very nature, mechanism seems to exclude any concern with the *individual*, and focuses instead on the generic *organism*. But the essence of creativity seems to be that all individuals do not think in the same way: that a Mozart or a Poincaré are anomalies.

Protocol Analysis offered a compromise: a way of looking at individual variations as well as regularities. For AI was searching for a *blueprint* of creativity: a set of rules for developing rules for solving problems that had been hardwired into the brain of *Homo sapiens* (in much the same way that cognitive scientists began to speak of a 'language organ' – a set of embodied 'super-rules' which enable the child to acquire the rules of any grammar – as being part of the human birthright). Thus, AI would show how the basic heuristics which cause an infant to hypothesise, e.g., that a partially occluded object is a chair, are not intrinsically different from the heuristics which led Poincaré to his discovery of fuchsian functions (although there will, of course, be the world of difference between the specific rules and knowledge-bases of these two extremes). And what better way to test this theory than by mapping the developmental trajectory leading from chess novice to Grand Master: i.e. from rote learning to *what we call* 'creative problem-solving'.

Chess thus came to provide the founders of AI with the means of synthesising a disparate body of thought ranging from mid-nineteenth-century responses to reasoning-machines, late nineteenth-century approaches to formalism, early twentieth-century developments in the psychology of thinking, and contemporary behaviourist attitudes towards problem-solving. Moreover, chess served as an obvious medium for the explanation/simulation of those processes which a subject's mind employs when solving problems, where this was seen as a matter of grasping a problem, tentatively experimenting with various methods of solution, selecting a favoured route, and then verifying the success of the chosen means.

What made chess so suitable for this purpose was the fact that the decision-making procedures leading up to a move are ideal for hierarchical recursive analysis: a player thinks through a problem by shuttling back and forth between sub- and primary goals as she formulates a plan, calculates the permutations, deduces whether any of these will implement the strategy she has in mind, and – if none of these succeeds in realising the overall goal – formulates a new plan and repeats the process.[16] Most important of all was the fact that chess afforded the perfect environment in which to map out the goal-directed pattern of the processes involved in problem-solving in a fixed domain, given the prior assumption that these processes must be *effective procedures*.

To be sure, the resulting models may be far removed from anything one might encounter in ordinary chess play; or, for that matter, in De Groot's verbal protocols. But as far as AI was concerned, the fact that we may not be aware of such processes is merely a confirmation of the limitations of introspection, not a reason to question the epistemological underpinnings of AI. Indeed, the AI position is even stronger than this suggests; for the key to Newell and Simon's explanation of the 'mystery of creativity' is that *we could not be aware* of the 'preconscious-processes' leading up to a 'moment of insight'. Certainly, the actual details of their theory seemed to bear this out.

§4 GPS and the assault on 'insight'

The task facing Newell and Simon was clear: if problem-solving is to be treated as the paradigm of thinking – or indeed, the core of all thinking – and if the atomic steps of a program must be such that they presuppose no intelligence, then neither can they presuppose insight. Yet the creativity and originality characteristic of thinking must somehow emerge from a program if it is to simulate human problem-solving. Hence Newell and Simon had to establish that 'novelty in problem solving comes about through ordinary

138

thought processes in interaction with the information available in the problem', and that 'there is no need to postulate a special process called insight' (Weisberg 1988: 155–6). In other words, Newell and Simon had to establish that there is nothing particularly *creative* about creativity: at least, not in the sense that we've been led to expect by Romantic myths.

Underlying Newell and Simon's view of problem-solving is a Darwinian picture of how the hominid brain evolved from the small organ possessed by *Australopithecus afarensis* – which must have had quite limited problem-solving capabilities – to the large and powerful brain of *Homo sapiens*. As Simon puts it, 'A human being is able to think because, by biological inheritance and exposure to a stream of experience in the external world, he has acquired a program that is effective for guiding thought processes. If we wish to seek an efficient cause for his behavior, it lies in that program in its interaction with ongoing stimuli' (Simon 1966a: 283). On this picture, the development of the hominid brain should not simply be seen in terms of size, or even of the enlargement of certain higher-order structures (such as the pre-frontal cortex). Instead, it should be seen as an evolution in the *information-processing design* of the primate brain. Organisms which, perhaps because of some mutation, acquired a more effective problem-solving program than their conspecifics would have bestowed a selective advantage on their offspring. Whether this process occurred gradually, or was one of 'punctuated equilibrium', it must have been the case that information-processing mechanisms which rely on fundamental heuristics to assign weightings were built up over the span of five million years.

The notion of informational complexity does not in itself, however, entail a computational view of cognitive heuristics. In order to get to the AI analysis of creativity, Newell and Simon had to introduce a quite specific picture of problem-solving as

> a process of searching through a tree (perhaps more precisely, a *directed graph*) whose nodes are states of affairs, or situations, and whose branches are operations that transform one situation into another. The graph contains a starting node and one or more goal nodes (alternatively, a test to determine whether any given node is a goal). To solve a problem is to find a sequence of operations that transforms the starting situation into a goal situation – that is, a path from the starting node to a goal node.
>
> (Simon 1972: 214)

Thus, according to GPS, problem-solving is rather like finding one's way through a maze in which we know where we are starting from, and approximately where to end up, but have no clear idea as to how to get there. You cannot get from a to ω without going through β,γ,δ . . . ; the very notion that a and ω lie on a continuous plane seems to demand this. But when it would require 10^{95} years just to compute the first move on a brute force approach, it is clear that some process must be involved that enables us to bypass trivial intermediary steps and go directly from a to β, if not from a to ξ.

Both the search rules which Newell and Simon developed, and the weighted tree structures on which these were supposed to operate, were directly culled from chess programming. Thus, on one heuristic, the mind/program proceeds from any given node to search the sub-branch with the highest value, while on the other heuristic, the mind/program erases nodes as soon as sub-nodes have been generated, and then proceeds to the next node of highest value. But, unfortunately, problems rarely come equipped with 'pre-weighted nodes'. In fact, the gifted thinker is distinguished by her ability to find – and forge – connections that no one else has seen: to explore undetected possibilities, whether this be in terms of discovering new methods for solving familiar problems, or discovering entirely new and significant problems.

Newell and Simon's response to this objection was that all discovery is the (possibly fortuitous) result of:

- applying established heuristics in new situations;
- modifying these heuristics to generate novel solutions;
- activating some form of random choice generator.

All that is needed to implement these possibilities is some form of program capable of reassigning node weightings, restructuring trees, and/or creating entirely new trees: perhaps *ab ovo*, perhaps by bridging what were previously regarded as disparate trees (see Simon 1972).

One can easily appreciate the appeal of chess for GPS. Chess provides the classic example of how a strategy must be built up which takes as its starting-point a single goal-state with nested sub-goals, whose weightings will be a function of their importance in the overall scheme. That is, a search tree for which the basic problem is how to get from a to ω as quickly (in as few moves) as possible. Chess thus constitutes the paradigm 'well-defined problem': there is a clearly-demarcated goal-state from the start, a predefined problem-space, stable transformation rules, and a combinatorial explosion of sufficient dimensions that the success of a program depends on the construction of a look-ahead approach that selects the most promising move from the multiple options available at every step, can alter its search depth according to the demands of each new situation, and can abandon or modify previously adopted sub-goals. Moreover, the nature of the tree is such that we can compute the 'heuristic power' of whatever procedure is adopted (in terms of the amount of search-time required as measured against the problem-solving effectiveness which it yields).

Chess programs are also capable of storing successful strategies and drawing on this constantly growing knowledge-base in new situations. The AI view of short-term memory thus comes into play here: viz., although STM may be confined to approximately seven pieces of information, this can refer to chunks as much as singular items. By 'chunking', 'a total structure of unlimited size can be assembled without the need for holding more than a few symbols in immediate memory at any given moment' (Simon 1966a: 295). Incubation, leading up to illumination, can then be explained in terms of 'selective forgetting'. In her first runs at a problem, a subject builds up ever more complex circuits through the problem-space that are stored in chunks. These chunks serve as the starting-point for subsequent attempts to solve the problem. Eventually, given sufficiently powerful maps, the problem-solver will experience what, in folk psychology, is referred to as 'a moment of illumination'.

The obvious question this argument raises is: How do we get from this highly formalised situation to a conception of problem-solving *simpliciter*? First, great emphasis must be placed on the fact that chess is an 'interactional activity': i.e. that an opponent's moves always have to be taken into account. On this basis, the AI scientist can hope to simulate the 'ill-structured' character of real-life problem-solving: the fact that problems are continually changing as new factors are introduced, or that, in many instances, the most one can strive for is a 'best possible position'. Furthermore, the notion of checkmate – or more generally, of discovery – must be broadened so as to prevent the argument from collapsing into a form of Platonism (which assumes that for all problems there exists a pre-defined solution waiting to be discovered). Hence the 'goal' for problem-solving *per se* must be defined in larger terms: e.g., as some form of deep-seated biological drive to persist in working at a problem, well beyond the point of what, for another species (e.g. an ape) would constitute a satisfactory 'solution'.

GPS thus represents an intriguing attempt to meld a mechanist analysis of 'creativity' with a Calvinist view of problem-solving. On the one hand, we can explain the differing abilities of problem-solvers (child versus adult, low versus high I.Q., etc.), up to and including genius, in terms of structural features (e.g., the size of a subject's knowledge base, or the more sophisticated programs embodied in her brain). But a place has also been reserved for effort; for the individual who abandons her attempt to solve a difficult problem at too early a stage will not have built up a sufficiently advanced search-procedure from which to advance much further on a subsequent attempt (rather like someone who sets aside a difficult crossword puzzle after failing to solve any of the clues, and finds himself unable to advance any further on a later try).

GPS seemed to offer a promising vantage-point from which to view certain aspects of creativity, such as the role that plans or heuristics play in problem-solving (although whether 'plans' or 'heuristics' are to be construed in computational terms is one of the central issues of this chapter). Yet the theory nonetheless attracted a great deal of criticism. To begin with, there were those who were sympathetic to Newell and Simon's computational paradigm, but worried about the various heuristics which they employed, and the weight they attached to *means–ends analysis* and *satisficing*. Within this camp, there were those who questioned their model of short- and long-term memory, and even the information-processing mechanisms which they postulated (viz., *familiarising* and *selective forgetting*). Then there were those who wished to see a paradigm-revolution within the computational framework, and thus challenged their serial/hierarchical approach. There were the psychologists of a different stripe who worried that GPS leaves no room for motivation or personality traits in the study of creativity. There were the humanists who saw this as a challenge and a threat to the sovereignty of the human imagination. And, of course, philosophers who saw in all this a return to the Homunculus Fallacy.

To this list might be added the worry that the argument either says too much, or else, not enough. Too much, because we are presented with a picture of discovery as a mental state that is the end-result of pre-conscious processes which a subject could not be (directly) aware of. And not enough, because creative thinking has been reduced to creative problem-solving; and, worse still, nothing has been said about the originality and unpredictability of discovery. For that matter, nothing has been said about the creative individual's desire to break rules, or to create new rules.

What is disturbing here is *not* the idea that, regardless of whether or not subjects are aware of the fact, a heuristic such as means–ends analysis might be evident in their problem-solving behaviour (i.e., that we might discover through protocol analysis that, in certain situations, subjects invariably demonstrate a distinctive strategy for solving a problem, testing its effectiveness, and formulating a new plan on the basis of its resulting shortcomings). What is worrying is rather the idea that we – that our brains – do this at a level that *could not* be accessed: and, further, that we do so according to the dictates laid down by recursion theory. And on the other hand there is the worry that the argument does not say enough, because, far from explaining what insight – as 'ordinarily understood' – consists in, it merely shifts the problem to a lower level, or else abandons insight altogether.[17]

To see exactly what the point under consideration is, we need first to clarify what it is not. To begin with, there is no reason to challenge the idea that invention is a rule-governed activity, or to dismiss the possibility of devising self-modifying algorithms that are capable of generating significant discoveries (*pace* BACON or Lenat's AM). There is no reason to object to the heavy reliance on trial-and-error in such generative procedures (although it is somewhat worrying to see what an orderly affair this becomes on computational models). There is no reason to deny the importance of psychological investigations into the causal factors influencing insight, or to confine such investigations to autobiographical sources. And, finally, there is no reason to deny that much of the process of discovery may be mechanical; nor is there any reason to follow Wertheimer in the charge that drill only serves to destroy creativity. On the contrary, part of the significance of training may well lie in the fact that this enables us to execute many of the basic tasks involved in problem-solving automatically, thereby freeing the mind for larger concerns.

But Newell and Simon's argument goes much further. On their account, whatever is involved in the process of creation – from *preparation* through *incubation* to *illumination* and *verification* – must be such that it can be mechanically simulated: i.e. must be such that it can be explained in terms which satisfy Turing's Thesis. Hence insight must be completely removed from a computational theory of creativity. For no one is about to attribute a special process of insight to chess programs, and neither, according to Newell and Simon, should we think that this 'vacuous concept' plays an explanatory role in psychology proper. From this perspective, one can appreciate how, for pre-computational psychologists, creativity would have seemed a mystery that invites Romantic myths about the mind's ability to *leap across gaps*. But a brain is a brain: it must solve problems [*sic*] one step at a time. Thus, GPS does not enable us to solve the mystery of creativity by providing us with a tool for bridging these 'gaps'. Instead, GPS removes all 'gaps' – and thus any need for 'insight' – from the mystery of creative reasoning.

What is most worrying about this argument is how, in true mechanist fashion, it forces us to bracket insight – and, indeed, creativity itself – in inverted commas. Thus, statements such as 'In a moment of insight, S saw how to solve the problem' are seen as saying nothing more than: 'S's brain did something to get from a to ω, but what that might have been is, at the present time, unknown'. Remove this reductionist starting point, however, and we are left with a very different question: Does GPS amount to anything more than a method for automating problem-solving procedures? Or, perhaps, a method for creating problem-solving procedures such as can be automated? Indeed, we might even ask: Does GPS really *remove*, or does it rather *presuppose*, insight?

At the level at which Newell and Simon's argument is operating, the questions that most need to be answered are:

1 how does the program decide how to (re)assign node weightings or to create new search trees?
2 how does the program decide which branches offer the most promising routes to discovery?

3 how does the program avoid storing unlimited amounts of useless information, since, presumably, the value of a selection is contingent on the
completion of a solution?

4 and most important of all, how does the program decide what constitutes a problem, let alone what constitutes a solution to that problem?

Do not each of these decisions – which the programmer must build in –
depend in some basic way on insight?

But even this way of presenting the problem is misleading; for it buys
into Newell and Simon's fundamental presupposition that problem-solving
is a mental process of searching through a tree. This already severely limits
the kinds of questions that one can ask about insight. But what about the
many different ways in which insight may be involved in the solution of a
problem? As Sternberg has shown, sometimes the great scientific insights
are simply that a problem is significant; sometimes that an existing problem
can be redefined in such a way that, not only can it be solved, but the solution opens up an entirely new domain of research; and sometimes what
really matters is the novel tool or technique that is created (see Sternberg
1988a). On rare occasions, such as in the case of Gödel's incompleteness
theorem, it can be all of the above (see Shanker 1988a).

Weisberg argues convincingly that many of the famous stories about leaps
of insight (such as that told about Darwin's discovery of the theory of
natural selection) can actually be shown to have proceeded in a systematic
manner which, for various reasons, the subject may not have been aware of,
or might have conveniently forgotten (Weisberg 1986). But, as Gruber has
meticulously demonstrated, the fact that Darwin did not discover the theory
of natural selection in a single flash does not entail that he did go through a
long creative process which led up to his great '"Malthusian insight", the
moment when, on September 28, 1838, he read the *Essay on Population* and
recognized the force of the idea of evolution through natural selection'
(Gruber 1981a: 7).

What Weisberg is saying is that we tend to romanticise stories of
discovery by overlooking prosaic details about the creative process. But this
important point is categorially different from the computational thesis; for
the argument that discovery is 'a long growth process', and that we often use
the term 'insight' to refer to 'the emotion of thought, to the surge of joy and
dread, excitement and fulfillment whenever the thinking person closes the
loop and discovers what he has done' (Weisberg 1986), is not at all the same
thing as Newell and Simon's premise that the notion of 'insight' as ordinarily understood not only has no bearing on, but is an actual obstacle to,
our understanding of 'creativity'.

Moreover, we use the term 'insight' to refer to a great deal more than just
the 'emotion of thought' (*ibid.*: 6). As Sternberg points out, we use it to refer
to a subject's abilities to:

- pick out the salient and ignore the irrelevant information in a problem
- seize on just the right way to combine information
- bring together diverse kinds of information (Sternberg 1988a).

Weisberg dismisses this argument as merely serving to isolate 'a mode of thinking that could be called insight' (Weisberg 1988: 169). Even if that were Sternberg's intention – and it is difficult to see what would actually be wrong with this idea – that is still not to treat insight as a *hidden mental process*. But, in fact, Sternberg wants to show how many different ways we speak about insight (see Sternberg 1988a). Or, indeed, the many different methods that have been proposed by psychologists to study the many different aspects of insight that are involved in getting a joke, or a pun; understanding a dream, or a painting, or a string quartet; grasping someone's motives, or seeing that they are lying; having an insight into one's own personality, or the meaning of life, or the nature of philosophy, and so on.

All of this goes missing on GPS. For that matter, GPS does not even seem able to account for the insight involved in rote problem-solving – e.g., for the moment of insight that comes to every student of geometry when the significance of a proof suddenly crystallises; or, indeed, for the insight which can occur when a student suddenly grasps the 'point' of an algorithm. Newell and Simon's strategy for dealing with these issues was to argue that 'processes that occur in human problem solving can be compounded out of elementary information processes, and hence . . . can be carried out by mechanisms' (Newell *et al.* 1958: 152). That is, however narrow the domain that applies to current models of discovery, the very fact that we can devise programs capable of delivering novel results proves that there is no *a priori* reason why AI should not one day be able to provide a comprehensive analysis of 'insight'. Thus, the immediate demand on computational theories is merely to show that insight does not remain a mysterious process residing at the atomic level of a program; the more exotic manifestations of 'insight' can be expected to succumb to computational analysis in due course.

Herein lies the explanation for what should be a very troubling question. Once again, we are confronted with the puzzling fact that the founders of the cognitive revolution should have embraced a theory with such pronounced mechanist and reductionist overtones. The attraction of the computational thesis *vis-à-vis* the problem of creativity seems simple enough to explain. Cognitive and educational psychologists at the time were profoundly interested in devising programmes that would best inculcate creative thinking. But then, how can one study something like the effects of competition on creativity, or the relative importance of intrinsic versus extrinsic motivation for creative thinking, unless one can first operationalize the concept of creativity? The last thing that these psychologists wanted, however, was to get bogged down in the aesthetic debates over the nature of creativity that have occupied the greatest philosophical minds for the past two millennia. Hence the strong appeal of AI; for it promised a working definition of creativity that would at least allow psychologists to get on with the business of designing their experiments.

The problem was, there is simply no logical space to ask questions about motivation or personality or effort in regard to a computer program. And the same point must, in light of the computational thesis, apply to creative human problem-solving. Questions about motivation, or personality, or attitude, must, like questions about 'insight' – or, indeed, 'creativity' – be reduced to mechanist terms. Thus, the issues that most concerned cognitive and educational psychologists were relegated to tangential issues regarding the causal factors affecting human problem-solving, in much the same way that one might speak, e.g., about the effect which the speed of the processor has on the running of a chess program.

We are clearly dealing with two very different pictures of creativity here: viz., a Romantic picture of the creative process, and a Cartesian picture of the mental process of creativity. The question is: do these two pictures represent – as AI claims – *rival theories of creativity* (i.e. a 'folk' theory versus a rigorously empirical theory)? Or do they rather represent entirely different ways of conceptualising creativity, and thus, raise different sorts of questions and call for different kinds of explanation of what we call creative thinking? Indeed, we might go still further and ask: does the Cartesian picture of creativity, which, as we shall see, underpins the computational thesis, exclude the very sorts of questions that lie at the heart of the cognitive revolution? Our task in the remainder of this chapter will be to look more closely at these issues, and thence, the reasons why the cognitive revolution was led down the path of mechanist reductionism.

§5 Converse responses to Köhler

In his 1959 Presidential address to the American Psychological Association, Köhler bemoaned the lack of influence that Gestalt psychology was having on the study of perception and learning theory in America. But, in point of fact, the impact of Gestalt psychology had only just begun, albeit in ways totally foreign to Köhler's intentions. For although Köhler's work on field theory was soon forgotten, his early writings on animal intelligence and the nature of insight played a key role in the evolution of AI.

The conception of problem-solving that Köhler developed in *The Mentality of Apes* was the culmination of developments in the psychology of thinking at the beginning of the century. *Denkpsychologie* had seen problem-solving as consisting in a tension between a goal and what is given, with the mind actively searching for a way to overcome this conflict. Köhler brought to this outlook his famous investigations into the phenomenon of insight as demonstrated by chimpanzees in the solution of simple problems.

146

Köhler's initial task in *The Mentality of Apes* is to convince the reader that the 'thoughtful' behaviour of the apes he had observed in Tenerife differed categorially from the frantic movements of the cats which Thorndike had enclosed in his puzzle boxes. In case after case, Köhler recounts how there was invariably a stage in his experiments in which the animal would cease its random efforts to obtain some fruit, quietly reflect on the situation, and then proceed to solve the problem in what Köhler describes as a 'smooth, continuous course, sharply divided by an abrupt break from the preceding behaviour' (Köhler 1925: 189). From this evidence he concludes that not even primitive forms of thinking can be satisfactorily explained on the crude associationist model which behaviourism had co-opted.[18]

Köhler takes great pains to clarify that he was not resorting to 'vital forces' to explain the apes' behaviour (*ibid.*: 102). But he also insists that the phenomenon of insight cannot be explained 'mechanically', simply because the processes of 'organization' underlying insight are far too complex to be accommodated on an S-R model (see Köhler 1947: 36). That is not to say, however, that insight cannot be explained 'dynamically', once the processes of the visual system are understood.

Köhler spells this idea out in the chapter on 'The Making of Implements'. He first describes a case where Sultan could only obtain a clump of fruit by joining two sticks together. Köhler emphasises that 'It is astonishing to note how, apparently, the "optics" of the situation is decisive for the animal' (Köhler 1925: 125). He concludes that 'to understand the [problem-solving] capacities and mistakes of chimpanzees in visually given situations is quite impossible without a theory of visual functions' (*ibid.*: 131). Insight, he feels, should not be seen as the end-result of hidden *cognitive* processes (i.e. 'unconscious inferences') but, rather, as the end-result of *physical* processes, the nature of which it would be up to future psychologists, working in close harmony with physiologists, to discover (see Köhler 1947: Chapter X).

The last impression Köhler wants to give is that he is succumbing to the fallacy of anthropomorphism (Köhler 1925: 17). Thus he cautions that he does not 'wish to affirm that a chimpanzee picks up a stick and says to himself, as it were (for speech is definitely beyond his powers): "All right, now I'm going to dig roots"' (*ibid.*: 78). He is even more explicit about this point in *Gestalt Psychology*, insisting that

> When I once used this expression [viz. 'insight'] in a description of the intelligent behavior of apes, an unfortunate misunderstanding was, it seems, not entirely prevented. Sometimes the animals were found to be capable of achievements which we had not expected to occur below the human level. It was then stated that such accomplishments clearly involved insight. Apparently, some readers interpreted this formulation as though it referred to a mysterious mental agent or faculty which was made responsible for the apes'

behavior. Actually, nothing of this sort was intended when I wrote my report.

(Köhler 1947: 200)

With the help of the argument presented in *Gestalt Psychology*, we can see that what Köhler is driving at in *The Mentality of Apes* is the idea that, given that 'visual experience corresponds to the totality of self-distributed processes in the visual sector of the brain' (*ibid.*: 126), the primitive sense in which chimpanzees can be said to *think* refers to the neural resolution of 'optical confusion' (Köhler 1925: 261). Thus, the pauses in an animal's behaviour manifest the critical stage in its perceptual experience in which its disjointed images suddenly begin to coalesce (see Köhler 1947: 260).

It was this argument which, as far as contemporary psychologists of thinking were concerned, separated *The Mentality of Apes* from the work of Romanes or Yerkes. For it was widely felt at the time that what was most needed was not a further demonstration *that* animals can think, but some indication of *what* such thinking consists in. Thus, the significance of *The Mentality of Apes* was seen as lying, not in Köhler's documentation of intelligent animal behaviour, but, rather, in his blueprint for a psycho-physical theory of insight.[19]

We have already seen how this was very much the problem that was at the forefront of Newell and Simon's mind when they developed GPS. Yet, far from seeking to resolve this issue on Köhler's visual grounds, they proposed to resurrect the theory of 'unconscious inference' which Köhler had assailed in his earliest major article, 'On Unnoticed Sensations and Errors of Judgment'. In fact, Köhler's theory of insight provided the jumping-off point for GPS in more ways than one. For Köhler's findings on problem-solving behaviour were quickly incorporated into the design of GPS (cf. Newell 1983: 207). Köhler had also ensured that any successful explanation of the mechanics of problem-solving would have to account for the goal-directed character of thinking, and, in so doing, would have to explain the phenomenon of insight on which he had based his critique of trial-and-error learning.

As far as AI was concerned, the need for a reductionist analysis of insight had been obvious from the start; for the whole point of the Lovelace–Gödel objection (see Chapter 1) was that a machine could never simulate the creative processes that occur in human thought (or, as Poincaré put it, the 'leap of intuition' upon which mathematical discovery depends). But even though mathematicians and psychologists were concerned with what was ultimately the same problem, there is little sign of any interaction between them before the time of the Second World War. If anything, the two disciplines had proceeded in the opposite direction, with mathematicians searching for ever more recherché problems that could not be proved in formal systems, while psychologists debated

148

whether primitive examples of problem-solving behaviour could be explained in mechanical terms.

Newell and Simon were the first to recognise that, from a mechanist point of view, the latter problem established the perfect framework for answering the former. Hence we get the argument that, if the simplest acts of insight could be mechanically simulated, then there is no *a priori* reason why AI should not climb the cognitive scale of problem-solving abilities, given that, as Newell *et al.* explained at the outset of one of their earliest papers on GPS, 'creative thinking is simply a special kind of problem-solving behaviour' (Newell *et al.* 1959: 3).

Newell and Simon were confident that 'we would have a satisfactory theory of creative thought if we could design and build some mechanism that could think creatively (exhibit behavior just like that of a human carrying on creative activity), and if we could state the general principles on which the mechanisms were built and operated' (*ibid.*: 2). To be sure, they were not about to predict the imminent simulation of 'activities like [the] discovery of the special theory of relativity or [the] composition of Beethoven's Seventh Symphony'. Nevertheless, they maintained that 'the success already achieved in synthesizing mechanisms that solve difficult problems in the same manner as humans is beginning to provide a theory of problem solving that is highly specific and operational' (*ibid.*). For all that was really needed was a mechanical procedure for solving problems as simple as how to obtain an object out of one's reach by joining two sticks together.

It goes without saying that Newell and Simon responded that the problem with Köhler's attack on mechanist theories of creativity lay in the pre-computational paradigm that he was addressing. And not without some justification. For there is little substantial difference between Köhler's conception of 'dynamically self-regulating systems' and cybernetic systems. Indeed, Köhler's attack on behaviourism foreshadows the argument that Rosenbleuth *et al.* presented in 'Behavior, Purpose and Teleology' (1943). Köhler argues that

> The right psychological formula is therefore: *pattern of stimulation–organization–response* to *the products of organization*. The operations of the nervous system are by no means restricted to primitive local processes; it is not a box in which conductors with separate functions are somehow put together. It responds to a situation, first, by dynamic sensory events which are peculiar to it as a system, i.e., by organization, and then by behavior which depends upon the results of the organization.
>
> (Köhler 1947: 97)

Newell and Simon had no quarrel with this argument as far as behaviourism was concerned; their objection was rather with what they saw as Köhler's failure to recognise that such 'processes of organization' must display their own internal logic, which, according to Newell and Simon, is computational.

Newell and Simon concluded that, far from undermining Helmholtz's theory of 'unconscious inference', Köhler's argument can actually be used to validate it. For Köhler had not questioned the premise that agents are unaware of the processes that occur during the crucial incubation period preceding the solution of a problem. His objection to the theory of the 'cognitive unconscious' was solely that it had placed too high a demand on existing mechanist models. Köhler's major shortcoming, therefore, was simply that he was unaware of the computational power that had been unleashed by Turing's thesis.

Wittgenstein also confronted Köhler over his attack on the 'cognitive unconscious', but from a completely different direction. The crux of Wittgenstein's critique hinges on the point that Köhler was not questioning Helmholtz's premise that insight (or perception) is the *end-result of unconscious processes*: only that these processes are inferential. Indeed, it was chiefly in response to Köhler's analysis of insight that Wittgenstein was led to formulate his notorious complaint that

> The confusion and barrenness of psychology is not to be explained by calling it a 'young science'; its state is not comparable with that of physics, for instance, in its beginnings. (Rather with that of certain branches of mathematics. Set theory.) For in psychology there are experimental methods and *conceptual confusion*. (As in the other case conceptual confusion and methods of proof.)
>
> The existence of the experimental method makes us think we have the means of solving the problems which trouble us; though problem and method pass one another by.
>
> (PI: 232)

Such a blanket indictment should not be treated lightly: not just because it is unclear whether Wittgenstein had read sufficiently widely to warrant such a sweeping generalisation, but, even more to the point, because the sentiments expressed here were far from novel. This is probably the reason why the uproar which one might have expected from this severe allegation never materialised. On the contrary, Wittgenstein's censure was greeted as confirming the significance of the post-computational revolution. In George's words, Wittgenstein's

> criticism of experimental psychology, at the time it was made, [was] almost entirely justified. Experimental psychologists were, at that time, struggling to unscramble their concepts and clarify their language and models: at worst they believed that as long as a well-

controlled experiment was carried out, the mere accumulation of facts would make a science. The relation, so vital to the development of psychology, between experimental results, by way of interpretation and explanatory frameworks, models, used largely to be neglected.

In fact, much of this conceptual confusion has now disappeared.

(George 1970: 21–2)

On this reading, what Wittgenstein was objecting to under the heading of 'conceptual confusion' was the lack of a comprehensive theoretical framework that could assimilate the fragmentary data yielded by Protocol Analysis. But then, the cognitivist sees the mechanist paradigm that Wittgenstein was attacking as having been fundamentally displaced by Turing's version of Church's Thesis, and speaking-aloud experiments as having been radically supplemented by computer models. Thus George concludes that Wittgenstein's objections are historically dated; for 'Almost everyone now acknowledges that theory and experiment, model making, theory construction and linguistics all go together, and that the successful development of a science of behavior depends upon a "total approach"' in which, given that the computer 'is the only large-scale universal model' that we possess, 'we may expect to follow the prescription of Simon and construct our models – or most of them – in the form of computer programs' (*ibid.*: 22).

George is relying on the classic two-fold division – which is seemingly along Wittgenstein's own lines – that the experimental psychologist tests theories while the 'pure' psychologist constructs them. To be sure, George is not about to suggest that Wittgenstein was engaged in the latter activity. But he sees the elimination of conceptual confusion as a key element in theory-construction. Thus, he regards Wittgenstein's strictures against the creation of philosophical theories as something of an eccentricity; for there is no *a priori* reason why the philosopher's activities should be confined in such a manner, and, in any event, the eradication of conceptual confusion is an essential step in the development of new theories. Hence, Wittgenstein can be seen as an important, albeit reluctant, participant in the evolution of AI, in so far as he exposed the conceptual confusions undermining introspectionism, behaviourism and Gestalt psychology.

The basic problem with such an interpretation is that it disregards Wittgenstein's insistence that the failings of experimental psychology to which he was drawing attention are 'not to be explained by calling it a "young science".' And it overlooks Wittgenstein's frequent admonition that what he was doing was philosophy *as opposed to* psychology. In the above attack on experimental psychology, Wittgenstein goes on to explain that: 'An investigation is possible in connexion with mathematics which is entirely analogous to our investigation of psychology. It is just as little a *mathematical* investigation as the other is a psychological one' (PI: 232).

In one sense, Wittgenstein's point is clear: the philosopher's sole concern is with logical, not technical or empirical issues (see GWL: 341). And just as the philosophy of mathematics cannot intrude into the affairs of mathematics proper, so, too, the philosophy of psychology cannot overstep its legitimate bounds (cf. Shanker 1987a: chapter V). But, of course, that still leaves us with the problem of identifying the nature of those parameters; and until this issue has been resolved, we cannot expect AI-theorists to be deeply troubled by Wittgenstein's insistence that 'The phenomena are not hidden; the concept is hidden. And the concept is surrounded by others. It occurs in a field and its relations give us trouble' (GWL: 247). But our chief concern in the following section is with the more immediate question of whether Wittgenstein's response to Köhler's theory of insight has any bearing on GPS.

§6 The relevance of Wittgenstein's remarks on Köhler for GPS

> Observing an animal, e.g. an ape that investigates an object and tears it to pieces, one may say: 'You see that something is going on in him.' How remarkable that is! But not more remarkable than that we say: love, conviction, are in our hearts!
>
> (RPP I)

Wittgenstein's remarks on thinking are central to his later writings in the philosophy of psychology, and somewhat atypical, in that, although the targets of his objections are generally cloaked in anonymity, there are frequent explicit references and easily discerned allusions to introspectionist, behaviourist and Gestalt theories. This enables us to see that, even if he had not read widely in the area, Wittgenstein was certainly familiar with the major positions in contemporary debates in the psychology of thinking. Thus, Wittgenstein takes us through discussions of:

- the elementarist dogma that, with training, one can perceive the workings of one's own mind, or at least, the 'mental states' which are the end-result of hidden inferential processes (RPP I: §§564f);
- James's discussion of 'wordless thought', and his argument that a thought is already complete before one describes it in a sentence (*ibid.*: §173, RPP II: §§183, 213);
- the behaviourist claim that 'thinking' is nothing more than talking to oneself (RPP I: §578, RPP II: §§8ff);
- Köhler's hypothesis that thinking and perceiving involve a form of cognitive/neurophysiological 'restructuring'.

The significance of these investigations goes far beyond the realm of the exegetical. While allowing us to see the depth of Wittgenstein's reading, they also invite the response that, as enlightening as Wittgenstein's remarks might be as a commentary on the history of experimental psychology, they have little relevance for AI. And nowhere could this problem be more pronounced than in regard to Wittgenstein's insistence that 'The confusion and barrenness of psychology is not to be explained by calling it a "young science"' (PI: 232).

The immediate problem which confronts us here is not so much to defend Wittgenstein's attack on experimental psychology as to understand its basis; for the very fact that, despite all his efforts to avoid such a misreading, Wittgenstein could still be seen as – and even applauded for – engaging in armchair psychology, is proof of just how intractable are the issues involved. The key to clarifying Wittgenstein's intentions in this widely quoted passage is to see this remark, not as an attack on prevailing experimental models and methods, but, rather, as a direct response to Köhler's reflections on the current – lamentable – state of psychology (see Köhler 1947: Chapter II). In the chapter entitled 'Psychology as a Young Science', Köhler argues that:

> At the present time [the methods which the psychologist employs] seem to be problems in themselves rather than aids for the solution of psychological problems. . . . Why does this difficulty beset psychology while it does not seem to exist in physics? The answer is simple enough: physics is an old science, and psychology is in its infancy.
>
> *(Ibid.: 27)*

It would not have been enough for Wittgenstein to have countered this argument with the bald statement that the problem with experimental psychology is not that it is in its early stages but, rather, that it contains conceptual confusions; for that was exactly what Köhler meant by calling psychology 'young'. Köhler felt that, like the early natural scientists, the pioneers of psychology had resorted to a metaphysical notion – viz., 'unconscious judgement' – in order to explain perception and problem-solving. But the Logical Positivists had established that there could be no more compelling proof of a burgeoning science's infancy than its resorting to metaphysical notions in place of verifiable processes. Thus, if psychology was to catch up with physics, it must rid itself of these 'conceptual confusions' (see Köhler 1947).

Far from overlooking this dimension of Köhler's argument, it was this very issue that Wittgenstein was addressing: *not* because he wished to lend any support to the theory of the 'cognitive unconscious' but, instead, because he felt that Köhler was attacking Helmholtz's theory on the wrong grounds. Indeed, it is clear that Wittgenstein's criticisms of Köhler, the theory of the 'cognitive unconscious', and experimental psychology in general, all stem from one and the same source.

The basis for the parallel which Köhler draws between physics and psychology is that, like the introspectionist psychologists to whom he was so opposed, Köhler construed the question 'What is thinking?' as being closely akin to the question 'What is digestion?'. In Wittgenstein's words, Köhler held that

> we know in general what [digestion] means, we want to be given a detailed account of what goes on when this process which we understand in a rough way occurs: we want more detail, the detailed working of the mechanism. 'What is thinking?' is similar in verbal form to 'What is digestion?' The answer is a matter of X-rays, clinical tests, etc., a matter of experimental procedure. Is this so with 'What is thinking?'
>
> (GWL: 236)

By responding affirmatively to this last question, Köhler was led to assume that 'The experimental method does *something*: its failure to solve the problem is blamed on its still being in its beginnings. It is as if one were to try and determine what matter and spirit are by chemical experiments' (RPP I: §1093).

Wittgenstein's criticism of experimental psychology at PI p. 232 can thus be seen as both an explicit response to the conception of thinking which underlies Köhler's argument in 'Psychology as a Young Science', and an implicit attack on Köhler's conception of how one goes about answering questions concerned with the nature of thinking. For Köhler's analysis of insight proceeds from the premise that ' "Thinking is an enigmatic process, and we are a long way off from complete understanding of it." And now one starts experimenting. Evidently without realizing *what* it is that makes thinking enigmatic to us' (RPP I: §1093). But then, this picture of the 'experimental method' has constituted the cornerstone of the psychology of thinking over the past century. And it is for precisely this reason that Wittgenstein's discussion of Köhler is not just a matter of considerable interest for the history of psychology, or for the exegesis of Wittgenstein's writings on the philosophy of psychology, but for the foundations of AI as well.

Köhler's criticisms of behaviourism and introspectionism stem from his Cartesian picture of the mind. Both behaviourism and introspectionism, according to Köhler, were led to distort the nature of the hidden processes involved in cognition: the former because it was working with too crude a model of the mind, and the latter because it was working without any serious model. But Köhler never questioned the fundamental premise that there must be some form of 'organisation' underlying conscious mental states. Thus, he presents a model of thinking which is based on a homeostatic system whose functional architecture determines how it responds to the welter of signals with which it is bombarded.

At the foundational level at which Wittgenstein's critique proceeds, the fact that Köhler ties this 'organisation' into the operations of the visual cortex is beside the point; all that matters is that Köhler illustrates the problems which result when, as Wittgenstein told his students, 'we compare "I think" with the wrong paradigm, e.g. with "I eat"' (GWL: 48). What Wittgenstein was thinking of here was the significance of the fact that 'eating' summons forth an explanation of the processes that occur during digestion. Not only had Köhler approached *thinking* as just this sort of dynamic activity, but he carried over exactly the same picture of the underlying processes involved. And this was because he construed thinking (and perceiving) as '*certain definite* mental processes [which] . . . seem to take place in a queer kind of medium, the mind; and the mechanism of the mind, the nature of which, it seems, we don't quite understand, can bring about effects which no material mechanism could' (BB: 3).

Having said that Köhler's conception of the mind is Cartesian, it is important to bear in mind that there was no end of psychologists for whom the same could have been said. But it was never Wittgenstein's practice to criticise an individual simply because he or she might illustrate some conceptual confusion in their thinking. So, given the amount of attention that he devotes to Köhler's writings – and in particular, to *The Mentality of Apes* – it is clearly incumbent on us to identify what Wittgenstein found so significant or instructive there.

To understand the full weight that Wittgenstein attached to Köhler's work, we need to look at the context in which he speaks of *The Mentality of Apes* in his 1946–7 *Lectures on the Philosophy of Psychology*. This occurs in the midst of a discussion on 'calculating in the head', in which Wittgenstein is talking about those expressions that lead one to treat thinking as a *hidden mental activity*. No better example of this tendency can be found than in *The Mentality of Apes*. But Wittgenstein then goes on to tell his students that 'Köhler makes important remarks only in parenthesis' (GWL: 168). That is, Köhler is at his best when he is describing psychological phenomena and not seeking to theorise about them; for it is in these moments that he sheds light on the 'condition under which a certain expression makes sense' (*ibid.*: 177).

We can glean some idea of what Wittgenstein is driving at here from a passage in *Remarks on the Philosophy of Psychology* in which we are asked to imagine

a human being, or one of Köhler's monkeys, who wants to get a banana from the ceiling, but can't reach it, and thinking about ways

155

and means finally puts two sticks together, etc. Suppose one were to ask, 'What must go on inside him for this to take place?' – This question seems to make some sort of sense. And perhaps someone might answer that unless he acted through chance or instinct, the monkey must have seen the process before its mental eye. But that would not suffice, and then again, on the other hand, it would be too much.

(RPP II: §224)

The reason such an argument would not suffice – which Köhler himself exploits in order to generate his reductionist analysis of 'insight' – is because it doesn't actually explain anything, but merely shifts the problem to a lower level. And the reason such an argument says too much is because we can imagine a case in which no images passed through the animal's mind, or even, where there was no discernible 'system of impulses going out from [its] brain and correlated with [its actions]' (RPP I: §903), but the animal was none the less seen to pause and reflect on the situation, as Köhler reports in several places in *The Mentality of Apes*.

The problem here is that, if reflection consisted, as Köhler assumes, of epistemically private events – e.g. the coalescing of images in one's 'mind's eye' – then this would mean that we could *never* know if the animal was genuinely reflecting on the problem or merely appeared to be doing so. Teaching the animal language – if that were possible – would be of no help, since we could never know if the animal was sincerely reporting its mental experiences. Moreover, exactly the same problem must apply to ourselves! So it looks as if the only way out of the sceptical dilemma in which Köhler lands himself is to embrace the eliminativist conclusion that his analysis of insight was originally designed to circumvent. Thus, suppose that what we call 'reflecting' is merely the name of certain neural processes that are localised in the occipital lobe. Then, should we observe a subject whom we would normally describe as 'reflecting' on a problem, but discover, through the use of a PET scan, that his occipital lobe was not lit up, this would mean that the subject was not, in fact, reflecting on the problem. In other words, only neuroscience can tell us whether a subject is *really* 'reflecting' on a problem; at the level of ordinary language, our use of 'reflection' is irretrievably vulnerable to epistemological scepticism.

For that matter, it is difficult to see how Köhler can avoid having his argument collapse into either associationism or anthropomorphism. For if he were to maintain: 'By "reflection" is meant the (possibly fortuitous) conjunction of these images, by "learning" is meant the stamping in of this unity, etc.', then the argument simply reduces to associationism. But what other alternative remains open to Köhler, other than the prohibited supposition that the chimpanzee 'says to himself, as it were, "That's how!", and then he does it with signs of full consciousness'? And if this, then why not: 'The animal says to himself, as it were, "if the distance to the bananas is about eight feet, and if this stick is only five feet long, then I will need an extension which is at least three feet long" '?

Is it any wonder, in light of this argument, that George was led to view Wittgenstein as a valuable ally of the post-computational revolution? But that this was far from Wittgenstein's intention is made clear in the following passage:

> I want the monkey to *reflect* on something. First he jumps and reaches for the banana in vain, then he gives up and perhaps he is depressed – but this phase does not have to take place. How can catching hold of the stick be something he gets to *inwardly* at all? True, he could have been shown a picture that depicts something like that, and then he could act that way; or such a picture could simply float before his mind. But that again would be an accident. He would not have arrived at this picture by reflection. And does it help to say that all he needed to have done was somehow to have seen his arm and the stick as a unity? But let us go ahead and assume a propitious accident! Then the question is: How can he *learn* from the accident? Perhaps he just happened to have the stick in his hand and just happened to touch the banana with it. – And what further must now go on in him?
>
> (RPP II: §224)

That is, it is only if the chimpanzee demonstrates that he has acquired a method of solving a problem that we are warranted in applying such concepts as reflecting, considering, insight, etc. Hence the importance of Köhler's reports on a chimpanzee's ability to repeat a performance, even after long intervals, with demonstrably improved efficiency. But, of course, each of these concepts introduces its own special problems. Thus, scattered throughout *Remarks on the Philosophy of Psychology* are what, in its present format, appear to be isolated passages in which Wittgenstein takes up the various concepts involved in Köhler's argument (see RPP I: §§560ff, RPP II: §§195f, 215f). In fact, these investigations form a seamless web in which Wittgenstein examines the manner in which these various concepts are used and interrelated.

Wittgenstein concludes that Köhler does indeed present us with circumstances in which, despite the fact that we are dealing with an animal, it is appropriate to use the term 'reflection'. For this very reason, Köhler's work forces us to consider 'The expression, the behaviour, of reflection. Of what do we say: It is reflecting on something? Of a human being, sometimes of a beast. (Not of a tree or a stone.) *One* sign of reflection is hesitating in what you do (Köhler). (Not just *any* hesitation.)' (RPP I: §561) The issue here has nothing to do with anthropomorphism: i.e. with reading 'human mental attributes' into the chimpanzee's behaviour. Rather, the issue here solely concerns the criteria governing the use of 'thinking' or 'reflecting'. For example,

> If [the chimpanzee] has made some combination in play, and he now uses it as a method for doing this and that, we shall say he thinks. – In *reflecting* he would mentally review ways and means. But to do this he must already have some in stock. Thinking gives him the possibility of *perfecting* his methods. Or rather: He 'thinks' when, in a definite kind of way, he perfects a method he has. It could also be said that he thinks when he *learns* in a particular way.
>
> (RPP II: §§224–5)

The argument presented in this passage is not empirical: i.e. it is not the sort of armchair philosophical theory that follows from George's interpretation of Wittgenstein's remarks on experimental psychology. Rather, Wittgenstein is drawing attention to the conceptual relations between *thinking* and *reflecting*, and to the fact that we could not describe the chimpanzee as 'thinking' about the problem unless we could also describe him as 'learning' from his mistakes and 'improving' his technique for getting the fruit.

So far, Wittgenstein has said nothing about whether the chimpanzees *did* learn from thinking about the problem. For his role, *qua* philosopher of psychology, should not be confused with Köhler's role, *qua* comparative psychologist. That is, Wittgenstein sees his primary task in regard to Köhler's work as that of clarifying, not that it is difficult to prove that apes are capable of reflecting on problems and experiencing moments of insight, but, rather, why Cartesianism finds it not just difficult but, in fact, impossible to describe their behaviour in these terms.

To be sure, we are dealing here with a highly problematic context; for, as Wittgenstein remarks:

> one might distinguish between two chimpanzees with respect to the way in which they work, and say of the one that he is thinking and of the other that he is not. But here of course we wouldn't have the complete employment of 'think.' The word would have reference to a mode of behaviour. Not until it finds its particular use in the first person does it acquire the meaning of activity.
>
> (*Ibid.*: §§229–30).

The absence of the first-person use of the verb 'to think' – which is an integral aspect of the concept of thought – underscores the limited sense in which the chimpanzee can be said to think. Thus, we might refer to the chimpanzee's behaviour as exhibiting a 'primitive' use of the verb 'to think'.

To illustrate what is meant by this, Wittgenstein asks us to

> Imagine a person who is taking a break in his work, and is staring ahead seemingly pondering something, in a situation in which we would ask ourselves a question, weigh possibilities – would we necessarily say of him that he was reflecting? Is not one of the prerequisites for this that he *be in command* of a language, i.e., be able to express the reflection, if called upon to do so?
>
> Now if we were to see creatures at work whose *rhythm* of work, play of expression etc. was like our own, but for their not *speaking*, perhaps in that case we should say that they thought, considered, made decisions. That is: in such a case there would be a *great deal* which is similar to the action of ordinary humans. And it isn't clear *how much* has to be similar for us to have a right to apply to them also the concept 'thinking', which has its home in *our* life.
>
> (RPP I: §§185–6)

What Wittgenstein is saying here is that: 'only of a living human being and what resembles (behaves like) a living human being can one say: it reflects, acts blindly, deliberates, acts capriciously' (cf. PI: §281, RPP II: §192). That is, human beings serve as the paradigm subjects for the use of psychological expressions: any question about the cognitive capacities of animals or infants demands that we compare their behaviour with the relevant actions underpinning the use of the psychological concept in question. And language-use – i.e. first-person and third-person psychological utterances – is clearly an integral part of this behaviour. But what we discover from work such as Köhler's is that, even though the possession of language is fundamentally bound up with the application of psychological expressions, we can also apply these terms to cases where, e.g., a subject is unable to explain his use of a symbol, or where a subject cannot use symbols but can respond appropriately to their use by others, or even cases where language-use is not involved.

Thus, once we get past the absolute premium which Cartesianism places on speech, we can only be struck by the commonalities between the apes' behaviour and our own in similar problem-solving situations. But then, what Köhler shows us in parentheses is that, even if an image did float before an ape's 'mind's eye' when he reflected on a problem, or his actions could be systematically correlated with a series of neural events, this is quite irrelevant to the fact that the ape's behaviour satisfies the criteria for describing him as 'reflecting on the problem', or as 'grasping how to solve it' in a 'sudden moment of insight'. So why does Köhler feel compelled to explain the ape's behaviour in terms of these sorts of epistemically private events?

The answer is: Because Köhler treats the ape's behaviour in these situations as *evidence* for the fact that he was reflecting on the problem, rather than as a *criterion* for describing the ape as 'reflecting on the problem'. And it is because of this Cartesian starting-point that Köhler's argument ultimately leads to the conclusion that the nature of insight *cannot* be explained: either because the 'processes' involved are unobservable, or else, because if what we call 'insight' reduces to certain neural events, then this entails that the ape did not actually *reflect* on and *grasp* how to solve the problem, but, rather, that these neural events caused the ape to do such-and-such, in the same way, e.g., that we can describe the chain of processes that caused an electric door to open.

Köhler's theory lands us in this predicament because Köhler misconstrued *ab initio* the *grammatical propositions* whereby we formulate the rules governing the application of the various terms that we use to talk about thinking as *empirical generalisations*. For example, we say that 'We cannot see what went on in a subject's mind when she solved the problem', or, 'Only the subject can know what, if anything, went on in her mind when she solved the problem'. Or we say that 'Stating that "In a moment of insight, the ape suddenly grasped how to solve the problem" just means that, "By reflecting on the problem the ape was able to see how to obtain the bananas".' We use such propositions to stipulate how one can talk about the mind, or to formulate the conceptual relations between, e.g., *reflecting* and *insight*. But Köhler treats these grammatical propositions as empirical generalisations, which leads him to ask such standard Cartesian questions as: 'How can one theorise about what went on in the ape's mind when these processes are unobservable?', or, 'How does reflection *bring about* insight?'

Wittgenstein is certainly not denying that there is a clear sense in which one can ask about the processes that led up to the ape's solving the problem. But what he shows us is that an appropriate answer to this question will be along the lines: 'He reflected on the problem, considered various possible solutions, suddenly saw how to fit the two sticks together, and so forth'. But as far as the Cartesian is concerned, this is not an answer; it is merely a restatement of the problem. For what the Cartesian wants to know is: what went on in the ape's mind *when he reflected, considered, and saw how to proceed*: what were the *mental processes* underlying these *mental states*?

The crux of the argument directed against Köhler at RPP II §§217–34 – as in so many other places in Wittgenstein's writings on the philosophy of psychology – is to wean us from this way of viewing an agent's behaviour as 'outward' signs of 'inner' mental processes and states (see Hacker 1990). For the answer to the above Cartesian question must at best be trivial, or non-explanatory, and, at worst, the source of 'philosophical theories' (such as eliminative materialism). This is not because Köhler's analysis of insight pushes us up against the limits of science, or into the arms of philosophical scepticism, but, rather, because it construes the question of 'What went on in the chimpanzee's mind?' as a question about the 'inner processes' leading up to the 'outer events' which we observe.

Wittgenstein concludes that 'The mistake, as usual, lies in the question, not in the answer' (GWL: 240). In this case, it is the question: 'What went on in the chimpanzee's mind/brain that enabled it to solve the problem?' It is in order to clarify the potentially misleading character of this question that Wittgenstein counsels us to investigate the use of psychological verbs. But this is hardly the sentiment of a semantic reactionary bent on retarding scientific progress. On the contrary, Wittgenstein repeatedly introduces thought-experiments which are designed to illustrate the different ways in which psychological concepts might develop. Rather, Wittgenstein's intention was to bring us to see that 'In describing the use [of "think"] we are misled by paradigms. Description depends on how we approach it' (*ibid.*: 122).

Köhler's basic problem, according to Wittgenstein, is that he assumed from the start that we can account for the 'mysterious processes underlying insight' in neurophysiological terms. It is in order to preclude Köhler's first step here that Wittgenstein warns us that 'In philosophy, the comparison of thinking to a process that goes on in secret is a misleading one' (RPP I: §580). For, once one adopts this fundamental Cartesian picture of thinking, one is ineluctably led to 'mistakenly locate this mystery in the nature of the process' (PG: 154).

Determined to place psychology on an equal footing with the natural sciences, Köhler naturally fell back on his early training in physics and produced a theory of psycho-physical isomorphism based on electro-dynamic models. Motivated by the same goal, Newell and Simon resorted to their training in mathematics and turned instead to a computational theory of information-processing. What matters here is not the contrast between their models, but rather the continuity in their presuppositions; for while the technologies – and thus the analogies on which they based their 'paradigm revolutions' – may have changed, the basic mechanist starting-point of 'interpreting the enigma created by our misunderstanding as the enigma of an incomprehensible process' remained constant (PG: 155). And therein lies the key to why Wittgenstein suggests, at PI p. 232, that 'problem and method have so persistently passed one another by' in experimental psychology. But then, that still leaves us in the dark as to how we are supposed to deal with the 'moment of insight'. Our next task in this chapter, therefore, is to examine Wittgenstein's response to the problem which lies at the heart of mechanist theories of creativity.

§7 The Cartesian shift from theory to the ethereal

> Philosophers have calculated the difference of velocity between sound and light; but who will attempt to calculate the difference between speech and thought! What wonder, then, that the invention of all ages should have been upon the stretch to add such wings to their conversation as might enable it, if possible, to keep pace in some measure with their minds.
>
> (John Horne Tooke, *Diversions of Purley*)

We ended the preceding section on the seemingly negative note that 'The mistake, as usual, lies in the question, not in the answer' (GWL: 240). But Wittgenstein is not suggesting that the question 'What is the nature of thinking, or insight?' should be framed in inverted commas, so as to signify that it isn't coherent (in a way that is comparable, e.g., to 'How much does $C^{\#}$ weigh?'), and accordingly, that any 'answer' to it must be nonsensical (must violate the bounds of sense). Rather, he is stressing the importance of clarifying the nature of the question, and thence, the answer.

Thus he tells his students: 'Sometimes the answers to the questions ["What is thinking?" "What is essential to thinking?" "What is insight?"] are called "theories". Here the use of the word "theories" is misleading' (*ibid.*: 122). The reason it can be misleading to describe some answers to these questions as 'theories' is because:

> A theory is a hypothesis; or in its more typical sense it is: it is perhaps a provisional statement about how phenomena work. But the word is used because those who choose it are not clear about whether it is a correlation in a science of phencmena, or a taking of phenomena to bits, or an investigation of the concept they want. They incline to put forward an attempt to 'find the nature of a phenomenon' as an alternative to an enquiry into a concept or, 'the use of a word'.
>
> (*Ibid.*: 240)

That is not to say, however, that psychology cannot investigate various aspects of, e.g., problem-solving or creativity. Rather, Wittgenstein's point is that we must be careful to distinguish between empirical and conceptual responses to empirical versus conceptual questions about the nature of thought.

In the former cases, the experimental psychologist seeks to discover 'general psychological propositions which are always true, for example, that no person could do certain calculations without writing, or that the

162

maximum one can remember is . . . ' But 'These features of the nature of thought will be described by propositions about thought, etc., and the use of the proposition would presuppose the exact technique of "I think . . . " etc.' (*ibid.*: 175). Thus, if psychology proceeds on the basis of implicitly comparing ' "I think" with the wrong paradigm, e.g. with "I eat" ' (*ibid.*: 48), the result will be, not a genuine theory or a hypothesis, but, rather, *metaphysics*.

This theme is spelt out in Nachlass writings from the early 1930s (see Typescript 213, Manuscript 117, both unpublished). Wittgenstein explains how:

> [The question] 'How does thought work, how does it use its expression?' [is approached] on the analogy: 'How does the Jacquard loom work, how does it use the cards?'
>
> The philosophical confusion concerning the idea of thinking together with the problems of psychology, is presented to us by the picture of a hidden (invisible) mechanism.
>
> This mechanism: is ~~perhaps the picture~~ the brain, translated into something ethereal.
>
> . . . It is absolutely not unexplored processes of belief [thought] that interest us, the ~~mechanism which we don't understand is no mental~~ but rather the use [*Gebrauch*] of our well-known processes of belief [thought], e.g. of the expression of the sentence 'I believe [think] . . . '
>
> To the question 'How does one do that', the one who answers perhaps through introspection will not come up with anything useful as an answer that one could use.
>
> . . . The mechanism which we don't understand is not anything in our mind, but rather of the activity in which this expression swims.
>
> (quoted in Hilmy 1987: 162–3)

If not for the date at which this was written (1932?), one would naturally assume that Wittgenstein was responding to rather than anticipating, Turing in this passage. But it seems far more likely that Wittgenstein was thinking here of classical associationism. So the basic issue that we must address in this and the following sections is: Does Wittgenstein's attack on pre-computational mechanism apply, *mutatis mutandur*, to AI?

The first thing to note is that there is nothing in Wittgenstein's argument forcing us to deny the possible gains to be realised by protocol analysis in the study of problem-solving or creativity. But the question which his argument raises is: How is 'protocol analysis' to be construed? Once again, Wittgenstein counsels us to be cautious; for

'Of course the psychologist reports the words, the behaviour, of the subject, but surely only as signs of mental processes.' – That is correct. If the words and the behaviour are, for example, learned by heart, they do not interest the psychologist. And yet the expression 'as signs of mental processes' is misleading, because we are accustomed to speak of the colour of the face as a sign of fever. And now each bad analogy gets explained by another bad one, so that in the end only weariness releases us from these ineptitudes.

(RPP I: §292)

That is, the danger in protocol analysis is that of construing a subject's words or behaviour as *evidence* of 'inner processes', and thus, to construe protocols on the paradigm, e.g., of a glucose tolerance test.

The source of the problem here, Wittgenstein argues, lies in the Cartesian picture of thinking as a hidden mental process that is (partially) disclosed to introspection. The main themes in Wittgenstein's discussion of thinking are:

1   we do not *perceive* what we think, and *a fortiori*,
2   there is no preconscious cognitive machinery which, because of the limits of our powers of introspection, we cannot perceive
3   thinking and speaking are internally related to one another
4   thinking is not an accompaniment of speaking
5   we do not use language to *describe* what we think, and thus,
6   we do not frame thoughts prior to *encoding* them in language
7   thinking and speaking are not separate, or – in the full mathematical sense of the term – 'dual' *processes* (see Hacker 1990).

The picture of thinking that Wittgenstein is attacking here clearly lies at the heart of GPS. In a passage which can be read as a direct response to Newell and Simon's view of protocol analysis, Wittgenstein asks us to:

Suppose we think while we talk or write – I mean, as we normally do – we shall not in general say that we think quicker than we talk; the thought seems *not to be separate* from the expression. On the other hand, however, one does speak of the speed of thought; of how a thought goes through one's head like lightning; how problems become clear to us in a flash, and so on. So it is natural to ask if the same thing happens in lightning-like thought – only extremely accelerated – as when we talk and 'think while we talk'. So that in the first case the clockwork runs down all at once, but in the second bit by bit, braked by the words.

(PI: §318)

We are concerned here 'with the queerness of psychological concepts as opposed to the queerness of psychological phenomena' (GWL: 289); for 'the phenomena are not hidden; the concept is hidden. And the concept is surrounded by others. It occurs in a field and its relations give us trouble' (*ibid.*: 247). Thus, we must be careful to differentiate the 'fields' in which the concepts of thinking and speaking are situated. For ' "Talking" (whether out loud or silently) and "thinking" are not concepts of the same kind; even though they are in closest connexion' (PI: p.217).

To see this, we might consider how one can think without talking, or talk without thinking; think about what one is saying or say what one is thinking; say the opposite of what one is thinking and think of things that are unrelated to what one is saying. If we exhort someone to think before speaking (or vice versa), we are not advising them to space the time between two separate experiences; and if we teach them to speak thoughtfully, we are not instructing them in the art of juggling two independent processes. A psychotherapist, a noviciate and a soldier must all learn how to refrain from saying what they are thinking; while a patient undergoing free association, a Zen Buddhist chanting a mantra and an aspiring politician must all learn how to speak without thinking.

The differences between the 'fields' surrounding *thinking* and *speaking* can be further illuminated if we compare their uses in such areas as:

* imperatives – for example, we can force ourselves or another to speak more slowly or more quickly, but it is not at all clear what this would mean in the case of thought
* error – we can fail to say what we mean, but can we fail to think what we mean?
* effort – one can tire oneself by thinking or speaking too much, but can one tire oneself by speaking too hard or thinking too loudly?
* learning – a child learns how to speak, but does a child learn how to think?
* duration – someone might set a record for non-stop talking, but for non-stop thinking? (see Hacker 1990).

All this may seem to be mere skirmishing with ordinary language, with little relevance for the foundations of AI; but Wittgenstein's point goes deeper. The fundamental issue he is exploring here is whether thinking and speaking are legitimately described as 'functionally interdependent processes', and that the relation between the two is akin to that which obtains between, e.g., the speed of one's metabolism and the frequency of hunger-pangs. If that were the case, then could we not measure the speed of thinking, as opposed to the speed of talking?

As far as AI is concerned, the answer to this last question is straightforward; for, as Simon explains, 'the human information-processing system . . .

operates almost entirely serially, one process at a time. . . . The elementary processes of the information-processing system are executed in tens or hundreds of milliseconds' (Simon 1978: 273). That is, given that thinking is a mechanical procedure, it *must* be possible to measure its speed; after all, one can do so with computers, so perhaps what De Groot's research really reveals is the different number of LIPS[20] which (the processors of) players of varying abilities are capable of executing. Moreover, it must be possible to calibrate and compare thinking on this basis (e.g., a player of USCF level 2200 will have completed 13/16th of the problem at t_i, whereas one of 1800 will only have reached the half-way point[21]).

But thinking, Wittgenstein remarks, unlike a bread roll, cannot be divided into segments (PG: 39). Thinking and speaking are not separate and asynchronous processes, the one inherently faster than the other. For thinking is not a 'process' in this sense at all (i.e. composed of 'elementary units'). One can quantify the speed of speaking, reading or typing (e.g. in terms of words per minute), but there is no comparable sense in which the speed of thinking can be measured (GWL: 171). To be sure, we can time how long it takes someone to solve a problem; but this provides a measure of their ability, not a measurement of some 'mental process'.

In order to appreciate the thrust of this argument, we need to get clear on what kind of statement Wittgenstein is making when he says that 'Thinking, unlike a bread roll, cannot be divided into segments', or that 'Thinking is not a process composed out of elementary units'. For that matter, we need to get clear on the nature of the statements in the above paragraphs outlining the contour of the fields in which 'think' and 'speak' are situated. The answer is that these are all grammatical propositions: they articulate various aspects of the uses of 'think'. That is, the statement 'Thinking can't be divided into segments' is like 'The bishop can't move horizontally in chess'. Both statements are normative: i.e. they stipulate how to make a move in a (language-) game. And it is precisely because the crux of Wittgenstein's argument is to bring us to see when – and that! – certain utterances are *reflexive*, that he is not developing the sort of 'philosophical theory' that the cognitivist envisages.

But that is exactly what the Cartesian does: viz., by treating these grammatical propositions as empirical generalisations, the Cartesian ends up developing a metaphysical thesis which cannot be *refuted*. Thus, the Cartesian will insist that we just won't know whether or not thinking can be divided into segments until we have finally discovered the nature of thinking – which, because of present technological limitations, still remains a mystery. But the source of this mystery does not lie in the fact that thinking is *hidden from our view*; rather, it lies in the fact that Cartesianism construes a question like 'Can the speed of thinking be measured?' as empirical, and then regards the ensuing difficulties that one has in answering this as due to the lack of a suitable model and/or the proper tools of measurement.

It is but a short step from this Cartesian picture of thinking to the 'computational *"must"*': i.e., to the idea that thinking must be an effective procedure, and that most of this computational process must lie 'beneath the threshold of introspection'. Thus, as far as cognitivism is concerned, a statement like 'The computer solved the problem in a flash' is *no different in kind* from a statement like 'In a moment of insight S solved the problem'. Both are seen as straightforward process statements. To be sure, that does not mean that the cognitivist is committed *nolens volens* to AI; only to the principle that the question whether computationalism, or some other mechanist thesis, provides the best model for the analysis of insight is an *empirical* matter. As we shall see in the following section, however, what is even more interesting here is how the computational analysis of creativity is grounded in a Cartesian picture of thinking.

§8 The nature of 'sudden understanding'

We have already examined some of the mechanist presuppositions underlying the description of a computer's operations in cognitive terms (see Chapter 1). Here, our concern is with the converse side of this issue: with the Cartesian presuppositions which lead one to look at *sudden understanding* in mechanist terms. For, as AI so richly demonstrates, by treating *sudden understanding* as the end-result of hidden mental processes, Cartesianism literally creates the gap that mechanism steps in to fill.

From a Cartesian point of view, the most curious feature of sudden understanding is the fact that ordinary-language-speakers have no trouble in identifying it. That is, the man on the Clapham omnibus has a seemingly sure grasp as to when he, or another agent, suddenly understands something. On what grounds do ordinary-language-speakers make these judgements? Indeed, what sorts of 'judgements' are they? Do ordinary-language-speakers *infer* when they or someone else has suddenly understood something? Do they possess an inchoate – a 'folk' – theory of sudden understanding? And if so, can cognitive science build a more rigorous theory of thinking and problem-solving on this foundation?

To answer these questions, we might first consider the kinds of situations in which we talk about 'sudden understanding'. As we saw in §3, Newell and Simon severely limited the scope of 'sudden understanding' to the solution of formal problems. But we speak of 'sudden understanding' in all sorts of different contexts. For example, one might suddenly understand the point of a social convention, or why someone is behaving the way they are, or what an idiomatic expression in a foreign language means. Sometimes an agent's behaviour serves as a criterion for saying that she suddenly understands something, and sometimes her failure to act can serve as such a criterion.

Sometimes two observers can have completely opposing views on whether an agent's behaviour signifies that she suddenly understands something. Sometimes an agent can insist that she didn't suddenly understand when observers insist – perhaps rightly – that she did. For that matter, even coming up with the right answer to a formal problem doesn't ensure that the agent suddenly understood it. For she might have made a lucky guess, or remembered having heard the answer, or known it was the right answer without knowing why.

It is difficult to see how one could possibly hope to ground our myriad uses of 'sudden understanding' in these – and countless other – cases in a theory as to what sorts of behaviour are 'signs' of sudden understanding. Indeed, how could a child possibly infer what is common to all these diverse situations when teams of cognitive scientists cannot come up with such a 'featural definition'? But the cognitivist might respond with a prototype-style argument: i.e. might argue that the above sorts of examples represent 'fringe' uses of the term, but that the 'core' or 'paradigmatic' use of 'sudden understanding' is in those cases where we wish to register our sense of surprise at suddenly finding the solution to a problem in a way that we cannot explain.

Ericsson and Simon, for example, pursue Durkin's argument (from 1937) that when a moment of illumination 'occurs, it comes with an onrush that makes it seem very sudden – an "out of the blue" experience. But it can always be found to have developed gradually. The suddenness must be regarded as due to the concealment of the background. It does not bring in a new *kind* of process' (Ericsson and Simon 1980: 238). The same point can be found in *Thought and Choice in Chess*. According to De Groot, a 'sudden flash of insight' is invariably accompanied by a feeling of surprise which is brought about by unexpectedly finding the solution to a problem, or a new way of formulating a problem. Even Wittgenstein remarks that it is conceivable that a flash of insight should always be accompanied by a distinctive experience (e.g. that agents who uttered 'Now I can go on' always registered a sense of surprise or excitement), and that this may be one of the reasons why we reserve a special term to distinguish insight from ordinary understanding: e.g. that it registers an agent's feeling of confidence that he has made a critical advance in his attempts to deal with some problem (PI: §321).

The problem with this type of 'ordinary language' argument, according to AI, is that it proceeds as if the goal of AI is to explain the nature of this experience, whereas the real goal of AI is to explain the processes that led up to this experience. But it is one thing to explain the processes in a subject's thinking – leading up to her feeling of surprise or elation at suddenly finding the solution to the problem – on the basis of statements in a verbal protocol which the subject cannot recall uttering; and quite another to explain this feeling of elation or surprise in terms of 'processes' (e.g. a linear chain of operations) that can only be *inferred* from the protocol, and are such that the subject *could not have been aware* of having gone through them.

The latter constitutes the crucial step in the mechanist analysis of 'sudden understanding'. According to De Groot, the 'moment of illumination' is to be explained as the consequence of subliminal mental operations that proceed far too quickly, or are too far submerged, for a subject to be aware of them. And it is for this reason that a subject is startled when she suddenly understands something; for what she *perceives* are the 'end-results' of 'imperceptible cerebral processes' (De Groot 1965: 312). In other words, the mechanist employs this observation about the feeling of surprise which characteristically accompanies sudden understanding to institute a reductionist analysis of what sudden understanding *consists in*: i.e. the 'preconscious processes' leading up to this 'experience'.

Thus, the question of 'What happens when a man suddenly understands?' (PI: §321) encourages the mechanist to search for an account of 'what has "happened" in the "cloudy gaseous medium" of the mind' (PG: 100). But the very question, Wittgenstein tells us, 'is badly framed. If it is a question about the meaning of the expression "sudden understanding", the answer is not to point to a process that we give this name to. – The question might mean: what are the tokens of sudden understanding; what are its characteristic psychical accompaniments?' (PI: §321). For example, suppose there were indeed some characteristic feeling of surprise which always accompanies sudden understanding: could this serve as a criterion for inferring that one has suddenly understood? If so, then, to teach a child when to use the expression 'sudden understanding', one would first have to teach her how to identify the feeling she is experiencing as surprise, and how to distinguish this feeling from similar emotions.

But then, this would only serve to shift the problem of explaining 'sudden understanding' to the problem of explaining how one teaches and correctly identifies what, according to Cartesianism, is an epistemically private mental state. Moreover, it also leaves us with the standard Cartesian problem of never knowing for certain whether another agent has suddenly understood something – is experiencing surprise – or only appears to have done so. Thus, if we are to avoid this relapse into epistemological scepticism, we need to recognise that

> the words 'Now I can do it!' don't express an *experience*. Any more than these: 'Now I am going to raise my arm.' – But why don't they express any experience, any feeling. – Well, how are they used? Both, e.g., are preliminary to an action. The fact that a statement makes reference to a point of time, at which time, however, nothing that it means, nothing of which it speaks, happens in the outer world, does not show us that it spoke of an experience.
>
> (RPP I: §244)

That is, the expression 'Now I suddenly understand' does not describe some experience or mental state with which only the subject is acquainted; nor does it represent an *inference* based on past experience. Both of these misconceptions – which are common in the Cartesian literature – result from the failure to recognise the categorial difference between psychological and empirical propositions.

Consider, for example, the difference between the statements 'Now I suddenly understand' and 'My pancreas is secreting too much insulin'. In the former case, the subject is not reporting on her condition or formulating a hypothesis. Rather, she is expressing her conviction – and thereby arousing certain expectations – as to what she can now say or do: she is indicating her ability or intention to proceed in a given manner.[22] *This*, Wittgenstein tells us, is a crucial aspect of what is involved when a child masters the expression 'sudden understanding' (PI: §§323f). Similarly, 'The words "It's on the tip of my tongue" are no more the expression of an experience than "Now I know how to go on!" – We use them in *certain situations*, and they are surrounded by behaviour of a special kind' (*ibid.*: 219). Whatever may have gone on in my mind 'was not what was meant by that expression. It is of more interest what went on in my behaviour. – "The word is on the tip of my tongue" tells you: the word which belongs here has escaped me, but I hope to find it soon' (*ibid.*).

Wittgenstein is not denying that 'There really are cases where someone has the sense of what he wants to say much more clearly in his mind than he can express in words.' Indeed, he confides that 'This happens to me very often. . . . [I]t is often as though the image stays there behind the words, so that they *seem* to describe it *to me*' (CV: 79). But:

> What happens when we make an effort – say in writing a letter – to find the right expression for our thoughts? – This phrase compares the process to one of translating or describing: the thoughts are already there (perhaps were there in advance) and we merely look for their expression . . .
>
> [Sometimes] I surrender to a mood and the expression *comes*. Or a picture occurs to me and I try to describe it. Or an English expression occurs to me and I try to hit on the corresponding German one. Or I make a gesture, and ask myself: What words correspond to this gesture? And so on.
>
> (PI: §335)

These utterances convey the manner in which a thought gradually crystallises as one struggles to articulate one's feelings, impressions, etc., or a thought emerges in the act of speaking and writing. The crucial point is that such phrases are not used to describe inchoate thoughts but, rather, to express one's thoughts inchoately. Hence our puzzlement if asked: ' "Do you have the thought before finding the expression?"' What could one reply to this? 'And what, to the question: "What did the thought consist in, as it existed before its expression?"' (*ibid.*).

As far as the AI-scientist is concerned, there is no reason why any of the above argument should preclude our inquiring into 'what a thought consisted in prior to its expression'. But it is precisely this way of viewing the matter that Wittgenstein is attacking. All of the above examples are designed to show us that we use the various utterances surveyed here to *express* (confide, clarify, explain, proclaim, reveal, conceal, etc.) our thoughts: not to *describe* or *encode* epistemically private mental events. The connection between sentences and the expression of thoughts cannot, however, be drawn too rigidly: not only because we can utter sentences without saying what we are thinking, but also because of the wide range of sentences used for other linguistic purposes (e.g., to disguise our intentions, beliefs, desires; to warn, chastise, correct; to flatter, encourage, cajole).

This Wittgensteinian view of linguistic behaviour – of 'learning how to do things with words' – is directly opposed to the Augustinian view of language as a system that is used to communicate epistemically private thoughts. For the Cartesian view reads a common function into all of the expressions of language, and describes the meaning of a sentence independently of the situation in which it is embedded. Thus, the Augustinian view of language treats all words as names and all sentences as descriptions (see Baker and Hacker 1980). Against this, Wittgenstein presents us with a picture of language in which words are seen, not as names (of mental representations or concepts), but as tools that are used for all different sorts of communicative purposes (see PI: §§10ff). And just as there are many different kinds of words, so, too, sentences should not all be treated as descriptions (e.g. of thoughts that language speakers encode and decode). For there are countless different kinds of sentences, used to do all sorts of things (e.g., to promise, order, request, command, invite, threaten, chide, etc.).

No better example of the linguistic diversity of words could be found than that of 'think'; for it can be used to confirm, qualify, or remove one's support; to convey one's uncertainty, certitude, or indignation; to evaluate, influence, or share another's opinions, etc. But the one use it does not enjoy, in first-person cases, is that of ordinary description. Thus,

> If someone wants to call the words the 'description' of the thought instead of the 'expression' of the thought, let him ask himself how anyone learns to describe a table and how he learns to describe his own thought. And that only means: let him look and see how one judges the description of a table as right or wrong, and how the description of thoughts; so let him keep in view these language-games in all their situations.
>
> (RPP I: §572)

That is, if we came to know our thoughts in a similar way to that in which we perceive objects – i.e. if it made sense to say that we are *acquainted* with our thoughts – then the same range of epistemic possibilities would apply to both. For example, it would make sense to speak of being mistaken or uncertain, or of learning, inferring, or misdescribing, what one is thinking; of never being certain about someone else's thoughts, no matter how sincere their speech. It would make perfectly good sense to say 'I think that I was (or was not) thinking', and to worry about how one could stop the regress which threatens here. But we can know what someone else is thinking regardless of what they say, or even, if they say nothing; for while the capacity to think is clearly bound up with the ability to express those thoughts, there are all kinds of behavioural as well as verbal criteria for what agents (or animals) are thinking.

The upshot of this argument, as far as understanding the nature of protocol analysis is concerned, is that if what is meant by 'protocol analysis' is an investigation of what a player thought, as opposed to what she merely said, then it is indeed the interpretation of the transcript that interests us.[23] For example, reading through the various protocols, De Groot reports finding expressions of the players' puzzlement, intentions, frustration, satisfaction, excitement; manifestations of their carelessness, meticulousness, ingenuity, limitations; evidence of their (in)experience and the manner in which this affected their approach to a problem, and so on. On this basis, De Groot formulates his theory that chess-thinking breaks down into four distinct phases:

1   In the first 'phase of orientation' the player is said to examine 'the consequences of moves.'

2   In the next 'phase of exploration' 'the subject tries out rather than 'investigates' possibilities for action. He calculates a few moves deep a few sample variations,' and 'if these are unsatisfactory he puts the move(s) in question temporarily aside.'

3   In the following 'phase of investigation . . . There is a deeper, more serious search for possibilities' which are 'quantitatively and qualitatively quite sharply defined.'

4   In the final 'phase of proof . . . The subject checks and recapitulates, he strives for proof.'

(De Groot 1965: 267)

Herein lies the major substance of De Groot's contribution to our understanding of the process of chess-thinking. He presents us here with what Wittgenstein has in mind when he speaks of 'general psychological propositions' (GWL: 175): i.e. psychological generalisations which we can indeed test to discover if they are always true. It is the next step in his argument, however, which is deeply problematic. For De Groot then goes on to treat

172

the players' utterances as partial descriptions of an underlying effective procedure which the subject is trying to experience and describe simultaneously. It is at precisely this point that De Groot ceases to interpret what the subjects thought (on the basis of their utterances and actions), and his mechanist preconceptions about the nature of thinking take over. We suddenly find ourselves thrust into the psychologistic assumption that, by mapping the protocol onto a formal model, we can use the latter to *fill in the gaps* in the former.

This shift is most clearly seen in the two (interrelated) phenomena which are De Groot's primary concern: the pauses in a transcript, followed by a fresh approach to a problem (possibly leading to its solution). It is not just natural for a computationalist to construe these phenomena as marking the stage at which the mind's program switches to a new level of processing: it is unavoidable. For if one sees thinking as a subliminal process, occasionally breaking through the surface of consciousness, then one is inexorably led to ask: 'What went on in the mind during these intervals?' Hence the post-computational mechanist seeks to infer the nature of these 'intervening processes' from the subject's reports as plotted against a program.

For example, one of the players was repeatedly observed to reach a point where he would look around and mutter 'Now let's see', while his eyes wandered over the board. De Groot interprets this as demonstrating that the subject's thinking consisted 'not so much of ordering, working out (calculating) or checking, but rather of reflecting, integrating, and most of all *abstracting*' (De Groot 1965: 113). That is, De Groot treats the transcript as manifesting the 'mental processes' (viz., *reflecting*, *integrating* and *abstracting*) which brought about the subject's 'moment of insight'. And, given that these 'mental processes' are hidden from all view – the subject's included – their nature can only be inferred from some formal model.

But the subject's utterances are not *evidence* of what he thought; rather, they serve as *criteria* for our describing a 'leap' in his thinking. To be sure, a pause in the transcript may (but need not) indicate a critical shift in an agent's thinking. But whether or not this is the case depends on what precedes and succeeds the pause. For there are certainly instances where this need not be the case (e.g. an inattentive student spasmodically responding to a teacher's questions); and there are instances where it simply makes no sense to ask whether an agent is thinking during the pauses.[24] In such cases, 'we say that the mind is not idle, that something is going on inside it' (RPP II: §217). But the point of such an idiom is to 'distinguish these cases from a state of stupor, from mechanical actions' (*ibid.*): i.e. to clarify that the agent is thinking about what he is doing, trying out various methods of solution, etc.

The crucial point here is that any explanation of how the subject made this leap is confined to the realm of the *subject*: to what she thought, or her previous experience, or her sudden intuition, and so on. If we are right to say that the subject 'reflected, integrated, and most of all, abstracted,' then this is because her behaviour satisfies the criteria for our describing her actions in these terms. That is, we do not *infer*, from the brute fact that she solved the problem, that her mind/brain must have done such-and-such. For it is not a necessary condition that a subject perform these acts in order to solve a problem.

But surely, the mechanist will object, something must have happened in her mind/brain that made this leap possible; and all that AI is trying to do is formulate a program/theory that will enable us to discover what that 'something' might have been. But then, this resulting 'theory' has absolutely nothing to do with neuropsychology. The 'brain', on this picture, is really the *ethereal mechanism* where the 'pre-conscious processes' stipulated by this latest version of the 'cognitive unconscious' must take place. This is why no mention has been made in this chapter of what we may or may not have learnt about creativity from PET scans, or advances in our understanding of the role of neurotransmitters. For the fact is that the 'black box' which behaviourism declared was incomprehensible, and which AI sought to break open, is a product of Cartesianism, and is not to be confused with empirical questions about the mechanics of the brain.

Where does that leave the psychological study of creativity? What about the problems with which we began this chapter: the role of 'incubation', the processes of 'unconscious selection' recorded by Poincaré and a host of other noted scientists? What about the factors that bring about a 'moment of insight'? If 'incubation' should not be treated as a process-noun, or 'sudden illumination' as an experience, how *should* they be treated? Is there a paradigm-use of 'insight', or are we dealing here with a family-resemblance concept whose proper explanation will depend on the context being studied? These are questions which demand that we respond to the practical concerns of psychologists of thinking: to the real problems on which they are working, and the advances which their theories afford us in the explanation of these phenomena. More importantly, it is the manner in which we respond to these questions which will ultimately determine the force of the preceding criticisms of computational models of discovery.

§9 The metaphor is the message

It is clear that Wittgenstein had no intention of rendering the human mind 'the final citadel of vitalism', and just as clear that he had no intention of following Watson down the path of insisting that there is 'no problem of discovery' for psychology to address (Watson 1925: 198f).[25] The preceding sections may seem, however, to have left the Wittgensteinian with little other alternative. For we have denied that the 'moment of insight' can be treated as the end-result of a pre-conscious process (that is comparable to the manner in which, e.g., the symbols that flash on a VDU are the end-result of several layers of mechanical operations). But the argument that expressions of insight should not be treated as descriptions of an experience, or that 'think' (and its cognates) should not be treated in the same way as physical activity-verbs, does not preclude the Wittgensteinian from talking about the antecedent processes leading up to the solution of a problem. The question is: what exactly is meant by 'process' here?

As we have seen, Wittgenstein's primary concern was with the confusions that result when 'mental process' is construed on a physiological paradigm. But that does not exclude the possibility that there is an important sense in which we can say that the psychology of thinking is concerned with the investigation of the processes that enable us to solve problems or have moments of insight. Indeed, there is even a sense in which we can accept that the psychologist of thinking can profitably engage in the construction of models that will evoke features of the mind hitherto undetected or unappreciated. But whether such models are to be interpreted in the manner proposed by AI is another matter (cf. BB: 6f).

At the dawn of the AI revolution, Simon optimistically reported that 'Today we have a substantial and rapidly growing body of knowledge about thinking processes, both at the neurological level and at the level of what I shall call elementary information processes' (Simon 1966b: 269). Here is a reminder that we must be careful, when discussing the AI view of psychological explanation, to distinguish between eliminative materialism and mechanist reductionism: a point on which, as this quotation demonstrates, AI-scientists themselves were not always clear. The reason why it is so important to keep this distinction in mind is because arguments directed against the idea that 'thinking is a set of processes like those now taking place in the central nervous system of that person' (*ibid.*: 268) do not in themselves address the theme that 'Thinking is a set of processes like those that enabled a person to produce this problem solution from this problem statement' (*ibid.*). That is, the objection that thinking is something done by agents, not by their brains, says nothing about the computational hypothesis that problem-solving is an effective procedure.

What we most want to avoid in this latter issue is question-begging: as is the case, e.g., with the familiar objection that computers can only do what they have been programmed to do. For our concern here is with mechanism in the psychology of thinking, and not with the strong version of the Mechanist Thesis. In this respect, the goal of GPS was not to persuade us that computers might one day think; rather, it was to establish that 'thinking is a hierarchically organized, serially executed symbol-manipulated process' (*ibid.*: 277). Thus, the basic issue which concerns the psychology of thinking is whether the introduction of computational models exemplifies the sorts of insights that a new technological metaphor can bring to our understanding of the mind.

It goes without saying that there can be no *a priori* objection to the introduction of new metaphors with which to discuss the mind; on the contrary, it is often difficult to know how else to characterise our mental acts and abilities. Organic metaphors are among the oldest forms for describing the discovery of solutions to a problem. The very term 'creativity' attests to this. So, too, do such expressions as the 'germination of ideas', 'nurturing creativity', solutions 'bursting forth' into consciousness. The presence of visual metaphors in the language of problem-solving are also archetypal, e.g., 'insight', 'see at a glance', 'moment of illumination', 'flash of understanding', Wordsworth's 'visionary gleam'. So, too, are bodily metaphors, e.g., we 'struggle' or 'wrestle with our problems', 'seize on possibilities', have 'leaps of intuition', 'penetrate to the heart of an issue', 'strike out in new directions'. But conspicuously missing from this list are any mechanical metaphors.[26] Indeed, if anything, their use undermines the usual connotations of creativity or insight (and thus, they might be employed for ironic purposes).

This is just what humanists are worried about when they challenge the Mechanist Thesis: i.e. that the introduction of what Turing referred to as a 'semantic' innovation would in fact entail a deep conceptual reorientation in our attitudes towards human imagination and creativity. It is undoubtedly the case that a metaphor can sometimes be of such power that it can change the course, not just of a science, but even of a civilisation (see Young 1985). Wittgenstein recorded in one of his notebooks that 'What a Copernicus or a Darwin really achieved was not the discovery of a true theory but of a fertile new point of view' (CV: 18). Perhaps, a hundred years hence, Turing's name will be added to this list? Certainly there are those around who feel this should be the case. But how fertile is the computational point of view?

The fruitfulness of computationalism in regard to the problem of creativity is largely a function of the principal metaphor of *searching through a problem-space*. The search metaphor is one of the oldest of the expressions that is used to talk about problem-solving. It goes back to the Judaeo–Christian theme that the perception of Divine Truth can only be attained after a prolonged struggle. The search for the solution of a problem is likened to an arduous physical search. Insight is one's reward for perseverance.

Opposed to this is the Romantic view of creativity which, as we saw in §1, can be traced back to the ancient Greek view of inspiration. On this picture, insight is a mystery which, like one of Zeus's lightning bolts, comes from 'out of the blue'. For reasons that we cannot hope to fathom, some are chosen to be the repositories of 'divine madness'. Neither they nor we can explain what happens to them when they are 'out of their senses'.

We commonly invoke both of these themes today, but with certain unspoken conventions. For example, we demand that an 'out of the blue' experience should not be too far out of the blue. The story of Newton's apple[27] provides an interesting illustration of the constraints that exist. The very fact that we should find the story so appealing is, perhaps, a residue of Romantic influences. And yet we would be reluctant to accept this story as true of anyone but a Newton – certainly not of someone who was not remotely interested or engaged in the problems of physics. Thus, we are predisposed to see creative problem-solving as a largely unconscious affair, and we are happy to accept the role of serendipity in 'sudden moments of insight'. But we are loath to separate insight from effort altogether; for, in modern eyes, only the prepared mind can recognise the significance of a chance event.

Computationalism represents a synthesis of the Judaeo–Christian with the Romantic view of creativity. *Searching through a problem-space* has retained many of the attributes of a physical search:

> In physical search, one often examines many items to find the right item ... Likewise in inventive thinking, one often finds and considers alternative ideas. In physical search, one often looks in different places. ... Likewise in inventive thinking, one looks in different 'conceptual places' – for instance, by taking different approaches to a problem that might lead to quite different solutions. Just as invention can be thought of as a process of search, so can effectiveness and efficiency in invention be understood as effectiveness and efficiency in search. In invention also, it makes sense to ask whether you've looked long enough, looked in the right places, dug deeply enough, ranged widely enough.
>
> (Perkins 1981: 131)

The computational version of the search metaphor brings several additional features into play: e.g., that one can search for several goals simultaneously, or engage in other activities while working on a problem; that one can employ different methods to solve a problem; that a search relies on pre-established routes (routines) and techniques; that the act of searching renders one sensitive to particular cues; that the parameters of a search constrain the set of possible solutions; that searching is cumulative and perhaps highly structured; that one can adopt either a bottom-up or a top-down approach to solving a problem; and, most important of all, that the success of a search often depends on various sorts of short-cut.

Although the search metaphor can be extended considerably, by its very nature all of the images which it calls to mind belong to the picture of effort meeting with its just rewards (e.g., the ideas that discovery demands training, commitment, fortitude, endurance and courage; that the search for the solution to an obdurate problem should be methodical, focused, sustained, etc.; that we progress by eliminating false routes). But on the computationalist version of this metaphor, it is not the agent who is doing the searching: it is his brain. Thus, not only does problem-solving not require effort on the subject's part: he need not even be awake. Preparation and incubation also fade into the background on the computationalist account; for the 'cognitive heuristics' which have become the engines of creativity are seen as the end-result of five million years of hominid evolution.

Thus, AI offers an entirely new picture of how the Judaeo–Christian view of creativity can be synthesised with the Romantic. But what seems to go missing on this approach is the individual whose 'courage, independence of thought and judgment, honesty, perseverance, curiosity, willingness to take risks, and the like' (Torrance 1988: 68) is rewarded with insight. This may come as no surprise given that, whereas the developmental, personality, or social psychologist is interested in such questions as the role of environment, intelligence, or character traits on creativity, the AI-scientist is concerned with the 'mechanics of the creative process'. But there is a far deeper issue at stake here: an issue which lies at the very heart of the post-computational mechanist thesis.

If problem-solving as conceived by Turing and elaborated by Newell and Simon is to be treated as the paradigm for thinking (or perhaps, the core of thinking), and if the 'atomic tasks' of a program must be such that they presuppose no intelligence, then neither can they presuppose insight. Yet the creativity and originality characteristic of thinking must somehow emerge from a program if it is to be used to simulate the processes of human problem-solving. Hence the post-computational mechanist has to persuade us that 'novelty in problem solving comes about through ordinary thought processes in interaction with the information available in the problem': that 'there is no need to postulate a special process called insight' (Weisberg 1988: 155, 156). Herein lies what we might call the 'hidden agenda' behind protocol analysis.

To be sure, the one thing which we have learnt from protocol analysis is just how easy it is for an agent to overlook the intervening stages whereby he has solved a problem. Given the charm of the Romantic picture of genius, it is little wonder that a subject should seize on the notion of inspiration to explain his own performance. The proof that his solution of the problem had proceeded in an orderly manner, or had been cued by some external stimulus, is somehow deflating when seen from this perspective. But the supposition that we can give a fairly complete explanation of the cognitive processes resulting in discovery does not mean that the agent did not experience a sudden moment of insight, or, as is more likely the case, many such moments (see Gruber 1981b). Nor does it mean that the notion of 'creative leap' is vacuous.

What it does tell us, however, is just how different 'thinking' and 'problem-solving' are from standard process-verbs, and thus, how different 'insight' and 'illumination' are from process-nouns. For 'The so-called *cognitive processes* include memory, thinking, interpreting, problem-solving, creativity and the like' (Reber 1985: 577). That is, the type of 'cognitive processes' which we are concerned with here are simply those that are studied by psychologists of thinking: viz., the processes of reflecting, remembering, imagining, guessing, observing, noticing, considering, searching, evaluating, testing, etc. But these are not hidden processes which we infer from an agent's behaviour; rather, they are the processes through which *the agent* goes when solving the problem (see §8). As Wittgenstein puts it: ' "There has just taken place in me the mental process of remembering . . . " means nothing more than: "I have just remembered . . . ". To deny the mental process would mean to deny the remembering; to deny that anyone ever remembers' (PI: §306).

As far as mechanism is concerned, this is merely to reiterate the problem, not to explain it. Classical mechanists resorted to association and apperception to explain what was going on 'inside the agent' (inside his brain). It was because of the obvious failure of this approach, and because they felt unequipped to deal with this problem, that behaviourists sought to bypass it. But this confined experimental psychology to the description of observable causal regularities; and the very notion of a 'black box' served as a challenge which AI could not ignore.

By defining 'cognitive process' as the preconscious information-transforming processes that bring about conscious mental states, 'post-computational' stands to 'pre-computational' mechanism in the way that Kepler stands to Copernicus, and not as Copernicus stands to Plotinus. The AI approach to explaining the nature of insight is thus the perfect illustration of how 'the philosophical problem about mental processes and states' arises: how

> The first step is the one that altogether escapes notice. We talk of processes and states and leave their nature undecided. Sometime perhaps we shall know more about them – we think. But that is just what commits us to a particular way of looking at the matter. For we have a definite concept of what it means to learn to know a process better. (The decisive movement in the conjuring trick has been made, and it was the very one that we thought quite innocent.)
>
> (*Ibid.*: §308)

The very premise that programs provide a means of 'learning to know these processes better' proceeds from the idea that 'psychology treats of processes in the psychical sphere, as does physics in the physical' (*ibid.*: §571). This presupposition results in the mechanist conception of insight as the termination of a causal chain, each link of which must, according to Turing's Thesis, be mechanically computable.

> And now the analogy which was to make us understand our thoughts falls to pieces. So we have to deny the yet uncomprehended process in the yet unexplored medium. And now it looks as

179

if we had denied mental processes. And naturally we don't want to
deny them.

(*Ibid.*: §308)

That is, we do not want our critique of mechanism to spill over into a
blanket condemnation of the psychology of thinking. There is even a crucial
sense in which we do not want to deny that insight is the consequence of
cognitive processes.

As Gruber explains in *Darwin on Man*,

> The fact that the formation of a new synthesis must be seen as a
> creative *process* rather than as a sudden creative act has a deep signifi-
> cance for the relation between the thinker and the intellectual and
> social milieu in which he works. An isolated and sudden act might
> conceivably be thought of as occurring out of all time and place.
> But a long growth process must be seen as rooted in its total human
> context.

(Gruber 1981a: 6)

Darwin's 'great insight' of 28 September 1838 exemplifies Gruber's point.
For Gruber shows that, first, it was really a '*re*-cognition of what [Darwin]
already knew or almost knew. Second, the moment is historic more in hindsight than it was at the time. . . . Third, the idea when it came did not
represent a rupture with his past, but a fulfillment of his own abiding
purposes' (*ibid.*: 42).

A similar point applies to the humbler and different species of insight; or
rather, to the 'different activities in which this expression swims' (MS: 117).
For to speak of different 'kinds' of insight immediately suggests different
types of mental process; but what we are really concerned with here is how,
to paraphrase what Wittgenstein says at §337 of the *Investigations*, 'an
insight is embedded in its situation, in the agent's abilities and intentions.'
That is, our use of 'insight' is highly context- and individual-relative, and to
clarify the nature of insight, the philosopher needs to survey the various
sorts of situations in which 'insight' ('illumination', 'incubation', 'creativity',
'discovery', etc.) are applied.

The very question 'What is sudden understanding?' is a product of the
physiological paradigm underpinning the mechanist/vitalist debate, and
thus the source of much of the trouble here. It was in order to forestall the
confusions that result from trying to define the 'essence of sudden understanding' – in terms, e.g., of an underlying process or a distinctive
experience – that Wittgenstein warns: 'The question is badly framed. If it is
a question about the meaning of the expression "sudden understanding", the
answer is not to point to a process that we give this name to' (PI: §321).
Rather, as we saw in §8, we use the term to indicate an agent's ability or

intention to proceed in a given manner. But such a use is defeasible; for the common experience of false (or forgotten) insights (which is conspicuously missing on the computational account) serves as a reminder that the concept must be seen against the background of an agent's 'doubts, retreats, detours, and impasses . . . impulsive moments of decision, leaps into the dark from points of no return . . . reasonable mistakes, non-essentials, and foolish blunders' (Gruber 1981a: 4).

This return to the physical search metaphor brings us back to the archetypal myths about genius and creativity that we have inherited. This, of course, is the central target of AI. Cognitivist attitudes are exemplified by Weisberg's *Creativity: Genius and other Myths*, where the various topics surveyed (e.g., the 'creativity myth', the 'myth of the unconscious', the ' "Aha!" myth') are all meant to illustrate the scientific naivety of earlier ages. But AI could no more *refute* our myths for talking about problem-solving and creativity than the theory of natural selection could refute the myth of Genesis. Indeed, computationalism stands on exactly the same level as the 'creativity myth' or the 'myth of the unconscious'. That is, computationalism is no more a *rigorous theory* than these earlier myths are *folk theories*. All provide us with metaphors with which to talk about the mind, and to assign established meanings to different aspects of our behaviour.

The reason why we find Wordsworth saying the same sorts of things as Plato about insight and creativity is not because both lived prior to the age of Turing Machines. More to the point (given the prominence which it has received in cognitivist writings on creativity), there is a way to read Coleridge's preface to 'Kubla Khan' other than as a (deliberate or inadvertent) fabrication. Drawing on Elizabeth Schneider's research, many cognitivists have seized on Coleridge's supposed duplicity to illustrate the manner in which Romantic preconceptions lead one to distort the creative process. But fortunately for Coleridge's reputation, it is clear that something very different is going on in the poem.

The Preface to 'Kubla Khan' should be seen as just that: i.e., it is part of the poem, and not a brief excursion into psychological theory. To understand why Coleridge presents 'Kubla Khan' in this manner, we have to look at the genre in which he hereby intended the poem to be read. Coleridge is identifying himself as a descendant of Tiresias; the poem we are offered is meant to provide us with a glimpse into a transcendental world, inaccessible to ordinary experience, but none the less immediately recognisable as a vision of the City of God. In this case, the whole meaning of the poem is constituted by the classical conventions which Coleridge invokes.

Similarly, when Poincaré maintains that 'Discovery is discernment, selection', he is not formulating a hypothesis; rather, his remark is a manifestation of the conventions guiding his understanding of creativity: not the product of introspection or inference. He frames his memoir with archetypal images of creativity: he is concerned, he tells us, with the genesis of mathematical knowledge, with the manner in which his mind was able to divine mathematical truths. There then follows a succession of metaphors, each chosen to convey some aspect of the creative process.

At the beginning of the memoir, the metaphors reflect the preliminary state of his thinking. Ideas are being canvassed, they are surging and jostling in his semi-conscious mind. The general impression conveyed is one of helplessness and a slightly overwhelmed feeling. As his thinking progresses, the metaphors become more dynamic (e.g. he speaks of verifying his finding); perceptual (e.g. he recognises an identity between two mathematical transformations); and physical (e.g. he struggles to work out the implications of his earlier insights). The over-arching metaphor of multiple paths signifies his feeling that many possible methods of solution lay open to him, and that the key to his success lay in his having (unconsciously) picked the best route.

The reason why our myths of creativity are of such importance is *not* because we are committed to some primitive theory of the 'inner workings of the mind' (itself a metaphor from another era), but because we invoke these pictures when we talk about 'sudden discovery'. There is a tendency to suppose that the role of metaphors in scientific writings is always heuristic: i.e. that they guide and are displaced by scientific theories. But when talking about something like 'sudden discovery', the metaphor is the message. Thus, the varying stages of metaphor through which Poincaré progresses are *expressions* of his evolving mastery of the problem, and his changing moods and expectations as this proceeds. What those who would dismiss the psychological import of his memoir fail to appreciate is how Poincaré uses these conventions to *create* a compelling picture of the 'unconscious processes of discernment, selection'. That is, he uses the 'myth of the unconscious' to draw attention to those crucial aspects of creativity which cannot be explained on a mechanist paradigm.

By the same token, the appeal of the computational myth lies in the fact that it draws attention to crucial aspects of creativity which are completely ignored by the 'myth of the unconscious'. Thus, by emphasising the step-by-step manner whereby agents typically solve problems, computationalism is highly effective at encouraging detailed scrutiny of the cognitive processes (as explained above, not as redefined by Turing) involved in problem-solving.[28] But it is quite striking to see how references to the information-processing metaphor in cognitivist writings are rarely accompanied by any genuine concern with its mechanics. Even those who write on the abilities of calculating prodigies from an information-processing perspective seldom draw on the details of chess- or theorem-proving programs.

There are, of course, other ways in which the computational myth has had a positive impact on the study of creativity. For example, it has led to a deeper understanding of the transfer of strategies to new situations, and the highly structured interplay between knowledge and problem-solving strategies. But the basic problem with the computational myth is that it is *too* structured. Given that what we say about problem-solving – which is a family-resemblance concept – is so intimately bound up with context, there is an ever-present danger of oversimplifying or even failing to recognise the creative processes displayed by an agent in a given circumstance.

Perhaps the greatest advances in our understanding of creativity over the past few years have been made in close observation of an agent's actions, and/or biographical research, and not in laboratory studies or computer simulations. For the explanation of creativity demands 'probing hermeneutical interpretation in order to reconstruct the events we hope to understand' (Gruber 1981b: 245). Such a conclusion is, of course, directly contrary to the principles and objectives of mechanism. For it places the emphasis on the individual as opposed to the universal; on the intentional as opposed to the automatic; on the cognisable as opposed to the 'inaccessible'; on the cultural as opposed to the neurophysiological; and on the interpretative as opposed to the predictive. Most important of all, it insists on the inclusion of insight in any adequate psychological explanation of problem-solving and creativity; on the gradual or sudden acquisition of an ability which may come about through natural endowments, practice, perseverance, reflection, or observation; on the acquisition of subsidiary skills; on strong intrinsic motivation; on personality traits; on well-placed encouragement and education; or perhaps, simply, on curiosity and a sense of wonder.

That hardly means, however, that psychology must abandon any hope of discovering significant regularities in problem-solving behaviour. This brings us back to the question of whether Wittgenstein wanted to argue that experimental psychology is *au fond* misconceived: that there can be no such thing as a 'science of thinking'. In 1938, Wittgenstein told his students that the attitude which he was battling was that which presupposed that the

> Paradigm of the sciences is mechanics. If people imagine a psychology, their ideal is a mechanics of the soul. If we look at what actually corresponds to that, we find there are physical experiments and there are psychological experiments. There are laws of physics and there are laws – if you wish to be polite – of psychology.
>
> (LA: 28f)

Thus, Wittgenstein had clearly set himself against the Boolean argument that a science of thinking is only possible if 'the operations of the mind are in a certain real sense subject to laws' (Boole 1947: 3) in exactly the same way that physical events are subject to the laws of nature. But Wittgenstein had no objection to treating psychology as akin to statistics (LA: 18) – i.e. of construing psychological laws on, e.g., the paradigm of epidemiology as opposed to pathology.

Seen in this light, Wittgenstein's remarks on the 'morphology of "thinking"' should be seen as a propaedeutic rather than an impediment to experimental psychology. This was precisely how Wittgenstein felt his remarks on the foundations of mathematics should be viewed. For, given that each discipline suffers from 'conceptual confusion', the benefit of philosophical therapy must be the same in each: viz., 'Philosophical clarity will have the same effect on the growth of mathematics and psychology as sunlight has on the growth of potato shoots. (In a dark cellar they grow yards long.)' (PG: 381). But there is also a striking difference between the philosophies of mathematics and psychology.

In the case of the former, the problems which we deal with only occur in the 'prose'; the mathematics itself must, as Wittgenstein constantly stressed, be left intact (see Shanker 1987a: chapter 5). But the philosophy of psychology is categorially different, for the simple reason that 'psychological concepts are just everyday concepts. They are not concepts newly fashioned by science for its own purpose, as are the concepts of physics and chemistry' (RPP I: §62). But this is exactly the point which AI disputes. For AI proceeds from the fundamental assumption that psychological concepts, *qua* concepts, are *theoretical constructs*. Psychological concepts should be compared to the earlier 'folk-theoretic' concepts of eighteenth-century natural science, and not to the rigorous concepts of present-day physics and chemistry. Indeed, this is precisely what is meant by calling psychology 'a young science' (see Wellman 1990). Thus, our investigation of Wittgenstein's remarks on the foundations of AI takes us to what is perhaps the ultimate foundation of AI: the Cartesian view of concepts.

5

THE NATURE OF CONCEPTS

It is with considerable difficulty that I remember the original
era of my being; all the events of that period appear confused
and indistinct. A strange multiplicity of sensations seized me,
and I saw, felt, heard, and smelt at the same time; and it was,
indeed, a long time before I learned to distinguish between
the operations of my various senses. By degrees, I remember, a
stronger light pressed upon my nerves, so that I was obliged
to shut my eyes. Darkness then came over me and troubled
me, but hardly had I felt this when, by opening my eyes, as I
now suppose, the light poured in upon me again. I walked
and, I believe, descended, but I presently found a great alter-
ation in my sensations. Before, dark and opaque bodies
surrounded me, impervious to my touch or sight; but I now
found that I could wander on at liberty, with no obstacles
which I could not either surmount or avoid.

(Mary Shelley, *Frankenstein*)

§1 What are concepts and how are they acquired?

This book is an exercise in what might be called 'philosophical archaeology':
a logical excavation of the foundations of AI. The guiding principle here is
the Wittgensteinian theme that, in order to understand the nature of AI –
what kind of theory it is and what kind of problems it raises – and in order
to understand the reasons why the cognitive revolution was so quickly
usurped by the post-computational mechanist revolution, we need to
examine not just the mathematical and psychological origins of AI but, also,
its philosophical roots. As we shall see in this chapter, this last point is especially relevant to the AI view of concepts, which has a distinctly Kantian
ring to it. It must be noted from the start, however, that merely establishing
the Kantian orientation of the AI view of concepts does not *ipso facto* constitute an indictment of AI. After all, Kant welcomed the 'confirmation or
refutation by experiment' of his theory of cognition; and Piaget was clearly

not disturbed by being labelled a Kantian (see Piaget 1965). So why should AI not claim for itself the honour of fulfilling Kant's vision of advancing the 'science of metaphysics'?

There is, however, a further dimension to this logical excavation. We are looking, not just for the presuppositions – and even the problems – which AI inherited from specific thinkers and schools of thought, but, also, for the fundamental epistemological view of the relation between thought and behaviour which lies at the heart of both pre- and post-computational mechanism. That is, we are struggling to understand the basic framework in which the very demand for AI is grounded. Putting together these two senses of 'origins' – the historical and the conceptual – enables us to see how AI is the product of a Cartesian picture of the mind which, as we saw in the previous chapter, leads one to postulate 'pre-conscious processes' in order to explain what are *epistemological*, not psychological, problems.

Throughout this book we have been concerned with AI's attempt to develop computational theories in order to analyse various psychological and logical concepts. Thus we have looked at such questions as: 'What is the nature of *calculating, thinking, reasoning, inferring, problem-solving* and *insight?*' In each case we have been at pains to understand what kind of question is being raised and to clarify how one might go about answering it: to distinguish psychological from philosophical responses, in order to identify and remove the sources of mechanist reductionism. Overshadowing all these investigations has been the implicit meta-question which has dominated cognitive psychology for the past forty years: viz., 'What are concepts and how are they acquired?' Our task in this chapter is thus fairly simply stated: viz., is the question 'What are concepts and how are they acquired?' any more the sort of question that can be resolved by a psychological theory than the previous questions that we have looked at in this book? The issue is complicated, however, by the fact that the shift from 'classical' to 'prototype' models in the theory of concepts is commonly attributed to Wittgenstein: specifically, to §§65–7 of *Philosophical Investigations*. In the course of this chapter we shall have to look closely at how Wittgenstein's argument in these passages relates to AI's view of concepts and concept-formation. But first we need to look more closely at how cognitive scientists have dealt with this issue.

In his overview of 'Concept Development', Flavell begins by stating that 'The search for a satisfactory definition of the term "concept" is a lexicographer's nightmare' (Flavell 1970). On first reading this may seem a sentiment that few philosophers or psychologists would wish to challenge: one of those truisms over which the eye glides. But on closer study it reveals an interesting tension. For it is unlikely that many lexicographers will share this sense of anxiety. After all, nothing could be more straightforward than to define 'concept'. In the words of the *Oxford English Dictionary*, 'concept' refers to 'an idea of a class of objects'. Of course, far from definitively explaining what a concept *is*, this merely serves to transfer the problem to a different term. And if you follow this up in the OED, you will find that the next step is to shift the problem on to 'notion', then to 'representation', then to 'image', which directs us back to 'idea'. But circularity was not one of the sins from which Dr Johnson sought to wean his craft.

There is nothing to suggest that cognitive scientists feel that this OED definition is in some deep sense *wrong*. In his recent survey of 'Concepts and Conceptual Structure', Medin is perfectly happy to proceed with this definition of 'a *concept* [as] an idea that includes all that is characteristically associated with it' (Medin 1989: 1469). But Medin then goes on to distinguish questions about 'how we define "concept"' from 'questions about the nature of [concepts and] categories,' where the latter 'may be psychological as much as metaphysical questions' (*ibid.*). Not surprisingly, it is in regard to the latter questions that the 'nightmares' surface.

It is not as though Flavell is unaware of the difference between the questions 'What is the definition of "concept"?' and 'What is a concept?' The point he is making is that a definition is merely the visible surface of an underlying theory. And, according to Flavell, it is because we do not yet have a satisfactory theory of concepts that each new proposed definition 'leaves the reader with a sense that something has been omitted, distorted, or oversimplified – that something he intuitively feels to be true of at least some concepts has simply not been captured' (Flavell 1970: 983).

On this view, the problem that confronts us in the definition of 'concept' is the same as the one that confronts us in the definition of any generic concept. A satisfactory scientific definition of 'plant', for example, must encompass all and only those organisms that are plants. Should we come across an organism like euglena, which defies straightforward classification as either animal or plant, the problem must lie in our theory of what constitutes a 'plant'. Likewise, if each new proposed definition of 'concept' proves inadequate, it can only be because we still do not have a satisfactory theory of what constitutes a concept. And the reason why no one has been able to come up with the latter is because 'these entities [*sic*] differ from one another in an astonishing number of ways; the dissimilarities are, in fact, far more striking, clear-cut, and important-looking than the similarities' (*ibid.*). That is, we cannot expect a satisfactory definition of 'concept' until we can say what, e.g., the concepts of furniture, plant, game, colour, natural number, irrational number, beauty, justice, truth, God, and concept itself, all have in common.

In short, the cognitivist's goal is nothing less than to discover 'the essential nature of concepts' (*ibid.*). And if the cognitivist is suffering nightmares in this endeavour, it is because the 'search for attributes common to this array gives meager returns' (*ibid.*). But here speaks the voice of the 'classical' model of concepts: the view that all the instances of a category must have some fundamental characteristic in common which determines their membership in that category. Perhaps what is needed is simply a different model of concepts: i.e. prototype theory.

The prototype theorist will respond that the fact that psychologists and philosophers have failed to come up with a set of the defining features of 'concept' hardly entails that we must resign ourselves to the fact that we shall never fully understand the very 'fabric of mental life' (*ibid.*). Instead, it suggests that the solution to this mystery must be to abandon the search for a set of singly necessary and jointly sufficient properties that define 'concept'. Rather, one needs to apply the shift from classical to prototype theory (that was initiated by Rosch in 'Cognitive Representations of Semantic Categories') to the concept of concept itself. That is, to treat the category of concept as organised around a set of attributes that are only characteristic of category-membership.

Whether prototype theory will prove any more lasting than the classical view, or, as is already occurring, there will be a further move to some form of a 'non-similarity based theory of concepts', we can see how Flavell's prefatory remarks highlight the central theme of this chapter. One can certainly appreciate how vexing it must be for cognitive psychologists to be unable to draw on a satisfactory definition of their basic construct. One can also appreciate how this issue became bound up in their eyes with a satisfactory explanation of the nature of concept-acquisition. And since lexicographers have never been responsible for the latter type of exercise, is it not reasonable that cognitive psychologists should take up this burden? But is the question 'What are concepts and how are they acquired?' any more a psychological than a semantic issue? And if it is neither, does that mean that it is metaphysical?

Once again, Flavell's overview is an invaluable place to which to turn. He brings into sharp relief the basic epistemological picture that underpins the demand for a theory of concepts, and the constraints which any satisfactory theory of concepts must meet. Flavell cites as his starting-point the fundamental presupposition that 'an individual interacts with his environment by breaking it down and organizing it into meaningful patterns congruent with his own needs and psychological make-up' (Harvey *et al.* 1961: 1). In Flavell's words, 'Concepts have the absolutely essential function of reducing the complexity of sensory input to manageable proportions' (Flavell 1970: 985).

As Rumelhart points out, this picture of concepts as 'the building blocks of cognition' can be traced directly back to Kant. For, as we saw in Chapter 2, Kant maintained that the mind is bombarded by a flux of sensations which must be synthesised and organised via concepts. On this view, concepts (schemata) 'are the fundamental elements upon which all information processing depends. Schemata are employed in the process of interpreting sensory data (both linguistic and nonlinguistic), in retrieving information from memory, in organizing actions, in determining goals and subgoals, in allocating resources, and, generally, in guiding the flow of processing in the system' (Rumelhart 1980: 33–4).

Given this Kantian picture of the mind forced to impose order on the intrinsically chaotic information it receives if it is to make sense of reality, it follows that 'The concept repertoire serves to carve up or "chunk" the organism's entire world into functional units, yielding a complete mapping of responses into stimulus sets for the length and breadth of the psychological environment' (Flavell 1970: 984). It is for this reason that the cognitivist maintains that the concept of concept can only be analysed by identifying the *functional similarities* which are either possessed by all concepts, or shared by all concepts to a greater or lesser degree.

The three 'functional similarities' most commonly cited by cognitive scientists are:

1 concepts serve to identify and classify input information;
2 concepts reduce the complexity of sensory input to manageable proportions;
3 concepts enable an organism to go beyond the information given.

On this view of cognition, the concepts that an organism forms as a result of its interactions with its environment capture the similarities that it perceives. Every time an organism sees something new it compares this with its stored repertoire of concepts, and if there is a match, it knows right away what it is seeing and what to expect: to the extent, that is, of its previous experiences. If a subject's only prior experience with dogs is with beagles, he will assume that the pit bull he has just identified as a dog will happily let him take food from its mouth and tug on its ears. Thus, experience quickly causes an organism's stored concepts to be modified. But the fact that concept-acquisition is a virtually endless process does not mitigate the usefulness of even the most primitive of concepts. For 'If we had no concepts, we would have to refer to each individual entity by its own name, and the mental lexicon required would be so enormous that communication as we know it might collapse.' Above all else, therefore, concepts 'decrease the amount of information that we must perceive, learn, remember, communicate, and reason about' (Smith 1989: 501).[1]

Given this 'functional' outlook, the most serious contender for the role of the 'common attribute' shared by all concepts (or prototypical property) is *equivalence response*. That is, concepts are said to consist in having similar or identical reactions to different environmental input. But then, if 'A minimal criterion for having a concept is that discriminably different objects be treated as similar',[2] it follows that 'even very unsophisticated animals will, of course, have concepts. For example, a pigeon can learn to peck at circles to be rewarded with food. Since the pigeon can see the differences between large and small circles yet treat them equivalently, it would be said to have the concept of circle' (Markman 1989: 138).

There are several things to observe at the outset about the 'functional definition of concepts'. First is the premise that to understand the function of a concept is similar to trying to understand the function of the prefrontal cortex: in both cases we have to establish 'what they accomplish for the organism' (Flavell 1970: 985). (Perhaps both emerged at roughly the same time on the evolutionary continuum, maybe even as a consequence of one another.) Second is the conspicuous return to the continuum picture. Whereas the pigeon example is exactly the sort of thing one might have resorted to as a *reductio* of this argument, we find it cited here as validating the theory. And finally, there is the pronounced commitment to mechanism (already implicit in the first premise); for concepts are treated as 'the mediating linkage between the input side (stimuli) and the output side (response)' (*ibid.*).

Flavell goes on to tell us that, 'psychologically speaking, [a concept is the result of] an act of colligation or drawing-together of disparate elements for response purposes' (*ibid.*: 984). Herein lies one of the key reasons why the founders of the cognitive revolution were so drawn to the co-occurring post-computational mechanist revolution. For, according to AI, 'in operating as a system of ordering, a concept may be viewed as a categorical schema, an intervening medium, or program through which impinging stimuli are coded, passed, or evaluated on their way to response evocation' (Harvey *et al.* 1961: 1). Thus, as we shall see in the following section, AI seemed to satisfy the most pressing need of the burgeoning cognitive revolution: a method for analysing the structure of concepts, and, thus, the mechanics of their acquisition, storage, retrieval, modification and organisation.

§2 Piaget and AI

The language used in the computational definition of 'concept' may be that of information-processing, but, as Rumelhart points out, the basic picture underlying the AI view of cognition is as old as Kant. Indeed, one of the central questions we shall have to explore in this chapter is whether the real reason why each new proposed definition of 'concept' is unsatisfactory is because each new stage in the theory of concepts is really just a reworking of classical Kantian themes. But there are marked differences between Kant's views and those of the cognitive revolution. For Kant thought that psychology – that considerations of *concept-acquisition* – could play no role in our explanation of the nature of a concept. But all this was changed by Piaget: most notably, in the latter's repudiation of the idea that the concepts that the mind imposes on reality are fixed. Instead, Piaget argued that concepts emerge from, and evolve through, a process of adapting to the environment.

The six stages of sensori-motor development that Piaget postulated are supposed to provide a bridge from elementary reflexes to the child's awareness of similarity relations (which appears in the later stages of sensori-motor development). The basis for the transition from *reflex mechanism* to *representation* – from *reacting to stimuli* to *possessing a concept* – is to be found in 'sensori-motor schemes', which are said to be the 'precursors' of concepts. According to Piaget, these begin to form in the earliest stages of intelligence – even at the initial stages, when a child cannot yet be said to be 'thinking' (in Piaget's terms, manipulating mental representations).

Piaget illustrated this idea with his account of the development of the grasping reflex. At first the grasping reflex is activated by any contact, but the child soon begins to differentiate between those objects which are graspable and those which are not. This leads the child to construct a mental scheme of graspable things: to search for things to grasp, to decide for any given object whether it is graspable (we observe a child about to pick up something, hesitate, pass it over), and to incorporate grasping in other goal-directed actions. The child's grasping reflex thus becomes attuned to its environment: the child extends the range of objects which it grasps ('generalised assimilation') and distinguishes between graspable and ungraspable objects ('recognitory assimilation').

Piaget argues that, in a sense, the child is already performing here a series of experiments, and constructing theories about reality. To 'conduct an experiment' at this level is to repeat an action while varying some of its elements. Intractable experiences then cause the child to revise its 'theory'. The outcome of these experiments is that the child's mind forms a sensori-motor scheme whose function is to guide grasping: i.e., presented with any object, it must decide whether or not it is graspable. This is said to involve 'making judgements' about the action and 'reasoning' from the effects. 'Judgement' at the sensori-motor level consists in assimilating an action to a scheme; 'reasoning' consists in the combining of several 'judgements'.

That is not to say that a sensori-motor child has an idea of or thinks about which objects are graspable; the latter are said to be cognitive processes that only emerge (in a rudimentary fashion) at the second stage of pre-operational thinking. Conversely, Piaget emphasises that attributing to the child possession of 'sensori-motor schemes' is not just a theoretical construct.[3] The sensori-motor child can be said to 'distinguish' (recall Turing's use of inverted commas) between graspable and ungraspable objects in a way that is not that far removed from the sense in which, e.g., a thermostat can be said to 'distinguish' between a hot and a cold room. So the transition from *reaction* to *cognition* is a mental process which proceeds from *sensori-motor schemes* to *concepts*. It consists in 'mapping similarity relations', which evolve as a result of interacting with and adapting to the environment.

We begin to get a deeper insight, here, into the significance of its epistemological framework for the cognitivist theory of concepts. Looking at concept-acquisition is supposed to reveal the nature of concepts *per se*. That is, if there is a functional similarity in the manner in which a child acquires its 'wide array' of concepts, this will reveal the essential nature of concepts. But, in actual fact, the exact opposite has transpired: a Kantian preconception of the nature of concepts has determined the manner in which the cognitivist looks at concept-acquisition. Thus, the presupposition that concepts identify and classify input information, reduce the complexity of sensory input to manageable proportions, and enable an organism to go beyond the information given, has predetermined the form which the cognitivist's explanation of *concept-acquisition* takes.

The crux of Piaget's theory of development is that, *contra* empiricism, *concept-acquisition* must be an 'active' mental process. Because of the Kantian epistemology, this takes the form of arguing that concepts emerge out of some form of *cognitive equilibration*: of *assimilation* and *accommodation* to incoming stimuli (i.e., modifying information to conform to pre-existing mental structures, and modifying mental structures so as to assimilate a broader range of incoming information). The 'equilibratory heart' of this mental process consists in some set of procedures that 'assess the match or mismatch between the input (whether example or counterexample) and the current state of the developing concept' (Boden 1979: 137). And, as Boden points out, it is precisely here where AI entered the picture; for Piaget had little to say about the actual mechanics of this process.

What could be a more compelling vindication of this epistemological picture than to build a system that actually demonstrates how, proceeding from a few schematic rules, it would be possible to *build up* certain concepts. But the point of such an exercise is not to defend Turing's views on strong AI; rather, it is to provide a formal model of the 'complex structure in terms of which [the mind makes] logically subtle comparisons and effect[s] appropriate transformations to the concept it is constructing' (*ibid.*). That is, according to AI, by modelling *concept-acquisition*, one analyses the nature of *concepts*. But the premise that a program constitutes a model of concept-acquisition turns on the Kantian preconceptions about the nature of concepts that lie at the heart of the AI view of cognition.

There is, of course, a significant divergence between the attitudes of cognitive psychologists and AI-scientists towards the theory of concepts. This comes through most clearly in Flavell's concern with the problem of how one distinguishes between *conceptual* and other kinds of equivalence response, such as tropisms. Flavell remarks that 'Even plants make what are essentially invariant responses to variant inputs', and we do not want to credit plants with the possession of concepts. So there must be some way of retaining the cognitive element which characterises concepts while showing how they emerge out of these simpler (mechanical) reactions. But 'What seems to be lacking so far is a *principled* distinction, one that suggests fundamental differences in process and mechanism between those equivalence responses we wish to call "conceptual" and all other kinds' (Flavell 1970: 985).

As we have repeatedly seen, AI had a powerful response to such reservations: according to AI, the longing for such a 'privileged distinction' is nothing more than a reflection of semantic conservatism. The difference between the 'higher-level' concepts possessed by man and the 'lower-level' concepts possessed by simpler organisms is indeed one of process and mechanism. All concepts are built up out of the same atomic units. Hence, on the AI view of cognition, we can extend the range of 'concept' downwards from man to animals to insects to plants to thermostats. For the slide into the mechanist continuum is the inexorable result of the premise that 'equivalence responses are intimately involved in adaptational patterns at all biological levels.' 'Concept-acquisition' applies to any organism – to any system – that adapts to its environment, and 'The centrality of [the study of] concepts is due to their playing major functional roles in any intelligent system, including human beings' (Smith 1989: 501).

With all the time and effort that was devoted to the problem of getting programs up and running, it was tempting in the early days to see AI as an attempt at bottom-up engineering, whose sole purpose, in Minsky's famous words, was to create machines capable of performing tasks that would require intelligence if done by humans (see Minsky 1968: v). But all of the work done on semantic nets, production systems, frames and scripts was intended to be seen as furthering our understanding of *concept-acquisition*. That is, what Winston (1975), Newell and Simon (1972), Minsky (1975), and Schank and Abelson (1977) all thought they were doing was simulating the manner in which concepts develop. For these pioneers of AI were guided by the premise that 'a concept may be viewed as a categorical schema, an intervening medium, or program through which impinging stimuli are coded, passed, or evaluated on their way to response evocation.'

In other words, a schema is literally a concept, and a self-modifying program is literally a model of internally-driven concept-acquisition. Consider, for example, the following schema, which is said to 'represent' a typical chair:

CHAIR
  SUBSET-OF: FURNITURE
  GOOD-FOR: Sitting, standing, working, eating, ruling, watching . . .
    DEFAULT: Sitting
  TYPE: Kitchen, Dining Room, Study, Lecture Hall, Garden . . .
    DEFAULT: Kitchen
  NUMBER-OF-LEGS: 1,2,3,4,5
    DEFAULT: 4

193

    IF-NEEDED: Use procedure COUNT-'EM
NUMBER-OF-ARMS: 0,1,2
    DEFAULT: 2
SEAT SHAPE: Flat, concave, convex
    DEFAULT: Flat
SEAT STRUCTURE: Solid, mesh, slats
    DEFAULT: Solid
BACK: Straight, angled, curved, missing
    DEFAULT: Straight
MATERIAL: Wood, plastic, chrome, leather, fabric
    DEFAULT: Wood
COLOUR: Black, white, red, brown, green, yellow . . .
    DEFAULT: Brown
STYLE: Modern, Baroque, Bauhaus, Sears, Frank Lloyd Wright . . .
    DEFAULT: Sears

What is meant by saying that the schema represents a typical chair is that the program will identify as chairs all those pieces of furniture which would most commonly be classified as chairs. But, then, this is precisely what was said to be the function of the concept chair. The program thus constitutes a preliminary analysis of the concept chair: i.e. of how the mind categorises chairs. The AI-theorist will hasten to concede that many more attributes can be added to this schema; that there is room for debate over the default values; and that most of the sub-categories are open-ended. But he will insist that the appeal of the program *qua* model of concept-acquisition lies in the fact that it seems to capture the most salient properties of chairs.

AI is what one might call 'developmental-neutral': i.e. it does not share Piaget's thesis that we can only understand the nature of a concept by charting its origins and evolution. But neither does it mark a return to the Kantian idea of fixed concepts. The AI-scientist's goal is to map the input–ouput patterns of the programs/concepts he constructs onto the behaviour of an organism. AI insists that the closer the fit, the more accurate the AI-scientist's analysis of the organism's concepts at the time of the comparison. The thrust of the toy domain argument is that, given that AI can already construct concepts that can be mapped onto primitive systems on the cognitive continuum, there is no *a priori* reason why it cannot construct and thereby analyse the higher-level concepts possessed by human adults, and, thus, no reason why it cannot model the developmental process incrementally (see Simon 1962).

The AI-scientist must work in close harmony, therefore, with the cognitive psychologist. For a program, *qua* analysis of a concept, will only be as good as the protocol onto which it is mapped. If the above chair program

has the same success as, say, a three-year-old child, when it comes to identifying different kinds of chairs, and if it makes the same kinds of mistakes
as the three-year-old, and, further, if the program can be designed to manifest the same sorts of typicality results (and whatever further constraints
one wants to add), then we may assume that the program serves as a model
of the schema whereby the three-year-old child assesses the match or
mismatch between an input and the current state of its developing concept
of chair.

Of course, if one approaches this issue from a narrow technical point of
view, the theory will seem to suffer from endemic underdetermination; after
all, any one of a number of programs might achieve the same results, so how
are we to say whether, e.g., production systems or frames are the right
approach? The answer is supposed to be provided by the fact that the AI-
scientist works hand-in-hand with the cognitive psychologist: the
justification for any given analysis is seen as lying, not in the sole criterion
of creating a successful program, but also in the type of responses which
subjects give to questions like: 'What is a chair?'; 'What is a chair most
likely used for?'; 'If a chair isn't used for sitting, what is it most likely used
for?'; and 'Think of a chair and describe it.'

From a cognitivist point of view, what AI brings to the analysis of
concepts and concept-acquisition is the simple fact that schema representations like the one shown above 'foster the kinds of computations that people
presumably execute. . . . [They provide] (1) a far greater set of potential
inductive inference, (2) a richer means for computing similarity to prototypes, and (3) a clearcut means for combining simple concepts into
composite concepts' (Smith 1989: 512). Whether or not a different type of
modelling should emerge which will prove even more effective when it
comes to these three conditions, all that concerns the cognitivist is that
these three conditions are seen as the criteria for justifying the analysis of a
concept.

The story of how the cognitive revolution was usurped by AI makes for a
fascinating study in the dynamics of normal science (see Bloomfield 1986).
But what our logical excavation is telling us is that 'usurp' is the wrong
word to use when talking about the relationship between the cognitive and
the computational revolutions. For, whatever the psychological or sociolog-
ical reasons for why the cognitive revolution seized on AI as its paradigm,
there is also this deep epistemological reason: AI proceeds from the same
Kantian framework as that which inspired the cognitive revolution. A
successful program would demonstrate the mechanics of the transition from
reflexes to cognition. Thus, far from imposing reductionism on the cognitive
revolution, AI simply explored different models of the reductionism that lies
at the heart of the cognitive revolution. Above all, what the rapidly-forged
union between AI and cognitive psychology reveals is how the question

'What are concepts and how are they acquired?' was seen by the cognitive revolution as an empirical matter: viz., a challenge to explain:

- How a subject forms a representation of a
- How S computes or infers whether x is an instance of a
- How S revises her representation of a to allow for borderline exemplars
- How S relates her knowledge of a to her knowledge of β
- How S is able to communicate her representation of a to others.

And it is precisely this picture of *concepts* as 'hidden mental constructs', and *concept-acquisition* as an 'active mental process' of 'abstracting and generalising' from experience that Wittgenstein was to scrutinise.

§3 Wittgenstein's 'discovery'

Wittgenstein's most significant contribution to our understanding of the nature of concepts is commonly said by cognitivists to be that he helped to bring about the demise of the classical theory of concepts when he 'discovered' family-resemblance concepts. This is said to occur in the argument at PI, §§65–7, in which Wittgenstein maintains that there is no single property common to all games in virtue of which we call them 'games'; instead, there is 'a complicated network of similarities overlapping and crisscrossing: sometimes overall similarities, sometimes similarities of detail' (PI: §66). But, from the cognitivist perspective, the chief drawback with Wittgenstein's argument is that he says nothing about the psychological dimensions of this issue. It is not just that there is no consideration in the *Investigations* of the differences between classical and prototype theories: no mention made of typicality ratings or reaction times. More importantly, it is that Wittgenstein seems content to describe the various 'complicated networks' that comprise language and leave the matter at that. As far as cognitive science is concerned, therefore, Wittgenstein's sum contribution to the theory of concepts amounts to a footnote, and, occasionally, an epigram.

There is an intriguing paper by Rosch, however, in which she struggles with the question of how Wittgenstein's 'view of language [as] part of our actions, part of the most basic problems which make up our physical and social "forms of life"' might serve as a starting-point for categorisation research (Rosch 1987: 153). She insists that 'This view has radical implications for categories. They are no longer objects of words or knowledge but are part of our delicately shifting forms of life' (*ibid.*). On this reading, Wittgenstein's argument does not just involve a paradigm-shift, with prototypes taking over the role hitherto played by *Merkmale*. For Wittgenstein successfully attacked the very framework that inspired classical theory: viz., the referential theory of meaning. Hence we must be careful, according to Rosch, not to repeat the same mistake of reifying prototypes: i.e. of supposing that all that is involved in the shift from classical to probabilist theories is a change in the *referent* of concept-words.

Rosch reminds us that 'For Wittgenstein the criterion for having reached the right focus point is the disappearance of the philosophical problem.' But that hardly means that categorisation research is about to disappear, for 'organisms still do treat discriminably different objects and events equivalently' (*ibid.*: 163). She thus ends her paper on an open note, querying whether, 'For empirical issues, perhaps this means rather that the problems are brought completely into view. And that is the beginning of the investigation' (*ibid.*: 164). There can be no gainsaying the importance of this point; Wittgenstein himself says much the same thing at PI, p. 232 (see Chapter 4). But what makes this issue so difficult is knowing where the philosophical problem ends and the empirical begins; and, more to the point, knowing how the two elements interact with one another in categorisation research.

A proper treatment of Wittgenstein's remarks on the concept of concept should respond to both of these demands. For, even if we can show how the 'functional definition of "concept"' is the unhappy legacy of Kantian presuppositions about the nature of cognition, having the right focus does not entail the disappearance of categorisation research. On the contrary, it should enhance it. The next section will broach the former task: viz., that of clarifying the substance and significance of Wittgenstein's discussion of the issue which concerned us in §1, the question 'What are concepts and how are they acquired?'. In the following sections I shall then try to relate Wittgenstein's concern with 'the way language works' to the cognitivist's goal of understanding 'how the mind works'.

§4. 'What we call "concept" comes into existence only by its incorporation in language'

The argument at PI §65 begins with the objection (voiced by the interlocutor) that Wittgenstein has so far said nothing of the essence of a language-game, 'and hence of language'. Wittgenstein responds that there is no 'common property'. This seems to suggest that one cannot talk about that which does not exist, and so the interlocutor's objection is meaningless. But elsewhere Wittgenstein makes it clear – in terms which are similar to those used by Flavell – that by no means is he abandoning the search for the 'essence of language'. ('We too in these investigations are trying to understand the essence of language – its function, its structure' (PI: §92).) But what he means by the 'essence of language' has undergone a radical change from when he wrote the *Tractatus*; he now regards this as 'something that already lies open to view and that becomes surveyable by a rearrangement', not 'something that lies *beneath* the surface. Something that lies within, which we see when we look *into* the thing, and which an analysis digs out' (PI: §92).

From his earliest work, Wittgenstein believed that questions about essence belong to logic (see NL). What changed was his view of logic (see PI: §108). Whereas in the *Tractatus* Wittgenstein believed that you *discover* the essence of a concept by logical analysis, in his later writings he argues that you *clarify* the essence of a concept by surveying the practice in which that concept-word is used.[4] Thus, in *Remarks on the Foundations of Mathematics* he maintains that 'if you talk about *essence*, you are merely noting a convention' (RFM: §74), and at PI §371 he asserts that 'Essence is expressed by grammar'.

When PI §§65–7 are read in the light of this larger argument, we can see that what he is saying there is that one cannot hope to answer the questions 'What is a game?' and 'What is language?' by delineating the set of necessary and sufficient conditions that every exemplar of the category must satisfy. That is, we must recognise that questions about the essence of a game, or of language, are not akin to questions about the chemical composition of a substance. Rather, to clarify the essence of a game, or of language, one must clarify the manner in which 'game' and 'language' are used.

The argument as so stated may seem to be redolent of ordinary-language philosophising; certainly it has been castigated as such often enough. But as PI §92 makes clear, Wittgenstein's goal is hardly to plot and preserve the manner in which we currently use concept-words. It is tempting, then, to argue that he must be presenting us with a different kind of theory about the nature of concepts from the theory that he had proposed in the *Tractatus*.

At TLP 3.341, Wittgenstein argued that 'what is essential in a symbol is what all symbols that can serve the same purpose have in common'. But immediately after the Second World War he told his students that 'A concept is the technique of using a word' (GWL: 50). Does this mean that the later Wittgenstein was proposing that concepts are simply the rules for using concept-words that are encoded in social practices? That is, was Wittgenstein proposing an anti-realist alternative to the realist view of concepts that he had embraced in the *Tractatus*? Or is it the *question itself*, which seems to invite an answer of the form 'A concept is a _____', that he is investigating in his later writings?

At PI §144, Wittgenstein suggests that to grasp the point that he is making about the analysis of concepts – the concept of concept included – demands an *Anschauungsweise*. That is, Wittgenstein is proposing to put a different picture of concepts before us. Not a different *theory of concepts*, but a different way of understanding and responding to questions about the nature of a concept. The key to grasping the import of this aspect-change hinges on our reading the argument at PI §§65–7, not as a psychological hypothesis but rather, as a 'grammatical investigation': 'an investigation [which] sheds light on our problem by clearing misunderstanding away' (PI: §90).

To overlook this distinction would be to read PI §65b as arguing: 'Instead of producing something common to all that we call language, I am saying that these phenomena have no one thing in common which causes us to use the same word for all – but that there are overlapping relationships (resemblances) which cause us to use the same word for all.' But the point of PI §65 is to shift us from viewing the issue in psychological terms to seeing it in grammatical terms. That is, the question he is asking is not whether we (our minds) have undergone a unitary experience, or have formed a schema of criterial attributes, or a cognitive representation of a prototype, or an ideal exemplar, which causes us to describe this activity as a 'language-game' (this object, this sample, this event as 'φ'). The question here is rather: 'What justifies us in using "language-game" for these disparate activities?' That is, the use of 'because' in the last line of PI §65 – 'it is because of this relationship, or these relationships, that we call them all "language"' – is used to mark a meta-linguistic observation, not to frame a psychological hypothesis.

The tendency to misconstrue what Wittgenstein is saying here as a psychological thesis is reinforced by the direction which the argument takes at PI §68. Like Piaget, Wittgenstein turns to concept-acquisition as a way of clarifying the nature of a concept.[5] One way to clarify the essence of a family-resemblance concept, Wittgenstein tells us, is to consider how someone acquires the concept: how someone is taught how to use a 'family-resemblance' concept as opposed to a sharply bounded concept. PI §69 makes this theme explicit in terms of the concept of number.

The reasoning behind PI §69 can be found at PG p. 114, where Wittgenstein argues that 'the concept of cardinal number can be called a rigorously circumscribed concept, that's to say it's a concept in a different sense of the word' than is number (where, once again, this is not a psychological hypothesis). To say that these are different kinds of concepts is to say that we play different language-games with these concept-words. That is not to say that these concepts *are* the language-games. Nor are we ruling out the possibility that 'number' and 'cardinal number' could be used in the same way. We could, e.g., teach 'number' as the logical sum of well-defined sub-concepts (cardinal numbers and rational numbers and real numbers . . .). To introduce a new number system would then be to change the meaning of 'number'. But, while we could proceed in this way, the fact is that we do not teach 'number' as a logical sum.[6] If someone claims to have created a new number system (e.g. transfinite cardinals) we do not check a table; rather, we see what sorts of things can be done with these new rules.[7]

To clarify the concept of number, Wittgenstein considers the different ways in which we use 'cardinal number' and 'number', and the parallels between the ways in which we use 'number' and the ways in which we use 'game'. There is no fixed set of rules which sets the meaning of 'number': which fixes the limit on what can count as a new number system. To learn how to use 'number' is to learn this feature of its rules: the freedom which one has to create new systems that enable us to do similar, but in some way new things from what has hitherto been possible.

199

It is in this sense that 'the range of the concept is *not* closed by a boundary'. That is, it is an essential feature of the concept of language (of game, number, etc.) that 'I'm now able to construct a new language, for instance to invent words. – So this construction too belongs to the concept of language. ... That's also what I meant when I said "there are surprises in reality but not in grammar".' The creation of a new language (a new game, a new number system) does not ' "broaden" (alter) the concept of language [of game, number]' (PG: 115). Whether the creation of a new language-game alters a concept 'depends on how the earlier concept was established'.

The focus in the discussion of family-resemblance concepts at PI §§65–7 is thus on conceptual clarification, not language-acquisition. This comes through particularly forcefully in the passage in *Philosophical Grammar* in which Wittgenstein asks:

> How did we learn to understand the word 'plant', then? Perhaps we learnt a definition of the concept, say in botany, but I leave out that of account [*sic*] since it only has a role in botany. Apart from that, it is clear that we learnt the meaning of the word by example; and if we disregard hypothetical dispositions, these examples stand only for themselves. Hypotheses about learning and using language and causal connections don't interest us. So we don't assume that the examples produce something in the learner, that they set before his mind an essence, the meaning of the concept-word, the concept 'plant'. If the examples should have an effect, say they produce a particular visual picture in the learner, the causal connection between the examples and this picture does not concern us, and for us they are merely *coincidental*.
>
> (PG: 117–18)

Just as this passage cannot be read as genetic theorising without completely ignoring Wittgenstein's intentions, no more can PI §69. There may well be cases where subjects all have the same experience, or make the same mistakes when learning a concept; but this has no bearing on an investigation into the 'essence' of that concept. That is, if what we are trying to explain is the nature of a concept, then our interest in how a word is taught or learnt is only in regard to the light this may shed on the type of language-game played with that concept-word.

PI §§69–71 are clearly intended as a direct attack on the *Tractatus* (Fregean) demand for determinacy of sense: on the idea that a concept is only usable if its boundaries have been sharply delineated – if we can give a straightforward Yes or No answer to the question of whether any object is an instance of that category. At PG p. 117, Wittgenstein presents the prototype-sounding argument that the fact that there are borderline cases where it is not clear whether something should be classified as a plant (Wittgenstein's example is coral) does not mean that the use of 'plant' is not perfectly clear to us in other cases. But it is not typicality that concerns him here; rather, Wittgenstein cites this example as evidence of the need to look at *concept-analysis* in a new light.

The discussion of this theme in *Philosophical Grammar* accentuates the further dimension of the issue with which we are most interested here; for the argument developed in PI §§65–88 is really meant to be self-reflective. It is not just the concepts of language, game or number that are meant to be seen as 'family-resemblance' concepts: it is, overall, the concept of concept itself. And the rationale behind this argument is to alert us to the dangers of seizing on some determinate concept as the paradigm for 'concept analysis', which in one environment led to the conclusion that ordinary language is 'defective' for scientific or philosophical purposes, and in another, to the classical theory of concepts and the inductivist theory of concept-acquisition and development.

In a passage which anticipates Flavell's opening remarks in 'Concept Development', Waismann explains:

> We have tried to clear our ideas about what are known as concepts, but we have not yet stilled our doubts. We try – in vain – to find out what it is that constitutes a concept, as if there must be something constituting its essence or nature. We do not realize that what we call 'concept' comes into existence only by its incorporation in language; that it is recognizable not by one feature but by a number, which, as it were, constitute its facets.
>
> (PLP: 227–8)

That is, to explain the essence of *concept* we need to clarify how 'concept' is used: to note the extraordinary heterogeneity that we saw Flavell alluding to in §1. In the above passage, Waismann goes on to describe how ' "Colour" and "primary colour" are concepts in very different senses, so also are "property", "cardinal number", "number" and "cause" ' (*ibid.*: 228). And what of aesthetic, religious, mathematical, political and psychological concepts: do all of these serve to 'reduce the complexity of sensory input to manageable proportions by identifying and classifying input information'? (cf. PI: §77).

The reason why the cognitivist is so troubled by passages like the above is because he feels that there are only two possible ways to read it: either Wittgenstein is saying that concepts are identical with language-games, or else he is saying that language-games refer to concepts (and may play a role in their development). The first option would reduce concepts to linguistic behaviour, and the second brings us no closer to understanding how we are to study the concepts themselves and not their verbal garb. But Wittgenstein is not suggesting that a concept is a linguistic as opposed to a mental entity – that the answer to the question 'What are concepts and how are they acquired?' is: 'Concepts are language-games, and they are acquired like any other rule-governed social practice'. To read Wittgenstein in this way would be to embrace the very picture of concept-analysis that he is attacking.

What we need to get away from here is the idea that Wittgenstein is presenting a family-resemblance definition as opposed to the classical definition of 'concept'. In *Philosophical Grammar*, Wittgenstein carefully spells out the point that we call 'The rule for "cardinal number" is [1, x, x + 1]', 'explaining the meaning of "cardinal number"', whereas we do not say that someone who points to the number series '1, 2, 3, . . . ' and says 'This *and similar things* are called "cardinal numbers"' has explained the meaning of 'cardinal number'. Similarly, at PI §69 Wittgenstein observes that what is most important in the language-game played with 'game' is that we call 'This *and similar things* are called "games"' '*explaining* the meaning of "game"'. This reflection on the *different kinds of explanations* – on the different kinds of practices that serve as 'grammatical explanations' – is a manifestation of the *different kinds of concepts* that there are: the different kinds of ways that concept-words are taught and used.[8]

This argument should be read in conjunction with PI §71b, for there is still a danger of reading this as a developmental thesis. The point is not that we can only teach a child the concept of game by listing some examples and then adding a rider like 'These *and similar things* are called "games"', thus leaving it to the child to 'see in those examples that common thing which I – for some reason – was unable to express'. The point is rather that, as Wittgenstein puts it at the end of PI §71b: '*this* is how we play the game. (I mean the language-game with the word "game".)' That is, this just is what we call 'explaining "game"'. And what we call 'understanding the explanation' consists in employing the word 'game' in the way intended.

AI presents us with a completely different response to this last point: viz., such an explanation does indeed fall short of a definition, but the mind is so constituted that it makes up for the limitations of verbal communication. Wittgenstein asks at PI §73: 'what does the picture of a leaf look like when it does not show us any particular shape, but "what is common to all shapes of leaf"?' Whereas Wittgenstein intends this as a rhetorical question, attacking the idea that there could be such a schematic representation independent of its use,[9] AI sees this as an empirical matter: one that can be answered by giving full rein to the wizardry of computer science.

As we saw in §2, therein lay the chief appeal of AI's view of concept theory for the founders of the cognitive revolution. For, according to AI, there is no *a priori* reason why a program cannot be designed that will learn how to identify all leaves, and only leaves, as leaves. The 'schematic representation' whereby the child's mind 'fills in the adult's partial explanation' could then be said to consist in the same kind of rules as were used in the program. That is, by mapping the child's behaviour onto the program, one can infer the nature of the 'pre-conscious rules' composing the child's schema of leaves. The fact that no competent language-user can cite such rules is totally irrelevant; for the pre-conscious is a blank cheque upon which AI can freely draw.

To back this argument up, the cognitivist can appeal to those cases where a subject's ability to use a concept outstrips her ability to explain that concept, or where the agent does not even possess the verbal ability to explain her use of a concept (e.g. animals or infants).[10] But the question Wittgenstein is asking at PI §69 is whether it really is the case that such an explanation of 'game' *falls short* of our knowledge of the concept. To be sure, we may know a great many more examples of games, and we may be able to say a great deal more about why certain games are played. But does that mean that there is a gap between my understanding of 'game' and the explanations I can give?[11]

There are many cases where one can say 'S understands "p"' even if she cannot define 'p'. '"To know it"', Wittgenstein argues, 'does not here mean to be able to say it. *This* is not our criterion of knowledge in this case' (PI: §67). That is, for some language-games, *explanation*, not *definition*, is the *correlate of understanding*. In such cases, if S is unable to define 'p', that is not a criterion for saying she does not understand 'p'; whereas her being unable to explain the meaning of 'p' would be such a criterion. To be sure, there are many cases where defining a word is a criterion for understanding it (e.g. technical terms). But one's ability to explain the meaning of 'game' – e.g. to describe various kinds of games – does not *fall short of*, but rather expresses one's grasp of the concept. The statement 'One can explain, but one cannot define "game"' is not an epistemological observation, inviting the construction of a model which will disclose a subject's 'tacit knowledge'. It is a grammatical proposition that formulates a rule in the language-game played with 'game'. It thus shows us what kind of concept *game* is.

§5 'Seeing what is in common'

Were Wittgenstein's argument to end at this point, would it amount to anything more than the damaging critique of classical theory which prototype theorists have claimed? Would this description of a normative practice even be that damaging? Wittgenstein's preoccupation with behaviourism – which dominates the *Blue and Brown Books*, and the first dozen or so passages of the *Investigations* (see Shanker 1996) – comes through in the passage from PG pp. 117–18 quoted in §4. Whether or not Wittgenstein is right to eschew 'hypotheses about learning and using language and causal connections', what about hypotheses about mental induction or theory-construction? Has this 'grammatical investigation' shed any light on the central question of how a subject comes to see what the instances of a category have in common? For this is surely the key to answering the question 'How did we learn to understand the word "plant"?' Indeed, has any of this clarified the nature of a concept which, by the very terms of the above passage, is the 'essence, the meaning [the intension] of a concept-word'?

This is the question to which Wittgenstein next turns as he begins to look more closely at the problems involved in the attempt to analyse what a concept is in terms of the Cartesian picture of what the mind *must* do: viz., the picture of concepts as the mental constructs which enable a subject to pick out instances of a category by capturing what is common to all those instances. The problem is, Wittgenstein's argument is phrased almost entirely in terms of classical theory.[12] So one of the questions we must ask ourselves is, how much does it matter to the discussion of concepts beginning at PI §72 if one is talking about *necessary and sufficient conditions* or *computing an exemplar's similarity to a prototype*. For the focus of the argument is on the fundamental idea that 'It is only in virtue of *seeing x* [however 'x' might be defined] that we can acquire or apply the concept φ'. That is, the focus is on the 'similarity function' which lies at the heart of the 'functional definition of concepts', and not, as Rosch points out, the particular theory which one slots into that function.

Wittgenstein's primary concern at PI §§72ff is to clarify the nature of 'seeing something in common'. One of the defining features of Cartesianism – if not *the* defining feature – is that this refers to the *mental process* of seeing what is common to the diverse instances of a category, or seeing that x is a member of the category φ. For 'seeing' and 'categorising' are both process-verbs, so what could be more natural than to assume that they refer to the 'mental processes' involved in the formation of a concept? Thus, on the Cartesian picture of concept-acquisition, when a subject encounters the exemplars of a category, she must abstract their common properties. The same sort of process must occur when she hears language-speakers using a concept-word. The reason why there must be such a process of *feature-detection* and *analysis* is because, otherwise, the subject would see every single object as unique, and would treat all words as proper names.

Suppose, then, that we are dealing with something like ostensive definition: how else, the Cartesian asks, can a subject get from this particular episode to the understanding that the concept-word applies to all the instantiations of the concept unless she constructs such a scheme (records the similarity between this and previous abstractions)? And this mental representation must be stored in such a way as to be easily accessed; otherwise, understanding would be limited to occurring in the presence of the sample. (A private scheme *must* take the place of the public object of comparison.) Furthermore, if the subject is to be able to join in public discourse about that concept, she must grasp the set of features that language-speakers are referring to when they use such-and-such a concept-word. Cartesianism sees two 'phenomena' here – viz., the possession of a concept, and the ability to talk about that concept – that are completely independent of one another. Accordingly, in order to know whether a subject possesses the concept φ, or what a subject understands by φ, it is not enough to observe how the subject uses the relevant concept-word (although this constitutes an important piece of evidence). One must also carefully observe the subject's behaviour in order to discover the nature of the epistemically private representation which she has formed.

The first step in Wittgenstein's argument is to clarify what it means to say: 'If S possesses the concept φ, S must see what is common to the exemplars of φ'. In *Philosophical Grammar* he asks:

> If someone says 'we understand the word "chair", [because] we know what is common to all chairs' – what does it mean to say we *know* that? That we are ready to say it (like 'we know that 6 3 6 is 36')? What is it that is common, then? Isn't it only because we can apply the word 'chair' that we say here we know what is common? Suppose I explained the word 'red' by pointing to a red wall, a red book, and a red cloth and in accordance with this explanation someone produced a sample of the colour red by exhibiting a red label. One might say in this case that he had shown that he had grasped the common element in all the examples I gave him. Isn't it an analogy like this that misleads us in the case of 'chair'?
>
> (PG: 118)

The first line in this passage serves as a recurrent theme in all that follows. If a child begins to use the concept-word 'chair' correctly, does one *infer* that this is because she (her mind) has successfully abstracted the salient properties of chairs and slotted this newly acquired concept into the appropriate concept-hierarchy? If so, one must figure out what sort of mental representation she has formed. Does it include dining room chairs, bridge chairs, rocking chairs, swivel chairs, armchairs, high chairs, deck chairs, hanging chairs, barbershop chairs, Italian designer furniture, recliners, thrones, and so on? Does it exclude stools, benches, bean bags, balans, wheelchairs, chaise longues, theatre seats, car seats, bicycle seats and orange crates? Does its application depend on context? Does it change over time?

But what if we should see the use of 'because' in the first line of the passage as meta-linguistic? In that case, the argument would be asking us to see a subject's 'overt behaviors' [*sic*], not as *evidence* of the concept that the agent possesses, but as constituting the *criteria* which license us in describing that agent as possessing (or not possessing) the concept φ. That is, it is on the basis of her use of 'chair', together with her use of chairs, that one is warranted in stating 'S possesses the concept *chair*', 'S sees what is common to dining room chairs and bridge chairs . . .'.

Like the cognitivist, Wittgenstein emphasises that: 'If S uses "light red" and "dark red" correctly she must have seen what is common to light red and dark red.' But whereas the cognitivist treats this statement as describing a mental phenomenon, Wittgenstein focuses on the logical character of the 'must' in this proposition. He argues that, to say 'S saw what is common to all the samples of φ' *is just to say* 'S uses "φ" correctly'. That is, to 'see what is common' to a sample of light red and dark red is to use 'red' correctly (BB: 130). 'To say that we use the word "blue" to mean "what all these shades of colour have in common" by itself says nothing more than that we use the word "blue" in all these cases' (*ibid.*: 135). The criterion for saying 'S sees what is common to all the samples of φ', or 'S understands what is common to a group of language-speakers' use of "φ"', is correct use of 'φ': the criteria for saying the one are the criteria for saying the other.

In other words,

> 'To see what is common to a group of samples of φ' =
> 'To use "φ" correctly' =
> 'To possess the concept φ'.

These are grammatical transformations, not inductive generalisations. They could not be falsified by any imaginable experience: i.e. it makes no sense to test their validity. We use them to formulate the rule of grammar:

> 'To say that S uses "φ" correctly *means* that S possesses the concept φ:
> that S sees what is common to the exemplars of φ'.

We could not understand what someone was trying to say who insisted that 'S possesses the concept φ but fails to see what the exemplars of φ have in common'. Thus, the statement 'S uses "light red" and "dark red" correctly because he sees what is common to light red and dark red' is not a *hypothesis* (viz., that S possesses the appropriate mental representation of red, causing him to use 'red' correctly); rather, this statement asserts that S has mastered the use of 'red'.

The cognitivist sees concepts as the *source* of an organism's ability to identify the instances of a category, to go beyond the information given, and to anticipate and adapt to its environment. This picture is a symptom of what Wittgenstein called 'a kind of general disease of thinking which always looks for (and finds) what would be called a mental state from which all our acts spring as from a reservoir' (*ibid.*: 143; cf. PG: 80). In one of his early discussions of rule-following, Wittgenstein suggests that the rule of a series is construed in causal terms as the mechanism which generates its applications (the rule determines that I call this a 'chair'):

> Here it can easily seem as if the sign contained the whole of the grammar; as if the grammar were contained in the sign like a string

of pearls in a box and he had only to pull it out. (But this kind of picture is just what is misleading us.) As if understanding were an instantaneous grasping of something from which later we only draw consequences which already exist in an ideal sense before they are drawn.

(*Ibid.*: 55)

So, too, the applications of a concept are thought to be contained in or to flow from possession of the concept. Against this, Wittgenstein argues that the relation between the possession of a concept and the applications of that concept is *internal*: i.e. we treat an agent's behaviour as the *criterion* for saying that she has acquired the concept φ. 'The application is still a criterion of understanding,' Wittgenstein concludes, not inductive evidence of the formation of a mental schema whose structure can only be inferred from the subject's behaviour (*ibid.*).

To treat concepts in the manner which Flavell advocates – viz., as the 'the mediating linkage between the input side (stimuli) and the output side (response)' (Flavell 1970: 985) – is to treat the relation between concept-possession and application as causal. Or, equally, we might phrase this: it is because the relation between concept-possession and application is seen as causal that the cognitivist treats concepts as 'intervening media, or programs through which impinging stimuli are coded, passed, or evaluated on their way to response evocation' (Harvey *et al.* 1961: 1). If we go back to the first line of the passage from PG p. 118 quoted above, we can see how the cognitivist construes the use of 'because' as causal. That is, he treats the proposition 'S possesses the concept *red* because he sees what all shades of red have in common' as an empirical generalization, rather than a metalinguistic utterance (articulating a rule for using the expression 'to possess the concept "red"'). This is the jumping-off point for the cognitivist's reductionist analysis of what a concept is: of the rules whereby 'impinging stimuli are coded, passed, or evaluated' by the brain.

It bears noting just how singular is the statement 'S possesses the concept φ'. Unlike 'knowledge', the use of this expression is almost exclusively confined to philosophical and psychological practices. If we lose sight of the kind of specialised language-games in which 'concept' is employed, then we do indeed, as Rosch cautions, run the risk of 'reifying concepts': i.e., of treating concepts as the 'mental analogues' of internal organs, which will thus be said to evolve uniquely in each organism according to the environmental pressures (i.e. the set of 'input stimuli') to which the organism is exposed.

In clarifying that 'concept' is not a referring term, Wittgenstein clarifies that the statement 'S possesses the concept φ' is not a hypothesis (about the existence or nature of a hidden mental state); rather, such a statement is used to attribute certain abilities to S.[13] 'Saying that S possesses the concept φ' =

'Saying that S can do *x,y,z*' (cf. *ibid.*: 162). For example, to say that S possesses the concept chair is to say that, if presented with a dining room chair, S will be able to identify it as a chair, be able to tell us what it is used for, be able to fetch an extra chair if asked to do so, be able to explain the meaning of 'chair', be able to distinguish chairs and tables, etc. Moreover, when we describe *concept* as a family-resemblance concept, what we are saying is that there is no univocal answer to the question: 'What must S be able to do in order to be described as possessing a concept?' For the skills required to license the statement 'S possesses the concept φ' are as various as the different kinds of language-games that we play.

But now the cognitivist might reply in objection: Why should treating a subject's behaviour as the *criterion* for describing her as possessing the concept φ undermine the possibility of using that same behaviour as *evidence* of the nature of the concept she possesses? Why can there not be two levels of explanation here? If I ask you how you know that S understands the concept φ and you answer, 'Because he behaves thus-and-so', in what sense have you explained the nature of S's representation of φ? All you have done is justify your attribution of the concept to S. But justifying the attribution of a concept (by means of invoking criterial relations) is not the same thing as explaining the nature of that concept. And how has any of this deepened our understanding of the nature of concepts *per se*?

This objection returns us to the theme that questions about essence belong to logic: i.e. Wittgenstein's argument that the question 'What is a concept?' is no more a psychological than a semantic or a metaphysical issue. The 'functional definition of "concept"' is the result of construing meta-linguistic propositions about the use of 'concept' as empirical generalisations about a hidden mental representation. The meta-linguistic utterance 'If S possesses the concept φ then S must see what all the instances of φ have in common' is treated as an hypothesis about a pre-conscious categorisation process. From here it is but a short step to the premise that the task of AI is to model how the mind assesses the match or mismatch between the input (whether example or counter-example) and the current state of a developing concept.

That is not to say that neurophysiologists can never hope to discover what occurs in the brain (which cells in the cerebral cortex are activated) when, e.g., a subject (any subject? every subject?) sees a chair (any chair? every chair?). What neurophysiology can never hope to explain, however, is what the nature of the concept chair consists in; for that issue belongs exclusively to philosophy. Conversely, one cannot employ an illicit reductionist analysis of the concept chair to tell us what *must* be occurring in the cerebral cortex when a subject sees a chair or calls something a 'chair'. For this is simply a variant of the cognitive psychologism that we have been examining throughout this book. And, finally, one cannot employ the bottom-up picture of neural processing that results from this manoeuvre to explain the processes of concept-acquisition: e.g., how a child acquires the concept *chair*, how a child sees that 'chair' refers to a class and not such-and-such an object. But it is not neurophysiology that is at issue here: it is the reductionism that ends up deflecting us from our real psychological concerns in the areas of cognitive and language-development.

It is important to bear in mind here that the only reason why Flavell was interested in discovering the 'essential nature of a concept' was because of the light he hoped this would shed on the processes of concept-acquisition and concept-development. The reductionist analysis of concept entails that the latter must be explained in terms of mental acts of colligation or induction, governed by the demands of cognitive economy and efficiency. It is precisely because of this epistemological framework that AI seemed such a boon to the fledgling cognitive revolution. For AI seemed to offer an invaluable tool for constructing and testing hypotheses about the mind's preconscious categorisation processes.

Our investigation of the origins of AI has thus brought us to the point where we can appreciate how the miscegenous union between AI and the cognitive revolution was forged in large part on the basis of a shared view of the functional nature of concepts. But this is only the beginning and not the end of what needs to be said about categorisation research. For nothing has been said here to deny the importance of studying how children or adults acquire category terms: only, that 'categorising' is not an internal mental process akin to digestion, and that concepts are not internal 'mental representations' akin to computer programs. What remains to be seen, therefore, is whether Wittgenstein's view of concepts sheds any light on the ongoing concerns of categorisation research.

§6 The cognitivist response to Wittgenstein's view of concepts

The standard cognitivist response to the Wittgensteinian line of argument pursued in the preceding sections is to downplay its significance by insisting that, even if the 'logical geography' of *concept* has been accurately plotted here – the reasons why the concept of concept was introduced, the manner in which 'concept' is used – then one can either reform that logical grammar, or else simply forsake 'concept' altogether and get on with the job at hand: the problem of explaining how an organism carves up or 'chunks' its world into functional units. What needs to be explained, according to the cognitivist, is a mental, not a linguistic, phenomenon: viz., how an organism is able to treat discriminably different, but in some respect similar, objects and events, equivalently. What the cognitivist wants to know is: *how* does a child see that such-and-such is a chair? What happens in her mind/brain when she sees a chair for the first time, or during an ostensive definition, that enables her to re-identify that object as a chair, or to pick out further exemplars of the category, sometimes quite distantly related? Charting the linguistic moves effected by 'S possesses the concept φ' cannot, the cognitivist insists, help us with this problem.

This objection is grounded in the Cartesian presupposition that thought is experientially prior to language. On this view, the child begins to acquire concepts before it begins to speak, and it is only on the basis of the 'conceptual primitives' she has acquired that she is able to learn how to speak. This means that the child is confronted early on with a 'mapping' problem: viz., acquiring the appropriate words to convey her concepts. 'As children, we learn which devices – which words – pick out, catch, hook which concepts and can thus be used to convey the concepts we are thinking about.' But 'the word meanings available are always fewer than the concepts they are used to talk about' (Clark 1983: 788). Or they may not be finely enough graded to pick out closely related conceptual categories.

We find ourselves confronted here with the following set of variations on the standard Cartesian problem of Other Minds:

- a child's concepts, or those of another culture, may be totally unlike our own, and may even be unlike anything we can presently express;
- we can never be certain about the concept onto which an agent has mapped a word;
- we can never be certain as to what common features an agent has abstracted from a group of exemplars;
- we can never be certain how an agent has organised her concepts.

Indeed, cognitivism goes still further; for the basic premise of cognitivism is that we do not have privileged access to our *pre-conscious* categorisation processes. This means that we must infer from our own behaviour, and the kind of judgements that we make, what concepts our own mind/brain has formed. Thus, cognitivism adds to the above list the further sceptical question:

- are our own concepts any less a mystery to ourselves than those formed by other organisms?

In the grip of this epistemological outlook, the cognitivist maintains that, by dwelling on existing language-use, the Wittgensteinian remains oblivious of these problems, oblivious of the fact that concepts and concept-words are externally related to each other. From a cognitivist perspective, Wittgenstein's approach to the study of concepts is at best a *descriptive* rather than an *explanatory* exercise: a form of social anthropology rather than psychology. To be sure, language-use constitutes an essential piece of evidence in our inferences about another organism's concepts; but Wittgenstein seems to treat this as an *alternative to*, rather than an *aspect of*, the psychological explanation of cognition.

Thus, the cognitivist will insist that this 'ordinary language argument' fails to explain:

- how it is that, without any training, a child suddenly begins to use a concept correctly;
- why children find some concepts easier to acquire than others;
- why certain concepts appear abruptly at certain ages, with no gradual build-up leading to their emergence;
- why children consistently make the same sorts of errors when they have to figure out how two words (e.g. 'oaks' and 'trees') apply to the same objects;
- why it is that, virtually from birth, infants habituate to familiar objects;
- why it is that a child spontaneously demonstrates sorting behaviour at 18 months;
- why this last phenomenon occurs at the very same time as the onset of the 'word explosion'.

From the cognitivist perspective, therefore, the problem with Wittgenstein's approach is that he over-accentuates the linguistic side of the equation. Far from explaining how a child sees that such-and-such is a chair, Wittgenstein's view seems to confine psychology to the description of when a child starts to use (and respond to the use of) 'chair' correctly. What is really needed, as far as cognitivism is concerned, is an account of the *matching and mismatching* processes that enable a child to treat discriminably different objects and events equivalently.

As the cognitivist conceives of concept-acquisition and concept-development, a child starts out life with a set of reflexes or predispositions, or even, possibly, primitive concepts that are modified as a result of adapting to her environment. That is, the child is forced to develop these reflexes or primitive constructs in order to increase her control over her environment, then to combine and modify the mental structures or schemes formed in these initial encounters, and so on. Each stage is a transformation of the preceding stage. Cognitive development is thus an autogenetic mental process: in Piagetian terms, interaction with the environment (social included) leads, through a continuous process of assimilation and accommodation, towards an ever more stable state of cognitive equilibrium. The schemes whereby a child constructs her concepts evolve from her earliest manipulations of objects, her interactions with agents, and the operations which are then abstracted from these actions.

On this view of concept-acquisition, developmental psychology becomes a means of resolving a fundamental *epistemological* problem: viz., how a child makes the transition from reacting to each new stimulus as an isolated event, to classifying and categorising stimuli. The harmony between the cognitive revolution and AI lay in the fact that both were concerned with the solution of this epistemological problem. Both interpreted the question of how a child acquires, e.g., the concept *chair* as the question of how a child builds up, in a step-by-step manner, a mental representation of chairs, which in turn determines her use of 'chair'. And the child's use of 'chair', *contra* Wittgenstein, is merely *evidence* of the child's mental representation of chairs.

The pivotal assumption here is that 'Because concepts and mental representations are intangible products of the human mind, they cannot be measured directly or observed spontaneously. Instead, we must depend upon overt behaviors' (Waxman 1990). That is, we can only infer the nature of the concept which an agent possesses from the behaviour which she manifests; the manner in which she uses a concept-word is but one element in this data. 'To elicit these overt behaviors, we introduce our subjects to events or problems of one kind or another' and then base our hypotheses on such things as 'reaction times, object labelling, classification, or typicality judgments' (*ibid.*). But these hypotheses are *always* subject to disconfirmation.

To back this argument up, the cognitivist presents us with a sceptical argument which has long been familiar to philosophy. For example, we are asked to suppose that a child begins to use 'red' correctly: this, according to the cognitivist, only counts as partial evidence for her possessing the concept *red*. For it is conceivable that the child begins to use 'red' correctly but does not possess the concept.[14] Maybe one day, when confronted with pink-coloured objects for the first time, she will label them as 'red'. Or maybe she will refuse to call a rubber ball 'red' because, so we discover, she only uses the term for hard objects. And this is not just a problem for the developmental psychologist. On this line of reasoning, I can never be certain that another agent's concept of *red* is the same as my own. Indeed, I cannot even be certain what my own concept is; in a sense I, too, have to wait to see how I categorise in the future before I can pronounce judgement on the nature of my concept of red.

Epistemological scepticism thus lies at the heart of the functional definition of concepts. As Flavell puts it, 'Concepts are fundamentally private, cognitive phenomena'; yet 'they of course can be and are externalized as social objects, and agreement can often be reached as to what their exact, "correct" meaning should be' (Flavell 1970: 986). But

> Knowing that a given concept, as a public entity, has certain attributes does not tell me what it means to you, how you represent it to yourself, how and under what conditions you can access and utilize it. . . . Just as concepts differ among themselves, so also do individuals differ in the way they apprehend, use, and otherwise 'relate to' any given concept. . . . The concept has one more or less definite meaning and individuals have various different approximations of that meaning.
>
> (*Ibid.*: 986–7).

For example, their category may be narrower or broader than the standard interpretation; or it may differ for individuals according to contexts. Communication is by no means an exact phenomenon, therefore, but we more or less succeed in knowing what each other is thinking, at least to the point where linguistic interaction is possible.

What Flavell is arguing here is that it is one thing to say that S has mastered the rules for the use of 'φ', but quite another to know how S mentally represents φ. For example, it is one thing to say that an infant has mastered the rules (within its limited routines) for the use of 'juice', but quite another to know how she conceptualises *juice*. To discover the latter phenomenon we must, as Waxman prescribes above, introduce the infant to various kinds of situations involving not just the use of juice but, also, various drinks, foodstuffs, objects, etc., and observe how she reacts. (For example, if we lay out milk, water, apple juice, tomato juice, cola, a banana, etc., in front of the child and say 'Bring me some juice', which will she choose, and will she always make the same choice? When we give her juice does she always drink it, or will she on occasion use it to wash her hands, water the garden, paint the walls?) But, no matter how stringent we make our tests, we can 'never be certain whether and how the effects we obtain and the behaviors we observe are related to the ever-intangible underlying cognitive processes and mental representations' (Waxman 1990: 109).

Far from seeing the epistemological scepticism which results from this theory of concepts as a flaw in the argument, the cognitivist seizes on this as the reason why Wittgenstein's view of language is of such limited importance for categorisation research. Wittgenstein, the cognitivist maintains, seems to have been oblivious of the basic fact that we use language to describe cognitive events as best we can. The cognitivist thus objects that Wittgenstein's normativity argument – his emphasis on the rules which we cite to license one's use of 'S understands "φ"' – only applies to linguistic conventions, not to cognitive phenomena. That is, cognitivism insists that there is a categorial divide between the criteria for using 'φ' correctly and the evidence for an organism's representation of φ. It is as conceivable that two subjects can master the rules for the use of 'φ' while inwardly forming very different impressions of φ, as that two subjects can agree on all the criteria that make for a good prime minister while forming a very different opinion of who best fits the bill.

To see what the cognitivist has in mind, we might consider the case of two agents, neither of whom speaks the other's language, but who share a third language. The problem is, each of the three languages in question draws subtly different conceptual boundaries (e.g. they classify different shades under the primary colour-terms). Hence, when trying to communicate a thought, A must try to find the closest approximation in the common language, while B must try to find the closest approximation when she translates A's utterance into her own language. Here we have what is supposed to be a clear instance of how, by virtue of their shared language, A and B can understand what the other is *saying*, but neither can ever be entirely sure that they know what the other is *thinking*.

It is important to note that, in the above passage, where he describes the privacy of concepts, Flavell deliberately – and correctly – places 'correct' in inverted commas. The thinking here is that the concept of *correct usage* only applies to linguistic conventions. Since, on the cognitive level, each subject may represent the same concept somewhat differently – e.g. each may see as red certain shades which another agent sees as blue – it makes no sense to say that a subject can be 'right' or 'wrong' in the manner in which he represents *red*. But then, this argument has quite puzzling consequences.

Why is it that we all agree that pink cannot be darker than red? How can we be so certain that it is impossible for someone to see red as lighter than pink? What do red and pink have in common that we call them both colours? How can we be so certain that it is impossible for someone to include C-sharp in this category; isn't this what happens to those who experience synaesthesia? For that matter, how can we be so certain that it is impossible for someone to see something as red and green all over? Gallistel, for example, suggests that

> the mutual exclusivity of certain color judgments (red-green, yellow-blue) is the result of this spatial representation of the reflectance spectrum. Colors cannot be both red and green simultaneously because the central tendency of activity in a cortical mapping of reflectance spectra cannot simultaneously lie on both sides of an anatomical axis of the mapping, the axis that divides the spectra judged red from the spectra judged green, nor on both sides of the orthogonal axis that separates the spectra judged yellow from the spectra judged blue.
>
> (Gallistel 1990: 10)

But then, isn't it possible for someone to have an idiosyncratic anatomical axis? And what if someone suffered a blow to the head, resulting in a dislocation of the axis: is it conceivable that the 'red and green spectra' could become superimposed on one another, so that that person could begin to see something as both red and green all over?

This reading of the colour-exclusion statement, and all of the above questions, returns us to the discussion of psychologism in Chapter 3: to Wittgenstein's remark that 'Here "I can't imagine [this]" doesn't mean: my powers of imagination are unequal to the task. These words are a defence against something whose form makes it look like an empirical proposition, but which is really a grammatical one' (PI: §251). That is, all of the above questions call for a grammatical, not an empirical, explanation. 'Red is darker than pink', 'Red and pink are both colours', 'Synaesthesia is a condition in which tones can cause a recurrent experience but cannot cause one to see tones *as* colours', 'Nothing can be red and green all over': all are grammatical propositions, they formulate rules for the use of 'colour', 'red', 'pink', 'green', and 'synaesthesia'. Hence our certainty in the preceding paragraph is normative, not inductive: it is that it makes no sense, given our rules for the use of colour-words, to speak of an object as being red and green all over – not that, to the best of our knowledge, the orthogonal axis that separates the spectra judged yellow from the spectra judged blue is the same in all human beings.

Suppose that language and thought were indeed, as the cognitivist contends, *externally related*: this would mean that someone could use 'red' correctly – could bring red objects when asked to do so, could explain the meaning of 'red' by pointing to red objects – and yet not possess the concept *red*: e.g. could correctly call something red while actually seeing it as blue! But in that case, how could she know that, according to linguistic custom, this sample is correctly labelled 'red'? Conversely, someone could possess the concept *red*, yet be incapable of mastering the use of 'red'. We might establish this by some form of sorting experiment in which, e.g., we present S with an array of differently coloured objects and observe her put all the red objects into one pile. But she is utterly bewildered if we ask her to bring us something red. It would be as if the parts of her brain in charge of processing colours and colour-terms (the colour and colour-terms spectra?) were not on speaking terms with one another.

Rather than seeing these paradoxical consequences of the functional definition of concepts as compelling reason to scrutinise the initial presupposition that language is externally related to thought, the cognitivist interprets 'the enigma created by our misunderstanding as the enigma of an incomprehensible process' (PG: 155). That is, the cognitivist treats these epistemological problems as further aspects of the *mystery of concepts*. And this sets the stage for AI. For what could be more tempting than to approach such a mystery at its simplest level, at the very bottom of the 'cognitive continuum'. Strip away the preoccupation with 'thinking machines' and this is precisely where the appeal of AI, *qua* exercise in mechanist reductionism, lay for the founders of the cognitive revolution.

§7 The 'cognitive continuum'

On the Cartesian picture of cognition, an organism's inability to enter into a community of language-speakers does not entail that it cannot share in their concepts. For example, we should have to say that any organism that is able to discriminate red circles, regardless of whether or not it possesses the capacity to use and to respond to uses of 'red', might possess the concept *red*. But far from treating this as an unfortunate consequence of the functional definition of concept, the cognitivist seizes on this point as an example of one of the theory's great benefits: viz., that it enables us to make sense of intelligent, non-linguistic behaviour. And it achieves this feat by extending the scope of *concept*.

Thus, it is pointless to object that, if cognitivism is right, this would mean that even a pigeon might possess colour concepts; for this is heralded as a virtue of the theory, not a drawback. To be sure, the cognitivist will hasten to add that a pigeon might not possess the same colour concepts as ourselves (although, as we have just seen, it is highly problematic, on the cognitivist account, to speak of the colour concepts which human beings possess). But the difference between a pigeon's and a human's colour concepts is held to be one of internal complexity, not of *kind*.

What the cognitivist has in mind here is a *cognitive continuum*, ranging from sensori-motor schemes, through percepts or frames, to schemata, concepts and theories.[15] These are all said to be instances of the category of 'mental representation', each a slightly more complex version of the previous construct on the continuum. At the primordial level are the simple 'intervening media' that regulate the behaviour of invertebrates. Then come the more intricate mechanisms which cause a plant to change the direction of its leaves or the depth of its roots; or which cause an insect to move up a plant or to return to the same location at the same time every day. At some point we arrive at the percepts or schemes that enable mammals and fish to identify specific features of their environment, or to anticipate and exploit periodic events. Then come the primitive constructs which non-human primates have about their environments, the members of their society and, perhaps, of themselves. And finally there are the concept hierarchies and theories possessed by human beings.

The whole point of calling this range of concepts a 'continuum' is to license the use of psychological terms to describe the activities of any living organism. Gallistel describes how:

> In the zoological or naturalistic tradition, the problem of learning arose incidentally in connection with investigations of how animals solve biological problems. When it is discovered that a digger wasp repeatedly returns to her nearly invisible nest to provision it with live food for her larvae, the question arises, How is she able to locate the nest again? This leads to experiments showing that she does so on the basis of remembered geometric relations between the nest location and the locations of surrounding landmarks. Similarly, when it is observed that animals seek to monopolize certain periodically available food sources by showing up in anticipation of the next period of availability, the question arises, How are they able to time their behavior in this way? This leads to experiments showing that they represent the daily time of occurrence.
>
> (Gallistel 1990: 7–8)

But one wants to ask: in what sense can a wasp be said to *remember* the location of its nest, or to navigate its way by *representing geometric relations*? Can a wasp also be said to *forget*, or to have a *dim recollection* of the location of its nest? Do wasps ever become *senile*? Can a wasp *guess* the location of its nest? Can it *summon up a mental image* of its nest and its surroundings? If we should move the nest in the presence of a wasp, or tell the wasp that we have moved its nest to such-and-such a spot, will it remember to return to this new location on its next foray?

One could, of course, argue that this sort of objection is unfair, in so far as the technical sense of 'remember' which Gallistel intends is specific to the zoological context he is discussing. But that is not his point. What Gallistel is saying is that, not only do we use psychological terms in the same way when speaking of wasps as when speaking of human behaviour, but, indeed, that such invertebrate examples may actually help us to understand the 'mechanics' of human psychological phenomena. For, as we saw in Chapter 1, the crux of the mechanist thesis is that to understand the nature of *learning* is to understand the mechanics of the programs which guide the response evocation of any organism. In this respect, a 'bottom-up' approach to psychological explanation is one which begins with the lower orders of the continuum, be it wasps or computers, and uses the resulting models as a starting-point for the explanation of 'higher-order' psychological phenomena.

Thus, from a cognitivist point-of-view, the problem with Wittgenstein's argument at PI §281 that human beings serve as the paradigm subjects for the use of psychological expressions – i.e. that any question about the cognitive capacities of animals or infants demands that we compare their behaviour with the relevant actions underpinning the use of the psychological concept in question – is that it fails to take this 'cognitive continuum' into consideration. Thus the cognitivist will say in objection: If that is how Wittgenstein insists on using 'concept', so be it; but call these more primitive stages on the cognitive continuum what you will, the important point is that all of these organisms are treating discriminably different objects as similar. Maybe the pigeon doesn't possess the *concept* red (and can we ever be sure of this?), but don't we at least have sufficient evidence to say that it possesses the *percept* red? After all, the pigeon can distinguish between red and green patches, and what's more, it can generalise from past experiences to different shades of red. So there is clearly some sort of perceptual learning going on, some sort of 'matching and mismatching' process. And the fact that pigeons cannot speak hardly means that we are powerless to infer the nature of their percepts.

By yoking 'percept' and 'concept' together in the manner dictated by the 'cognitive continuum', it follows that 'percepts' are just a more primitive kind of 'intervening media through which impinging stimuli are coded, passed, or evaluated' than 'concepts'. For 'What the bird learns is not a response but rather a representation' (*ibid.*: 364). Thus, Gallistel explains how the brain can be 'said to represent an aspect of the environment when there is a functioning isomorphism between an aspect of the environment and a brain process that adapts the animal's behavior to it' (*ibid.*: 3). Accordingly, we would hope to explain a pigeon's acquisition of the 'percept' circle in terms of a functional isomorphism between the points on the circumference of a circle and the spatial relations between the cells firing in the hippocampus when the pigeon's head is oriented towards the circle. And, in virtue of the continuum picture, something similar must hold true of learning in the human infant: i.e. the explanation of a child's acquisition of the 'concept' circle must also be in terms of such 'functional isomorphisms' between spatial configurations and the firing-pattern in some cell-assembly in the brain.

This gives a whole new meaning to the notion of a *family-resemblance concept*. It means that, for any given concept, there will be a 'cognitive continuum', ranging from sensori-motor schemes, through percepts, to full-bodied concepts. Each of the stages on this continuum will be defined according to the processing mechanisms of the organism that possesses the mental representation in question. After all, the question 'What is the difference between the *percept* circle and the *concept* circle?' cannot be answered directly, since these are epistemically private constructions. But what we can compare are neurological structures, from which we can infer how complex an internal representation the organism in question would be capable of forming. The more primitive an organism's brain, the more schematic will be the mental representations it is capable of forming. It is as if, corresponding to the descent down the evolutionary scale, there is a descent down the 'cognitive continuum'. Thus, for any given concept, one must strip away its defining features until one arrives at a representation that has a minimal amount of information; if we begin, e.g., with the concept of man, we shall end up at some point with an image of a stick man.

Recall how, on the cognitivist picture, one of the most important functions of concepts is that they are said to enable an organism to 'go beyond the information given': e.g. to form expectations on the basis of past experiences. Thus, in the case of pigeons, their 'mental representation' of men might be limited to such information as *potential source of harm* and *potential source of food*. But we infer this, not by examining their hippocampus, but by observing their behaviour: e.g., do they flee when a man approaches but not a woman or child, or do they stay within visual range and return to the spot as soon as the man leaves, and begin searching for food? In other words, it makes sense, according to cognitivism, to say that the pigeons recognise a man as a man, but what it is *for a pigeon* to recognise a man as a man is something of a mystery.

Once one embraces the premise that 'since [a] pigeon can see the differences between large and small circles yet treat them equivalently, it would be said to have the concept of circle' (Markman 1989: 138), one has placed oneself on a slippery slope which leads inexorably and swiftly into the Mechanist Thesis. But by no means did the founders of the cognitive revolution go down this route unwillingly. For AI promised to supply what was perhaps the single most important factor missing in the cognitivist approach to categorisation research: an explanation of the mechanics of the 'matching and mismatching process' which, on the cognitivist picture, lies at the heart of concept-application.

On the cognitivist view of concepts, every application of a concept involves a mental act of recognition: to apply a concept is to recognise exemplars of the criterial attributes that one has previously abstracted and stored. But, of course, according to Cartesianism, an organism's internal representation of ϕ is epistemically private. Thus, an organism might not recognise as a sample of red – where 'recognition' refers to the mental process of 'matching and mismatching' – what, according to linguistic convention, is correctly described as 'red'. Yet the organism will recognise samples which accord with its own, possibly idiosyncratic, representation of red.

But then, how does the organism know that its representation of red hasn't changed since its last experience? On this argument, it would make sense to say that 'red' means such-and-such a colour on one occasion, and such-and-such a colour on another, each time pointing to a different colour sample according to the organism's changing perceptual experiences. But 'red', we want to say, means this ↗ colour (pointing to a sample of red), regardless of when, where, or by whom it is said.

For that matter, how does an agent know that a sample she is observing *accords* with her representation of red? In his 1936 lectures 'The Language of Sense Data and Private Experience', Wittgenstein makes the point that, in order to speak of 'recognising' that x is an instantiation of ϕ, it must be logically possible to speak of 'misrecognising' y as an instantiation of ϕ. But, for that to be possible, there must be an *independent* – a public – criterion which enables one to identify when *x* is the *same* colour (object, experience, sensation, event, etc.) as before. For it only makes sense to speak of 'recognising that *x* is ϕ' when there exist independent and public criteria for describing something as 'ϕ'.

But what criterion does the agent possess on the cognitivist picture? 'Here the criterion is *that* you recognize it. . . . This really means that it is impossible to recognize it wrongly – in fact that there is not any such thing as recognition here' (LSD: 341). That is, on the cognitivist picture, 'x is ϕ' really states: 'It appears to me that x is ϕ'. But *what appears to me* can hardly act as an *independent criterion of identity*. And if that is the case, then what this means is that it is impossible to *misrecognise x*. But if it is impossible to misrecognise something, then in what sense can you speak of 'recognising' it?

The cognitivist answer to this question lies in the mechanist gloss which AI imposed on the notion of *matching and mismatching*. The obvious problem with the cognitivist argument at this point is that it has merely shifted the problem of explaining the nature of concept-application (categorisation) to the problem of explaining the nature of 'recognition'. The latter is said to consist in 'seeing' a match between an input and its internal representation. But how does one explain what this mental act consists in without at some point deploying those very cognitive concepts which the theory is supposed to explain? And what does the 'match' consist in? Perhaps the cognitivist would answer: If x is the same as y, then there must be a match. But what is the nature of this 'must': isn't this just a grammatical proposition stipulating how one is to use 'match'? And what is the nature of this use of 'same as'?

On the epistemological framework which underpins the cognitivist theory of concepts, *recognition* refers to the perceptual experience of seeing what is common to the diverse instances of a category. It thus turns out that our 'questions about the nature of [concepts and] categories' rest on questions about the nature of recognition; and, like the former, these questions 'may be psychological as much as metaphysical questions' (Medin 1989: 1469). This is precisely where the appeal of AI lay for the cognitive revolution. For it offered what seemed to be the perfect way to remove these questions from the realm of the metaphysical: viz., it would explain the experience in question in computational terms.

As we saw in Chapter 2, in his earliest writings on the Mechanist Thesis, Turing assumed that the concept of *recognition* can be analysed in such a way that equivalent responses to invariant stimuli can be said to constitute a primitive instantiation of recognition. Thus, a Turing Machine is said to 'recognise' '0s' and '1s', just as a parking meter, which uses a sophisticated coin-testing device, can be said to 'possess enough knowledge' to 'recognise' a round metal disc, but not to 'distinguish' between coins and slugs. This reductionist premise provides a straightforward explanation of the 'mental process' of matching and mismatching: viz., this refers to a mechanical fitting together of two different pieces.

The resulting theory demands, first, that we distinguish between sensory 'input' and 'representation', and, second, that both the input and the representation be encoded in some form which allows the mind to compare like with like. Of course, all of these terms – 'matching', 'mismatching', 'compare' – still rest on the rules governing the use of 'same as' in various contexts. But Wittgenstein's private language argument (that it makes no sense to suppose that someone could follow a rule that it is logically impossible for anyone else to follow) will not be seen as damaging to what the AI theorist has in mind. For what he means by 'recognition' is a causal process analogous to, e.g., a key opening a lock. When there is a 'match' between input and representation, the door opens: the subject 'recognises' x as an instantiation of φ. But what this really means is that it makes no sense to speak of 'recognition' and 'misrecognition' as such: only of 'matching', 'mismatching' and 'malfunctioning'. And this, presumably, is a consequence which the AI-theorist will greet as proof of 'semantic progress'.

The problem with this argument, however, is that, by definition, if a door doesn't open for whatever reason (e.g. the key jams), then there wasn't a match; and conversely, anything that opens the door (e.g. a jemmy) consti- tutes a match. AI soon discovered just how pertinent this problem is in Pattern Recognition studies. Any number of things – e.g., the intrusion of background or foreground objects, subtle variations in scanned objects, unforeseen consequences of self-modifying algorithms – can result in a bug in a Pattern Recognition program. The most significant aspect of this state- ment is the presence of the term 'bug'; for the sole criterion for speaking of a 'match' or a 'mismatch' lies in our rules for the use of the concept in question.

In the case of an agent, the criterion for such a match would be that the agent *recognised x*. But this is established by the manner in which S responds to *x*, not by whatever mental or neurophysiological events she might be experiencing. That is, it is only possible to speak of matching *x* and *y* if we possess an independent criterion for identifying the act of 'recognising x'; and it is by clarifying this criterion, and the manner in which 'recognise' is used, that we explain the nature of *recognition* (see Coulter 1983). As far as the AI view of concepts is concerned, what we would have to say in the case of 'bugs' is not that the program had *malfunctioned* but, rather, that the 'concept' (program) had been modified in such-and-such a way. For we would no longer have any criteria to establish when the input and represen- tation match each other in the *prescribed* manner.

Likewise, we would have no reason to correct a child who classifies a table as a chair; for who are we to argue with her mental categorisation processes? Moreover, recall that, on the cognitivist picture, thought and language are externally related to one another. It follows that, provided we observe a neurophysiological match between input and representation, then, regard- less of an agent's sincere avowal that she does not know if x is ϕ, the contrary must be the case. And, conversely, despite an agent's ability to use and respond to uses of 'ϕ' correctly, should we discover a mismatch at the neuro- physiological level between input and representation, we must conclude that, linguistic appearances notwithstanding, she does not possess the concept ϕ.

The various 'musts' which govern this argument lead to Wittgenstein's warning that what we are really dealing with here is 'a primitive conception, viz., that [when we recognize someone] we are comparing the man we see with a memory image in our mind and we find the two to agree. I.e., we are representing "recognizing someone" as a process of identification by means of a picture' (BB: 165). What AI contributed to this 'primitive conception' is the thesis that to see, e.g., a chair is a compound mental process in which the recognition of a sensory array as an instance of *chair* is the end-result of hypothesis-generating or template-matching procedures. Hence, the use of an expression like 'I immediately recognised S' is treated, not as an avowal, but, rather, as an hypothesis. Phenomenologically speaking, it may have *felt* like an 'immediate experience', but, in fact, a complex series of information-processing steps, performed in an instant, preceded this 'state of consciousness'.

What Wittgenstein refers to as a 'primitive conception' of recognition is the consequence – or perhaps one of the sources – of the cognitivist picture we are addressing in this chapter, of the mind forced to 'make sense of' reality. On this epistemological picture, the question of how a child acquires the concept *chair* is construed as asking: 'What happens in the child's mind/brain when she sees a chair for the first time that enables her to re-identify that object as a chair, or to pick out further exemplars of the category, sometimes quite distantly related?' There are two key elements in Wittgenstein's attempt to overturn this approach to the theory of concepts. In this section we have dealt with the negative side: the demonstration that the barriers to answering these questions are logical, not empirical. The view of epistemic privacy which lies at the heart of cognitivism is not some sort of technical obstacle which AI tried but failed to overcome: it is an epistemo-logical confusion which needs to be clarified as such, and thence removed. But if, as Rosch hoped, Wittgenstein's view of language is to provide us with an alternative starting-point for categorisation research, he needs to show us a different way of looking at questions about the nature of concepts and concept-acquisition. And it is to this constructive aspect of his argu-ment which we shall now turn.

§8 The harmony between thought and language

The main reason why AI strikes cognitivists as so much more attuned to their concerns than Wittgenstein is because AI is willing to tackle the epis-temological problems that Wittgenstein seems to be neglecting in his preoccupation with language-games. From the cognitivist perspective, even though it has failed to explain the nature of concepts, or the process of concept-acquisition, at least AI has stimulated research in these areas; but the same can hardly be said of Wittgenstein's approach. Perhaps Piaget was right to complain that philosophy's failure to have any significant impact on psychology is the result of its isolation from empirical matters (see Piaget 1965). Certainly, as far as the cognitivist is concerned, Wittgenstein's apparent obsession with word-use only magnifies this failing by confusing one of the scientist's tools for her object of study.

To answer this charge, we need to understand the relevance of Wittgenstein's remarks on the *harmony between thought and language* for cate-gorisation research. The target of Wittgenstein's argument is the Cartesian premise that thought and language constitute independent and externally related realms. This picture can be broken down into five basic cognitivist presuppositions:

1 we use language to encode and decode thoughts;
2 a child must learn which words hook onto which concepts;
3 concepts are private mental phenomena which, as such, cannot be measured or observed directly;
4 anything that we see must be categorised;
5 categorising is a mental process which enables an organism to go beyond the information given.

We come back, ultimately, to the question of *how* a child sees that this ↗ is a chair. The upshot of the foregoing sections is that this question – this way of looking at concept-application – is a product of the Cartesian picture that Wittgenstein is attacking. According to Wittgenstein, the resolution of this issue lies, not in a new theory of concepts, or in the development of a new technology for examining concepts (*sic*), but in philosophical clarification. This therapeutic endeavour is not supposed to result in the demise of categorisation research, but, rather, in the emergence of a new perspective from which to view concept-acquisition and development.

As we saw in §1, the fundamental question driving categorisation research is: What happens in an organism's mind/brain when it reacts in the same way to discriminably different instances of φ? But what if nothing happened in S's mind when using 'φ' correctly or responding correctly to its use: would this mean that, contrary to appearances, S didn't possess the concept φ? What if a subject experienced synaesthesia for a number of years but this suddenly disappeared: would this mean that her concept of φ had abruptly changed? And what if the exact same sequence or pattern of neural events never occurs twice in a subject's brain when using 'φ', or it changes over time, perhaps as a result of maturation or injury, even though the subject continues to use 'φ' correctly throughout: does this mean that our judgements about a subject's understanding of φ can be overturned by a PET scan? If a subject's 'mental representation' is embodied in a specific location in the brain, does this mean that we might one day be able to perform concept transplants? And, ignoring the question of what counts as *acting in the same way*, what about this troubling use of 'discriminably different instances of φ'?

Cognitivism presupposes that the concept-word 'φ' *refers* to a mental representation, and that the *instances of* φ only count as such on the basis of an organism's experiences. But, in that case, we are only entitled to ask: what causes an organism to react to x,y,z in the same way? That is, we cannot presuppose that which the theory is supposed to explain: viz., what counts as an 'instance of φ', what constitutes φ for S. We cannot assume that a child who refers to lamps, tables and chairs as 'chairs' has made a mistake, or is reacting in the same way to discriminably different instances of different concepts. On the cognitivist thesis, if a pigeon should consistently peck at circles, squares and rhomboids, then these are all 'instances of its concept φ', and the task of the comparative psychologist is to discover what this φ might be (e.g., perhaps it is a *bounded figure*, perhaps it is simply *food*).

It is not enough, however, merely to highlight the sceptical consequences of treating concepts as private mental phenomena: we also need to scrutinise virtually every term in the above 'fundamental question' driving categorisation theory. For example, we must consider whether the use of 'organism' as opposed to 'subject' is the illicit product of the 'cognitive continuum' picture. We must question whether the use of 'react' is grossly overgeneralised. To be sure, an infant may react to sounds, or to sudden movements, or to the sight of certain objects or people. But in what sense can a child performing match-to-sample tests (e.g. selecting a photograph of a chair when it hears the word 'chair') be said to be 'reacting in the same way to a discriminably different instance of *chair*'? Likewise, we must consider this indiscriminate use of 'recognise'. Does the child who cries out 'Mama' every time it sees its mother *recognise* her afresh each time? If the child calls its aunt 'Mama', has it *misrecognised* her?

None of this is intended to subvert the study of how a child acquires a given concept: only the presupposition that the answer to this problem must lie in a formal model of *pre-conscious matching and mismatching processes*. It is in order to wean us from the epistemological picture underpinning this presupposition that Wittgenstein lays so much stress on the theme that the relation between thought and language is *internal*, not *external*. In contrast to the five basic cognitivist presuppositions listed above, Wittgenstein's argument can be summarised by the five following points:

1   there is a categorial difference between treating an agent's behaviour as a *criterion* of what she understands, or as *evidence* of what she is thinking;
2   we use language to *express*, not to *encode* and *decode* thoughts;
3   concepts are neither private nor public phenomena;
4   we use 'concept' to attribute certain abilities to an agent, and not as a referring term: i.e., not as the name of a mental representation;
5   what we see in the world are tables and lamps and chairs, and human beings acting in ways which satisfy the criteria for describing their behaviour in psychological terms: we do not see objects or events or 'colourless movements' which we infer are members of classes whose criterial attributes we have previously abstracted and recorded.

The cognitivist picture of concepts as *the repositories of featural analysis* is the result of conflating two very different language-games. On the one hand, doing x,y,z may constitute a criterion for saying that 'S possesses the concept φ'. On the other hand, a subject's actions – or for that matter, her failure to act – may provide us with evidence of what she thinks. This distinction between

- the criteria for saying S possesses the concept ϕ, and
- the evidence for saying S thinks such-and-such

is often highly pertinent to developmental studies. For example, correctly referring to all the chairs in the house as chairs is a criterion for saying 'S possesses the concept *chair*'. But if a child calls her high-chair 'chair', and nothing else, this may count as evidence that she thinks that 'chair' only refers to her high-chair. But cognitivism disregards the distinction between these different language-games: it treats the evidence that a subject thinks such-and-such as evidence of the concept which the subject's mind has constructed. It thus treats the evidence that a child thinks that 'chair' refers to her high-chair as 'evidence that *the child's concept of chair*' consists in a 'mental representation' of her high-chair.

We must also be careful not to confuse Wittgenstein's grammatical observation that the concepts of thought and language are internally related with the much stronger claim that the attribution of thought presupposes the ability to speak a language. One of the more important points that cognitivism has stressed – and possibly one of the reasons why it was drawn to the continuum picture – is that it makes sense to speak of pre- and even non-linguistic behaviour in cognitive terms. But this, too, is a grammatical observation – in this case, about the concept of *cognition* – and not a hypothesis about the cognitive processes or mental states of lower organisms. The last thing Wittgenstein wanted to claim was that it makes no sense to speak of animals or infants as *thinking such-and-such*. On the contrary, he often capitalises on this very point when examining the light which primitive contexts can shed on the nature of some concept (see Savage-Rumbaugh *et al.* in press). But whether it makes sense to speak of infants or animals as *possessing such-and-such a concept* is a much more complex issue.

The emphasis in Wittgenstein's discussion of the various rules whereby we regulate the disparate uses of 'concept' is on *behaviour*, not *verbal behaviour*. The question which this raises is: are we ever licensed to say of an organism which does not possess the capacity to acquire language that it none the less possesses the capacity to acquire the concept ϕ? That is, how critical is linguistic behaviour to our uses of 'concept'? While the attribution of many, if not most, of our concepts requires the ability to speak a language, are there some concepts, or some uses of 'the concept ϕ', so primitive that even a non-linguistic creature could be said to possess them?

This is not an issue that can be decided *a priori*. That is, there is no formal set of rules governing the use of 'concept' which forbids us from describing an animal or an infant as possessing, e.g., the concepts of cause and effect, even though they cannot use or respond appropriately to the use of 'cause'.

Nor is this just an issue for comparative psychologists to debate. For the fact is that developmental psychologists have drawn freely on the idea that an infant acquires fairly complex concepts prior to its ability to speak, and, indeed, that it is on the basis of these concepts that the child is able to begin to speak. But all too often such attributions are based on an *a priori* model which dictates what concepts an organism *must* possess if it is to make sense of its environment, rather than on close scrutiny of that organism's behaviour.

Just as in the case of attributing primitive linguistic skills, so, too, our judgements about a subject's possession of a concept are based on how she behaves in certain contexts. We are not dealing here with some mysterious realm whose constructs we can at best infer from an organism's behaviour. Nor are we trying to 'get inside' the mind of animals or infants: to understand inductively how they 'see the world'. Rather, we literally observe – or at least, we can observe, if we have been properly trained and if we look carefully enough – what they think. We can see their emotions, intentions, thoughts, and desires: what they want, what they believe, and what they think other agents want or believe or intend.

Thus, we might infer from his actions that the bonobo Kanzi thinks that the vet has come to hurt him, but we do not *infer* that Kanzi understands the request 'Go to the refrigerator and get some melon' when we observe him proceed to the refrigerator and rifle through its contents until he finds a melon which he then hands over to his trainer (see Savage-Rumbaugh *et al.* 1993). For this just is what is called 'understanding the request'. To be sure, a sceptic might require further criteria before he is prepared to sanction this description of Kanzi's behaviour (e.g., that Kanzi is able to do this with different kinds of fruits, that he can pick out the melon from a table laden with fruit, that he understands the relation between *melon* and *fruit*, etc.). But this merely signifies that the application of 'understands the request' demands greater behavioural complexity than might be afforded by a simple or a single comprehension task, and not that comprehension is some mental process or state hidden behind the veil of an organism's behaviour.

The same point applies to the attribution of concept-possession. As a child or an animal's behaviour becomes increasingly complex, so, too, do the terms used to describe that behaviour. That is, we have varying criteria for our uses of 'S possesses the concept ϕ' in primitive contexts, and in the increasingly more advanced contexts involved in language-use. These criteria are the background – the 'form of representation' – against which any conjectures about a child's or an animal's ability to acquire and apply certain concepts can be formulated. But what happens if we construe the *justificational criteria* for describing S as possessing the concept ϕ as *inductive evidence* for the concept she (her mind) has acquired? That is, what happens if, instead of seeing the statement 'S possesses the concept ϕ' as grounded in normative practices, we treat it as a hypothesis that a representation has formed in S's mind as a result of an abstraction and generalisation process? As we shall see in the following section, one answer is provided by *constraint theory*.

§9 Constraint theory

Constraint theory is sister to the study of 'cognitive heuristics' in the psychology of reasoning. For example, a close parallel can be drawn between the 'class-inclusion' experiments performed on young children and the Wason selection tasks. In both cases, cognitivists are looking for consistent types of error. The starting-point is the hypothesis that these mistakes reflect 'biases' which manifest hidden cognitive processes. But it is hardly surprising that we should find this close parallel. After all, both groups are concerned with explaining the nature of thinking *qua* (partially) pre-conscious process. *Category-systematisation* and *reasoning* are seen as inter-connected sub-domains in this broad subject.

Constraint theory begins with the premise that children must systematise concepts by creating category taxonomies. But the inferences they make or the hypotheses they frame are said to be highly idiosyncratic. In the case of concept-organisation, however, the end-point is at least defined – or is in the process of being defined – as the category hierarchies that occur in the adult mind (*sic*). Thus, constraint theory proceeds from the given that children must learn hierarchically organised class-inclusion relations, and that, to do so, 'they must figure out how two words (e.g., "oaks" and "trees") apply to the same objects' (Markman *et al.* 1980: 227).

There are thought to be several options which the child must consider here:

- the two terms might label the same object at two different levels of a hierarchy;
- the two terms might be synonyms;
- the two terms might refer to partially overlapping categories.

'On encountering a new word, then, children must differentiate between a number of plausible hypotheses about how it fits into their current concep-tual structure' (Callanan and Markman 1982: 1093).

In light of the ubiquity of class-inclusion relations in natural language, we might expect that 'inclusion should be the first hypothesis children would consider when confronted with a novel hierarchy' (Markman *et al.* 1980: 228). But categorisation experiments suggest that children have difficulty with class-inclusion, which they see as violating the principle of mutual exclusivity (i.e. as assigning the same object to two different classes on the same catego-rial level). These experiments also suggest that children find it easier to acquire and operate with part–whole hierarchical relations. Perhaps when 'children are relatively free to impose their own structure on a novel hierarchy, they might prefer a collection to a class organization' (*ibid.*: 229).

This is the hypothesis which underlies Markman *et al.*'s attempt to demonstrate that children misinterpret superordinate category terms as referring to collections. One such experiment begins with ostensive definitions of nonsense syllables. The child is told: 'These ↗ are oaks' (pointing to a group of oak figurines), 'These ↗ are pines' (pointing to pine figurines), and 'These ↗ are trees' (pointing to the entire array). Subsequent questioning reveals that, while she has no trouble using 'oaks' and 'pines' correctly, the child uses 'trees' in the same way as she would use a collective noun like 'forest'. For example, if asked 'Show me an oak', she will pick up a single oak figurine, but, if asked 'Show me a tree', she will pick up a bunch of the figurines, rather than one of the oak or pine figurines – and indeed, will deny that a single oak or pine figurine is a 'tree'.

Markman also cites evidence (see Markman 1989) which she claims suggests that, when children are taught new superordinate category terms as mass nouns (e.g. 'An oak is a part of trees'), they master the relation between subordinate and superordinate concepts more readily than if count nouns are used to teach superordinate category terms ('An oak is a tree'). This is seen as corroborating the hypothesis that collections help children to learn and reason about hierarchies: that it is easier for children to deal with collections (part–whole relations) than class-inclusion relations, and that the former establish a sound cognitive footing for the acquisition of the latter.

Instead of treating these results as a criterion of *misunderstanding*, they are treated as evidence of a *primitive mode of understanding*: viz., that a child's mind treats novel hierarchical categorial relations as part–whole relations. That is, instead of concluding from this experiment that, in certain situations, children may have trouble grasping relatively simple conceptual relations, or the plural use of superordinate count nouns, we get the conclusion that some different form of *mental categorisation process* must underlie the children's behaviour: that the errors *must* have some significance as to *the hypotheses which the child's mind generates*, or *the inferences it draws*, in the organisation of its concepts.

The crux of this argument lies in the rider that it is only 'when minimal information is supplied' that children are said to have trouble assimilating the class-inclusion relation; for no such problems were seen to arise when 'the relation was explicitly specified' (Markman *et al.* 1980: 238). But were these results due to the fact that 'ostensive definition gives limited information', or because the way the experiment has been set up confuses the way in which 'oaks', 'pines' and 'trees' are to be used? After all, we would normally say to a child to whom we were trying to teach the relation between *oak*, *pine* and *tree*: 'This ↗ is an oak tree', 'This ↗ is a pine tree', and 'These ↗ are all trees'. Rather than helping the child to distinguish between the different categorial levels involved, the use of the undifferentiated plural demonstrative in all three ostensive definitions suggests categorial homogeneity. From another point of view, the child's 'mistakes' might in fact appear to be perfectly appropriate, and it was the protocol that was at fault.

The constraint theorist will readily concede that much more needs to be done here, but will insist that, just as with a selection-task experiment, we create an unusual problem for a subject precisely in order to observe how she reacts. The whole point of this exercise is to see how a child will attempt to 'resolve the apparent conflict between x *is an* A and x *is a* C' (*ibid.*: 239). But did the children really experience this particular 'conflict'? Here the manner in which the data are presented is overladen with epistemological presuppositions which need to be teased out.

Broadly speaking, there are two basic issues here:

1 Do these experiments tell us anything about the way children think, how their thought-processes develop?
2 Do these experiments manifest the manner in which the developing human mind systematises concepts?

Our question is: how did (2) become equivalent to (1)? How did an ambiguous use of a plural demonstrative become evidence of a *class-membership conflict*? Why does the constraint theorist assume that the child is 'organising its concepts', much less 'constructing a hierarchy'? Indeed, what is the source of the fundamental premise that 'Very young children assume that category terms are mutually exclusive' (Markman 1989: 161)?

Consider once again what Markman says about a pigeon's acquisition of the concept *circle* (quoted in the opening section). According to Markman, 'a pigeon can learn to peck at circles to be rewarded with food. Since the pigeon can see the differences between large and small circles yet treat them equivalently, it would be said to have the concept of circle' (*ibid.*: 138). Now, suppose a pigeon can be successfully trained to peck at round keys, but cannot be trained to peck at round buttons: would this constitute evidence of its tendency to assume that category terms are mutually exclusive? Obviously, we need to get clear what sorts of criteria license us in saying of a subject: 'S thinks that p and q are mutually exclusive'.

Perhaps the first question we need to ask here is: Why should one suppose that the statement 'S thinks that x can't be both ϕ and ϕ' (e.g. S thinks that John can't be both tall and Canadian) *means the same thing* as: 'S thinks that nothing can be both a member of the set ϕ and a member of the set ϕ (S thinks that nothing can belong to both the set of tall people and the set of Canadians)? Surely these statements belong to different language-games with different justificational criteria? The latter demands that the subject be able to explain why she thinks the formal definitions of two sets conflict. Are we to assume that the ostensive definition of a concept-word is categorically identical to the explicit definition of a set?

Still more to the point, what is it in this experiment that licenses the assumption that 'The child thinks that p and q are mutually exclusive'? The child doesn't actually insist that nothing can be both an oak and a tree (or a group of oaks and a group of trees); she only denies that a single oak figurine is a tree. Yet this, together with the (putative) fact that she used 'oaks' as a count noun and 'trees' as a collective noun, is said to constitute sufficient evidence of a *conflict in her mind* between 'x *is an* A and x *is a* C'. But there is a huge difference between saying that the child denied *that an object can be both an oak and a tree* and that she denied *that that ↗ is a tree*.

The 'mutual exclusivity' interpretation turns on the epistemological premise that the child is presented with *objects* which must be labelled and categorised. As Markman puts it, 'Children have several choices when confronted with a label (say, "animal") for an object for which they already have a label (say, "dog") (*ibid.*: 162). And why just synonymy, hierarchy, or overlapping sets? Doesn't the child also have to rule out the possibility of metaphor, or metonymy, or a bilingual parent, or a mistake, or simply alternative proper names? And once it has settled that it is confronted with a category hierarchy (and why it should have settled on this is totally obscure), why just class-inclusion (which entails that she grasps that one of the categories is included in the other, and hence, violates the principle of mutual exclusivity between category terms), or part–whole collections (thereby maintaining mutual exclusivity)?

Let us grant, however, that Markman and her colleagues have discovered that, in some situations, a child treats a superordinate category-term as if it were a collective (or a mass) noun. (We would need to sharpen the criteria for this – for what it is to treat a class-inclusion term as if it were a collective or a mass noun – but let us suppose that this has been done.) The point is not to deny the possible psychological significance of this discovery, but to understand and assess it. And the problem here is that, because of the epistemological framework underpinning constraint theory, this description of children's behaviour – of their reasoning or conceptual abilities and biases – automatically becomes a hypothesis about *the logical architecture of the child's 'categorizing processes'* (viz., 'The child represents the relation between 'φ' and 'Φ' as part–whole').

The principle operating here is thoroughly reductionist. Having first assumed that the child can be legitimately described as thinking that p and q are mutually exclusive, we get the following analysis:

- the statement 'S thinks that p and q are mutually exclusive' means:
- 'S thinks that the category terms "p" and "q" are mutually exclusive', which in turn means:
- 'S thinks that no object can be both a member of the set "φ" and a member of the set "Φ"'.

This provides us with both the question that drives this theory, and its answer: viz., in answer to the question 'Why do children have trouble grasping class-inclusion relations when minimal information is supplied?' we get the answer: 'Because their minds naturally represent

'$(\exists x)(\exists \phi)(\exists \Phi)(x \in \phi \ \& \ x \in \Phi)$' as
'$(\exists x)(\exists \phi)(\exists \phi) \ (x \in \phi \ v \ x \in \phi)$'' (where '$\phi$' and '$\phi$' are treated as same-level categories).

But the child is able to see 'ϕ' and 'Φ' as first- and second-order concepts if the superordinate relation is represented as part–whole rather than class-inclusion: i.e. as governed by something like an 'is a piece of' or 'is a part of' rather than the 'is a member of' operator (i.e. '$(\exists x)(\exists \phi)(\exists \Phi)(x \in \phi \ \& \ x \ \iota \ \Phi)$').

This introduction of different 'operators' marks an interesting development in classical Piagetian theory. The constraint theorist is searching here for the most appropriate logic with which to model the child's mind. The mistake of earlier approaches is said to be that, following Piaget's lead, psychologists continued to look for a single logic with which to chart the mind's development. But why not adopt different logics to model the different stages of the mind's development? Within any given stage, the various conceptual relations will still be seen as uniform: i.e. the mind will still be said to use a common denominator – a common operator – to systematise its concepts. The relation between *yellow* and *colour* will still be treated as the same as that between *oak* and *tree*. But what that relation is will depend upon the logic which characterises the stage in question. Hence, the relation between *yellow* and *colour*, or *oak* and *tree*, at stage$_1$ will be different from the relation between them at stage$_2$: i.e. there will be a succession of *subordinate/superordinate* relations in the development of categorisation.

But do categories really display the sort of formal unity which this theory demands? In what sense is the relation between *yellow* and *colour* the same as that between *oak* and *tree*? It is not enough to answer that *yellow* and *oak* are basic-level concepts while *colour* and *tree* are superordinate concepts, and that the relation between the two levels is asymmetric: i.e. that all that is meant by saying that *yellow* and *oak* are 'basic-level', and *colour* and *tree* 'superordinate' concepts, is that, just as something that is yellow is coloured, but something coloured need not be yellow, so too something that is an oak is a tree, but something that is a tree need not be an oak. For this presupposes – it does not explain why – the relation between 'subordinate' and 'superordinate' concepts (whatever these two terms might mean) is invariant.

Moreover, this argument presupposes that *colour* is a more generalised concept than *yellow* in exactly the same sense that *tree* is a more generalised concept than *oak*. But are questions like

1   'What do *green* and *yellow* have in common that we call them both "colours"?', or

2   'What do *happiness* and *sadness* have in common that we call them both "emotions"?', the same as questions like

3   'What do *oaks* and *pines* have in common that we call them both "trees"?' and

4   'What do negative numbers and natural numbers have in common that we call them both "numbers"'?

With (3) and (4) the cognitivist will feel he is on solid ground when it comes to theorising about how the child formulates her concept on the basis of her encounter with a small sample of the extension of the concept (i.e. the list of common features which her mind abstracts). But how do 'feature-detection and analysis' apply to the first two questions? Do (1) and (2) even have (non-tautological) answers? Or do we simply draw a blank cheque on reductionism in order to conceal the embarrassment which such examples cause constraint theory?

For that matter, we certainly do not want to conclude from the fact that grass is green, but not all green things are grass, that *grass* and *green* are subordinate/superordinate concepts. We are looking here for the stronger relation that φ *must be* Φ. These are supposed to be in some sense necessary, not contingent, relations. But what is the source of this 'necessity': does it lie in the structure of the mind? Are the statements 'Yellow is a colour' and 'An oak is a tree' *psychological generalisations*? Do the conceptual relations between *yellow* and *colour*, or *oak* and *tree*, vary over the course of development? It is one thing to say that one's understanding of the relation between two concepts may change over time, but quite another to say that the *conceptual relation* itself changes over time. But how does the categorisation argument allow us to draw this distinction if the conceptual relation just is the structure which the mind imposes on the two categories?

The very notion of a *category hierarchy*, built up out of uniform subordinate/superordinate conceptual relations, is troubling. It suggests a rigid mathematico-logical structure, both within category levels and from the lowest to the highest orders of categorisation, when in fact language, in Wittgenstein's famous phrase, 'is a labyrinth of paths' (PI: §203). But the cognitivist is prepared for this objection: perhaps the answer to this problem lies in Wittgenstein's earlier remark, at PI §108, that 'Language has not the formal unity' which he envisaged in the *Tractatus*, but is rather a 'family of structures more or less related to one another'.

That is, perhaps the solution to the problems that confront us here is to institute still further complexity: e.g. to argue that *part–whole* and *class-inclusion* are second-level *theoretical* concepts which only apply to *stages* in categorisation; but each concept can be broken down into first-level theoretical concepts (e.g., *discreteness*, *parthood*, *overlap* and *fusion*), which in turn can be used to model the concept-specific categorisation processes used within each stage (e.g., *colours*, *emotions*, *animals* and *numbers* might each have a different logic). Development could then be seen as a cumulative process rather than one of displacement. Categorisation would be said to consist in the gradual accretion and systematisation of multiple *subordinate/superordinate* relations (e.g., *colour* might be assigned to *overlap*, and *emotions* to *fusion* within part–whole logic, while *trees* and *numbers* are assigned to class-inclusion logic). Provided there are ways to systematise these first-level logics (and perhaps there is a way to map part–whole onto class-inclusion, yielding a still more all-embracing logic at the third level), we would have a way to contain the mounting complexity which confronts us here.

In any event, whether or not the child understands something logically different by the two statements 'yellow is a colour' and 'oaks are trees', what matters here is that the child understands something logically different from the adult when the adult says that 'yellow is a colour' or 'oaks are trees'. The cognitivist's problem is thus to discover what 'S thinks that "yellow" is a "colour" or "oaks" are "trees"' means when applied to an *x-year-old child* (which is accomplished by observing how the child uses 'yellow', 'colour', 'oak' and 'tree' in various situations).

Constraint theory rests on a phenomenon which is familiar to every parent: what looks like nonsense may make perfectly good sense once you get to know the child. But is the distinction that has to be drawn here between *adult* and *infant* modes of understanding, or between *nonsensical* and *idiosyncratic* uses of words? There is a crucial distinction between the two statements:

1   'S thinks that "trees" means the same thing as "forest"'; and
2   'S thinks that "oaks" are a part of (or a piece of) "trees"'.

We can have all sorts of criteria for (1), but what exactly does (2) mean? Is this an example of Frege's 'hitherto unknown kind of madness': of different kinds of logic? Does the child – as Markman suggests – exemplify what Quine had in mind with his 'radical translation' argument (see Shanker 1996)?

How should we respond if a child says to us 'oaks are a part of trees'? On constraint theory, instead of correcting her we should confirm this. For recall that, on the educational methodology formulated according to this theory, our primary goal is to enhance category systematisation. The child's mistake is apparently nothing of the sort; it is evidence of her natural categorisation processes, and were we to respond, 'No. Oaks *are* trees', we would risk impeding her cognitive development. For all that matters here is that, if we say to the child, 'Those ↗ are maples', she will know automatically that they are ligneous, have some form of foliage, a self-supporting trunk, give off oxygen . . . . And even if the child can't supply us with any such defining features, the very fact that she uses 'trees' correctly – e.g., upon first seeing a stand of maples she observes, 'Those ↗ are trees' – entails that her *mind* must have gone through some such process (where, again, the psychologist's task is to discover what defining features the child's mind might have processed).

What this really means is that, on the functional definition of concept, one cannot talk about *category systematisation* independently of knowing what it is that is being systematised: i.e. what concepts *are* constrains how one goes about systematising them. For, obviously, the mind will seek out ways that will augment, and certainly not conflict with, the basic function of concepts. Thus, whatever method of category systematisation a child settles on *must* satisfy the demands of cognitive economy and efficiency.[16]

This last point is crucial; for the function of taxonomic systems must be an extension of the function of concepts. Recall that, according to constraint theory, 'When learning a new concept, children first encounter a small sample of the extension of the concept' (Markman 1989: 6). The child is supposed to have formulated its concepts of *yellow* and *oak* on the basis of its initial encounters with a few exemplars (accompanied, perhaps, by ostensive definitions and/or more explicit information); then used its primitive concepts of *yellow* and *oak* to acquire the concepts of *colour* and *tree*; and then used its superordinate concepts to facilitate further basic-level acquisitions and revised its superordinate concepts as a result of these encounters. Taxonomic systems are thus said to play a vital role in the concept-acquisition process, enabling us to organise and pass on a large amount of information, thereby 'saving us from having to learn anew for each object' (*ibid.*: 15). But the key question is, learn what?

According to this theory, the statement 'If S has acquired the concept *tree* he will be able to point to trees' is utterly vacuous. It simply reiterates the problem which confronts us here: the problem of *how* S is able to identify maples as trees. At some level of representation he *must* have abstracted a sufficient number of common features to enable him not only to re-identify oaks as oaks and maples as maples, but, also, to identify oaks and maples as trees and to identify new species of trees as trees. (How the same argument is supposed to apply to *colour* is an even greater mystery.) But there is an obvious problem with a statement like 'If S has acquired the concept *tree* he will know that maples are ligneous, have some form of foliage, a self-supporting trunk, give off oxygen . . . '. For it is not at all unreasonable to suppose that a child might be able to use 'tree' in the manner stipulated – can correctly identify trees as 'trees' – yet cannot understand any of the terms used in this statement, and, indeed, is unable to give any answer to the question, 'What do trees have in common?'

At this point the theory has two options: it can argue that, appearances notwithstanding, the child does not possess the concept *tree*; i.e. correct use of 'trees' is only *evidence* of concept-possession. Or it can resort to the notion of 'preconscious inference': viz., although the child cannot explicitly respond to questions about any of these terms, she *must*, at some cognitive level, have recorded a set of common features.

The danger here, of course, is that one does not want to describe the child as abstracting features that are beyond her conceptual abilities. But the constraint theorist will claim that we are not totally helpless when it comes to discovering what common features the child might have abstracted. We can do things like show the child pictures of various parts of trees and ask her 'Where do you find these?' Or show her pictures of trees that are missing their leaves or branches and ask her 'Is this a tree?' On a still more extreme line of reasoning, we might simply show her photographs of trees, and, when she has habituated to these, show her photographs of trees missing various parts and record whether she manifests dishabituation towards any. The point is, it should be possible, according to cognitivism, to design some form of experiment that will provide us with evidence as to what the abstracted features might be.

But how do you stop the regress which threatens here? We started out by stating that the explanation for the child's possession of the concept *tree* – of her being able to pick out the same things as *exemplars of trees* – is that she could pick out some feature which trees have in common: e.g., could point to leaves, even though she may not understand the word 'leaf'. But to be able to pick out common features presupposes that the agent possesses a criterion of identity for that feature. What, then, is the criterion for her possessing the concept *leaf*? The same argument must come into play: at some level of representation she *must* have abstracted a sufficient number of common features to enable her not only to re-identify oak leaves and pine needles, but, also, to identify new species of leaves. So now we need a set of experiments to establish what common features she abstracted when she observed oak and pine leaves. And so on.

Constraint theory contributes to the functional definition of concept the corollary that category-hierarchies must mirror the course of cognitive development. That is, a child *cannot* acquire the concept of *tree* before she has acquired the concepts of *leaf* and *branch* (or whatever the common features whereby she grasps the concept of *tree*). The growth of knowledge must be an orderly – a logical – affair. Here, then, is the definition of 'superordinate' in the context of cognition (as opposed to linguistics, where its meaning is strictly taxonomic): it means, 'Built up out of previous knowledge'.

This returns us to the picture of a cognitive continuum; for, according to this theory, 'All animals must have some ability to classify objects in their world: they must be able to identify food, predators, and shelter, tasks that certainly require classification. Even pigeons, trained using discrimination learning procedures, appear capable of learning categories, including "trees", "oak leaves", "fish", "humans", and the letter "A"' (*ibid.*: 137). Thus, the question 'When does concept-possession *per se* occur on the continuum?' is an idle philosophical issue. For the answer is: at every stage. Self-modifying programs, neural nets, accommodation, habituation, and even tropisms, have all been cited as primitive forms of concept-acquisition.

This theory is not only resilient: it is seemingly invulnerable. And that is more than just a little worrying. For example, the objection, 'By these criteria a thermostat would possess the concepts *warm* and *cool*' is *not seen as an objection*. Normative and causal concepts have not been inadvertently conflated: the reductionism is both explicit and deliberate. Similarly, it is fruitless to object that a child can understand 'tree' before she can understand 'leaves' or 'branches'. For this will be seen as confusing linguistic with cognitive phenomena, eliciting the response: it is possible that a child may be able to use the concept-word 'tree' before she can use 'leaves' or 'branches', but she cannot possess the concept of *tree* before she possesses the concepts of *leaves* or *branches* (or whatever the common features whereby she builds up her concept of *tree*).

The use of 'can' and 'cannot' in both of these statements is meant to be psychological. Just as a parrot can utter the sound 'tree' without possessing the concept *tree*, so, too, a young child can parrot its parents' use of the word 'tree'. *Concept-acquisition* and *category-term acquisition* are thus seen as distinct phenomena. The former is seen as experientially prior to the latter in so far as concept-possession is concerned: first we see what two things have in common, then we (may or may not) learn names for both the features they have in common and the group of things that have these things in common. Even if we learn a name first, it remains just a meaningless mark until we have mapped it onto a concept. Thus, only concept-acquisition and category-systematisation must be linear; category-term-acquisition can occur in any order.

Ostensive definition enters into this picture as a catalyst for concept-acquisition. The starting-point for the functional definition of concepts is that the subject who hears an ostensive definition must figure out what two exemplars have in common. The starting-point for the categorisation experiments discussed in this section is that the subject must figure out how two words apply to the same object. There is thus an interaction between linguistic and psychological phenomena: but that is all. For, as we have seen throughout this chapter, *concept-possession* and *category-term possession* have been rendered externally related: i.e. how we think is said to be fundamentally different from how we speak. Hence, the above objection that semantic categories do not display the sort of formal unity which this theory demands – that the relation between 'yellow' and 'colour' is not the same as that between 'oak' and 'tree' – will be dismissed as the cavilling of ordinary-language philosophy. For whether or not *language* is a 'family of structures more or less related to one another' will be dismissed as irrelevant to questions regarding the structure of *cognition*.

How we use and explain a concept-word may count as a *criterion* for

236

category-term possession, but language-use only serves as *evidence vis-à-vis* cognition. That is, the fact that an agent correctly uses and explains how to use 'tree' does not entail that the agent possesses the concept *tree*. *Qua* evidence, it can be overturned; e.g., we might discover through reasoning experiments, which expose the agent's 'cognitive biases', that she did not in fact possess the concept. Or we might discover that her concept is different from ours, or different from the semantic rules which define the range of the category-term. Indeed, we might discover that how we explain 'tree' falls short of our knowledge of the concept.

The cognitivist speaks of mapping words onto concepts. But we can never be certain what the concept is onto which an agent has mapped a word, or what the common features are which she has abstracted from a group of exemplars, or how an agent has organised her concepts. For example, an agent who has pointed to oaks and pines and maples as examples of 'trees' one day calls a telephone pole a 'tree'. Do we conclude that she has suddenly made a mistake, or that her concept was not what we inferred? Indeed, are our own concepts any less a mystery to us than those formed by pigeons? Doesn't Quine's radical translation argument apply just as forcefully to ourselves as to other agents (see Shanker 1996)? For we certainly don't have privileged access to our brain's operations. Do we thus infer from our own behaviour and the kind of judgements that we make what concepts our brain has formed?

A whole series of questions naturally present themselves here: does a baby make a *mistake* if it tries to grasp a soap bubble? Does a brain make a *mistake* if it groups together oaks and pines and maples and telephone poles? Do we make a mistake in our semantic category if we map 'trees' onto oaks and pines and maples but exclude telephone poles? Or is this whole obsession with the possibility of error *vis-à-vis* the application of a concept itself a mistake: the consequence of confusing the rules that we cite for the use of 'concept' with the nature of *concepts*? But what happens to the concept of *concept* when correct and incorrect usage are abandoned? Clearly we need to look yet again at the basic presuppositions driving the functional definition of concept.

§10 The 'constitutional uncertainty of the mental'

If the function of a concept is to enable an organism to 'go beyond the information given', and if the need for 'cognitive economy' in a complex world such as ours demands some sort of efficient system for classifying and categorising a given stimulus, then it would seem that if we are ever to understand how the mind works we are going to have to discover the order in which concepts are acquired and the manner in which they are organised. Herein lies a further reason why we see the simultaneous rise of both AI and developmental psychology in the 1960s, for the obvious place to begin this complex task is with 'toy domains', whether this be in the realm of computer programs, or of the child's cognitive development.

The cognitive revolution was committed to the principle that one should be able to analyse concept-acquisition using either a 'bottom-up' or a 'top-down' approach; but, in practice, the emphasis was solely on the latter. As a result, a large part of cognitive psychology became *a priori*. For, on this approach, the psychologist has to develop formal models about the order in which concepts are acquired and the manner in which they are organised, onto which she then attempts to map behaviour. Clearly, all sorts of anomalies are going to arise that will have to be explained away (e.g. by exploiting some such notion as *décalage* or *content-effects*). But, in principle, the question of whether a subject possesses a given concept at any given stage is supposed to be clear-cut: i.e., if the formal model dictates that the concept φ presupposes the concept φ, then one first has to establish whether S can classify exemplars of the concept φ before going on to consider whether S can classify exemplars of the concept φ.

One of the most striking consequences of this psychologistic approach to psychological explanation is that it promotes a *discontinuity* view of cognitive development. This is because it postulates a discrete hierarchy of psychological concepts. The developmentalist then has to decide whether an organism possesses the concept φ or the 'lower-level' concept φ, where there is thought to be a clear break between φ and φ. For example, there is said to be such a gap between the concepts of *pretence* and *feigning*: i.e., to be capable of feigning, a subject need only believe that doing *x* will lead to her getting *y*, but to be capable of pretence a subject has to believe that if she does *x* another agent will believe something false and act accordingly. But, to be capable of the latter feat, the subject must be able to represent another agent's mental states: that is, the subject must possess the concept of *false belief* (and all that this entails). Either a subject does or does not possess the concept of false belief. Hence there is no intermediary between *feigning* and *pretence*; for without the concept of false belief, it is *impossible* for S to be capable of pretence.

The so-called logical gap between *feigning* and *pretence* means that the mind must make a 'cognitive leap' to get from feigning to pretending. More fundamentally, the Cartesian view of concepts has led cognitivists to postulate a discontinuity between non-linguistic and linguistic behaviour, and between not possessing and possessing a 'theory of mind'. To explain these phenomena, cognitivism has resorted to some sort of LAD (language acquisition device) or TOMM (theory of mind mechanism), which are said to be activated when the relevant mechanism reaches a certain threshold of experience (see Savage-Rumbaugh *et al.* in press).

Wittgenstein presents us with a radically different way of speaking about 'how concepts are organised' when he remarks that: 'Only of a living human being and what resembles (behaves like) a living human being can one say:

it has sensations; it sees; is blind; hears; is deaf; is conscious or unconscious' (PI: §281). That is, 'concept hierarchies' are not built up from atomic (non-cognitive) units in the manner prescribed by AI. Rather, human beings serve as the paradigm subjects for the use of psychological concepts: any question about the psychological capacities of animals or infants demands that we compare their behaviour with the relevant actions underpinning the use of the concept in question.

We enjoy considerable latitude, however, when it comes to using psychological terms. That is, we freely apply many psychological terms in primitive contexts: in cases, e.g., where a subject is unable to explain his use of a symbol, or where the subject cannot use symbols but can respond appropriately to their use by others; or cases of 'proto-linguistic' communication (such as have been documented by developmental interactionists and primatologists); and even, cases of behavioural prototypes (as in Wittgenstein's example of how a cat stalking a bird constitutes 'a natural expression of intention' (*ibid.*: §647)).

We might say that, far from being able to represent psychological concepts as having clearly demarcated boundaries, psychological concepts are characterised by the fuzzy contours of their use.[17] That is, there is no point at which the use of *feigning* suddenly ends and that of *pretending* just as suddenly begins. In more general terms, there is no sharp break between what we call 'pre-linguistic' and what we call 'linguistic' behaviour (and no point at which 'syntax' abruptly appears); or between describing a subject as knowing what another agent *thinks, wants*, or *believes*. And there is no set of formal rules which a child must – tacitly, or explicitly – master in order to become proficient in the 'authorised' use of a psychological term.

The fact that we engage in endless debates over how best to characterise animal and human behaviour is part of what, in *Last Writings on the Philosophy of Psychology*, Wittgenstein refers to as the 'constitutional uncertainty of the mental'. So, too, is the fact that human actions can be so unpredictable; or that two people watching the same action can disagree profoundly on its meaning; or that psychological judgements are so often imponderable (i.e., the fact that we can be certain that someone is in pain, or is sad, but cannot specify what it is in their behaviour that makes us so sure of this). Far from being a liability – a relic from the dawn of folk psychology – this 'indeterminacy of the mental' is the source of the richness of mental life (LW: §246).

Wittgenstein is not, however, proposing that, contrary to the classical theory, concepts are organised according to some alternative (e.g. non-monotonic) logic. Rather, he is suggesting that the very question 'In what order are concepts acquired and how are they organised?' is born from the same Cartesian picture as that which inspires the functional definition of concept. One of the most significant consequences of 'reifying concepts' is that, if these epistemically private mental constructs are going to serve their appointed function, then they must be logically organised. Thus, one might want to argue that constraint theory first appeared in Kant's *First Critique*, and not, as Markman suggests, in Quine's *Word and Object*. But what really matters here is not which philosopher should be credited with the birth of constraint theory, but simply, that the origins of constraint theory lie in philosophy and not in psychology.

In place of the idea of 'concept taxonomies' – rigid concept hierarchies that can be modelled set-theoretically – Wittgenstein urges us to look instead at the language-games that are played with psychological terms, which range from primitive to quite sophisticated uses of psychological concepts. As one moves away from paradigmatic cases, the criteria for applying 'ϕ' correspondingly vary, depending upon the circumstances in which the concept is being applied. (Compare the use of 'pretence' when said of a young child to its use in diplomatic circles.)

This suggests a different way of viewing the relation between 'higher' and 'lower' concepts: i.e. cases where the possession of ϕ presupposes the possession of φ. We are dealing here with those asymmetric conceptual relations where it makes no sense to say that S possesses the concept ϕ unless one can also say that S possesses the concept φ, but the reverse grammatical proposition does not hold.[18] But we should not expect to be able to model the relation between ϕ and φ in terms of the notion of class-inclusion or the intersection of sets. For, when we survey the uses of 'ϕ' and 'φ', we find that they shade into one another, or that, in many instances, it is not at all clear which is the more appropriate term. That is, there may be some cases where one wants to state categorically that x constitutes feigning and y constitutes pretence, yet other cases where we are not at all clear which is the more appropriate term, even when spoken of a very young child. Thus, we can hardly hope to learn from a formal model of conceptual relations how a child's mind must develop.

To speak of 'language-games' is to draw attention to the fact that our use of psychological terms is in a constant state of flux, and, in a sense, is constantly evolving. That is, we are constantly extending or altering the use of psychological terms, as we reinforce or challenge one another's uses of these terms. This does not, however, mean that a state of linguistic anarchy exists, such that any form of causal regularity (e.g., a thermostat, or a tropism) can be regarded as exhibiting evidence for possessing a rudimentary concept of belief. Similarly, the reason why pecking consistently at different sizes of circles does not constitute possession of the concept circle is grammatical, not epistemological. That is, the point is not that we lack *sufficient evidence* to know what the pigeon is or is not thinking; it is that the language-game played with 'circle' demands greater behavioural complexity than is displayed by the pigeon in this example.

We are not being 'semantically conservative' if we say that such behaviour only constitutes a conditioned response; for this just is what is called 'reacting to a stimulus': a language-game that highlights the inapplicability of psychological terms for reflexive behaviour. A dog which, bell or no bell, incessantly salivates, has no more made a *mistake* than has a pigeon who fails to peck a circle or begins to peck at squares. Typically, we regard a subject's ability to respond to, and to use, 'φ' appropriately as licensing our description of her as possessing the concept φ. That does not mean that we are *a priori* ruling out the possibility that a pigeon might be taught the concept of circle; but we need a clear grasp of just how complex its behaviour must be to warrant such an attribution before we can claim to have taught a pigeon geometry.[19]

The point here is not to deny the possibility of describing animal behaviour in psychological terms: it is to see that the use of such terms is not grounded in any neurophysiological similarities between lower and higher organisms. Do wasps *remember* where their nest is? Do pigeons *recognise* circles? Do apes *understand* sentences? Such questions cannot be answered by studying cerebral phenomena. Rather, we need to look carefully at what sorts of things wasps and pigeons and apes can do, or can be brought to do, and clarify on that basis whether it makes any sense to speak of wasps as 'remembering such-and-such', or pigeons as 'recognising such-and-such', or apes as 'understanding such-and-such'.

Where behaviourism was particularly effective was in forcing us to recognise that the stronger the analogy between lower life forms and machines, the more unfitting it becomes to use psychological terms to describe the movements of an organism. For example, merely returning to a specific location does not satisfy the criteria governing the application of 'remember'. (This was Skinner's point when he conditioned pigeons to dive-bomb a target: i.e. he showed us that it no more makes sense to describe their actions in cognitive terms than it does that of a guided missile.) Similarly we might ask: does a wasp remember the location of its nest any more than a boomerang remembers where it was thrown from, or a pilotless spy plane remembers where its home base is?

The manner in which AI dealt with this behaviourist strategy was to defend – via the mechanist continuum – the exact opposite thesis: viz., the stronger the analogy, the more it makes sense to describe both a machine's and an organism's operations in cognitive terms: and, what is more, thereby come to understand the mechanics of cognitive processes higher up on the continuum. On this reading, wasps can be said to remember where their nests are, or pigeons to recognise circles, precisely because of the continuity between the logical structure of their neurophysiological processes and those of the human being when she remembers and recognises things (however this might eventually be explained).

What are we to say of a dog when it digs up a bone that it buried the previous week? Does the concept of memory obtain a foothold here, or should the dog's actions be compared to a squirrel's (which is guided by its sense of smell to dig up nuts that it buried the previous winter)? To answer a question like this, we need to look closely at the sorts of things the dog does in this and related contexts. What makes these issues so complicated is that there is no hard and fast rule for where it does or does not make sense to use psychological concepts in primitive contexts. It many cases it is clear that the explanation of an organism's movements can only be explained neurophysiologically. But, in those cases where there is indeed a primitive sense in which we can speak of an animal as *remembering* or *recognising* things, or *understanding* sentences, this does indeed cast important light on the nature of *memory*, *recognition* and *language*.

What all this means, as far as the epistemological framework underlying cognitivism is concerned, is that the transition from using causal to using psychological concepts to describe an organism's or a subject's behaviour is subtle, and constantly shifting. If there is a 'continuum' here, it is to be found in grammar, and not in the phylogeny of the brain. That is, behaviour that we describe in causal terms shades into behaviour that we describe in psychological terms. Describing behaviour in terms of instincts, automatic or conditioned responses, associations, imitating, repeating, or memorising sounds, merges into describing behaviour in terms of understanding, intending, believing, hoping, wishing, expecting. But despite the intrinsically problematic nature of applying psychological concepts in primitive contexts, the transition from using causal to using psychological concepts to describe behaviour involves a fundamental categorial shift: the terms that apply to conditioned responses do not carry over into the description of cognitive or linguistic skills, even though it may at times be difficult to distinguish between where 'reacting' ends and 'understanding' begins (in the case of the child as much as that of the non-human primate).[20]

§11 The nature of concept-acquisition

The crux of Wittgenstein's view of concept-acquisition is that, to understand how a child acquires a concept, we need to look at the routines whereby the child first begins to master a normative practice. For we treat the child's mastery of such a practice as that which satisfies our criteria for describing her as possessing such-and-such a concept. And, conversely, one clarifies the nature of a concept by surveying the normative practices in which it is used.

This way of presenting concept-acquisition rests on the grammatical observation that 'S possesses the concept φ' *means* 'S can do x,y,z'. For example, we might explain the statement 'S possesses the concept circle' as meaning: 'S can use and respond to the use of "circle" correctly and can explain what "circle" means by pointing to circles'. This example is particularly illuminating, in so far as *circle* is a family-resemblance concept. That is, we distinguish between defining a circle as:

- a figure that is perfectly round;
- a construction in which every point on the circumference is equidistant from the centre;
- a plane curve that is the locus of a point moving at a fixed distance (r) from a given point (the centre);
- $(x - a)^2 + (y - b)^2 = (r)^2$ *(where r is the radius and (a, b) is the centre);*
- a conic with zero eccentricity (i.e. a special case of an ellipse).

And, of course, we also talk of squaring the circle; arguing in a circle; coming full circle; circling one's quarry; a circle of friends; the Vienna Circle; watching a play from the dress circle; using circular files in computing, etc.

Needless to say, the criteria for saying of someone that she has mastered these diverse uses of 'circle' are related, yet quite distinctive. But the root of a child's mastery of the geometric concept, and thence, of many of these uses, may lie in simple interindividual routines. Thus, to understand how a child acquires the concept of circle, what we need to look at is not how to define 'circle', or the properties which various geometrical figures might have in common, but the function that 'circle' plays when it is introduced in a normative practice.

For example, we say of a young child that she possesses a primitive concept of circle if she can identify the correct flash card (can both call out its name and find the circle from a pile of cards); can respond appropriately to the command 'Gather round in a circle'; can draw circles when asked to do so; can distinguish between circles and squares; and so on. But our criteria for saying of a grade school pupil that she possesses a more advanced concept of circle might be that she can produce the appropriate Euclidean definition, and can perform simple operations like constructing a circle using a compass or calculating its area. Our criteria for a high school student might be that she can construct a circle in analytic geometry. And so forth.

This way of looking at the family of normative practices in which the expression 'S possesses the concept circle' is embedded removes any need for speaking about how a child's 'mental representation' of circle is 'progressively constructed'. For, when we describe a child as possessing, e.g., a 'primitive' concept of circle, we are simply alluding to the limited practices in which 'circle' is first used. Thus, Wittgenstein's way of looking at 'concept-acquisition' amounts to a fundamental challenge to the most basic of Cartesian tenets about the nature of cognition.

This can clearly be seen if we compare Wittgenstein's approach to concept-acquisition to that of Piaget. Piaget would argue that the uses that have been sketched above would amount to 'merely verbal knowledge' (as Piaget says of counting; see Piaget 1965). That is, mastering the use of 'circle' in a simple interindividual routine does not amount to understanding the formal nature of circles: i.e. a 'fully operational' understanding of *circle*. The child in the early stages described above is unable to make the appropriate correspondences between lengths, or to divide a length into equal subsections. She will not even have gone beyond the second, 'pre-operational' stage, in which she is still basing her judgements on appearances. (For example, a child asked to build a tower the same height as another will base her judgement on a perceptual comparison.)

On Piaget's approach, only if a child is able to ignore conflicting percep-tual cues, and can make the correct judgement in any condition, can she be said to have reached the fully operational stage of geometric knowledge. (For example, this might involve using a third object, different in length from either of the two towers, as a standard of comparison.) And only when a child has reached the formal stage of calculating areas and volumes (i.e., of grasping that, whereas multiplying two numbers yields a product which is another number, multiplying two lengths yields a product which is composed of entirely different units – i.e. an area and not a length) can we speak of her possessing a geometric concept.

But why should we not say of a child who satisfies the sorts of rudimen-tary criteria described above, but fails these more advanced tests, that she possesses a *primitive* concept of circle? As with the case of his theory of number development, Piaget's argument is top-down: his starting-point is a group-theoretic definition of geometric concepts, which then drives his analysis of cognitive development. The 'stages' in a child's understanding are thus said to be marked by the emergence of logical operations (changes of position and subdivision of lengths) whereby the child is said to make sense of the world.

Accordingly, to test the stage which a child has reached in her cognitive development, we must test her mastery of these operations. For the defini-tion of the concept is presented in terms which the child can only be said to be capable of acquiring at a specific point in her cognitive development: viz., as marked by her ability to perform formal logical operations. Hence, the formal model determines how we talk about the course of a child's cognitive development: e.g. what constitutes a 'primitive' understanding and what a 'fully operational' understanding of the concept in question.

Piaget's great insight was that it makes no sense to speak of a child as acquiring a concept that presupposes other concepts before she has acquired the latter. For example, in order to grasp the concept of geometry, a child must first have grasped certain geometrical concepts. But this is not an inductive generalisation about the 'basic concepts' which provide a 'cogni-tive foundation' for the concept of geometry; rather, it is a grammatical proposition which stipulates that, in order to speak of a child as grasping the nature of geometry, we have to be able to speak of the child as being familiar with circles, squares, triangles, rectangles, etc.

Whether this sort of grammatical proposition can provide the foundation for a theory of 'formal stages' in cognitive development is quite another matter. We find Wittgenstein[21] toying with this idea in the early 1930s when he argues:

> The learning of language is achieved by stages. The first stage consists in learning the use of expressions like 'cube', 'column', 'white', 'red', '1', '2', '3'. At the second stage the meaning of second-order concepts like 'shape', 'colour', 'number' are explained with the help of the words already learned. At the third stage these second-order concepts are used to shorten the process of ostensive definition and to prevent it being misunderstood.
>
> (PLP: 106)

The problem with the argument that 'One might here speak of a stratification of concepts', Wittgenstein immediately cautions, is that

> the order of the strata is not quite unambiguously determined. A person can first be taught the words 'oak', 'maple', 'fir', and taught the word 'tree' *afterwards*; or this order might be reversed. But can the meaning of 'number' be explained before the particular numbers are taught? Why not? What about the intermediate case of 'colour' and particular colours?
>
> (*Ibid.*)

What Wittgenstein is saying here is that, although it makes no sense to suppose that a subject could understand the meaning of 'number' without being able to count, our criteria for stating that 'S understands the meaning of "tree"' may not require that the agent know the name of any particular tree. That is, there may well be cases where we insist that a subject cannot acquire the concept ϕ until she has acquired the concept φ, but one cannot draw from this the psychologistic generalisation that a subject can never acquire a second-order concept until she has acquired a first-order concept. Indeed, one cannot even assume that a clear categorial boundary can be drawn, independent of use, between 'first-order' and 'second-order' concepts.

Piaget was quite right, therefore, to question the criteria whereby we can describe a child as, e.g., possessing a primitive concept of circle; I have done much the same thing myself with pigeons. To say that a child possesses a concept of circle, no matter how primitive, presupposes that she does more than simply responds in a consistent manner to circles, or runs around in circles. But Piaget's argument – and in general, discontinuity theories – admit of no possibility of treating *circle* as a family-resemblance concept: no possibility of having different justificational criteria for saying of a subject that she possesses the concept circle. Instead, Piaget's theory proceeds from a unitary concept which serves as the metric whereby the psychologist assesses the logical stage which a child has reached in his cognitive development: a metric which lies at the uppermost reaches of the 'grammatical continuum'. But the fact that a group-theoretic definition of 'circle' represents one of the higher levels of abstraction in the understanding of geometric concepts does not entail that anything prior to this achievement must constitute partial stages towards its attainment.

Indeed, Piaget's psychologistic analysis of the acquisition of mathematical concepts conflicts with what close empirical study is beginning to reveal about the nature and origins of mathematical knowledge. As Miller puts it, 'The extent of extant evidence running counter to the Piagetian description of number development is such . . . that it may be necessary to reconstruct the study of number development on a new foundation' (Miller 1992). In line with the argument sketched in this chapter, Miller goes on to suggest that: 'As applied to number development in children, Wittgenstein's approach emphasises description of the rules or systematic techniques that children use in the number-games they actually play' (*ibid.*: 12, 14).

The same point applies to the language-games which the child plays with 'circle': i.e. to the increasingly abstract concepts of *circle* which the child masters in the increasingly complex practices it is taught. This may also have been one of the points that Rosch had in mind when she recommended Wittgenstein's view of language as a starting-point for categorisation research: viz., that Wittgenstein's approach enables us to focus on the child's development of those skills which Piaget dismisses as 'merely verbal knowledge.'

A further point that needs to be noted here is how this argument bears on the so-called 'problem of reference' made famous by Quine. If a child's acquisition of the concept of circle is looked at in isolation from the function which 'circle' plays in specific practices, we would seem to be confronted with the dilemma – which Wittgenstein himself raises at PI §§29ff[22] – that it is unclear how a child knows that 'circle' refers to an object's shape and not to its colour, texture, size, etc. (and why to the object?). Surely, the Cartesian insists, there must be some sort of 'constraint' built into the child's cognitive system which limits the number of possible hypotheses that can be framed.[23]

But suppose the function of 'circle' is to initiate a routine in which a child and its caretaker draw similar shapes with crayons, or find objects which are the same shape as the picture on a flash card. The child then starts to use 'circle' to initiate this routine (e.g. saying 'circle' while drawing one). Of course, at this stage the child may think that 'circle' only refers to comparisons with the drawing; requests to a group of young children to 'form a circle' are met with a blank stare. But the difficulty that we have in answering a question like, 'At what point does a child's behaviour become sufficiently complex to satisfy the criteria for describing him as possessing a primitive concept of circle?' attests to the context-sensitive criteria whereby we assess a child's developing mathematical abilities.[24]

What is really going on in the child's acquisition of *circle* is, of course, part of a much more far-reaching interactional process: one whose roots extend far beyond some lone moment when the child may first have heard the word 'circle' used or explained. Wittgenstein makes a highly relevant point in regard to this issue at PI §27: 'In languages (2) and (8) [of the *Investigations*] there was no such thing as asking something's name. This, with its correlate, ostensive definition, is, we might say, a language-game on its own. That is really to say: we are brought up, trained, to ask: "What is that called" – upon which the name is given.' In other words, to be able to grasp an ostensive definition (what Wittgenstein refers to at PI §31 as a *Worterklärung*) demands the mastery of a practice (cf. PI: §7). But in saying this, we are referring to the child's mastery of certain practices, and not to some structural change in the child's mind or brain such that we can speak of 'concept-acquisition' in the same way that we speak of, e.g., 'the onset of menarche'.

This is the point behind the easily overlooked rider 'in another sense' in the argument: 'we shall only say that it tells him the use, if the place is already prepared. And in this case it is so, not because the person to whom we give the explanation already knows rules, but because in another sense he is already master of a game' (*ibid.*: §31). We are operating here in the realm of grammatical explanation, not epistemology:

> In this case we shall say: the words 'this is the king' (or 'This is called the "king"') are a definition [a word-explanation] only if the learner already 'knows what a piece in a game is'. That is, if he has already played other games, or has watched other people playing 'and understood' – *and similar things*.
>
> (*ibid.*)

We might make a comparison between saying 'This is the king' to the type of subject described here – one who already knows something about game-playing – and saying it to a parrot; merely squawking 'What is this called', or repeating our words, will not satisfy the criteria for describing the parrot as understanding an ostensive explanation. (Cf. *ibid.*: §33: 'Just as a move in chess doesn't consist simply in moving a piece in such-and-such a way on the board – nor yet in one's thoughts and feelings as one makes the move: but in the circumstances that we call "playing a game of chess", "solving a chess problem".')

But, further, without the behavioural capacity to demonstrate such abilities, it makes no sense to speak of trying but failing to explain the meaning of a word to an organism. That is, it makes no sense to describe an utterance as an 'ostensive explanation' unless the hearer has already mastered a practice.[25] Thus 'We may say: only someone who already knows how to do something with it can significantly ask a name.' The emphasis here is on 'significantly': i.e., someone can only be described as asking for a name if she has mastered a technique, and only if the subject can be so described does it make sense to speak of 'ostensively explaining' a word to her.[26] Thus, ostensive definition can hardly be treated as marking the start of language-learning; this would be a caricature of the techniques that the child must already have mastered to have taken her to the point where it makes sense to speak of explaining, or even of trying to explain, the meanings of words to her.

Exactly the same point applies to speaking about 'concept-acquisition'. If one ignores the complex overlap between social, affective, linguistic and cognitive development, and looks at the question 'How does a child acquire the concept ϕ?' ('How does it identify or re-identify instances of ϕ?') a-contextually, as it were, then it may well seem that we are confronted with a mystery buried deep in the mechanics of the mind/brain. It would be like asking 'How is a seasoned dancer able to pick up the most complicated steps in a flash?' without paying any attention to the years of practice underlying this ability, and then supposing that the answer must lie in 'cognitive maps' embodied in the dancer's brain. The *depth* that is missing in both of these cases is of a completely different order.

Far from entailing that the child is a passive participant in the acquisition of its concepts – as is the case on both nativist and behaviourist theories – what really emerges on Wittgenstein's view of language is an entirely different conception of what it means to be 'active': i.e. of the nature of *concept-acquisition*. On the epistemological framework we have been addressing, *concept-acquisition* is defined in terms of *induction* and *inference*. Since none of the child's actions satisfy the criteria for applying these concepts, the cognitivist concludes that these must be 'pre-conscious' mental processes, whereby the child's *mind* classifies and categorises the various stimuli it encounters. But 'concept-acquisition' does not function in the same way as a term like 'digestion': it does not refer to some form of 'hidden' process. Rather, it draws attention to the dynamic role played by both a child and her caregiver in dyadic interaction: to the fact that an infant is responsive to this interactive process and soon begins to initiate interindividual routines.

Recall that Flavell was only interested in discovering the 'essential nature of a concept' because of the light he believed this would shed on the processes of concept-acquisition. What we have done is reversed this way of looking at the issue: viz., we study the way a concept is acquired in order to understand the essential nature of that concept. The basis for this shift rests on a categorial transformation in our understanding of *the kind of processes* referred to by 'the processes of concept-acquisition'. That is, they are the kind of processes which one explains by studying every aspect of a child's development, not by constructing computer models. Even more importantly, the question 'What is a concept?' returns to the philosophical fold, and, in so doing, loses much of its urgency for understanding the nature of concept-acquisition. Perhaps the ultimate service that AI has performed is just this: it shows us how important it is to free psychology from its obsession with classic epistemological problems, in order to get on with the business of explaining the complex interrelations involved in a human being's social, affective, cognitive and linguistic development.

NOTES

1 WITTGENSTEIN'S RESPONSE TO TURING'S THESIS

1 Cf. the discussion of Russell's paradox in *Remarks on the Foundations of Mathematics* I App 3 and VII.

2 This might make it seem all that much more surprising that Wittgenstein and Turing never touched on the Mechanist Thesis in *Lectures on the Foundations of Mathematics*. But there are two important points to be noted in this respect: first, that *Lectures on the Foundations of Mathematics* is exactly that; and second, that even when he attacked Turing's version of CT, Wittgenstein did not tie this in to the Mechanist Thesis. Rather, what Wittgenstein addressed in *Remarks on the Foundations of Mathematics* was solely that part of 'On Computable Numbers' which inspired the assumption that the Mechanist Thesis is entailed by Turing's version of CT.

3 It is interesting to note that this caution slips slightly in what follows:

> However, by altering its m-configuration the machine can effectively remember some of the symbols which it has 'seen' (scanned) previously. The possible behaviour of the machine at any moment is determined by the m-configuration q_n and the scanned symbol G(r). This pair $q_n, G(r)$ will be called the 'configuration': thus the configuration determines the possible behaviour of the machine.
>
> (Turing 1936: 117)

Here the words 'remember', and perhaps even more significantly, 'behaviour', were given without inverted commas.

4 Note that we could just as easily ask: Would we say of an ant that had wandered through some paint, and then in its subsequent perambulations somehow traced out the outline of the Notre Dame, that it had *sketched* the Notre Dame?

5 And informally; see his 1935 letter to Kleene (quoted in Davis 1982: 9).

6 The equivalence is Church's (see Church 1938: 224, and Kleene 1981a: 56).

7 This was the argument which Church pursued in 'The Constructive Second Number Class'; he there defends his proposed definition of effective ordinals on the grounds that for 'those who do not find this convincing the definition may perhaps be allowed to stand as a challenge, to find either a less inclusive definition which cannot be shown to exclude some ordinal which ought reasonably to be allowed as constructive, or a more inclusive definition which cannot be shown to include some ordinal of the second class which cannot be seen to be constructive' (Church 1936: 224).

8 Suppose 'a mistake is not possible. But what kind of possibility is that? Mustn't mistake be *logically* excluded?' (OC: §194; see Shanker 1987a).

9 So much is clear from Church's review of 'On Computable Numbers' and the account he gave of Turing's Thesis in 'The Constructive Second Number Class' (see Church 1938: 227, and Davis 1978).

10 Turing was convinced the conjecture was false. In 1936 E. C. Titchmarsh had used a mechanical calculator to demonstrate that the first 104 zeros all lie on the real line. Turing's plan was to examine the next few thousand zeros in the hope of coming across a counterexample to Riemann's Hypothesis.

11 See Hamming 1980: 8f. See also Donald Knuth's explanation – which reads as a direct comment on the early founders of recursion theory – that 'computing machines (and algorithms) do not only compute with *numbers*: they can deal with information of any kind, once it is presented in a precise way. We used to say that sequences of symbols, such as names, are represented in a computer as if they were numbers; but it is really more correct to say that numbers are represented inside a computer as sequences of symbols' (Knuth 1976).

12 Hodges reports that

> Shannon had always been fascinated with the idea that a machine should be able to imitate the brain; he had studied neurology as well as mathematics and logic, and had seen his work on the differential analyser as a first step towards a thinking machine. They found their outlook to be the same: there was nothing sacred about the brain, and that if a machine could do as well as a brain, then it *would* be thinking – although neither proposed any particular way in which this might be achieved. . . . Once Alan said at lunch, 'Shannon wants to feed not just *data* to a Brain, but *cultural* things! He wants to play *music* to it!' And there was another occasion in [t]he executive mess, when Alan was holding forth on the possibilities of a 'thinking machine'. His high-pitched voice already stood out above the general murmur of well-behaved junior executives grooming themselves for promotion with the Bell corporation. Then he was suddenly heard to say: 'No, I'm not interested in developing a *powerful* brain. All I'm after is just a *mediocre* brain, something like the President of the American Telephone and Telegraph Company.'
>
> (Hodges 1983: 251)

13 This is corroborated in Michie's memoir on 'Turing and the Origins of the Computer':

> The game of chess offered a case of some piquancy for challenging with irreverent shows of force the mastery which rests on traditional knowledge. At Bletchley Park, Turing was surrounded by chess-masters who did not scruple to inflict their skill upon him. The former British champion Harry Golombek recalls an occasion when instead of accepting Turing's resignation he suggested that they turn the board round and let him see what he could do with Turing's shattered position. He had no difficulty in winning. Programming a machine for chess played a central part in the structure of Turing's thinking about broader problems of artificial intelligence. In this he showed uncanny insight. As a laboratory system for experimental work chess remains unsurpassed. But there was present also, I can personally vouch, a Turing streak of iconoclasm: what would people say if a machine beat a master? How excited he would be today when computer programs based on his essential design are regularly beating

masters at lightning chess, and producing occasional upsets at tournament tempo!

Naturally Turing also had to build a chess program (a 'paper machine' as he called it). At one stage he and I were responsible for hand-simulating and recording the respective operations of a Turing–Champernowne and a Michie–Wylie paper machine pitted against each other. Fiasco again! We both proved too inefficient and forgetful. Once more Alan decided to go it alone, this time by programming the Ferranti Mark 1 computer to simulate both.

(Michie 1982: 35)

14 Davis concludes that Gödel found in Turing's Thesis a satisfactory rendering of the 'generally accepted properties' of effective calculability of which he had complained to Church in 1934 (Davis 1982: 14). While this is an important point, it merely restates the problem which concerns us.

15 For example, in the case of the Doubling Program which Davis outlines in Davis 1978 (246ff), we would want to say that someone has only mastered the program when they understand *why* it is called a 'doubling program', and how this relates to the shift from step 9 to step 10 when the program terminates.

16 Cf. Haugeland's account of the 'paradox of mechanical reasoning':

Reasoning (on the co[m]putational model) is the manipulation of meaningful symbols according to rational rules (in an integrated system). Hence there must be some sort of manipulator to carry out those manipulations. There seem to be two basic possibilities: either the manipulator pays attention to what the symbols and rules *mean* or it doesn't. If it does pay attention to the meanings, then it can't be entirely mechanical – because meanings (whatever exactly they are) don't exert physical forces. On the other hand, if the manipulator does not pay attention to the meanings, then the manipulations can't be instances of reasoning – because what's reasonable or not depends crucially on what the symbols mean.

(Haugeland 1985: 39)

17 See Note 15 above.

18 One of the factors which complicates this issue is the ambiguous nature of computer programs – itself a product of their evolution. In one respect a program can be seen as a set of instructions (e.g., upwards to the user, and originally downwards to machine operators when they were in service). With the development of compilers, however, the 'downwards' function of the program has been restricted to that of a set of ciphers (see Shanker 1987b: 88ff).

2 THE BEHAVIOURIST ORIGINS OF AI

1 In fact, they refused to use the term for several years, preferring instead to describe their work as 'complex information processing'.

2 This theme was clearly expressed by Shannon in 'A Chess-Playing Machine':

The thinking process is considered by some psychologists to be essentially characterized by the following steps: various possible solutions of a problem are tried out mentally or symbolically without actually being carried out physically; the best solution is selected by a mental evaluation of the results of these trials; and the solution found in this way is then acted upon. It will be seen that this is almost an exact description of how a chess-playing computer operates, provided we substitute 'within the machine' for 'mentally'.

(Shannon 1956: 2132–3)

3 Peirce was to develop this theme in several important papers on 'logical machines'. I am indebted to Kenneth Ketner for drawing this to my attention.
4 The overlap appears to be coincidental, although that in no way diminishes its significance. Wittgenstein had already formulated his argument by 1934 (see BB: 117ff), and it seems unlikely that Turing had read this before he composed 'On Computable Numbers'.
5 In §162 of the *Investigations*, Wittgenstein advances a definition of 'reading' as 'deriving a reproduction from the original'. The argument is about whether the pupil's behaviour warrants saying that he derived his action from a rule we have taught him: e.g., if he can be seen to check the rule in the process of reading a text, if he cites the rule to justify what he has read. But the 'definition' proposed in the first line of §162 is after something much stronger: viz., you can only be said to be 'reading' if this intermediary 'inferential' process occurs, and if you are not conscious of this process then it *must* have occurred unconsciously. The thesis under attack here is that of 'secondarily automatic actions'. Since learning how to read demands that we be conscious of such intermediary processes, they must have become automated in the adult reader. Hence, we can deploy a protocol of the child's behaviour as the paradigm for the 'unconscious processes' that must occur in a skilled reader. Wittgenstein often touches on this theme in his discussions of 'calculating in the head': e.g. we use the long-hand calculations that would be done on paper as the paradigm for what *must have gone on in an agent's mind* when the answer to a problem suddenly occurs to him.
6 But note that not all causal uses imply a lack of understanding. Cf. 'He reacted with alarm when he saw the sign of the four'.
7 Note also the subtle distinction drawn in the last line of PI §157 between 'change in his behaviour' and 'state-transformations'. If there were no difference between these two uses then 'change in behaviour' would be taken as a sign of an underlying change in the hypothetical internal mechanism.
8 Note the picture of learning here. Cf. the argument presented at BB p. 118 with Turing's conception of 'learning programs'.

3 THE RESURGENCE OF PSYCHOLOGISM

1 This begins inauspiciously enough with an attempt to relate Boole's classic psychologistic conception of the Laws of Thought to Wittgenstein's conception of language-games which, according to Gregory, renders language 'a kind of machine which by operating generates understanding – and sometimes confusions, which need to be made explicit and sorted out by philosophers' (Gregory 1987: 430). But the whole point of language-games is to challenge this very picture of language (see Baker and Hacker 1980).
2 This sounds very much like Mary Henle's argument that the source of reasoning errors lies, not in the rules which the mind follows, but in their misapplication: e.g., in the subject's misunderstanding of the meaning and/or logical form of the problems he is trying to solve, or simply, reasoning correctly from false premises (see Henle 1962).
3 That is not to say that subsequent Kantians would not pursue such a course. For example, many were to argue that 'logical relations' or 'numbers' serve as such a domain.

4 Cf. Simon's constant refrain that 'The apparent complexity of [man's] behavior over time is largely a reflection of the complexity of the environment in which he finds himself' (Simon 1969b: 65).

5 But not entirely. Sigwart, for example, is classed by Husserl as one of the naturalists, yet he presents his argument as Kantian. Even Erdmann, who exemplifies German naturalist thought, often seems more sympathetic to Kant than Mill.

6 Cf. Spencer's explanation in 'Mill versus Hamilton', which Mill quotes in *System of Logic*: 'The law of the Excluded Middle, then, is simply a generalization of the universal experience that some mental states are directly destructive of other states' (Mill 1963: 279).

7 There are, however, important differences in content as well as style between their approaches to psychologism. One of the most striking is how much more conciliatory Husserl is than Frege. He suggests that 'the truth [in the debate between Kantian and naturalist psychologicians] lies in the middle': that the naturalists' argument 'only proves one thing, that psychology *helps* in the foundation of logic, not that it has the only or the main part in this, not that it provides logic's *essential foundation*' (LI: 96).

8 'I therefore think it better to avoid the expression "laws of thought" altogether in logic, because it always misleads us into thinking of laws of thought as laws of nature. If that is what they were we should have to assign them to psychology' (PW: 145). In the first version of 'Logic' he referred to them as 'laws of valid inference' (*ibid.*: 4).

9 'Thinking, as it actually takes place, is not always in agreement with the laws of logic any more than men's actual behaviour is in agreement with the moral law. . . . Don't we automatically judge in accordance with these laws? No! *Not* automatically; normally, yes, but not always!' (*ibid.*: 145, 147).

10 The 'first prejudice' of psychologism, according to Husserl, is that 'Prescriptions which regulate what is mental must obviously have a mental basis' (LI: 168).

11 Husserl is even more forthright. *Logical Investigations* begins with an outline of Mill's position in his polemic with Hamilton.

12 At one point Frege suggests that 'to present the process of thinking in its natural form . . . we should presumably have to resort to observing primitive peoples' (PW: 146).

13 This argument prompted Husserl to object that, far from confronting this difficult issue, Mill sought to evade it, with the relativist and sceptical consequences that Husserl spells out in Chapter VII of *Logical Investigations*. Husserl insists that a universal law of mental nature could not be extrapolated from subjective experience; for 'How could [self-reports] provide inner evidence for a universal *law* which transcends persons and times?' (LI: 120). Citing Frege, Husserl explains that the contrast involved in the Law of Contradiction is between *objects of thinking*, not between acts of thinking. That is, we do not infer from self-observations that it is impossible to believe and disbelieve p. We see or grasp that p and not-p cannot both be true.

14 What Frege says is that 'With the psychological conception of logic we lose the distinction between the grounds that justify a conviction and the causes that actually produce it. This means that a justification in the proper sense is not possible; what we have in its place is an account of how the conviction was arrived at, from which it is to be inferred that everything has been caused by psychological factors' (PW: 147).

15 Cf. Oliver Sacks's account of the Twins' ability to see the most extraordinary number of matchsticks (Sacks 1985: 189).

16 Cf. Sacks's account of the painter Jonathan I in *An Anthropologist from Mars*.

17 This psychologistic move is as widespread today as it was one hundred years ago. To take a recent example, the Theory of Mind treats the fact that we can't imagine another culture speaking a language but not understanding that other people have intentions, desires or beliefs as empirical. Seen as such, it seems conceivable that there could be a society of solipsists, capable of communicating with one another but not of realising that other agents have minds; but *we* can't imagine what it would be like to live in such a world because we are born with a 'mindreading module' which forces us to construe each other's behaviour in terms of intentions, desires, and beliefs (see Baron-Cohen 1995). But the relation between speaking a language and knowing that other people have intentions, desires and beliefs is *internal*, not external. That is, the statement 'one can't imagine another culture speaking a language but not understanding that other people have intentions, desires or beliefs' is a grammatical proposition: it formulates a rule governing uses of the term 'language'. The consequence of this rule of grammar is not that we can't conceive of what it would be like for two solipsists to talk to one another, but rather, that we could not describe their behaviour as 'talking to one another' (see Savage-Rumbaugh, Shanker and Taylor in press).

18 'If you follow other rules than those of chess you are playing another game; and if you follow grammatical rules other than such and such ones, that does not mean you say something wrong, no, you are speaking of something else' (PG: 184–5).

19 For some idea of the trouble in which Frege lands himself on this issue, cf. his attempt in 'Compound Thoughts' to explain how 'Since only thoughts can be true, this compound sentence ["If A, then A"] must express a thought; and, despite its apparent senselessness, the negation of this thought is also a thought' (Frege 1923: 75).

20 For example, 'If A knows that B is lying, then A knows that B intends to deceive him' is a rule of grammar, not an empirical proposition. Should this be treated as an empirical proposition, it seems to create the problem of how one is able to make the connection between knowing that B is lying and knowing what B intends: i.e., it seems to presuppose that one knows that other agents can have intentions, which then raises the question, what is it to know what intentions are? And so on.

21 Detlefsen cautions that, while others may have seen Hilbert's 'earlier' formalism as idealist, there is insufficient evidence to determine Hilbert's own views on the matter. But, as we shall see in this section, no such doubts can arise in regards to Hilbert's 'later' formalism (see Detlefsen 1992).

22 'Thinking parallels speaking and writing: we form statements and place them one behind another' (Hilbert 1927: 475).

23 The key to his argument lies in the tacit reference to Helmholtz – a clear sign, as far as his audience would have been concerned, of the larger overtones which Hilbert intended. The proof to which Hilbert alludes had at one and the same time provided a key element in the overthrowal of the vitalist theory of animal heat and created a new focus of attention in the conservation of energy. Helmholtz's proof thus served as a classic example of the role of a transitional impossibility proof: a proof with profound epistemological consequences in so far as, in closing off one problem, it served to open up an entirely new domain of thought.

24 Consider, e.g., the difference between trying but failing to come up with the answer to a problem and merely saying the first thing that pops into one's head.

25 Rips, for example, maintains that inference is 'a particular type of mental process through which conviction in one set of beliefs comes to affect conviction in another' (Rips 1988: 119). How different is this from Mill's claim that the law of contradiction refers to the psychological generalisation that it is impossible to have contradictory mental states: viz., believing and disbelieving p? Only, if this is a rule of cognitive processing – which the AI-scientist sees as debatable – it is not discovered by introspection. What is clear, however, according to Rips, is that 'Deductive reasoning has a special status among cognitive processes' (*ibid.*: 146).

26 Indeed, assuming that it even makes sense to speak of '*sequential* neural processes'.

27 The very notion of a 'Turing Machine' is grounded in Hilbert's argument; for it is used to signify both a formal system and a machine: i.e. both the rule-governed transformation of a string of symbols and a series of causal operations. And, of course, it has the added appeal that it removes the role of intuition at the 'atomic' level of inference [*sic*]. Hence it is not surprising to find AI insisting that, given that inferring is a process, then it *must* be possible to measure its speed; for one can do so with computers, so why not with human systems? As Simon puts it: 'the human information-processing system . . . operates almost entirely serially, one process at a time. . . . The elementary processes of the information-processing system are executed in tens or hundreds of milliseconds' (Simon 1978: 273).

4 MODELS OF DISCOVERY

1 'The mind,' James explains in 'Are We Automata', 'is at every stage a theatre of simultaneous possibilities. Consciousness consists in the comparison of these with each other, the selection of some, and the suppression of the rest by the reinforcing and inhibiting agency of Attention' (James 1879: 13).

2 As opposed to the notion of the unconscious that interested the pioneers of the first dynamic psychiatry. Where the latter were primarily concerned with the pathology of mental disease or the nature of such abnormal behaviour as somnambulism, mesmerism, hypnosis, etc., Helmholtz's interest, like that of other nineteenth-century mechanists, was in the causes of ordinary experience.

3 We can get some idea of how serious an issue this must have appeared to Helmholtz from James's observation that 'We find the Kantian philosophers everywhere hailing him [Helmholtz] as the great experimental corroborator of their master's views' (James 1879: 10).

4 Helmholtz only mentions the resurgence of interest in Schopenhauer's *Ur-will*, but he must have been highly distressed by von Hartmann's use of his argument in *The Philosophy of the Unconscious* (see von Hartmann 1931: 40).

5 In his 1881 memorial to Faraday, Helmholtz remarked that 'It is in the highest degree astonishing to see what a large number of general theorems, the methodical deduction of which requires the highest powers of mathematical analysis, he found by a kind of intuition, with the security of instinct, without the help of a single mathematical formula' (Koestler 1975: 170). Speaking of himself in his 'Autobiographical Sketch', Helmholtz described how 'useful ideas often steal into one's train of thought without their significance being at first understood; afterward some accidental circumstance shows how and under what conditions they originated. Sometimes they are present without our knowing when they came. In other cases they occur suddenly, without effort, like an inspiration' (Helmholtz 1971a: 474).

6 Cf. Baldwin's remark that 'What was once pure intelligence now becomes mechanism' (Baldwin 1889: 57).

7 This and the previous quotation were taken from Ketner (1988).

8 For example, 'An individual, at any given time, is confronted with more stimulation from within and from without than can be managed adaptively.' Thus 'Some degree and kind of selection must occur' (Shevrin and Dickman 1980: 423).

9 Indeed, this debate continues to this day, as can be seen in the Henle–Skinner exchange on the problem of creativity (see Henle 1986: 168f).

10 As Watson saw it, 'If the behaviorists are right in their contention that there is no observable mind–body problem and no separate entity called mind – then there can be no such thing as consciousness and its subdivision' (Watson 1923: 94). Thus, what appear to be acts of insight are either the result of applying old associations to new situations, or blind responses to new situations (see Watson 1925: 198f).

11 Cf. Poincaré's account of his discovery of fuchsian functions as a result of the fact that 'One night I took some black coffee, contrary to my custom, and was unable to sleep. A host of ideas kept surging in my head; I could almost feel them jostling one another, until two of them coalesced, so to speak, to form a stable combination' (Poincaré 1913: 52–3; see *ibid.*: 55–8).

12 Cf. Shannon's proof that, if one tried to design a chess-program using strictly logical procedures, it would require over *1095* years for the machine to decide on its first move (Shannon 1956).

13 Although *Thought and Choice in Chess* was not translated into English until 1965, Simon recounts how, in 1954, he had taught himself Dutch solely in order to read it (see Simon 1982: 149).

14 In Simon's words, 'Thinking is a dynamic process – using that term in its technical sense. . . . The *state* of the system at any given moment of time is specified by the values of a set of variables, the state variables, at that moment. Then the differential equations determine how the state variables will change; they predict the state of the system at the "next" moment as a function of the present state' (Simon 1966b: 271–2).

15 As Miller put it: 'It is the *result* of thinking, not the process of thinking, that appears spontaneously in consciousness' (Miller 1966: 56).

16 In Shannon's words: 'The thinking process is considered by some psychologists to be essentially characterized by the following steps: various possible solutions of a problem are tried out mentally or symbolically without actually being carried out physically; the best solution is selected by a mental evaluation of the results of these trials; and the solution found in this way is then acted upon. It will be seen that this is almost an exact description of how a chess-playing computer operates, provided we substitute "within the machine" for "mentally"' (Shannon 1956: 2132–3).

17 Cf. Perkins: 'If, by *insight*, we mean simply a good understanding of the problem achieved in the process of seeking a solution, then insight becomes confounded with understanding generally, losing its distinctive character, which was the very thing to be explained' (Perkins 1988: 327).

18 For example, Köhler tells the story of how 'a local colleague, convinced, like most students, of the general value of the chance theory for animal psychology, came to see the anthropoids. I chose Sultan for the demonstration. He made one attempt at solution, then a second, and a third; but nothing made so great an impression on the visitor as the pause after that, during which Sultan slowly

scratched his head and moved nothing but his eyes and his head gently, while he most carefully eyed the whole situation' (Köhler 1925: 192).

19 Köhler's argument was bolstered by the growing evidence that there is a significant body of creative thinkers who solve problems by visualising a solution. For one of the most fascinating autobiographical accounts of what it is like to 'think in pictures', see Grandin 1995.

20 Logical inferences per second.

21 This suggests that, not only do 'great minds think alike', but they do so at the same speed!

22 That obviously does not entail that the subject really has solved or understood the problem. Yet there is a definite bias towards success in the use of this expression; for what we would say of someone who habitually exclaimed 'Now I have it' but could never demonstrate this in practice: how often could this be repeated before we began to question the sincerity or the sanity of these reports? (PI: §323).

23 This can be an extremely subtle matter. Wittgenstein brings this point out nicely when he asks: 'The psychologist in his laboratory is investigating psychological phenomena. What does he observe? The answer is not at all obvious. Is he observing my face, listening to what I say, and watching how I react?' (GWL: 172) (Cf. Jackson's memoir of Wittgenstein lecturing in 1946–7 with his record of those lectures.)

24 For example, the subject-matter alone of Wittgenstein's lectures was enough to exclude such doubts, but, when compounded by his behaviour during these frequent periods of silence, such a question could at best be treated as a poor joke.

25 Watson argued that what appear to be acts of insight are either the result of applying old associations to new situations, or blind responses to new situations.

26 Just imagine if Coleridge were to have written:

And what if all of animated nature
Be but Jacquard looms diversely fram'd,
That tremble into thought, as o'er them sweeps
Plastic and vast, one intellectual breeze,
At once the Soul of each, and God of all?

27 Originally reported by Voltaire, who claimed to have heard it from Newton's cousin.

28 But then, as we saw in §3, this was very much the central theme in Selz's approach to problem-solving. Hence the question which this raises is whether computationalism has been effective because it originates, or because it appeals to an already existing conception of problem-solving. The same point applies to the blurring of the distinction between problem-solving and creating. Getzels and Csikszentmihalyi, for example, have explored at some length the manner in which creating can be elucidated in problem-solving terms (Getzels and Csikszentmihalyi 1976), while Gruber has shown how scientific discovery can be profitably treated as a poetic activity (Gruber 1981b). Whether this shift should be laid at the door of AI is another matter, however; for, as was pointed out in the opening section, we can already detect evidence in Helmholtz's and Poincaré's memoirs of the growing urge to renounce Mill's sharp distinction between poetic and scientific inspiration.

NOTES

5 THE NATURE OF CONCEPTS

1 Can we even imagine what life without concepts would be like for an organism? Could there be a story, like Musil's *Mann ohne Qualität*, of a *Mann ohne Begriffe* (the sort of thing that one encounters in *The Man Who Mistook his Wife for a Hat*)? But life without concepts would not just be cumbersome: it would be pathological. For without concepts an organism would quickly starve to death. And note just how appropriate the term 'organism' has become.

2 It bears noting that what Markman really means here is: 'A minimal criterion for having a concept is that discriminably different objects which are similar in some fundamental respect be treated as similar in that respect'. Far from being an omission, this constitutes a grave problem for the functional definition of concept.

3 'The essence of Piaget's operatory theory is that the structures revealed through structural analysis should possess a functional reality. They exist in some sense in the mind of the subject, not merely in the mind of the psychologist-observer [Piaget 1941]. The question is how the formal properties of the structures described by the observer are mapped onto the functional properties of the structures active in the mind of the subject' (Chapman 1988: 357).

4 For example, in the PPI version of PI §143, Wittgenstein begins by counselling that 'In order to clarify our concepts, let us examine this kind of language-game.'

5 I say 'like Piaget' because of the latter's frequent insistence that he was only interested in developmental psychology in so far as it could be used to resolve the problems of genetic epistemology.

6 Armstrong *et al.* (1983) found that they could obtain the same kind of typicality responses for classical as for family-resemblance concepts (e.g. 'odd numbers'). Subjects felt that 7 was a better example of an odd number than 23. They would respond more quickly that 7 was an odd number than 23. Thus, if typicality results were our sole criterion, we should be forced to conclude that all concepts are to a lesser or greater extent family-resemblance concepts: that *family-resemblance concept* is itself a family-resemblance concept, with philosophers and psychologists more likely to choose *game* as an example of a family-resemblance concept than *odd number*.

7 But note that, just as the introduction of the transfinite cardinals does not change the meaning of 'number', neither does it change the meaning of 'cardinal number': i.e. 'fill in a gap' in the cardinal number system (see Shanker 1987a).

8 PI §77b – a residue of LA 1–2 – returns to this theme. If we look at how we learn 'good', we see that it is by examples that admit of different interpretations (viewpoints). We learn that the game played with 'good' is a wholly different practice from the game played with a term like 'cardinal number'. It is different, not only in that people can disagree on its application, but in that using it entails further demands on the speaker; e.g. that you can defend or justify its use. Moreover, a concept like *good* spans many different realms, and we learn a shifting 'family of meanings' in mastering these different uses. ('The enormously complicated situation in which the aesthetic expression has a place.')

9 See PI §73. What makes a representation schematic (think of a stick man or a smiley) is not some intrinsic feature of the representation, or its position in a system: it is its use in a language-game (see BB: 17–18). Prototype theory seems to offer a far simpler answer to the follow-up question Wittgenstein poses in PI §73: viz., 'Which shade is the "sample in my mind" of the colour green – the sample of what is common to all shades of green?' But then, this still leaves the

259

question of how subjects compute similarity to prototype up in the air; or rather, beneath the threshold of consciousness.

10 What Flavell describes as the distinction between 'cognitive object' and 'instrument' (Flavell 1970: 989).

11 PI §82 adds to this theme in a way that turns the focus on itself. Whereas in the preceding sections Wittgenstein has been concerned with such specific questions as 'What do we call "game", "blue", etc.?', which invited the answer 'What are the rules for the use of "game", "blue"?', he now looks at the question: 'What do we call "what do we call"?' – i.e. 'What are the rules for the use of "What are the rules which he uses"?'. Wittgenstein is primarily concerned with the case where neither an external observer nor a speaker can formulate *the* rule the speaker is following because the speaker is employing a family-resemblance concept. This does not signify an epistemological shortcoming on the theorist's part to rival the subject's; it is rather that, here, there is no such 'clear rule' for either speaker or observer to articulate. Yet the subject can *explain* what he understands by 'N'. To say that we cannot describe his use as governed by a 'clear rule' does not entail that we cannot describe his use as rule-governed. (This point is reinforced by the use of the same metaphor in PI §30 and §82.)

12 Johnson-Laird and Wason cite an interesting example of a precursor of prototype ideas in Gestalt psychology (see Johnson-Laird and Wason 1977). But there is nothing in Wittgenstein's work to suggest he was aware of any alternatives to classical theory of concepts.

13 PI §150 makes the point that what we call 'knows' ('understands', 'possesses the concept φ') is similar to what we call 'can'. That is, to say that 'S possesses the concept φ' is similar to saying 'S can identify x,y,z as instances of φ'.

14 Or, conversely, possesses the concept *red* but cannot use 'red' correctly.

15 One of the appeals of AI was that it enabled the cognitivist to speak of 'programs' *simpliciter* without having to worry about individuating the various stages on this continuum.

16 This immediately raises a problem for constraint theory, since collective nouns do not transfer knowledge to new exemplars in inductive and deductive inferences. Hence we find Markman pursuing a further elaborate argument showing how it is really mass nouns with which the child's mind deals.

17 Cf. LW §267: 'A sharper concept would not be the same concept. That is: the sharper concept wouldn't have the *value* for us that the blurred one does. Precisely because we would not understand people who act with total certainty when we are in doubt and uncertain.'

18 Wittgenstein gives as an example of this 'primary' and 'secondary' sense of a word: 'Only if you have learnt to calculate – on paper or out loud – can you be made to grasp, by means of this concept, what calculating in the head is' (PI: p. 216).

19 It is conceivable that this argument fails to do justice to the complexity already present in the pigeon's behaviour. The truth is that we just don't have enough information here to form any judgement. The same can be said of the classical conditioning experiments on which we ourselves have been conditioned. We have grown so accustomed to the mechanist orientation of radical behaviourism that we easily accept the crude S-R (or S-O-R) picture that it portrayed. Moreover, AI also accepted this crude picture, and then tried to build cognition out of the elements which it furnishes. But if a dog is kept trussed up and is forced to endure open wounds, how can we possibly speak of this as a *learning experiment*, let alone one that has the greatest significance for our understanding of the nature of human learning? For that matter, it is hardly surprising that the

sound of a bell should have caused the dog to salivate; the ringing of the dinner bell has the same effect on me. But that hardly means that it makes no sense to speak of dogs as learning the significance of the bell. For all we know, the bell may have come to play an important communicative role between Pavlov and his dogs. Maybe their attention picked up the moment they saw Pavlov move towards the bell. Perhaps they glanced at Pavlov and then at the bell when they were hungry? Is it possible that, had they been left free, a bitch weaning her pups could begin teaching them how to ring the bell? In our fixation on the sound–saliva sequence, have we overlooked what may have been most interesting about these experiments?

20 For example, one of the earliest sounds that a child makes in its babbling is 'dada' (for reasons which we still do not fully understand). Interestingly, many cultures have seized on this sound as a name for the father, which encourages caregivers to treat this early vocalisation as the child's first recognition of its father. This in turn leads them to reinforce the very behaviour which they read into the child's vocalisation, thereby helping the child reach this linguistic milestone.

21 Or is it Waismann speaking here? The theory of language strata is now closely tied to Waismann, but was it perhaps Wittgenstein who first touched on this idea?

22 In PI §29, Wittgenstein suggests, first, that explanations of category terms are no more immune from possible misunderstanding than ostensive definitions, and second, that it makes no sense to speak of explaining, e.g., the concept of *number* before one has grasped 1,2,3 . . . (cf. PLP: 98ff). Given the prior claim that 'an ostensive definition can be variously interpreted in *every* case' (PI: §28), it is no wonder that the argument has been construed by some as a sceptical attack on theories of shared understanding. But, far from intending a sceptical thesis in PI §28, Wittgenstein's point is that ostensive definition stands on the same footing as any other form of grammatical explanation – that it is an intrinsic feature of *grammatical explanation* that it does not guarantee success (understanding), where this is a grammatical proposition about the concept of *grammatical explanation*, not a sceptical attack on the possibility of communication. And it is this theme – with its obvious overlap with the argument that an 'explanation of meaning is not an empirical proposition and not a causal explanation, but a rule, a convention' (PG: 68) – that provides the key to reading PI §30: to seeing the continuity between this and the earlier sections in the *Investigations* on *training* and *explaining*.

23 From here it is but a short step to the argument that, in acquiring concepts, children must learn hierarchically organised class-inclusion relations. But, to do so, 'they must figure out how two words (e.g., "oaks" and "trees") apply to the same objects' (Markman *et al.* 1980: 227). But there are several options which they must consider: the two terms might label the same object at two different levels of a hierarchy; they might be synonyms; or they might refer to partially overlapping categories. 'On encountering a new word, then, children must differentiate between a number of plausible hypotheses about how it fits into their current conceptual structure' (Callanan and Markman 1982: 1093).

24 Cf. Locke's discussion of 'The Emergence of Reference' in *The Child's Path to Spoken Language*: 'Low-level referencing may not wait for words. In the second year of life, sound–meaning associations may occur at the segmental level, embedded in utterances that sound very much like babbling, suggesting the presence of de facto sound–meaning associations prior to the expression of words. . . . Although it is difficult to say which early words children produce

with the intention of communicating, analyses of children's initial lexicons suggest that they may deploy some words for this reason' (Locke 1993: 342–3).

25 This is the point behind the remark in PI §27 that ostensive definition is the *correlate* of asking for a name.

26 We should not, however, expect a hard and fast distinction here, not just in regard to the abilities of subjects (e.g. at what age is it possible to explain a word to a child ostensively? What kinds of word? Is it possible to explain a word to a chimpanzee ostensively? What kinds of word?) but, also, in terms of what we will call ostensive explanations:

Compare the definitions 'Red', 'That is red', and 'this colour is red', where the person giving the definition points to a sample of the colour in each case. Are these all definitions in the same sense? Perhaps there will be an inclination to deny that the first is a definition at all (at least in certain circumstances), and to call it instead an early stage in a training. The second is what might be called an articulate definition, but is liable to be misunderstood in various ways. It is only the third that is given to someone familiar with language. Accordingly, we can distinguish between primitive and fully developed forms of ostensive definition – without indeed being always able to specify the point exactly where the 'definition' begins and 'training' ceases. And this constitutes a further uncertainty which we find in our concept {viz., *ostensive explanation*] (PLP: 106).

BIBLIOGRAPHY

Abrams, Meyer (1953), *The Mirror and the Lamp*, New York: Oxford University Press.

Agar, Michael (1994), *Language Shock*, New York: William Morrow and Company, Inc.

Aristotle (1938), *Selections*, W. D. Ross (ed. and trans.), New York: Scribner.

Armstrong, S. L., L. R. Gleitman and H. G. Gleitman (1983), 'On what some concepts might not be', *Cognition*, 13.

Ayer, A. J. (1935), *Language, Truth and Logic*, London: Victor Gollancz.

Baker, G. P. (1988), *Wittgenstein, Frege and the Vienna Circle*, Oxford: Basil Blackwell.

Baker, G. P. and P. M. S. Hacker (1980), *Wittgenstein: Understanding and Meaning*, Oxford: Basil Blackwell.

—— (1984), *Frege: Logical Excavations*, Oxford: Basil Blackwell.

—— (1986), *Rules, Grammar and Necessity*, Oxford: Basil Blackwell.

Baldwin, James Mark (1889), *Handbook of Psychology*, New York: Henry Holt and Company.

Baron-Cohen, Simon (1995), *Mindblindness*, Cambridge, Mass.: The MIT Press.

Bell, D. (1990), *Husserl*, London: Routledge.

Binet, Alfred (1894), *Psychologie des grands Calculateurs et Joueurs d'Echecs*, Paris: Deuxieme Partie.

Birch, Herbert G. (1945), 'The relation of previous experience to insightful problem-solving', *Journal of Comparative and Physiological Psychology*, 38.

Black, Max (1965), 'Verificationism and Wittgenstein's reflections on mathematics', *Revue Internationale de Philosophie*, 23.

Bloomfield, Brian (ed.) (1986), *The Question of Artificial Intelligence*, London: Croom Helm.

Boden, Margaret A. (1979), *Piaget*, Brighton: The Harvester Press.

—— (1981), 'Real-World Reasoning', in *Minds and Mechanisms*, Ithaca: Cornell University Press.

—— (1988), *Computer Models of Mind*, Cambridge: Cambridge University Press.

Boole, George (1947), *An Investigation of the Laws of Thought*, New York: Dover.

Born, Rainer (ed.) (1986), *Artificial Intelligence: The Case Against*, London: Croom Helm.

Bower, Gordon H. and Ernest R. Hilgard (1981), *Theories of Learning*, 5th edn, Englewood Cliffs, N.J.: Prentice-Hall.

Bowers, Kenneth S., Glenn Regehr, Claude Balthazard and Kevin Parker (1990), 'Intuition in the context of discovery', *Cognitive Psychology*, 22.

Bruner, J. S. (1959), 'Inhelder and Piaget's *The Growth of Logical Thinking*', *General Psychology*, 50.

—— (1960), 'Individual and Collective Problems in the Study of Thinking', *Annals of the New York Academy of Science*, 91.

—— (1983), *In Search of Mind*, New York: Harper and Row.

—— (1990), *Acts of Meaning*, Cambridge, Mass.: Harvard University Press.

Bruner, J. S., J. J. Goodnow and G. A. Austin (1967), *A Study of Thinking*, New York: John Wiley and Sons.

Byrne, Richard (1983), 'Protocol analysis in problem solving', in Jonathan St B. T. Evans (ed.), *Thinking and reasoning*, London: Routledge and Kegan Paul.

Callanan, M. A. and E. M. Markman (1982), 'Principles of organization in young children's natural language hierarchies', *Child Development*, 53.

Carpenter, B. E. and R. W. Doran (eds) (1986), *A. M. Turing's ACE Report of 1946 and Other Papers*, Cambridge, Mass.: The MIT Press.

Carpenter, William (1891), *Principles of Mental Physiology*, New York: D. Appleton and Company.

Chaitin, G. (1975), 'Randomness and mathematical proof', *Scientific American*, CCXXXII.

Chapman, Michael (1988), *Constructive Evolution*, Cambridge: Cambridge University Press.

Chase, W. G. and K. A. Ericsson (1981), 'Skilled Memory', in J. R. Anderson (ed.), *Cognitive Skills and their Acquisition*, Hillsdale, N.J.: Lawrence Erlbaum.

Church, Alonzo (1936), 'An unsolvable problem of elementary number theory', *American Journal of Mathematics*, 58, reprinted in Martin Davis, *The Undecidable*, New York: Raven Press (1965).

—— (1938), 'The constructive second number class', *Bulletin of the American Mathematical Society*, 44.

Clark, Eve (1983), 'Meanings and concepts', in J. H. Flavell and E. M. Markman (eds), *Handbook of child psychology*, vol. 3, *Cognitive Development*, New York: Wiley.

Cleveland, Alfred A. (1907), 'The Psychology of Chess and of Learning to Play it', *The American Journal of Psychology*, XVIII.

Cobbe, Frances Power (1883), 'Unconscious Cerebration', in *Darwinism in Morals*, Boston: George H. Ellis.

Cohen, L. J. (1981), 'Can human irrationality be experimentally demonstrated?', *The Behavioral and Brain Sciences*, 4.

Coulter, Jeff (1983), *Rethinking Cognitive Theory*, London: Macmillan.

Danziger, Kurt (1980), 'The history of introspection reconsidered', *Journal of the History of the Behavioral Sciences*, XVI: 3.

Davis, Martin (1965), *The Undecidable*, New York: Raven Press.

—— (1978), 'What is a computation?', in Lynn Arthur Steen (ed.), *Mathematics Today*, New York: Springer Verlag.

—— (1982), 'Why Gödel didn't have Church's Thesis', *Information and Control*, 54.

De Groot, Adriaan D. (1965), *Thought and Choice in Chess*, The Hague: Mouton.

Dennett, Daniel (1978), 'Why the law of effect will not go away', in Daniel Dennett (ed.), *Brainstorms*, Sussex: The Harvester Press.

—— (1983), 'Artificial Intelligence and the Strategies of Psychological Investigation', in Jonathan Miller (ed.), *States of Mind*, New York: Pantheon Books.

Detlefsen, M. (1992), 'Poincaré against the logicians', *Synthèse*, 90.

Dreyfus, Herbert (1972), *What Computers Can't Do*, New York: Harper and Row.

Du Bois-Reymond, Emil (1874), 'The Limits of our Knowledge of Nature', J. Fitzgerald (trans.), *The Popular Science Monthly*, 5.

Du Bois-Reymond, Paul (1882), *Die allgemeine Funktionentheorie*, vol. I.

Dummett, M. A. E. (1973), *Frege: Philosophy of Language*, London: Duckworth.

—— (1991), *Frege and Other Philosophers*, Oxford: Clarendon Press.

Duncan, Carl P. (1959), 'Recent Research on Human Problem Solving', *Psychological Bulletin*, 56.

Ellenberger, Henri (1970), *The Discovery of the Unconscious*, New York: Basic Books.

Ericsson, K. Anders and Herbert A. Simon (1980), 'Verbal Reports as Data', *Psychological Review*, 87.

—— (1984), *Protocol Analysis*, Cambridge, Mass.: The MIT Press.

Evans, J. St B. (1989), *Biases in Human Reasoning*, Hillsdale, N.J.: Lawrence Erlbaum and Associates.

Fearing, Frederick (1930), *Reflex Action: A Study in the History of Physiological Psychology*, New York: Hafner.

Feigenbaum, Edward A. (ed.) (1963), *Computers and Thought*, New York: McGraw-Hill.

Flavell, John (1970), 'Concept Development', in P. H. Mussen (ed.), *Carmichael's Manual of Child Psychology*, vol. 1, New York: Wiley.

Føllesdal, D. (1958), *Husserl und Frege*, Oslo: Aschehoug.

Frege, Gottlob (1918), 'Thoughts', in P. T. Geach (ed.), P. T. Geach and R. H. Stoothoff (trans), *Logical Investigations*, Oxford: Basil Blackwell.

—— (1923), 'Compound Thoughts', in P. T. Geach (ed.), P. T. Geach and R. H. Stoothoff (trans), *Logical Investigations*, Oxford: Basil Blackwell.

—— (1959), *Foundations of Arithmetic*, John L. Austin (trans.), Oxford: Basil Blackwell [1884].

—— (1969), *Nachgelassene Schriften*, Hans Hermes, Friedrich Kambartel and Friedrich Kaulbach (eds), Hamburg: Felix Meiner.

—— (1972), 'On the Scientific Justification of a Conceptual Notation', T. W. Bynum (trans.), Oxford: Clarendon Press.

—— (1979), 'Boole's Logical Calculus and the Concept-script', in Hans Hermes, Friedrich Kambartel and Friedrich Kaulbach (eds), Peter Long and Roger White (trans), *Posthumous Writings*, Oxford: Basil Blackwell [1880/81].

—— (1980), *Philosophical and Mathematical Correspondence*, G. Gabriel (ed.), Hans Kaal (trans.), Oxford: Basil Blackwell.

Gallistel, C. R. (1990), *The Organization of Learning*, Cambridge, Mass.: The MIT Press.

Gardner, Howard (1985), *The Mind's New Science*, New York: Basic Books.

George, F. H. (1962), *Cognition*, London: Methuen and Co.

—— (1970), *Models of Thinking*, London: George Allen and Unwin.

Getzels, J. and M. Csikszentmihalyi (1976), *The Creative Vision*, New York: Wiley.

Gödel, Kurt (1931), 'On formally undecidable propositions of *Principia mathematica* and related systems', in Solomon Feferman *et al.* (eds), *Kurt Gödel: Collected Works*, vol. 1, Oxford: Oxford University Press (1986).

—— (1934), 'On undecidable propositions of formal mathematical systems', in Solomon Feferman *et al.* (eds), *Kurt Gödel: Collected Works*, vol. 1, Oxford: Oxford University Press (1986).

—— (1946), 'Remarks before the Princeton bicentennial conference on problems in mathematics, 1–4', first published in Martin Davis, *The Undecidable*, New York: Raven Press (1965).

Grandin, Temple (1995), *Thinking in Pictures*, New York: Doubleday.

Gregory, R. L. (1973), 'The Confounded Eye', in R. L. Gregory and E. H. Gombrich (eds), *Illusion in Nature and Art*, London: Duckworth.

—— (1981), *Mind in Science*, Harmondsworth: Penguin Books.

—— (1986), *Odd Perceptions*, London: Routledge.

—— (1987), 'Laws of Thought', in Richard L. Gregory (ed.), *The Oxford Companion to the Mind*, Oxford: Oxford University Press.

Gruber, Howard E. (1981a), *Darwin on Man*, Chicago: The University of Chicago Press.

—— (1981b), 'On the relation between "Aha Experiences" and the construction of ideas', *History of Science*, xix.

—— (1988), 'Evolving-systems approach', in Robert J. Sternberg, *The Nature of Creativity*, Cambridge: Cambridge University Press.

Hacker, P. M. S. (1990), *Wittgenstein: Meaning and Mind. Volume 3 of an Analytical Commentary on the Philosophical Investigations*, Oxford: Basil Blackwell.

Hadamard, Jacques (1945), *The Psychology of Invention in the Mathematical Field*, New York: Dover Publications.

Hallett, Garth (1977), *A Companion to Wittgenstein's "Philosophical Investigations"*, Ithaca: Cornell University Press.

Hamming, R. W. (1980), 'We would know what they thought when they did it', in N. Metropolis, J. Howlett and Gian-Carlo Rota (eds), *A History of Computing in the Twentieth Century*, New York: Academic Press.

Hardy, G. H. (1967), *A Mathematician's Apology*, London: Cambridge University Press.

Harré, R. (1990), 'Explanation in Psychology', in D. N. Robinson and L. P. Mos (eds), *Annals of Theoretical Psychology*, vol. 6, New York: Plenum Press.

Harvey, O. J., D. E. Hunt and H. M. Schroder (1961), *Conceptual Systems and Peronality Organization*, New York: Wiley.

Haugeland, John (1985), *Artificial Intelligence: The Very Idea*, Cambridge, Mass.: The MIT Press.

Helmholtz, Hermann von (1971a), 'An Autobiographical Sketch', in Russell Kahl (ed.), *Selected Writings of Hermann von Helmholtz*, Middletown, Conn.: Wesleyan University Press.

—— (1971b), *Selected Writings of Hermann von Helmholtz*, Russell Kahl (ed.), Middletown, Conn.: Wesleyan University Press.

—— (1977), *Epistemological Writings*, R. S. Cohen and Y. Elkana (eds), Malcolm F. Lowe (trans.), Dordrecht: Reidel.

Henle, Mary (1962), 'On the Relation between Logic and Thinking', *Psychological Review*, 69.

—— (ed.) (1971), *The Selected Papers of Wolfgang Köhler*, New York: Liveright.

—— (1986), *1879 and All That*, New York: Columbia University Press.

Hilbert, David (1917), 'Axiomatic Thinking', (trans. J. Fang), *Philosophia mathematica*, VII.

—— (1923), 'Die logischen Grundlagen der Mathematik', *Mathematische Annalen*, Bd 88.

—— (1927), 'Logic and the Knowledge of Nature', (trans. Don Howard), unpublished.

—— (1930), 'Naturerkennen und Logik', *Die Naturwissenschaften*, 18.

—— (1935), *Gesammelte Abhandlungen*, Berlin: Springer.

—— (1967a), 'On the Foundations of Logic and Arithmetic', in Jean van Heijenoort (ed.), *From Frege to Gödel*, Cambridge, Mass.: Harvard University Press [1904].

—— (1967b), 'Foundations of Mathematics', in Jean van Heijenoort (ed.), *From Frege to Gödel*, Cambridge, Mass.: Harvard University Press [1928].

—— (1967c), 'On the Infinite', (trans. Stefan Bauer-Mengelberg), in Jean van Heijenoort (ed.), *From Frege to Gödel*, Cambridge, Mass.: Harvard University Press [1925].

—— (1984a), 'Mathematical Problems', in *Mathematics: People. Problems. Results*, Douglas M. Campbell and John C. Higgins (eds), vol. I, Belmont, Cal.: Wadsworth International.

—— (1984b), 'Paris lecture', in *Mathematics: People, Problems, Results*, Douglas M. Campbell and John C. Higgins (eds), vol. 1, Belmont, Cal.: Wadsworth International [1900].

Hilmy, S. Stephen (1987), *The Later Wittgenstein*, Oxford: Basil Blackwell.

Hodges, Andrew (1983), *Alan Turing*, London: Burnett Books.

Hofstadter, Douglas (1980), *Gödel, Escher, Bach, An Eternal Golden Braid*, Middlesex: Penguin Books.

Howe, Michael J. A. (1989), *Fragments of Genius*: London: Routledge.

Hull, Clark L. (1962), 'Psychology of the Scientist, VI', *Perceptual and Motor Skills*, 15.

Humphrey, George (1951), *Thinking*, London: Methuen and Co.

Husserl, E. (1903), 'Reply to Palágyi', in Peter McCormick and Frederick A. Elliston (eds), *Shorter Works*, Brighton: Harvester Press.

James, William (1879), 'Are We Automata', *Mind*, 13

—— (1890), *Principles of Psychology*, London: Constable and Co. (1950).

Johnson-Laird, P. N. (1988), *The Computer and the Mind*, London: Fontana.

Johnson-Laird, P. N. and P. C. Wason (1977), *Readings in Cognitive Science*, Cambridge: Cambridge University Press.

Kant, Immanuel (1933), *Critique of Pure Reason*, Norman Kemp-Smith (trans.), London: Macmillan [1781].

Kenny, A. J. P. (1976), *Will, Freedom and Power*, Oxford: Basil Blackwell.

Ketner, Kenneth Laine (1988), 'Peirce and Turing: Comparisons and conjectures', *Semiotica* 68.

Kitcher, Patricia (1990), *Kant's Transcendental Psychology*, New York: Oxford University Press.

Kleene, Stephen C. (1943), 'Recursive predicates and quantifiers', *Transactions of the American Mathematical Society*, 53.

—— (1950), *Introduction to Metamathematics*, Princeton, N.J.: D. Van Nostrand Company.

—— (1981a), 'Recursive function theory', *Annals of the History of Computing*, 3.

—— (1981b), 'The theory of recursive functions, approaching its centennial', *Bulletin of the American Mathematical Society*, 5.

Klein, D. B. (1977), *The Unconscious: Invention or Discovery?* Santa Monica, Cal.: Goodyear Publishing Company.

Knuth, Donald (1976), 'Computer science and mathematics', *Science*, 194, reprinted in *Mathematics: People. Problems. Results*, vol. III, Douglas M. Campbell and John C. Higgins (eds), Belmont, Cal.: Wadsworth International (1984).

—— (1977), 'Algorithms', *Scientific American*, CCXXXIV.

Kochen, Manfred and Eugene H. Galanter (1958), 'The Acquisition and Utilization of Information in Problem Solving and Thinking', *Information and Control*, 1.

Koestler, Arthur (1975), *The Act of Creation*, London: Pan.

Köhler, Wolfgang (1925), *The Mentality of Apes*, Ella Winter (trans.), New York: The Humanities Press (1951).

—— (1947), *Gestalt Psychology*, Toronto: The New American Library.

Kripke, Saul (1982), *Wittgenstein on Rules and Private Language*, Oxford: Basil Blackwell.

Kusch, Martin (1995), *Psychologism*, London: Routledge.

Lachman, Roy, Janet L. Lachman and Earl C. Butterfield (1979), *Cognitive Psychology and Information Processing*, Hillsdale, N.J.: Lawrence Erlbaum Associates.

Lesgold, A. (1988), 'Problem solving', in Robert J. Sternberg and Edward E. Smith (eds), *The Psychology of Human Thought*, Cambridge: Cambridge University Press.

Lewes, G. H. (1877), *The Physical Basis of Mind*, Boston.

Locke, J. (1690), *An Essay Concerning Human Understanding*, John Yolton (ed.), London: Dent (1961).

Locke, John L. (1993), *The Child's Path to Spoken Language*, Boston: Harvard University Press.

Loeb, Jacques (1912), 'The Significance of Tropisms for Psychology', in Donald Fleming (ed.), *The Mechanistic Conception of Life*, Cambridge, Mass.: The Belknap Press (1964).

Lotze, Hermann (1887), *Microcosmus*, Elizabeth Hamilton and E. E. Constance Jones (trans), Edinburgh: T. and T. Clark.

Lovelace, Ada Augusta (1842), 'Sketch of the Analytical Engine Invented by Charles Babbage by L. F. Menabrea', in Charles Babbage, *On the Principles and Development of the Calculator*, New York: Dover Publications (1961).

Lyons, William (1986), *The Disappearance of Introspection*, Cambridge, Mass.: The MIT Press.

Machlup, Fritz and Una Mansfield (eds) (1983), *The Study of Information*, New York: John Wiley and Sons.

Mandler, Jean Matter and George Mandler (1964), *Thinking: From Association to Gestalt*, New York: John Wiley and Sons.

Markman, Ellen (1989), *Categorization and Naming in Children*, Cambridge, Mass.: The MIT Press.

Markman, E. M., M. S. Horton and A. G. McLanahan (1980), 'Classes and collections: principles of organization in the learning of hierarchical relations', *Cognition* 8.

McCorduck, Pamela (1979), *Machines Who Think*, New York: W. H. Freeman and Company.

Meadows, A. J. (1982), *Dictionary of Computing and New Information Technology*, London: Century Publishing.

Medin, D. L. (1983), 'Structural principles in categorization', in T. J. Tighe and B. E. Shepp (eds), *Perception, cognition, and development: Interactional analyses*, Hillsdale, N.J.: Lawrence Erlbaum.

—— (1989), 'Concepts and Conceptual Structure', *American Psychologist*, 44.

Metcalfe, Janet and David Wiebe (1987), 'Intuition in insight and noninsight problem solving', *Memory and Cognition*, 15.

Michie, Donald (1982), *Machine Intelligence and Related Topics*, New York: Gordon and Breach.

Mill, J. S. (1963), *System of Logic*, Toronto: University of Toronto Press [1865].

—— (1979), *An Examination of Sir William Hamilton's Philosophy*, Toronto: University of Toronto Press [1873].

Miller, George (1966), *Psychology, the Science of Mental Life*, Harmondsworth: Penguin Books.

Miller, Jonathan (1992), *States of Mind*, New York: Pantheon Books.

Minsky, M. L. (ed.) (1968), *Semantic Information Processing*, Cambridge, Mass.: The MIT Press.

—— (1975), 'Frame-system theory', in P. N. Johnson-Laird and P. C. Wason, *Thinking: Readings in Cognitive Science*, Cambridge: Cambridge University Press (1977).

Mischel, Theodore (1967), 'Kant and the possibility of a science of psychology', *The Monist*, 51.

Mohanty, J. J. (1982), *Husserl and Frege*, Bloomington: Indiana University Press.

Montmasson, Joseph-Marie (1931), *Invention and the Unconscious*, H. Stafford Hatfield (trans.), London: Kegan Paul, Trench, Trubner and Co.

Münsterberg, Hugo (1910), *Subconscious Phenomena*, Boston: Richard G. Badger, The Gorham Press.

Neisser, Ulric (1967), *Cognitive Psychology*, New York: Appleton-Century-Crofts.

Neumaier, Otto (1986), 'A Wittgensteinian view of artificial intelligence', in *Artificial Intelligence: The Case Against*, Rainer Born (ed.), London: Croom Helm.

Newell, Allen (1983), 'Intellectual Issues in the History of AI', in Fritz Machlup and Una Mansfield (eds), *The Study of Information*, New York: John Wiley and Sons.

Newell, Allen and Herbert A. Simon (1956), *Problem-solving in Humans and Computers*, Rand Corporation Paper P-987, Santa Monica, Cal.: The Rand Corporation.

—— (1957), 'The Logic Theory Machine: A Complex Information Processing System', *Transactions on Information Theory*, Institute of Radio Engineers.

—— (1961a), 'Computer Simulation of Human Thinking', *Science*, 134.

—— (1961b), 'The Simulation of Human Thought', in Wayne Dennis (ed.), *Current Trends in Psychological Theory*, Pittsburgh: University of Pittsburgh Press.

—— (1963), 'GPS, A Program that Simulates Human Thought', in Edward A. Feigenbaum (ed.), *Computers and Thought*, New York: McGraw-Hill.

—— (1972), *Human Problem Solving*, Englewood Cliffs, N.J.: Prentice-Hall.

—— (1979), 'The Processes of Creative Thinking', in Herbert A. Simon, *Models of Thought*, New Haven, Conn.: Yale University Press [1962].

Newell, Allen, J. C. Shaw and Herbert A. Simon (1958), 'Elements of a Theory of Human Problem Solving', *Psychological Review*, 65.

—— (1959), 'The Processes of Creative Thinking', Rand Corporation Paper P-1320, Santa Monica, Cal.: The Rand Corporation, September 16, 1958, revised January 28, 1959.

Nisbett, R. E. and T. D. W. Wilson (1977), 'Telling more than we can know: verbal reports on mental processes', *Psychological Review*, 84.

Osherson, Daniel N., Michael Stob and Scott Weinstein (1982), 'Ideal learning Machines', *Cognitive Science*, 6.

Pavlov, I. P. (1927), *Conditioned Reflexes*, B. V. Anrep (trans. and ed.), New York: Dover Publications.

Perkins, D. N. (1981), *The Mind's Best Work*, Harvard: Harvard University Press.

—— (1984), 'Creativity by design', *Educational Leadership*, 42.

—— (1988), 'Creativity and the quest for mechanism', in Robert J. Sternberg and Edward E. Smith (eds), *The Psychology of Human Thought*, Cambridge: Cambridge University Press.

—— (1990), 'The nature and nurture of creativity', in B. F. Jones and L. Idol (eds), *Dimensions of thinking and cognitive instruction*, Hillsdale, N.J.: Lawrence Erlbaum Associates.

Piaget, Jean (1941), 'Le mécanisme du développement mental et les lois du groupement des opérations', *Archives de Psychologie*, 28.

—— (1965), *Insights and Illusions of Philosophy*, W. Mayes (trans.), New York: Meridian Books.

Poincaré, Henri (1903), 'Review of Hilbert's "Foundations of Geometry",' E. V. Huntington (trans.), *American Mathematical Society*, XII.

—— (1913), 'Mathematical Creation', in *The Foundations of Science*, G. Bruce Halsted (trans.), New York: The Science Press.

Posner, Michael I. and Gordon L. Shulman (1979), 'Cognitive Science', in Eliot Hearst (ed.), *The First Century of Experimental Psychology*, Hillsdale, N.J.: Lawrence Erlbaum Associates.

Post, Emil, 'Absolutely unsolvable problems and relatively undecidable propositions', in Martin Davis, *The Undecidable*, New York: Raven Press.

Reber, Arthur S. (1985), *The Penguin Dictionary of Psychology*, London: Penguin Books.

Resnik, Michael D. (1980), *Frege and the Philosophy of Mathematics*, Ithaca: Cornell University Press.

Richards, Robert J. (1980), 'Wundt's early theories of unconscious inference and cognitive evolution in their relation to Darwinian biopsychology', in W. G. Bringmann and R. D. Tweney (eds), *Wundt Studies: A Centennial Collection*, Toronto: C.J. Hogrefe.

Rignano, E. (1923), *Psychology of Reasoning*, W. A. Holl (trans.), London: Kegan Paul, Trench, Trubner and Co.

Rips, Lance J. (1988), 'Deduction', in Robert J. Sternberg and Edward E. Smith (eds), *The Psychology of Human Thought*, Cambridge: Cambridge University Press.

Rosch, E. (1987), 'Wittgenstein and categorisation research in cognitive psychology', in *Meaning and the Growth of Understanding: Wittgenstein's Significance for Developmental Psychology*, M. Chapman and R. A. Dixon (eds), New York: Springer-Verlag.

Rosenbleuth, Arturo, Norbert Wiener and Julian Bigelow (1943), 'Behavior, Purpose and Teleology', *Philosophy of Science*, 10.

Rosser, J. B. (1984), 'Highlights of the history of the lambda-calculus', *Annals of the History of Computing*, 6.

Rumelhart, David E. (1980), 'Schemata: The Building Blocks of Cognition', in R. J. Spiro, B. C. Bruce and W. F. Brewer (eds), *Theoretical Issues in Reading Comprehension*, Hillsdale, N.J.: Lawrence Erlbaum.

Sacks, Oliver (1985), *An Anthropologist from Mars*, New York: Knopf.

Samuel, Arthur L. (1962), 'Artificial intelligence: a frontier of automation', *The Annals of the American Academy of Political and Social Science*, 340.

Savage-Rumbaugh, E. S., S. G. Shanker and T. J. Taylor (in press), *Apes, Language and the Human Mind*, New York: Oxford University Press.

Savage-Rumbaugh, E. Sue, Jeannine Murphy, Rose A. Sevcik, Karen E. Brakke, Shelly L. Williams and Duane M. Rumbaugh (1993), *Language Comprehension in Ape and Child*, *Monographs of the Society for Research in Child Development*, Serial No. 233, 58:3–4.

Schank, R. C. and R. P. Abelson (1977), *Scripts, Plans, Goals and Understanding*, Hillsdale, N.J.: Lawrence Erlbaum.

Searle, John (1980), 'Minds, brains and programs', *The Behavioral and Brain Sciences*, vol. 1, reprinted in Rainer Born (ed.), *Artificial Intelligence: The Case Against*, London: Croom Helm (1986).

Shanker, S. G. (1986), 'The decline and fall of the mechanist metaphor', in Rainer Born (ed.), *Artificial Intelligence: The Case Against*, London: Croom Helm.

—— (1987a), *Wittgenstein and the Turning-Point in the Philosophy of Mathematics*, London: Croom.

—— (1987b), 'Wittgenstein versus Turing on the Nature of Church's Thesis', *Notre Dame Journal of Formal Logic*, 28.

—— (1988a), 'The Dawning of Machine Intelligence', *Philosophica*, 42.

—— (1988b), 'Wittgenstein's Remarks on the Significance of Gödel's Theorem', in *Gödel's Theorem in Focus*, London: Croom Helm.

—— (1992), 'In Search of Bruner', *Language and Communication*, 12:1.

—— (1993a), 'Locating Bruner', *Language and Communication*, 13:4.

—— (1993b), 'Wittgenstein versus Russell on the Analysis of Mind', in Andrew Irvine and Gary Wedekind (eds), *Bertrand Russell and the Rise of Analytic Philosophy*, Toronto: University of Toronto Press.

—— (1994), 'Ape Language in a New Light', *Language and Communication*, 14:1.

—— (1996), 'Wittgenstein versus Quine on the Nature of Language and Cognition', in R. L. Arrington and H. J. Glock (eds), *Wittgenstein and Quine*, London: Routledge.

—— (1997a), 'Reassessing the Cognitive Revolution', in David M. Johnson and Christina Erneling (eds), *Reassessing the Cognitive Revolution*, New York: Oxford University Press.

—— (1997b), 'The Mechanist Continuum', in S. G. Shanker (ed.), *Philosophy of the English Speaking World in the Twentieth Century. 1: Logic, Mathematics and Science*, G. H. R. Parkinson and S. G. Shanker (eds), *Routledge History of Philosophy*, London: Routledge.

Shanker, S. G. and T. J. Taylor (forthcoming), 'The House that Bruner Built', in David Bakhurst and Stuart Shanker (eds), *Jerome Bruner's Philosophical Psychology*, London: Sage.

Shannon, Claude E. (1956), 'A Chess-Playing Machine', in James R. Newman (ed.), *The World of Mathematics*, New York: Simon and Schuster.

Shevrin, Howard and Scott Dickman (1980), 'The Psychological Unconscious', *American Psychologist*, 35.

Simon, Herbert A. (1961), 'Modelling Human Mental Processes', in *Proceedings of the Western Joint Computer Conference*, May 9–11, 1961.

—— (1962), 'The Processes of Creative Thinking', in Herbert A. Simon, *Models of Thought*, New Haven: Yale University Press (1979).

—— (1966a), 'Scientific discovery and the psychology of problem solving' in Herbert A. Simon, *Models of Discovery*, Dordrecht: Reidel (1977).

—— (1966b), 'Thinking by Computers', in Herbert A. Simon, *Models of Discovery*, Dordrecht: Reidel (1977).

—— (1969a), 'Adapting to the Need to Understand Thought', in James F. Voss (ed.), *Approaches to Thought*, Columbus: Charles E. Merrill Publishing Company.

—— (1969b), *The Sciences of the Artificial*, Cambridge, Mass.: The MIT Press.

—— (1972), 'The theory of problem solving', in Herbert A. Simon, *Models of Discovery*, Dordrecht: Reidel (1977).

—— (1977), *Models of Discovery*, Dordrecht: Reidel.

—— (1978), 'Information processing theory of human problem solving', in W. K. Estes (ed.), *Handbook of learning and cognitive processes*, vol. 5, Hillsdale, N.J.: Lawrence Erlbaum.

—— (1979), *Models of Thought*, New Haven: Yale University Press.

—— (1982), 'Otto Selz and Information-Processing Psychology', in Nico H. Frijda and Adriaan D. De Groot (eds), *Otto Selz: His Contribution to Psychology*, The Hague: Mouton.

—— (1983), 'Why Should Machines Learn?', in R. S. Michalski (ed.), *Machine Learning*, Berlin: Springer-Verlag.

—— (1984), *The Sciences of the Artificial*, Cambridge, Mass.: The MIT Press.

Sloboda, John A. (1985), *The Musical Mind*, Oxford: Oxford University Press.

Smith, Edward E. (1989), 'Concepts and Induction', in M. I. Posner (ed.), *Foundations of Cognitive Science*, Cambridge, Mass.: The MIT Press.

Sternberg, Robert J. (1988a), 'A three-facet model of creativity', in Robert J. Sternberg, *The Nature of Creativity*, Cambridge: Cambridge University Press.

—— (1988b), *The Nature of Creativity*, Cambridge: Cambridge University Press.

Sternberg, Robert J. and Edward E. Smith (eds) (1988), *The Psychology of Human Thought*, Cambridge: Cambridge University Press.

Tolman, Edward C. (1926), 'A Behavioristic Theory of Ideas', *Psychological Review*, 33.

Torrance, Paul E. (1988), 'The nature of creativity as manifest in its testing', in Robert J. Sternberg, *The Nature of Creativity*, Cambridge: Cambridge University Press.

Trevarthen, Colwyn (1993), 'The self born in intersubjectivity: the psychology of an infant communicating', in U. Neisser (ed.), *The Perceived Self*, Cambridge: Cambridge University Press.

Turing, Alan (1936), 'On computable numbers, with an application to the Entscheidungsproblem', *Proceedings of the London Mathematical Society*, vol. 42 (1936–1937), reprinted in Martin Davis, *The Undecidable*, New York: Raven Press (1965).

—— (1939), 'Systems of logic based on ordinals', *Proceedings of the London Mathematical Society*, vol. 45, reprinted in Martin Davis, *The Undecidable*, New York: Raven Press (1965).

—— (1946), 'Proposal for development in the mathematics division of an automatic computing engine (ACE)', in B. E. Carpenter and R. W. Doran (eds), *A. M. Turing's ACE Report of 1946 and Other Papers*, Cambridge, Mass.: The MIT Press (1986).

—— (1947), 'Lecture to the London Mathematical Society on 20 February 1947', in B. E. Carpenter and R. W. Doran (eds), *A. M. Turing's ACE Report of 1946 and Other Papers*, Cambridge, Mass.: The MIT Press (1986).

—— (1948), 'Intelligent machinery', in B. Meltzer and D. Michie (eds), *Machine Intelligence 5*, Edinburgh: Edinburgh University Press (1969).

—— (1950), 'Computing Machinery and Intelligence', in Alan Ross Anderson (ed.), *Minds and Machines*, Englewood Cliffs, N.J.: Prentice-Hall (1964).

—— (1959), 'Intelligent Machinery: A Heretical View', in Sarah Turing, *Alan Matheson Turing*, Cambridge: Heffers.

—— (1992), *Collected Works*, D. C. Ince (ed.), Amsterdam: North-Holland.

Turing, Sarah (1959), *Alan Matheson Turing*, Cambridge: Heffers.

van Heijenoort, Jean (ed.) (1967), *From Frege to Gödel*, Cambridge, Mass.: Harvard University Press.

Vitruvius Pollo (1934), *On Architecture*, Frank Gagner (ed. and trans.), Cambridge, Mass.: Harvard University Press.

von Hartmann, Eduard (1931), *Philosophy of the Unconscious*, New York: Harcourt, Brace and Company.

Wallas, Graham (1926), *The Art of Thought*, London: Jonathan Cape.

Wang, Hao (1960), 'Toward mechanical mathematics', *IBM Journal of Research and Development*, 4.

—— (1974), *From Mathematics to Philosophy*, London: Routledge and Kegan Paul.

—— (n.d.), 'Between Meaning and Science', unpublished MS.

Warren, Richard M. and Roslyn P. Warren (eds) (1968), *Helmholtz on Perception*, New York: John Wiley and Sons.

Wason, P. C. (1980), 'On the failure to eliminate hypotheses in a conceptual task', *Quarterly Journal of Experimental Psychology*, 12.

Watson, John (1923), 'The Unconscious of the Behaviorist', in *The Unconscious: A Symposium*, New York: Alfred A. Knopf.

—— (1925), *Behaviorism*, London: Kegan Paul, Trench, Trubner and Co.

Waxman, Sandra R. (1990), 'Contemporary Approaches to Concept Development', *Cognitive Development*, 6.

Webb, Judson (1980), *Mechanism, Mentalism, and Metamathematics*, Dordrecht: Reidel.

Weisberg, Robert W. (1986), *Creativity: Genius and other myths*, New York: Freeman.

—— (1988), 'Problem solving and creativity', in Robert J. Sternberg, *The Nature of Creativity*, Cambridge: Cambridge University Press.

Wellman, Henry (1990), *The Child's Theory of Mind*, Cambridge, Mass.: The MIT Press.

Whyte, L. L. (1978), *The Unconscious Before Freud*, New York: St Martin's Press.

Winston, P. H. (ed.) (1975), *The Psychology of Computer Vision*, New York: McGraw-Hill.

Woodworth, Robert S. (1938), *Experimental Psychology*, New York: Henry Holt and Company.

Young, Robert M. (1985), *Darwin's Metaphor*, Cambridge: Cambridge University Press.

NAME INDEX

SUBJECT INDEX

I AUW 9057 h.11   8/7/95

2